German Immigrants, Race, and Citizenship in the Civil War Era

This study of Civil War–era politics explores how German immigrants influenced the rise and fall of white commitment to African-American rights. Intertwining developments in Europe and North America, Alison Clark Efford describes how the presence of naturalized citizens affected the status of former slaves and identifies 1870 as a crucial turning point. That year, the Franco-Prussian War prompted German immigrants to reevaluate the liberal nationalism underpinning African-American suffrage. Throughout the period, the newcomers' approach to race, ethnicity, gender, and political economy shaped American citizenship law.

Alison Clark Efford is Assistant Professor of History at Marquette University. Her 2008 doctoral dissertation won the Friends of the German Historical Institute's Fritz Stern Prize.

German Immigrants, Race, and Citizenship in the Civil War Era

ALISON CLARK EFFORD
Marquette University, Wisconsin

GERMAN HISTORICAL INSTITUTE

Washington, D.C.

and

 CAMBRIDGE
UNIVERSITY PRESS

CAMBRIDGE UNIVERSITY PRESS
Cambridge, New York, Melbourne, Madrid, Cape Town,
Singapore, São Paulo, Delhi, Mexico City

Cambridge University Press
32 Avenue of the Americas, New York, NY 10013-2473, USA

www.cambridge.org
Information on this title: www.cambridge.org/9781107031937

First published 2013

Printed in the United States of America

A catalog record for this publication is available from the British Library.

Library of Congress Cataloging in Publication Data

Efford, Alison Clark, 1979–
German immigrants, race, and citizenship in the Civil War era / Alison Clark Efford.
pages cm. – (Publications of the German Historical Institute)
Includes bibliographical references and index.
ISBN 978-1-107-03193-7 (hardback)
1. German Americans – History –
19th century.   2. Immigrants – United States – History – 19th century.   3. German Americans –
Politics and government – 19th century.   4. Citizenship – United States – History – 19th century.
5. African Americans – Suffrage – History – 19th century.   6. United States – Race relations –
History – 19th century.   7. Reconstruction (U.S. history, 1865–1877)   8. United States – Politics and
government – 1857–1861.   9. United States – Politics and government – 1861–1865.   10. United
States – Politics and government – 1865–1877.   I. Title.
E184.G3E29   2013
973′.0431–dc23   2013010248

ISBN 978-1-107-03193-7 Hardback

Cambridge University Press has no responsibility for the persistence or accuracy of URLs for external
or third-party Internet Web sites referred to in this publication and does not guarantee that any
content on such Web sites is, or will remain, accurate or appropriate.

Contents

Acknowledgments

The scholarly journey of writing this book was entangled with a personal one, making a home for myself in the United States. I now have the pleasure of acknowledging the guides along the way. The challenge is not to gush. Mitchell Snay was closer to the project than anyone. His warm advice, incisive questioning, and scrupulous attention to detail shaped more than my writing. At Ohio State University, John Brooke was an exemplary adviser. I found his boundless enthusiasm, passion for theory, and individual support indispensable. Michael Les Benedict was unstintingly generous with his penetrating critiques, and Kevin Boyle led by example.

A wider group of scholars also guided my work. Before I had even settled on a topic, Walter Kamphoefner's expert probing and professional magnanimity encouraged me. As I finished the manuscript, Andrew Zimmerman's insightful reading reinvigorated my revisions. In between, colleagues at Ohio State, Marquette University, and elsewhere prodded and inspired me. I am particularly grateful for the interventions of David Roediger, Kathleen Neils Conzen, A. J. Aiseirithe, Michelle Wolfe, Jessica Pliley, Andrew Kahrl, and Andrew Slap. They changed how I understood significant aspects of the book. I am also indebted to Tyler Anbinder, Daniel Nagel, Mischa Honeck, Jonathan Zatlin, David Quigley, Adam Arenson, Thomas Bahde, Sameena Mulla, Peter Staudenmaier, and Geeta Raval for acute and substantive suggestions. I benefited greatly from stimulating conversations with Audra Jennings, Jane Berger, David Dzurec, John McKerley, Greg Downs, and Lezlie Knox.

Institutional debts feel less poignant than personal ones, but they are no less important. A Dean's Distinguished University Fellowship and other grants at Ohio State allowed me to indulge in spells of undistracted research and writing. I also received funding from the Deutscher Akademischer Austausch Dienst (German Academic Exchange Service) and the German

Historical Institute in Washington, DC. I have the institute to thank for facilitating this publication and especially for providing the services of David Lazar, an editor of uncommon skill and dedication. The staff of libraries and archives in Washington and around the Midwest introduced me to their collections and entertained my requests. Parts of Chapter 3 first appeared in "Race Should Be as Unimportant as Ancestry: German Radicals and African American Citizenship in the Missouri Constitution of 1865," *Missouri Historical Review* 104, no. 3 (2010): 138–58. Editor Gary R. Kremer kindly granted permission to use this material.

The History Department at Marquette feels more like an academic home than an institution. I have stumbled into a department of mentors. The College of Arts and Sciences provides welcome support to junior faculty, but I am not alone in believing that James Marten works special magic as History chair. And who can explain the good fortune of finding an accomplished historian of German America, John Jentz, working at Marquette's library?

I owe the most to people outside the academy. Murray Efford, Ramona Clark, Neil Efford, and teachers, friends, and family on both sides of the Pacific have taught me the value of reflection, debate, compassion, and reason. Final thanks go to Brandon Walton for the practical joys and emotional sustenance of shared homemaking.

Naturalized Citizens, Transnational Perspectives, and the Arc of Reconstruction

On a June day in 1906, thousands of St. Louisans gathered in Forest Park for the unveiling of a statue of General Franz Sigel.[1] A group of immigrants, having commissioned the bronze likeness of their Civil War hero, now displayed the pageantry for which German Americans were renowned. Elderly veterans who had fought "mit Sigel" marched in formation, choirs of men sang German folk songs, and local dignitaries addressed the crowd from a platform decked with American flags. One after another, they recounted how "our naturalized fellow-citizens of German birth" had helped defeat the Confederacy, saving the Union and securing its "free institutions."[2]

The entire dedication celebrated the nineteenth-century nation-state. The officiants made much of Sigel's decision to swear his loyalty to his adopted country. They also linked his battle to preserve the United States in the 1860s to his efforts to unify Germany in 1848. Yet the proceedings largely neglected the political ideology that the general had considered inseparable from his nationalism during those years – liberalism. Sigel, like revolutionaries and reformers around the world, had assumed that nation-states would enshrine the individual rights of their male residents in law. Although the speakers in Forest Park referred obliquely to Sigel's "noble ardor for human rights," no one explained that the German republic he had envisioned in 1848 was altogether different from the authoritarian German Empire that Otto von Bismarck had eventually founded in 1871. No one mentioned his opposition to slavery or his support for African-American suffrage after emancipation. Indeed, the only man who alluded to the postwar years expressed relief that Americans had put the troublesome

---

1 On the sculpture itself, see Caroline Loughlin and Catherine Anders, *Forest Park* (Columbia: Junior League of St. Louis and University of Missouri Press, 1986), 97, 261.
2 *St. Louis Mississippi Blätter* [Sunday edition of the *Westliche Post*], June 24, 1906. All translations are my own unless a translator is identified.

1

issues of the conflict behind them. "Those who once fought each other," he said, "now stand together, unified."[3] Most white Unionists were pleased that the federal government no longer antagonized white Southerners by upholding black citizenship.[4] Contemplating the Civil War era from their vantage point at the turn of the century, the immigrants testified that the nationalism of 1848 and the 1860s had prevailed. Liberalism was more in doubt.[5]

This book argues that the activities of German Americans not only reflected the rise and fall of liberal nationalism in the mid-nineteenth-century United States, they helped ensure it. I take up the subject that the ceremony in Forest Park pointedly ignored: the debate over African-American citizenship. Black rights were most fiercely contested during the twelve years that followed the American Civil War, the extraordinary period known as Reconstruction. Between 1865 and 1877, white Republicans first threw themselves into equal rights for black Southerners and then quickly retreated from the cause.[6] The German-American Republicans who animate this study – men such as Franz Sigel – played a unique role in these developments for two main reasons, both of which were on display decades later in Forest Park. As new American citizens themselves, they possessed a distinctive insight into citizenship, and as people who had lived on two continents, they brought a transnational perspective to Reconstruction politics. Ultimately, German Americans, who were politically divided but formed by far the largest immigrant group in the ruling Republican Party, would see to it that the fate of the nation-state and individual rights in North America on the one hand and in Europe on the other were intertwined.

German Americans suggest a new interpretation of the arc of white commitment to African-American citizenship, which ascended during the 1860s, reached its zenith around 1870, bowed downward during the 1870s,

---

3 Ibid.

4 David Blight, *Race and Reunion: The Civil War in American Memory* (Cambridge, MA: Belknap Press of Harvard University Press, 2001).

5 For a similar framing, see Thomas Bender, *A Nation among Nations: America's Place in World History* (New York: Hill and Wang, 2006). See also David M. Potter, "The Civil War in the History of the Modern World: A Comparative View," in *The South and the Sectional Conflict* (Baton Rouge: Louisiana State University Press, 1968), 298, which emphasizes Lincoln and Bismarck's "contrasting styles of nationalism." Approaching the subject with a focus on the Confederacy, Carl N. Degler has pointed out that Lincoln and Bismarck each in his own way forged national unity with blood and iron. Degler, "One among Many: The United States and National Self-Determination," in *Lincoln, the War President: The Gettysburg Lectures*, ed. Gabor S. Boritt (New York: Oxford University Press, 1992), 91–119.

6 Stephen D. Engle, *The Yankee Dutchman: The Life of Franz Sigel* (Fayetteville: University of Arkansas Press, 1993), 226.

and sunk to its nadir at about the time of the festivities in Forest Park in 1906.[7] Of course, the freed people themselves propelled lawmakers forward, demanding equality and asserting control over their work, leisure, relationships, sexuality, mobility, religion, and education.[8] Since Southern whites generally resisted these endeavors, however, the attitudes of the Northern whites who controlled the federal government became vitally important. Republicans in Congress, it turned out, would recognize suffrage as the "fullest manifestation" of American citizenship.[9] In 1866, they drafted the Fourteenth Amendment, which conferred national citizenship on all persons born or naturalized in the United States. Congressmen then passed legislation requiring the states of the former Confederacy to enfranchise African-American men and proposed the Fifteenth Amendment to outlaw racial discrimination in electoral law. But soon after the states ratified this final amendment in 1870 the Northern will to protect black men's suffrage began to subside. Although Republicans did not repudiate the revised Constitution, it became difficult for them to muster enough support to defend African-American rights. Republicans essentially ended an era in

7 The so-called post-revisionist historians flattened the arc of Republican Reconstruction, emphasizing that Northern racism and constitutional conservatism hampered it from the outset. C. Vann Woodward, "Seeds of Failure in Radical Race Policy," in *New Frontiers of American Reconstruction*, ed. Harold M. Hyman (Urbana: University of Illinois Press, 1966), 125–47; William S. McFeely, *Yankee Stepfather: General O. O. Howard and the Freedmen* (New Haven: Yale University Press, 1968); William Gillette, *The Right to Vote: Politics and the Passage of the Fifteenth Amendment* (Baltimore: The Johns Hopkins Press, 1969); Gillette, *Retreat from Reconstruction, 1869–1879* (Baton Rouge: Louisiana State University Press, 1979); Michael Les Benedict, *Compromise of Principle: Congressional Republicans and Reconstruction, 1863–1869* (New York: Norton, 1974); Benedict, "Preserving the Constitution: The Conservative Basis of Radical Reconstruction," in *Preserving the Constitution: Essays on Politics and the Constitution in the Reconstruction Era* (New York: Fordham University Press, 2006), 3–22; Phillip S. Paludan, *A Covenant with Death: The Constitution, Law, and Equality in the Civil War Era* (Urbana: University of Illinois Press, 1975); Earl M. Maltz, *Civil Rights, the Constitution, and Congress, 1863–1869* (Lawrence: University of Kansas Press, 1990).

8 Kate Masur's distinction between equality and citizenship is useful here, although immigrants offer good reasons to focus on the latter. Masur, *An Example for All the Land: Emancipation and the Struggle over Equality in Washington, D.C.* (Chapel Hill: University of North Carolina Press, 2010), 3–7. Examples of an extremely rich literature include W. E. B. Du Bois, *Black Reconstruction: An Essay toward a History of the Part which Black Folk Played in the Attempt to Reconstruct Democracy in America, 1860–1880* (New York: Russell & Russell, 1935); Leon Litwack, *Been in the Storm So Long: The Aftermath of Slavery* (New York: Knopf, 1979); Steven Hahn, *A Nation under Our Feet: Black Political Struggles in the Rural South from Slavery to the Great Migration* (Cambridge, MA: Belknap Press of Harvard University Press, 2003); Julie Saville, *The Work of Reconstruction: From Slave to Wage Laborer in South Carolina, 1860–1870* (Cambridge: Cambridge University Press, 1994); Laura F. Edwards, *Gendered Strife and Confusion: The Political Culture of Reconstruction* (Urbana: University of Illinois Press, 1997); Leslie A. Schwalm, *Emancipation's Diaspora: Race and Reconstruction in the Upper Midwest* (Chapel Hill: University of North Carolina Press, 2009).

9 Mitchell Snay, *Fenians, Freedmen, and Southern Whites: Race and Nationality in the Era of Reconstruction* (Baton Rouge: Louisiana State University Press, 2007), 163; Derek Heater, *A Brief History of Citizenship* (New York: New York University Press, 2004), 65–87.

1877, when they settled the previous year's disputed presidential election by agreeing to withdraw federal troops from the South almost completely.[10]

During Reconstruction, German-American Republicans were motivated to promote and then abandon racially inclusive policies for many of the same reasons as other white Unionists. Most of them were initially adherents of "free labor ideology" who believed that arming black men with the vote would allow African Americans to exact fair compensation for their work and remake the South as a region of independent farmers, craftsmen, and shopkeepers. As historian Eric Foner has argued, when industrialization and labor conflict in the North eroded this vision during the 1870s, Northern politicians' sympathy for Southern workers dissipated.[11] German Republicans were also intent on unifying the war-torn country. During the 1860s, they thought that African Americans would safeguard the Union by acting as a political counterweight to disloyal white Southerners, but as time passed, they increasingly longed to reconcile with former Confederates. The unveiling in Forest Park showed how this latter urge could undercut the war's emancipatory legacy.[12] Meanwhile, the most violent white opponents of black rights wore down the resolve that would have been necessary to enforce the Fifteenth Amendment.[13]

10 Some scholars point out that Republicans continued to make some attempts to defend African-American rights. See for example Xi Wang, *The Trial of Democracy: Black Suffrage and Northern Republicans, 1860–1910* (Athens: University of Georgia Press, 1997); Brooks Simpson, *The Reconstruction Presidents* (Lawrence: University of Kansas Press, 1998). More than half the essays in a 2006 historiographical collection argue that the issues of Reconstruction persisted past 1877. Thomas J. Brown, ed., *Reconstructions: New Perspectives on the Postbellum United States* (Oxford: Oxford University Press, 2006), 7.

11 Eric Foner, *Reconstruction: America's Unfinished Revolution, 1863–1877* (New York: Harper & Row, 1988), 525. Foner drew on a generation of revisionist work written on Reconstruction during the 1970s and 1980s, but he was especially inspired by Du Bois, *Black Reconstruction*. Foner distinguished his position from David Montgomery's argument that Northern labor conflict undid the Republican coalition. Montgomery, *Beyond Equality: Labor and the Radical Republicans, 1862–1872* (New York: Knopf, 1967). Extending Foner's interpretation, see Heather Cox Richardson, *The Death of Reconstruction: Race, Labor, and Politics in the Post-Civil War North, 1865–1901* (Cambridge, MA: Harvard University Press, 2001); Richardson, *West from Appomattox: The Reconstruction of America after the Civil War* (New Haven, CT: Yale University Press, 2007); Amy Dru Stanley, *From Bondage to Contract: Wage Labor, Marriage, and the Market in the Age of Slave Emancipation* (New York: Cambridge University Press, 1998); Sven Beckert, *The Monied Metropolis: New York City and the Consolidation of the American Bourgeoisie, 1850–1896* (Cambridge: Cambridge University Press, 2001); David Quigley, *The Second Founding: New York City, Reconstruction, and the Making of American Democracy* (New York: Hill and Wang, 2004); Nancy Cohen, *The Reconstruction of American Liberalism, 1865–1914* (Chapel Hill: University of North Carolina Press, 2002).

12 Blight, *Race and Reunion*. For alternative views of reconciliation, see Nina Silber, *The Romance of Reunion: Northerners and the South, 1865–1900* (Chapel Hill: University of North Carolina Press, 1993); Robert W. Burg, "Amnesty, Civil Rights, and the Meaning of Liberal Republicanism," *American Nineteenth Century History* 4, no. 3 (2003): 29–60.

13 Allen Trelease, *White Terror: The Ku Klux Klan Conspiracy and Southern Reconstruction* (New York: Harper & Row, 1971); George Rable, *But There Was No Peace: The Role of Violence in the Politics of Reconstruction* (Athens: University of Georgia Press, 1984); Richard Zuczek, *State of Rebellion:*

Although German-American Republicans valued free labor and reunification just as their colleagues did, their peculiarities would also influence the trajectory of Reconstruction. First of all, the immigrants were, like the people freed from bondage, new citizens. In fact, I propose that immigrants from Europe were the *archetypal* new citizens in the eyes of Americans.[14] Individuals such as Sigel declared that they embodied citizenship's essence. Their naturalization, as feted in Forest Park, symbolized the liberal notion that men who pledged their fealty to the nation would be guaranteed individual rights. Sometimes immigrant men's acquisition of citizenship could even serve as a template for other aspiring citizens. During the 1860s, leading German-American Republicans explicitly argued that emancipation should bring the freedmen the same political rights that naturalization had effectively secured for male immigrants. Black men should be able to tread the path to voting citizenship that they had pioneered.[15]

While describing the emergence and then eclipse of arguments likening immigrants and African Americans, I probe the limitations inherent in an understanding of citizenship centered on German immigrant men. Preconceptions about race, gender, and political economy inhibited German-American Republicans. Many historians have found that as male Europeans claimed American citizenship, they acted to reinforce the rhetorical line between whiteness and blackness.[16] During Reconstruction, German

Reconstruction in South Carolina (Columbia: University of South Carolina Press, 1996); LeeAnna Keith, *The Colfax Massacre: The Untold Story of Black Power, White Terror, and the Death of Reconstruction* (New York: Oxford University Press, 2008); Hannah Rosen, *Terror in the Heart of Freedom: Citizenship, Sexual Violence, and the Meaning of Race in the Postemancipation South* (Chapel Hill: University of North Carolina Press, 2009).

14 James H. Kettner argued that the development of naturalization in Britain's North American colonies influenced the model of "volitional allegiance" adopted in the independent United States. Kettner, *The Development of American Citizenship, 1608–1877* (Chapel Hill: University of North Carolina Press, 1978), 9–10, 106–28.

15 Donna R. Gabaccia uses the label "immigrant paradigm" for the idea that the experience of male Europeans was normative and represents the thrust of American history. She points out that scholars are quite aware that white men were exceptionally privileged, so historians are suitably skeptical of this paradigm. Gabaccia, "Is Everywhere Nowhere? Nomads, Nations, and the Immigrant Paradigm of United States History," *Journal of American History* 86 (1999): 1115–34. Another historian discusses a similarly self-congratulatory approach to the immigrant past, the "Ellis Island paradigm." Paul Spickard, *Almost All Aliens: Immigration, Race, and Colonialism in American History and Identity* (New York: Routledge, 2007), 4–11.

16 Descriptions of immigrants using this technique can be found in Du Bois, *Black Reconstruction*, but they have been further developed under the rubric of "whiteness studies." Significant contributions include David R. Roediger, *Wages of Whiteness: Race and the Making of the American Working Class* (London: Verso, 1991); Noel Ignatiev, *How the Irish Became White* (New York: Routledge, 1995); Matthew Frye Jacobson, *Whiteness of a Different Color: European Immigrants and the Alchemy of Race* (Cambridge, MA: Harvard University Press, 1999). For evidence of historians' reception of whiteness studies, see Jon Gjerde, "'Here in America There Is Neither King nor Tyrant': European Encounters with Race, 'Freedom,' and Their European Pasts," *Journal of the Early Republic* 9 (1999): 673–90; Eric Arnesen, "Whiteness and the Historians' Imagination," *International Labor and Working Class History*

Republicans denounced their Democratic countrymen who appealed to immigrants as white men, but they perpetuated more subtle discursive distinctions between European immigrants and black Americans. At a time before ethnicity and race were clearly differentiated, German immigrants insisted that they belonged to an ethnic group. As scholars of the twentieth-century have observed, ethnicity, viewed as cultural and malleable, was defined in contradistinction to race, which was understood as more biological and fixed.[17] Even the German Americans who attacked this dichotomy championed ethnicity in ways that inadvertently encouraged the belief that race constituted a more legitimate basis for exclusion. An ethnic identity predicated on the difference between culture and biology encumbered their work. German-American constructions of ethnicity and their effect on Reconstruction politics consequently form central themes of this book.

Privileging the experience of immigrant men also produced a narrow form of citizenship that revolved around male voting rights during the 1850s and 1860s. Few Americans supported women's suffrage, but German immigrants were especially keen to prevent it. Unpropertied men had first won the right to vote as potential soldiers and heads of household, roles that any man could theoretically assume precisely because no woman could.[18]

60 (2001): 3–32. On German Americans and whiteness, see Russell Kazal, "Irish 'Race' and German 'Nationality': Catholic Languages of Ethnic Difference in Turn-of-the-Century Philadelphia," in *Race and the Production of Modern American Nationalism*, ed. Reynolds J. Scott-Childress (New York: Garland Publishing, 1999), 149–68; Kazal, *Becoming Old Stock: The Paradox of German-American Identity* (Princeton, NJ: Princeton University Press, 2004).

On the general argument that the inclusion of some was predicated on the exclusion of others, see Linda K. Kerber, "The Meanings of Citizenship," *Journal of American History* 84 (1997): 833–54; Barbara Young Welke, *Law and the Borders of Belonging in the Long Nineteenth Century United States* (Cambridge: Cambridge University Press, 2010); Rogers M. Smith, *Civic Ideals: Conflicting Visions of Citizenship in U.S. History* (New Haven, CT: Yale University Press, 1997); Rogers Smith, "The 'American Creed' and American Identity: The Limits of Liberal Citizenship in the United States," *Western Political Quarterly* 41 (1988): 225–51; Ned Landsman, "Pluralism, Protestantism, and Prosperity: Crevecoeur's American Farmer and the Foundations of American Pluralism," in *Beyond Pluralism: The Conception of Groups and Group Identities in America*, ed. Wendy F. Katkin, Ned C. Landsman, and Andrea Tyree (Urbana: University of Illinois Press, 1998), 105–24; Eric Kaufmann, "American Exceptionalism Reconsidered: Anglo-Saxon Ethnogenesis in the 'Universal' Nation, 1776–1850," *Journal of American Studies* 33 (1999): 437–57; Uday Mehta, "Liberal Strategies of Exclusion," *Politics and Society* 18 (1990): 427–54.

17 Victoria Hattam, *In the Shadow of Race: Jews, Latinos, and Immigrant Politics in the United States* (Chicago: University of Chicago Press, 2007); Hattam, "Ethnicity: An American Genealogy," in *Not Just Black and White: Historical and Contemporary Perspectives on Immigration, Race, and Ethnicity in the United States*, ed. Nancy Foner and George M. Fredrickson (New York: Russell Sage Foundation, 2004), 42–60; Mae Ngai, "The Architecture of Race in American Immigration Law: A Reexamination of the Immigration Act of 1924," *Journal of American History* 86 (1999): 67–92; Ngai, *Impossible Subjects: Illegal Aliens and the Making of Modern America* (Princeton, NJ: Princeton University Press, 2004).

18 Nancy F. Cott, "Marriage and Women's Citizenship in the United States," *American Historical Review* 103 (1998): 1440–54; Kerber, "The Paradox of Women's Citizenship in the Early Republic: The Case of *Martin vs. Massachusetts*, 1805" *American Historical Review* 97 (1992): 349–78; Joan R. Gunderson, "Independence and Citizenship and the American Revolution," *Signs* 13 (1987): 59–77; Nancy

Men's rights rested on their authority over women who were subordinated according to heterosexual social norms.[19] Traditional family structures held a special place in a community dislocated by migration. German Americans prized their reputation for harmonious male-headed households. The fact that many Anglo-American feminists sought to curb social drinking also distanced immigrants from the campaign for women's rights, leading the majority to conclude that gender equality was antithetical to ethnic and racial inclusivity. The Republicans among them advocated patterning the citizenship of African-American men after that of male immigrants, *not* non-voting women.

Finally, immigrant men's tendency to see their own experience as normative discouraged a view of citizenship that included economic rights beyond the freedom to enter a labor contract. German Americans were thus ill prepared to support the freed people in their quest for economic justice. Most of them, familiar with Europe's hereditary nobility and North America's government-sanctioned slavery, believed that state interference in the marketplace profited only the wealthy. Protections for workers encroached on the principle of limited government, most German Americans thought during the 1860s, and were unnecessary at best. German-born socialists complained that even struggling working-class immigrants accepted the "delusion" that free markets and political rights were enough to give every industrious individual a fair shot at wealth.[20] Those very socialists, of course, provided a counterpoint to the reigning liberal nationalism of the Civil War decade.[21] A small yet vocal cast of German-American activists critiqued liberal ideology and followed their own political strategy. It is not incidental to this book's argument that they decided to collaborate with liberals and black Southerners *up until* about 1870. Political economy was as relevant to Reconstruction citizenship as race or gender.

Isenberg, *Sex and Citizenship in Antebellum America* (Chapel Hill: University of North Carolina Press, 1998), 6–13, 22–23, 28–32; Carol Pateman, *The Sexual Contract* (Stanford, CA: Stanford University Press, 1988).

19 Specifically on sexuality, see Martha Gardner, *The Qualities of a Citizen: Women, Immigration, and Citizenship, 1870–1965* (Princeton, NJ: Princeton University Press, 2005); Margot Canaday, *The Straight State: Sexuality and Citizenship in Twentieth-Century America* (Princeton, NJ: Princeton University Press, 2009); Welke, *Borders of Belonging*, 145–46, 150–51.

20 North American Federal Council to the General Council of the International Workingmen's Association (IWA), Aug. 20, 1871, reel 1, fr. 1013, IWA Papers (microfilm), Wisconsin Historical Society (hereafter WHS), Madison.

21 On the constraints of free labor ideology, see Eric Foner, *Free Soil, Free Labor, Free Men*, rev. ed. (Oxford: Oxford University Press, 1995), xxxv–vi; Foner, *Reconstruction*, 236–37. Arguing that free labor ideology did not preclude government action to advance economic equality, see Adam Tuchinsky, *Horace Greeley's* New-York Tribune: *Civil War Socialism and the Crisis of Free Labor* (Ithaca, NY: Cornell University Press, 2009). On liberalism's theoretical compatibility with state action, see James T. Kloppenberg, *The Virtues of Liberalism* (New York: Oxford University Press, 1998), 13–14.

German-American Republicans such as Sigel were not only conscious of being new citizens, they were also instinctively transnational in outlook. This second proclivity contributed to Republican Reconstruction's astonishing rise and precipitous fall.[22] The women and men who fled German Europe after the Revolutions of 1848 – dubbed "Forty-Eighters" – infused the American Republican Party with a passionate liberal nationalism.[23] In Europe, they had found it difficult to conceive of a united Germany that would not recognize the rights of men to participate in their own governance and freely dissent, organize, worship, work, and trade. In the United States, naturalization only reaffirmed the refugees' conviction that the nation-state and individual rights were tightly bound. Forty-Eighters were quick to concur with Abraham Lincoln that the survival of the Union intact was essential to the maintenance of its free institutions.[24] Largely lacking the president's moderation, however, they argued that abolishing slavery and, later, enfranchising African-American men would strengthen the nation still further.

22 On transnational histories of the period, see W. Caleb McDaniel and Bethany L. Johnson, "New Approaches to Internationalizing the History of the Civil War Era," *Journal of the Civil War Era* 2 (2012): 145–50; David Armitage et al., "Interchange: Nationalism and Internationalism in the Era of the Civil War," *Journal of American History* 89 (2011): 455–89; Douglas R. Egerton, "Rethinking Atlantic Historiography in a Postcolonial Era: The Civil War in a Global Perspective," *Journal of the Civil War Era* 1 (2011): 79–95; Mark M. Smith, "The Past as A Foreign Country: Reconstruction, Inside and Out," in *Reconstructions*, ed. Brown, 117–40; Jay Sexton, "Toward a Synthesis of Foreign Relations in the Civil War Era, 1848–1877," *American Nineteenth Century History* 5 (2004): 50–73. Examples include Andre M. Fleche, *The Revolutions of 1861: The American Civil War in the Age of Nationalist Conflict* (Chapel Hill: University of North Carolina Press, 2012); Matthew Pratt Guterl, *American Mediterranean: Southern Slaveholders in the Age of Emancipation* (Cambridge, MA: Harvard University Press, 2008); Philip Katz, *From Appomattox to Montmartre: Americans and the Paris Commune* (Cambridge, MA: Harvard University Press, 1998); Snay, *Fenians, Freedmen, and Southern Whites*; Rebecca J. Scott, *Degrees of Freedom: Louisiana and Cuba after Slavery* (Cambridge, MA: Belknap Press of Harvard University Press, 2005); Frederick Cooper, Thomas Holt, and Rebecca Scott, *Beyond Slavery: Explorations of Race, Labor, and Citizenship in Postemancipation Societies* (Chapel Hill: University of North Carolina Press, 2000); Steven Hahn, "Class and State in Postemancipation Societies: Southern Planters in Comparative Perspective," *American Historical Review* 95 (1990): 75–98.
23 There is a substantial literature on the activities of the Forty-Eighters before and during the Civil War. Daniel Nagel, *Von republikanischen Deutschen zu deutsch-amerikanischen Republikanern: Ein Beitrag zum Identitätswandel der deutschen Actundvierziger in den Vereinigten Staaten, 1860–1861* (St. Ingbert: Röhrig Universitätsverlag, 2012); Mischa Honeck, *We Are the Revolutionists: German-Speaking Immigrants and American Abolitionists after 1848* (Athens: University of Georgia Press, 2011); Bruce Levine, *The Spirit of 1848: German Immigrants, Labor Conflict, and the Coming of the Civil War* (Urbana: University of Illinois Press, 1992); Charlotte L. Brancaforte, ed., *The German Forty-Eighters in the United States* (New York: Peter Lang, 1989); Carl F. Wittke, *Refugees of Revolution: The German Forty-Eighters in America* (Philadelphia: University of Pennsylvania Press, 1952; reprint, Westport, CT: Greenwood Press, 1970); A. E. Zucker, ed., *The Forty-Eighters: Political Refugees of the German Revolution of 1848* (New York: Columbia University Press, 1950). On the broader repercussions of the European revolutions in the United States, see Timothy Mason Roberts, *Distant Revolutions: 1848 and the Challenge to American Exceptionalism* (Charlottesville: University of Virginia Press, 2009).
24 Bender, *Nation among Nations*, 124–27.

More significantly, I contend that the same German immigrants who connected liberalism and nationalism facilitated their decoupling. Just months after the ratification of the Fifteenth Amendment, Forty-Eighters were transfixed by an undisputedly illiberal nationalist, Bismarck.[25] My argument hinges on the German-American response to the Franco-Prussian War, which united Germany on the terms dictated by Bismarck's Prussia. Proud of Germany's manifest might, German Americans would toy with a model of national greatness that privileged racial hierarchy over individual rights. In the United States, the immigrants who had campaigned for African-American suffrage would lead the Liberal Republican challenge to Republican race policy.[26] Defending the citizenship rights of African Americans, the Liberal Republicans said in 1872, had become an obstacle to national unity. Although the name of the new party suggested otherwise, Liberal Republicanism subverted liberal nationalism well before the Compromise of 1877.

The immigrant story, with its emphasis on citizenship and international comparison, generates a new narrative of postwar politics that integrates ethnicity, race, gender, and political economy. German Republicans accentuated cultural trends and tightened political turning points, making the contours of Reconstruction much more dramatic than they would have been in the immigrants' absence. This feat was possible only because their actions were, at times, decisive.

German immigrants overestimated their influence, exaggerating their political clout and overrating Sigel's military skill, but they did indeed play a crucial part in Reconstruction. The Irish were the largest immigrant group in the country, but the second-place Germans outnumbered them considerably in the Union Army. At the beginning of the Civil War, more than 1,300,000 residents of the United States hailed from Europe's German-speaking lands.[27] By its end, about one-tenth of Union soldiers had been German-born.[28] Although sizable numbers of Germans settled along the

25 The existing work does not address how the immigrant reaction affected American politics. John G. Gazley, *American Opinion of German Unification, 1848–1871* (New York: Columbia University, 1926; reprint, New York: AMS Press, 1970); Hans L. Trefousse, "The German-American Immigrants and the newly Founded Reich," in *America and the Germans: An Assessment of a Three-Hundred-Year History*, ed. Frank Trommler and Joseph McVeigh, 2 vols. (Philadelphia: University of Pennsylvania Press, 1985), 1: 160–75.

26 For a brief German-language article on the German involvement in the Liberal Republican movement, see Jörg Nagler, "Deutschamerikaner und das *Liberal Republican Movement*, 1872," *Amerikastudien/American Studies* 33 (1988): 415–38.

27 U. S. Bureau of the Census, *Abstract of the Eighth Census* (Washington, DC: Government Printing Office, 1865), 620–23.

28 Engle, "Yankee Dutchmen: Germans, the Union, and the Construction of a Wartime Identity," in *Civil War Citizens: Race, Ethnicity, and Identity in America's Bloodiest Conflict*, ed. Susannah J. Ural

eastern seaboard, the heart of German America lay in the Middle West.[29] The immigrants made up a particularly high proportion of the population in the region's "German triangle." This area stretched from Cincinnati in the east to St. Louis in the west and then north to Milwaukee, incorporating broad swaths of land in between.[30] I concentrate on the states at the tips of the triangle, Ohio, Missouri, and Wisconsin. In 1860, 7.2, 7.5, and 16.0 percent of the people living in these respective states had emigrated from German Europe, and Germans were overrepresented in the largest cities.[31] When observers factored in the immigrants' American-born children, they reckoned that Milwaukee was roughly half German and Cincinnati and St. Louis were each around a third Teutonic.[32]

To Anglo-American politicians, German-American Midwesterners appeared to be an important bloc of swing voters. Republicans would attest to their interest in a German constituency by inserting a pro-immigrant plank in their 1860 platform and commissioning numerous German-born army officers. One of the generals, Carl Schurz, gave the keynote address at the Republican national convention in 1868. In private letters, Republican politicians would fret revealingly about losing immigrant support in 1872 and 1876. That a little more than half of all German-American voters probably continued to side with the Democrats only made German Republicans more valuable to their party.[33] It is important to acknowledge that the opposition attracted immigrants too, but the Republicans seized the initiative during the Civil War era. Democrats had to scramble to respond.

The partisan allegiances of German Americans varied from state to state. Ohio, overwhelmingly white and densely populated, was an electoral battleground whose German residents were as politically divided as Ohioans as

(New York: New York University Press, 2010), 19; William L. Burton, *Melting Pot Soldiers: The Union's Ethnic Regiments* (Ames: Iowa State University Press, 1988), 110.

29 Kathleen Neils Conzen, "Germans," in *The Harvard Encyclopedia of American Ethnic Groups*, ed. Stephan Thernstrom, Ann Orlov, and Oscar Handlin (Cambridge, MA: Belknap Press of Harvard University Press, 1980), 311–13.

30 Colman J. Barry, *The Catholic Church and German Americans* (Milwaukee: Bruce Publishing Company, 1953), 44.

31 U. S. Bureau of the Census, *Abstract of the Eighth Census*, 620–23.

32 Conzen, *Immigrant Milwaukee, 1836–1860* (Cambridge, MA: Harvard University Press, 1976), 15–19; James G. Heller, *Isaac M. Wise: His Life, Work and Thought* (New York: The Union of American Hebrew Congregations, 1965), 242; Henry Boernstein, *Memoirs of a Nobody: The Missouri Years of an Austrian Radical, 1849–1866*, trans. and ed. Steven Rowan (St. Louis: Missouri Historical Society Press, 1997), 247. For the actual numbers, see Conzen, "Germans," 413; U. S. Bureau of the Census, *Abstract of the Eighth Census*, 539, 381, 297.

33 Walter D. Kamphoefner, "German-Americans and Civil War Politics: A Reconsideration of the Ethnocultural Thesis," *Civil War History* 37 (1991): 232–45. For some comparison to other immigrant groups, see Frederick C. Luebke, ed., *Ethnic Voters and the Election of Lincoln* (Lincoln: University of Nebraska Press, 1973). Much less numerous than the Germans, Scandinavian and English immigrants also tended to vote Republican. The more numerous Irish were confirmed Democrats.

a whole.[34] Missouri, where nearly 10 percent of inhabitants were black in 1860, became a literal battleground. The slave state never joined the Confederacy, but Missourians sympathetic to the South engaged their Unionist neighbors in bitter guerilla warfare.[35] In this context, German immigrants became some of Missouri's most committed white Republicans. Wisconsin, in contrast, was home to few African Americans, and its native-born population leaned Republican.[36] Anglo-American Republicans there alienated most immigrants from the party with their hostility to immigrant customs such as beer drinking. Taken together, these three states capture the variety of German politics in the Midwest. Missouri, with its hub in St. Louis, was the epicenter of German Republicanism, while Wisconsin represented the Democrats' enduring hold on immigrants, and Ohio dramatized the interactions between the two parties.

For all their diversity, Germans in Ohio, Missouri, and Wisconsin engaged in a common German-language debate over American citizenship. *German Immigrants, Race, and Citizenship* focuses on an arena of public life that was segmented by language, an arena I call the German-language public sphere. The speeches and songs at the unveiling of Sigel's statue exemplify the sorts of performances that filled this space.[37] More routinely, immigrants heard German-language campaigning, read German-language newspapers, and spoke German in club halls, churches, and bars. The German-language public sphere also encompassed the strikes and demonstrations that challenged the German-American establishment. My formulation of the public sphere draws on adaptations of the work of theorist Jürgen Habermas,[38] especially the thinking of historian John L. Brooke, who recognizes the

34 U. S. Bureau of the Census, *Abstract of the Eighth Census*, 598, 595.
35 William E. Parrish, ed., *A History of Missouri*, vol. 3, *1860–1875*, by Parrish (Columbia: University of Missouri Press, 1973), 7; U. S. Bureau of the Census, *Abstract of the Eighth Census*, 596, 598.
36 In 1860, 1,171 African Americans lived in Wisconsin, amounting to 0.15 percent of the population. U. S. Bureau of the Census, *Abstract of the Eighth Census*, 531.
37 The 1906 speeches appear to have been delivered in English and then translated for the German-language press, but Civil War-era speeches were commonly given in German.
38 Jürgen Habermas, *The Structural Transformation of the Public Sphere: An Inquiry into a Category of Bourgeois Society*, trans. Thomas Burger (Cambridge, MA: MIT Press, 1989). My spatialized, democratized, and cultural public sphere departs from the notional, bourgeois, and exclusively rational *Öffentlichkeit* Jürgen Habermas originally theorized. Opposing such a redefinition, see Harold Mah, "Phantasies of the Public Sphere: Rethinking the Habermas of Historians," *Journal of Modern History* 72 (2000): 153–182. Examples of a reworked public sphere appear in Jeffrey L. Pasley, *The Tyranny of Printers: Newspaper Politics in the Early American Republic* (Charlottesville: University Press of Virginia, 2001); David Waldstreicher, *In the Midst of Perpetual Fetes: The Making of American Nationalism, 1776–1820* (Chapel Hill: University of North Carolina Press, 1997); James M. Brophy, *Popular Culture and the Public Sphere in the Rhineland, 1800–1850* (Cambridge: Cambridge University Press, 2007).

Literary scholar Brent O. Peterson has argued that German-language publications created ethnic identity by forming a community of readers. Peterson, *Popular Narratives and Ethnic Identities: Literature and Community in* Die Abendschule (Ithaca, NY: Cornell University Press, 1991). For reference to

power of the concept of the public sphere to bridge the gap between "the old political history of law and the new political history of language." Brooke argues that the public sphere was a communicative domain of both authority and dissent, involving both persuasion (the unequal exchange of cultural signals, particularly language, that "set boundaries on the possible") and deliberation ("the structured and privileged assessment of alternatives among legal equals leading to a binding outcome").[39]

Understanding the public sphere as a site of persuasion *and* deliberation lends itself to an investigation of the Civil War era, a period during which the *language* of citizenship intersected with the *law* of citizenship. German-speaking Americans created their own language of citizenship. Bounded by the linguistically circumscribed public sphere, immigrants enumerated the traits that they shared with other Americans and the qualities that set them apart from their fellow citizens. Bilingual politicians then transferred these ideas into the larger political contest over citizenship. The leaders of German America disagreed among themselves and could not prescribe public opinion, but I have gauged the popularity of different positions by consulting an array of German-language sources, both published and archival. The immigrant press was especially rich, including everything from uncontroversial reports of cultural events to divisive editorial feuds. Ordinary immigrants responded to editors and politicians (and most editors were also politicians) in personal letters and street protests as well as at the ballot box. Immigrant leaders, for their part, were always attentive to their subscribers, constituents, and opponents, adjusting their arguments over time.

The language of citizenship informed binding political and legal decisions. At its core, Reconstruction entailed a rewriting of the *law* of citizenship. White immigrant men were among the relatively few individuals for whom national citizenship held much legal significance before the Civil

a German-American partial public sphere ("Teilöffentlichkeit"), see Nagel, *Von republikanischen Deutschen zu deutsch-amerikanischen Republikanern*, 25–27.

For other explorations of marginalized groups pushing their way into the public sphere or establishing autonomous sites of debate, see Nancy Fraser, "Rethinking the Public Sphere: A Contribution to the Critique of Actually Existing Democracy," in *Habermas and the Public Sphere*, ed. Craig Calhoun (Cambridge, MA: MIT Press, 1991), 109–42; Oskar Negt and Alexander Kluge, *Public Sphere and Experience: Toward an Analysis of the Bourgeois and Proletarian Public Sphere*, trans. Peter Labanyi, Jamie Owen Daniel, and Assenka Oksiloff (Minneapolis: University of Minnesota Press, 1993); Joanna Brooks, "The Early American Public Sphere and the Emergence of a Black Print Counterpublic," *William and Mary Quarterly* 62 (2005): 67–92.

39 John L. Brooke, "Consent, Civil Society, and the Public Sphere in the Age of Revolution and the Early American Republic," in *Beyond the Founders: New Approaches to the Political History of the Early American Republic*, ed. Jeffrey Pasley, Andrew W. Robertson, and David Waldstreicher (Chapel Hill: University of North Carolina Press, 2004), 209.

War.[40] Originally, the Constitution had charged Congress with passing laws to govern naturalization, but the document left American citizenship undefined. Prior to Reconstruction, the states had taken the lead in deciding which rights citizens would enjoy.[41] Since most states stipulated that foreign-born voters must be naturalized citizens, citizenship seemed to be tied to suffrage, but it was not that simple. In Wisconsin, for example, male aliens who had begun the naturalization process and had lived in the state for at least one year could vote, but native-born free blacks and women – presumably citizens – could not.[42] In legal fact, there were different types of citizen, as well as state-to-state variations in the practice of citizenship. German Republicans who hoped to grant black men the franchise would have to grapple with these complications.

German Immigrants, Race, and Citizenship charts the rise and fall of Republican Reconstruction chronologically, emphasizing the pivotal year of 1870. Laying the antebellum foundations, Chapter 1 shows how immigrants developed a German language of American citizenship as they reacted to the Revolutions of 1848 and made a home in an English-speaking land. They split over the meaning of German ethnicity but united in constituting themselves as a specifically ethnic group, a cultural minority within a plural nation. Before the war, the implications of this cultural pluralism were unexplored. Was it expansive enough to include African Americans or did it proscribe them based on biology? The results for women were less ambiguous. Most German-American liberals construed women's suffrage as contrary to the multiethnic spirit that now suffused their nationalism, and few socialists embraced it either. Anglo-American advocates of women's rights, with their disdain for alcohol consumption and Sabbath recreations, made enemies of German immigrants, including the Forty-Eighters who endorsed other unpopular reforms.

Chapter 2 argues that in the 1850s a cohort of German immigrants stamped their masculine multiculturalism onto the new Republican Party, which was otherwise Anglo-Protestant in tone. Agreeing on the near-term goal of ending slavery, socialists allied with the dominant liberal nationalists to surmount, partially and temporarily, differences of class and in some places even religion. German-American Republicans popularized one personification of German ethnicity, the "freedom-loving German" who abhorred

---

40 Emphasizing the role of Irish immigrants in the formation of national citizenship during the Civil War era, see Christian G. Samito, *Becoming American under Fire: Irish Americans, African Americans, and the Politics of Citizenship during the Civil War Era* (Ithaca, NY: Cornell University Press, 2009).

41 Kettner, *Development of American Citizenship*, 218–24; Smith, *Civic Ideals*, 115–36.

42 Alexander Keyssar, *The Right to Vote: The Contested History of Democracy in the United States* (New York: Basic Books, 2000), 353.

slavery as much as he prized immigrant rights. Without specifying the commonalities between immigrants and African Americans, the foreign-born Republicans prepared their native-born colleagues and later their German-American opponents to compare the two groups.

The next chapters follow Republican Reconstruction's ascent between 1865 and 1869, years when most German Americans in the party decided that the principle of liberal nationalism, which had circulated during 1848 and triumphed in the Civil War, required them to support enfranchising black men. Pro-suffrage immigrants cited their own attainment of citizenship and asserted their transnational authority, adding ideological consistency and popular weight to a much wider movement. In the postwar environment, Republicans could put the idea that the immigrant man was the archetypal new citizen to work in the service of African Americans. Chapter 3 covers the German arguments for black enfranchisement in the Missouri constitutional convention of 1865, and Chapter 4 maps the spread of such Radicalism among Midwestern Republicans from 1865 to 1869. At each step, the politics of ethnicity also constrained Reconstruction. Although German-American Radicals pronounced that race and ethnicity must be conflated, their campaigning played on the idea that cultural bonds connected their own community, while racial characteristics marked African Americans. When they told German-speaking audiences that universal manhood suffrage could become an emblem of their fabled devotion to "principle," the freed people seemed almost an afterthought. The self-referential statements of immigrant Republicans occasionally implied that enfranchising African Americans might not be such a good idea *in practice*. All along, their politics of citizenship was grounded in a version of German-American identity, one that was subject to change.

The three final chapters of *German Immigrants, Race, and Citizenship* trace how the Franco-Prussian War and German unification altered the German language of American citizenship and helped reverse Republican Reconstruction's legal momentum after 1870. The immigrants' jubilant reception of the news from Europe dominates Chapter 5. In their excitement, German Americans began to consider the advantages of a less liberal nationalism in which racial destiny and effective administration loomed larger than citizenship rights and representation. Chapter 6 argues that German Americans deployed some of Europe's lessons in *Volk* and state in the Liberal Republican Party. Liberal Republicans espoused reconciliation between Northern and Southern whites and civil service reform, two priorities that led them away from African-American citizenship. Chapter 7 looks ahead to the concerns of the late nineteenth century. During the 1870s, some immigrants called on the state to guarantee a living wage or support Catholic education. These new citizenship demands reoriented German-American politics. Discussions of economic and cultural equality incorporated women in new ways and could have benefited all African Americans, but both supporters and opponents of the new economic and cultural rights saw black suffrage as an outmoded cause. The interests of German immigrants no longer coincided with the needs of African Americans.

German Americans approached black citizenship through the lens of their own experience. They were conscious of being new citizens themselves, and they introduced Americans to foreign ideas. If this political style was one of Reconstruction's constants, however, its consequences for African Americans changed markedly over time. During the 1860s, black men capitalized on the energy of 1848 and the norm of a voting male citizenship. After 1870, new nationalisms – German and American – exposed the risks of making the self-conceptions of white Americans the basis for African-American rights. The German Missourians who erected Sigel's statue in 1906 still presented themselves as archetypal new citizens, but that identification no longer motivated them to work to sustain equal citizenship for all men. White Americans' understanding of their better selves had transformed the Constitution, but it had not secured racial justice.

1

The German Language of American Citizenship

When Jacob Müller came to write his memoirs in 1896, he remembered arriving in Cleveland, Ohio, after the Revolutions of 1848 had failed in Europe. He had been among the political refugees who were, he said, "saturated with the feeling that their free qualities made them the best citizens of the Great [American] republic." According to Müller, the Forty-Eighters believed that "they could not perform a better service to their new country than to retain the positive qualities of German spirit and nature, and to hone, improve and domesticate their German characteristics, particularly through using the German language." They certainly were not to be "used simply as raw material for the construction of a Yankee nation." In orienting himself toward the European revolutions and extolling the German *Volk*, the ever-passionate Müller brought together two of the defining features of the German language of American citizenship in the mid-nineteenth century: German immigrants drew on the legacy of 1848, and they asserted the value of German culture in their adopted home.[1]

This chapter establishes exactly how the upheavals of 1848 and the process of migration shaped the immigrants' views of citizenship. Müller was the sort of minor politician who came to represent the revolutions in the United States. A young law student in 1848, he had interrupted his studies to take up arms against the Bavarian king and serve as a commissioner under the short-lived revolutionary government in the Bavarian Palatinate.[2] Being prepared to fight for a unified German republic made him a "radical

---

1 Jacob Mueller, *Memories of a Forty-Eighter: Sketches from the German-American Period of Storm and Stress in the 1850s*, trans. Steven Rowan (Cleveland, OH: Western Reserve Historical Society, 1996), 114–15.
2 German-American Biographical Pub. Co., *Cleveland and Its Germans*, trans. Steven Rowan (Cleveland, OH: Western Reserve Historical Society, 1998), 74–75.

democrat," in local parlance. Europeans usually reserved the label "liberal" for moderates who would have been content with a constitutional monarchy. In the transatlantic context, however, Müller is best understood as an intensely committed liberal nationalist. He was one of a growing number of Germans who believed that the redress of age-old grievances would come only when a united nation-state guaranteed individual freedoms. The revolutions were complex, including peasants who protested economic change, socialists who opposed the emerging capitalist order, and bureaucrats who preferred piecemeal reforms, but liberal nationalists came to dominate German politics – however briefly – in 1848 and 1849. A national parliament would promulgate a culturally inclusive definition of the German *Volk* and seek to enfranchise all German men regardless of their background. These impulses, along with the gendered hierarchy that the revolutions perpetuated, would be carried across the Atlantic.

Thwarted by state governments in Europe, Germans faced a different challenge in the United States. There they would have to find a place for themselves within an English-speaking nation. Migration did not erase ideological, class, gender, or religious differences, but it did elicit common yearnings for meaningful interactions in a land that Germans found individualistic and culturally barren. Leading German Americans harnessed these emotions as they set about revising the meaning of the indispensable word *Volk*. In the United States, the German *Volk* was not the population of an unrealized polity but an ethnicity, a group of loyal Americans with their own culture. With rival leaders producing competing versions of what it meant to be German American, the actual content of German ethnic identity was dynamic and contested. But the fundamental structure of ethnicity held important implications for the debate over race. As historian Kathleen Neils Conzen has argued, German immigrants helped "invent ethnicity itself as a category within American society."[3] Other scholars have shown how this classification featured in twentieth-century clashes over citizenship. It could serve as a counterpoint to race, suggesting that although culture was not a valid basis for exclusion, biology was.[4] During the Civil War era, before either the word "ethnicity" had taken on its modern meaning or the line between ethnicity and race had hardened, ethnic pluralism provided a framework that members of minorities deemed racial could potentially, although not necessarily, exploit.

3 Conzen, "German-Americans and the Invention of Ethnicity," in *America and the Germans*, ed. Trommler and McVeigh (Philadelphia: University of Pennsylvania Press, 1985), 1: 133.
4 Hattam, *In the Shadow of Race*, 3, 21–43.

German-American ethnicity would also give rise to a distinctive gendering of American citizenship. Few immigrants questioned the cultural pluralism that newspaper editors formalized when they defended naturalized men's right to vote and right to drink. Reexamining these two rather predictable positions illuminates the fact that the citizenship claims of German-American men rested on customs that German-American women were expected to nurture. Forty-Eighter Mathilde Franziska Anneke would try to mold German-American ethnicity to accommodate her feminism, but without much success. It is no shock that most German immigrants opposed women's suffrage, but they went further, specifically treating women's voting rights as inimical to multiethnic republicanism. All told, the revolutionary inheritance and the construction of ethnicity would reinforce the assumption that male voting rights epitomized the promise of the era's liberal nationalism, one step on the way to enfranchising African-American men with the Fifteenth Amendment.

LIBERAL NATIONALISM AND CITIZENSHIP IN 1848

Although Germans later became infamous for defining citizenship by blood, the men and women who participated in the Revolutions of 1848 brought other ideas to the United States.[5] During the pre-revolutionary decades, known as the *Vormärz* period, Europeans living throughout the loose confederation of German-speaking countries accumulated a long list of economic and religious complaints with monarchal rule. Some Germans, especially members of the burgeoning middle classes, articulated liberal nationalist solutions to the problems of German Europe. Before liberals could adapt their ideas for America, however, socialists challenged their economic theories, and feminists broached the issue of gender. The very definition of the German *Volk* was up for debate until the uprisings empowered liberal lawmakers to pen a legal outline of citizenship.

Any account of the Revolutions of 1848 must begin with the difficulties that had wracked the largely agrarian economy of Central Europe since the early nineteenth century. As a swelling population outstripped the resources of German farms, manufactured goods from other regions undercut the sales of German workshops. Feudalism no longer ordered economic life in most parts of the German Confederation, but its dismantling had created new hardships. In western German states, many emancipated serfs had become

---

5 Rogers Brubaker, *Citizenship and Nationhood in France and Germany* (Cambridge, MA: Harvard University Press, 1992); Eli Nathans, *The Politics of Citizenship in Germany: Ethnicity, Utility and Nationalism* (Oxford: Berg, 2004).

landless laborers. Peasants with marginal holdings were forced to supplement their livelihoods by selling goods, such as textiles, that they produced at home. With guilds losing power, more craftworkers were free to open their own shops, but economic independence often proved elusive. Vulnerable to taxes and competition, numerous master artisans found themselves reduced to working on consignment for better-capitalized concerns. All of these changes, historian Jonathan Sperber argues, resulted in the formation of "unfree market economies," where authorities controlled access to the markets on which producers depended. Taxation, tariffs, contract law, and land restrictions exacerbated economic inequality in agriculture and the trades.[6]

Endemic religious conflict also plagued German Europe during the nineteenth century. Each German state had an established church, so secular priorities entered the selection of senior clergy. A disputed appointment could stoke tensions within and among denominations. In Prussian territory, the Protestant Union Church struggled to balance the interests of its Lutheran and Reformed factions and antagonized Roman Catholics. Although Catholics ran their own publicly funded school system, they bristled at state intrusions into religion, especially the requirement that all army conscripts attend Protestant services. Matters of faith could turn Germans against state officials without automatically promoting individualism or nationalism, but religious dissent contributed to the revolutionary mood of the late 1840s.[7]

During the *Vormärz*, Germans' protest against economic and religious injustice was taking new forms. The ban on political organizing fell hardest on poor and rural Germans, but they used song, almanacs, pre-Lenten carnival celebrations, and religious festivals to evade censorship and circumvent restrictions on public assembly. Widely disseminated folk calendars, for example, sometimes offered subtle political commentary. In one case, a calendar marking the fiftieth anniversary of U.S. independence praised

6 Jonathan Sperber, *Rhineland Radicals: The Democratic Movement and the Revolutions of 1848–1849* (Princeton, NJ: Princeton University Press, 1991), 63. My description of the German economic crisis also draws on Bruce Levine, *Spirit of 1848: German Immigrants, Labor Conflict, and the Coming of the Civil War* (Urbana: University of Illinois Press, 1992), 19–41; James J. Sheehan, *German History, 1770–1866* (Oxford: Clarendon, 1989), 451–524; and Timothy Anderson, "Proto-Industrialization, Sharecropping, and Outmigration in Nineteenth-Century Rural Westphalia," *Journal of Peasant Studies* 29 (2001): 1–30.

7 Sperber, *Rhineland Radicals*, 43–52; Dagmar Herzog, *Intimacy and Exclusion: Religious Politics in Pre-Revolutionary Baden, 1803–1849* (Princeton, NJ: Princeton University Press, 1996); Sperber, "Churches, the Faithful, and the Politics of Religion in the Revolutions of 1848," in *Europe in 1848: Revolution and Reform*, ed. Dieter Dowe et al., trans. David Higgins (New York: Berghahn Books, 2001), 708–31.

the democratic government of the United States.[8] Some Germans acted on the percolating ideas. In 1844, Karl Krumrey, a grape grower in Rhenish Bavaria, joined a mutual aid society, where he began to make public speeches. Years later in Sheboygan County, Wisconsin, Krumrey wrote that this political awakening had prepared him for revolution.[9] August Kleinert regretted that "Germans were still too backward" in his region.[10] As a carpenter – an "ordinary worker" – in the town of Stettin in Prussian Pomerania, Kleinert believed that he had been denied the education that might have made him more political. His years in the United States must have influenced this retrospective analysis, but his statement also hinted that even this "backward" Pomeranian had been starting to reframe long-standing problems in the 1840s. Workers in Cologne, the capital of Prussia's industrializing Rhine Province, were at the forefront of a distinctly novel, class-based mobilization. One measure of their success was the state's constant surveillance of their activities.[11] Across Europe, Germans who were unhappy with the economic and religious policies of their governments were beginning to stir.

Before 1848, the professionals, bureaucrats, and business owners who made up about 5 percent of the German population were the most likely to offer liberal nationalist remedies to the German plight.[12] Benefiting from the end of feudalism, members of the upper middle class tended to blame Germany's economic crisis on government interference. They sought to reform tariffs, taxes, and regulations, along with the agencies that enforced them. At the same time, many of these men and women tried to liberate personal faith from state orthodoxies and hierarchies. Economic and religious change was unlikely, however, while power remained concentrated in the hands of an old elite. To achieve progress, liberals believed, individual political rights would have to replace inherited political privilege. The freedom to dissent would be a good start, especially given that middle-class life relied on newspapers and *Vereine* (associations), including informal discussion groups, singing and sports clubs, and student

---

8 James M. Brophy, *Popular Culture and the Public Sphere in the Rhineland, 1800–1850* (Cambridge: Cambridge University Press, 2007), 37.

9 Karl Krumrey, "Journal, 1842–1870," box 3, folder 7, Germans in the United States Collection, WHS. For biographical information, see Carl Zillier, *History of Sheboygan County, Wisconsin, Past and Present*, 2 vols. (Chicago: S. J. Clarke Publishing Co., 1912), 2: 246.

10 "Autobiography of August Friedrich Kleinert," box 1, folder 2, Gladys Dieruf Papers, WHS.

11 Sperber, *Rhineland Radicals*, 118–22.

12 Jürgen Kocka, "The European Pattern and the German Case," in *Bourgeois Society in Nineteenth-Century Europe*, ed. Jürgen Kocka and Allan Mitchell (Oxford: Berg, 1993), 4; Sperber, *Rhineland Radicals*, 92.

societies.[13] Periodically, authorities would clamp down on these organizations, signaling that their mere existence threatened Europe's traditional order. Even so, everyone knew that real change would come only with enlarged electorates and accountable governments.

Liberals generally ensconced all of their objectives in an emotive German nationalism. U.S. Senator Carl Schurz later reflected on his youth in 1840s Germany: "We young people [believed] that the disintegrated Fatherland must be moulded [sic] into a united empire with free political institutions. The fermenting, restless spirit permeating the minds of the educated classes, and finding expression in the literature of the day, aroused in us boys the warmest enthusiasm."[14] Individual rights and the unity of the *Volk* were interdependent in liberal nationalist thought.

Germany's middle-class liberal milieu produced its own most trenchant critic – Karl Marx. Born in the Rhineland city of Trier to a lawyer and his wife, Marx pursued doctoral studies at the University of Berlin before working briefly in Cologne until he left to live abroad in 1843.[15] The *Manifesto of the Communist Party*, which he published with Friedrich Engels as the Revolutions of 1848 were about to ignite Europe, identified a "selfish misconception" at the heart of liberal ideology. The authors argued that the ideas that liberals presented as "eternal laws of nature and reason" were actually "the outgrowth of the conditions of your bourgeois production and bourgeois property." Middle-class liberals advocated political rights only in order to defend their economic interests, Marx theorized. He believed that universal manhood suffrage would be of little consequence if free-market capitalism compelled individuals to work in dehumanizing circumstances for subsistence wages. For Marxists, true freedom lay in the transformation of labor and the abolition of private property, attacks on the free market that liberalism would not countenance.[16] Many socialists differed with Marx on

---

13 Thomas Nipperdey, *Germany from Napoleon to Bismarck, 1800–1866*, trans. Daniel Nolan (Dublin: Gill & Macmillan, 1996), 231–36, 522–24; Sperber, *Rhineland Radicals*, 92–94; Sheehan, *German Liberalism in the Nineteenth Century* (Chicago: University of Chicago Press, 1978), 19–34; Otto Dann, ed., *Vereinswesen und bürgerliche Gesellschaft in Deutschland* (Munich: R. Oldenbourg, 1984); David Blackbourn and Geoff Eley, eds., *The Peculiarities of German History: Bourgeois Society and Politics in Nineteenth-Century Germany* (Oxford: Oxford University Press, 1984); Kocka, ed., *Bürger und Bürgerlichkeit im 19. Jahrhundert* (Göttingen: Vandenhoeck & Ruprecht, 1987).

14 Carl Schurz, *The Reminiscences of Carl Schurz*, 3 vols. (New York: The McClure Company, 1907), 1: 73.

15 Marx actually submitted his dissertation to the University of Jena, which granted his degree. David McLellan, *Karl Marx: A Biography* (New York: Palgrave Macmillan, 2006), 33.

16 Karl Marx and Friedrich Engels, "Manifesto of the Communist Party" (1848), in *The Collected Works of Karl Marx and Friedrich Engels*, trans. Richard Dixon et al., 47 vols. (New York: International Publishers, 1975–2004), 6: 501.

how to end economic alienation, but they too saw the wide distribution of political rights as necessary *but not sufficient*.

Although socialists rebuked liberalism, their activities in *Vormärz* Germany only augmented it. This irony is critical to the politics of mid-nineteenth-century Europe and North America. According to Marx's linear view of history, middle-class liberals would have to eliminate the remnants of feudalism before working-class socialists could stage their own revolution. Some other German socialists were not prepared to wait, but they were equally interested in the advent of a German state in which men could wield political power regardless of their wealth. Some of the socialist leaders who would later join liberals in lobbying for African-American suffrage in Ohio, Missouri, and Wisconsin worked with them to replace German kingdoms and principalities with a centralized Germany governed by male citizens. Fritz Anneke, Joseph Weydemeyer, and August Willich were all Prussian army officers who joined the Communist League in 1840s Cologne. Anneke and Willich inspired workers with visions of a society that upheld their dignity, and the two men helped organize them to demand economic relief and the franchise.[17] Weydemeyer, the most orthodox Marxist of the three, moved to Trier and assailed liberal capitalism from the pages of the *Trier'sche Zeitung* in 1845 and 1846, but his attacks on absolutism and inherited privilege were much more likely to provoke the Prussian censors.[18] Despite their critique of free markets, socialists often acted as though they were unusually dedicated liberals. Because the German governments of the 1840s clearly advantaged the wealthy by distorting markets and curtailing political rights, the immediate goals of socialists coincided with the ultimate aspirations of liberals.

Women also contributed to the pre-revolutionary ferment without managing to place their own rights firmly on the liberal agenda. Several female writers established themselves in print, and a few even added the subjugation of women to the mounting indictments against German rulers. The most radical *Emanzipirtin* ("emancipated woman") of the 1840s was Louise Aston, who scandalized Berliners by wearing trousers, divorcing her

---

17 Wilhelm Schulte, *Fritz Anneke: Ein Leben für die Freiheit in Deutschland und in den USA* (Dortmund: Historischer Verein Dortmund, 1961), 15–38; Loyd Easton, *Hegel's First American Followers: The Ohio Hegelians: John B. Stallo, Peter Kaufmann, Moncure Conway, and August Willich* (Athens: Ohio University Press, 1966), 159–70; Levine, *Spirit of 1848*, 41; Dieter Dowe, *Aktion und Organisation: Arbeiterbewegung, sozialistische und kommunistische Bewegung in der preußische Rheinprovinz, 1820–1852* (Hanover: Verlag für Literatur und Zeitgeschehen, 1970), 69–74, 113–29; Sperber, *Rhineland Radicals*, 118–22.

18 Ibid., 122–26; Karl Obermann, *Joseph Weydemeyer: Ein Lebensbild, 1818–1866* (Berlin: Dietz Verlag, 1968), 28–59.

industrialist husband, and claiming that women suffered the same sort of exploitation as factory workers.[19] When Aston was exiled from Berlin in 1846 for her political organizing and outspoken atheism, Mathilde Franziska Anneke's written response showcased a more moderate feminism. Anneke, who would become the leading German feminist in the United States, was the daughter of a respected Prussian civil servant. By 1847, she was married to Fritz Anneke and living in Cologne, where she wrote for opposition newspapers and hosted political discussions in her home.[20] Although she too had left her first husband, Anneke condemned Aston's decision to engage in sexual relationships outside of marriage. She did, however, ask her female readers to reflect on how "social relations," including the conventions of marriage, straitened their lives. She argued that Prussian authorities had persecuted Aston because of her gender. Women's speech frightened them, Anneke wrote, "because with [women's] heart blood they nurture the higher creed of human dignity." Anneke specifically included patriarchy among the arbitrary and illegitimate hierarchies that states supported by limiting political speech. She told German mothers, "You can pass on to coming generations a healthy, free sex of women who will never again let themselves be reduced to chattel slaves."[21] Her own protest simultaneously challenged the tyrannical state and women's oppression, demanding that her audience consider women's writing – Aston's and her own – an act of emancipation and an exercise in citizenship.

Anneke would become an important figure in the United States, but it is important to note that her feminism, while supported by some in socialist circles, was not representative of liberal thought in Germany.[22] Marxists described "traditional" marriage as an institution designed to control women and appropriate their labor, but they were usually careful to add that they had no plans to "interfere in the personal relationship between

---

19 Lia Secci, "German Women Writers and the Revolution of 1848," in *German Women in the Nineteenth Century: A Social History*, ed. John C. Fout (New York: Holmes & Meier, 1984), 151–71; Hans Adler, "On a Feminist Controversy: Louise Otto vs. Louise Aston," in *German Women in the Eighteenth and Nineteenth Centuries: A Social and Literary History*, ed. Ruth-Ellen B. Joerres and Mary Jo Maynes (Bloomington: Indiana University Press, 1986), 193–214.

20 Sperber, *Rhineland Radicals*, 94.

21 Mathilde Franziska Anneke, "Das Weib im Konflikt mit den sozialen Verhältnissen," in *Frauenemanzipation im deutschen Vormärz: Texte und Documente*, ed. Renate Möhrmann (Stuttgart: Philipp Reclam, 1978), 85; Anneke, *Mathilde Franziska Anneke in Selbstzeugnissen und Dokumenten*, ed. Maria Wagner (Frankfurt am Main: Fischer, 1980), 38–46.

22 Stanley Zucker, "Female Political Opposition in Pre-1848 Germany: The Role of Kathinka Zitz-Halein," in *German Women*, ed. Fout, 133–50; Zucker, *Kathinka Zitz-Halein and Female Civic Activism in Mid-Nineteenth-Century Germany* (Carbondale: Southern Illinois University Press, 1991); Möhrmann, *Die andere Frau: Emanzipationsansätze deutscher Schriftstellerinnen im Vorfeld der Achtundvierziger-Revolution* (Stuttgart: Metzler, 1977).

men and women."[23] Many liberals called for women to have greater influence within marriage, but most of them still assumed that women could best serve the nation as dutiful mothers, wives, and daughters.[24] In the classic *Staats-Lexikon*, published in fourteen volumes between 1834 and 1843, theorist Carl Theodor Welcker laid out a popular position. Convinced that "the subordination of women to men" was good for everyone, Welcker glorified the heterosexual relationships that confined women to domestic tasks. He judged societies by their commitment to gender difference. American men, Welcker wrote, confirmed that the United States "led in the most essential features of true civilization" because they recognized that "women's honor" was entirely different from men's rights.[25] In Welcker's mind, the North American republic was a model of liberal nationalism *because* women were restricted from political activity, not despite the fact. Liberals who wrote about gender before 1848 did not conclude that their political philosophy necessitated sexual equality.

A brief examination of one of *Vormärz* Germany's most influential organizations, the Turnverein, shows how the public sphere blended competing ideologies into a roughly coherent political culture that the Forty-Eighters could transport to the United States. Originating in the German resistance to the French occupation during the Napoleonic Wars, the Turnverein had used gymnastics as a cover to train men for military action. After a decades-long ban, the club resurfaced in 1842, with chapters proliferating as Germans grew more restive.[26] Turners would disagree among themselves on political economy and how to define the German *Volk*, but as long as the old regime remained in place, they could unite publicly around individual rights for men and the related goal of unifying the German nation.

The masculine tone of the Turners' German nationalism was striking. During the 1840s, they resumed their performances of physical strength, male sociability, and German nationalism. The high point of any regional

23 Marx and Engels, "Manifesto of the Communist Party" (1848), in *Collected Works*, 6: 502–03; Engels, "Draft of a Communist Confession of Faith" (1847), in *Collected Works*, 6: 103; Engels, "The Principles of Communism" (1847), in *Selected Works of Karl Marx and Frederick Engels*, 2 vols. (Moscow: Foreign Languages Publishing House, 1955–1958), 1: 81–97.

24 Gabrielle Hauch, "Women's Spaces in the Men's Revolution of 1848," in *Europe in 1848*, ed. Dowe et al., 654–62; Herzog, *Intimacy and Exclusion*, 85–110, 140–66.

25 Carl Theodor Welcker, "Geschlectsverhältnisse," in *Das Staats-Lexikon*, ed. Carl Theodor Welcker and Karl von Rotteck (Altona: J. F. Hammerich, 1838), 6: 658, 630. On gender and nineteenth-century liberalism, see Herzog, *Intimacy and Exclusion*, 140–66; Carola Lipp, "Frauen und Öffentlichkeit: Möglichkeiten und Grenzen politischer Partizipation im Vormärz und in der Revolution 1848," in *Schimpfende Weiber und patriotische Jungfrauen: Frauen im Vormärz und in der Revolution 1848/49*, ed. Carola Lipp (Moos: Elster, 1986), 270–301.

26 Dieter Düding, *Organisierter gesellschaftlicher Nationalismus in Deutschland*, 1808–1847 (Munich: R. Oldenbourg, 1984), 249–57.

Turnfest was always the men's gymnastics competition, but attendees also indulged in days of dances, feasts, toasts, political speeches, and torch-lit processions. These activities, which would later become familiar sights in Midwestern cities, were accompanied by patriotic songs and framed by decorations in the outlawed colors of the nationalist movement – red, black, and gold.[27] If anyone could unify the German nation, these displays suggested, it would be vigorous young men. Enacting a martial and fraternal ideal of citizenship, the Turners in no way shared Anneke's objections to patriarchy.

If the masculinity embedded in the Turners' nationalism was easy to spot, their economic ideas were more elusive. With a membership composed chiefly of clerks and artisans, many chapters became bastions of working-class solidarity. They also provided a forum for the debate of political economy. The Cologne Turnverein included several socialist leaders, and Düsseldorf Turners published a magazine that condemned capitalism. But one student of the movement found that Turners, especially in the southwestern German states that saw heavy out-migration, usually directed their ire at feudalism and absolutism.[28] At a large Heidelberg festival in 1847, a speaker declared, "Equality! Freedom! That is the watchword of the day, and those wealthy elites, those rapacious usurers . . . sit on soft chairs while we pine from hunger. So away with the estates. There is only one estate: the *Volk*."[29] This Turner assumed economic inequality would fall away with the passing of monarchal governments that manipulated the economy. Working-class energies could be channeled into liberal nationalist crusades.

Turner nationalism also included a spectrum of racial or ethnic messages. Its crux lay in the word *Volk*, which can be rendered in English as "nation," "people," "ethnicity," or "race." On the one hand, German nationalists appealed to the unity of the *Volk* in hopes of overcoming the authoritarian and hidebound governments of the individual German states. In that sense, the word *Volk* was inclusive, drawing together people who had traditionally been divided. The Turners' favorite patriotic song, Ernst Moritz Arndt's "Des Deutschen Vaterland," opened with five verses on the geographical scope of Germany.[30] In combination with their calls for equality

27 Ibid., 263–66, 282–99; Daniel A. McMillan, "Germany Incarnate: Politics, Gender, and Sociability in the Gymnastics Movement" (PhD diss., Columbia University, 1997), esp. 384–93, 408–11.
28 Sperber, *Rhineland Radicals*, 96–97; Ralf Wagner, "Turner Societies and the Socialist Tradition," in *German Workers' Culture in the United States, 1850–1920*, ed. Hartmut Keil (Washington, DC: Smithsonian Institution Press, 1998), 221–40; Levine, *Spirit of 1848*, 91–95.
29 Düding, *Organisierter gesellschaftlicher Nationalismus*, 291.
30 Ibid., 102, 270–71.

and freedom, this geographical focus indicated that Turners believed that the German *Volk* could encompass all the people who resided within the political boundaries of a future German state.

The German *Volk* did not yet have its own state, however, so the Turners also spoke of the biological and cultural attributes of prospective citizens. Here the strains within liberal nationalism were evident. The Turners were anti-French, and although they were not consistently anti-Semitic, some chapters were hostile to Jews. Turner literature sometimes mentioned German "blood," but biological descriptions of the *Volk* were overshadowed by references to the cultural markers that Americans would much later call "ethnic": a shared language, a sense of historical destiny, and a purported predisposition for honesty, justice, and courage.[31] Arndt's song celebrated such cultural characteristics without referring to biology at all, and Turner rituals emphasized culture over race. Not until the revolutions came would liberal nationalists need to settle the question of whether the German *Volk* would be defined in terms of culture, biology, or politics.

When the French deposed their king in February 1848, men and women in the German Confederation rose up against their own leaders. Peasants marched on the castles of local lords, tearing down symbols of authority and attempting to burn official records. They called for tax relief, forestry and hunting rights, and the chance to elect their own representatives. Some rural Germans targeted Jews, driving them from the villages in which they lived.[32] In large cities such as Berlin and Vienna, revolutionaries took to the streets. One future American, Friedrich Hassaurek, was just sixteen when he sustained minor injuries fighting troops in the Austrian capital.[33] Karl Marx rushed back to Cologne, where workers were massing outside government buildings and interrupting council meetings.[34] In many towns, women were among the Germans who demonstrated, built barricades, and brandished weapons.[35]

Although various local motives spurred the spontaneous actions, the opposition movement became a liberal nationalist one. Intent on uniting

---

31　Ibid., 139, 266–89.
32　Christof Dipper, "Rural Revolutionary Movements: Germany, France, Italy," in *Europe in 1848*, ed. Dowe et al., 420; Reinhard Rürup, "Progress and Its Limits: The Revolution of 1848 and European Jewry," in *Europe in 1848*, ed. Dowe et al., 751–54; Sperber, *Rhineland Radicals*, 166–67.
33　Wittke, "Friedrich Hassaurek: Cincinnati's Leading Forty-Eighter," *Ohio Historical Quarterly* 68 (1959): 2–3.
34　McLellan, *Karl Marx*, 177–81; Levine, *Spirit of 1848*, 41–42.
35　Hauch, "Women's Spaces in the Men's Revolution of 1848," 638, 662–75. Describing women's participation in street fighting, riots, and other protests, see Zucker, *Kathinka Zitz-Halein*, 70–93; Lipp, ed., *Schimpfende Weiber*. General accounts de-emphasize women. See for example Veit Valentin, *Geschichte der deutschen Revolution von 1848–1849*, 2 vols. (Berlin: Ullstein, 1931), 2: 579–82.

Germany, liberal nationalists set about advancing their political views. At university in Bonn, Carl Schurz signed up for a democratic association whose members addressed each other as "citizen." After being elected to its executive committee, he represented the organization at a congress in Cologne.[36] Peter Engelmann, who would become an eminent Milwaukeean, "sought out a number of like-minded companions...for the purpose of spreading liberal ideas."[37] They founded a Turnverein and a democratic club. Groups in southwestern Germany rallied around politicians such as Friedrich Hecker, a Baden assemblyman who led campaigns for freedom of the press, jury trials, and political representation. Hecker's part in raising an army to forcibly establish a republic would soon send him too to the United States.[38] Portraits of Hecker were on display at public meetings, and men like Karl Krumrey modeled their speeches after his writings.[39] Working-class demonstrators were also swept up in the liberalism of the moment. Marx and Engels made the creation of a German republic with universal manhood suffrage their first priority, assigning socialist policies such as state-owned transportation and public works a secondary status.[40] Around German Europe, protestors hewed to the red, black, and gold German tricolor.[41] A surprising number of Germans showed that they expected that reform would come through the consolidation of a democratically governed nation-state.

Alarmed by the unrest, German monarchs conceded in March 1848 to the election of a national parliament. Although the body seemed far too moderate to most of the Germans who would wind up in the United States, its proposed constitution is a useful guide to the Forty-Eighters' ideas of citizenship. When delegates met in Frankfurt am Main to give legal form to a German nation-state, they had to resolve the tension between their understanding of the *Volk* as a culturally demarked group and their commitment to a geographically bounded polity in which all men had equal rights. Historian Brian E. Vick persuasively argues that in response to this dilemma, the liberals imagined the nation as an "organic unity" that constantly evolved to incorporate different groups and realize its cultural

36 Schurz, *Reminiscences*, 1: 137–40.
37 Peter Engelmann, "Autobiography," box 1, page 6 of typed translation, Milwaukee County Historical Society (hereafter MCHS).
38 Sabine Freitag, *Friedrich Hecker: Biographie eines Republikaners* (Stuttgart: Steiner, 1998), 103–13.
39 Sperber, *Rhineland Radicals*, 243; Krumrey, "Journal, 1842–1870," box 3, folder 7, Germans in the United States Collection, WHS.
40 Marx and Engels, "Demands of the Communist Party in Germany" (1848), in *Collected Works*, 7: 3–4.
41 Sperber, *Rhineland Radicals*, 151–54.

potential. They hoped that free institutions would facilitate cultural cohesion and cultural progress, which in turn would purify the political expression of the nation.[42]

The parliamentary discussion of the place of Jews in a future Germany illustrates how liberals delimited the *Volk*, an exercise that would inform the Forty-Eighters' take on American pluralism. Just as many white Americans did not include people of African descent in their imagined nation, many German liberals indulged in vicious anti-Semitic stereotypes.[43] Hecker, for example, rhetorically excluded Jews from the German *Volk*, describing them as parasitical and backward.[44] Yet by 1848, his native Baden and several other German states were repealing the laws that barred Jews from some occupations and curbed their political activities.[45] Jewish Germans were elected to numerous legislatures in 1848, seven practicing Jews sat in the Frankfurt Parliament, and ten other delegates had Jewish ancestry.[46] Hamburg's Gabriel Riesser, the most vocal of these parliamentarians, persuaded his colleagues to include Jews who lived within the geographical boundaries of the proposed German state on equal terms with Catholics and Protestants.[47] Brian Vick explains that "as a result of the mixing of cultural and political ideas of nationality in mid-nineteenth-century German thought, liberal nationalists did not have to insist on either total exclusion or total absorption of a culturally distinct population in order to achieve a comfortable and workable degree of national and political unity."[48] Liberals who retained a jaundiced view of Jewishness hoped that making Jews part of the German *Volk* would transform their character and eradicate their traditions.[49] German Forty-Eighters would apply some of these lessons in the United States, although they would be much more enthusiastic pluralists when they were in the minority.

---

42 Brian E. Vick, *Defining Germany: The 1848 Frankfurt Parliamentarians and National Identity* (Cambridge, MA: Harvard University Press, 2002), 15, 28. On the definition of *Volk* (plural *Völker*) during the middle decades of the nineteenth century, see also Reinhart Koselleck, "Volk, Nation, Nationalismus, Masse," in *Geschichtliche Grundbegriffe: Historisches Lexikon zur politisch-sozialen Sprache in Deutschland*, ed. Otto Brunner, Werner Conze, and Reinhart Koselleck (Stuttgart: Ernst Klett Verlag, 1972–1992), 7: 380–89.

43 Léon Poliakov, *The History of Anti-Semitism*, trans. Miriam Kochan, 4 vols. (London: Routledge & Kegan Paul, 1965–1985), 3: 380–429; Eleonore Sterling, *Judenhass: Die Anfänge des politischen Antisemitismum in Deutschland, 1815–1850* (Frankfurt am Main: Europäische Verlagsanstalt, 1969).

44 Vick, *Defining Germany*, 97; Herzog, *Intimacy and Exclusion*, 55, 56, 65, 74, 75.

45 Ibid., 59; Nipperdey, *Germany*, 217–19.

46 Rürup, "Progress and Its Limits," 758. Jews, who made up 1.5 percent of the population of the German Confederation, were certainly underrepresented among the 649 deputies. Nipperdey, *Germany*, 220; Frank Eyck, *The Frankfurt Parliament, 1848–1849* (London: Macmillan, 1968), 57.

47 Ibid., 241–44. 48 Herzog, *Intimacy and Exclusion*, 85.

49 Vick, *Defining Germany*, 79–109; Herzog, *Intimacy and Exclusion*, 53–84.

As they tied membership in the nation to residence within the state, not cultural background, liberals in Frankfurt also debated whether all Germans would hold the same legal status. German legal precedent was not well suited to drafting citizenship law for a nation-state. Historically, a German *Bürger* was a member of the small group of artisans and merchants who lived within the self-governing towns of the Holy Roman Empire. These politically active men formed a privileged estate within the traditional polity.[50] The rise of absolute monarchies in the eighteenth century had supplemented this old usage of *Bürger* with another. By the early 1800s, the constitutions of Prussia and Austria used the term *Staatsbürger* synonymously with "subject" to refer to an inhabitant who received protection from the sovereign in return for taxes, obedience, and military service. The inadequacy of such a minimalist citizenship reverberated through the uprisings of 1848. Liberals rejected both the declining estate-based order and the authoritarianism of the new monarchical states, calling for a citizenship that allowed men to participate actively in government through the franchise.[51]

Like similar institutions that had devised fundamental law in France and the United States, the Frankfurt Parliament framed citizenship in vague terms. The parliament's constitution proposed that the German *Volk* comprise current "members" (*Angehörigen*) of all the states that joined the new empire. It proceeded to promise "citizenship of the empire" (*Reichsbürgerrecht*) to "every German."[52] The central and state governments

---

50 Manfried Reidel, "Bürger, Staatsbürger, Bürgertum," in *Geschichtliche Grundbegriffe*, ed. Brunner, Conze, and Koselleck, 1: 676–78; Mack Walker, *German Home Towns: Community, State, and General Estate, 1648–1871* (Ithaca, NY: Cornell University Press, 1971); Sheehan, *German History*, 24–40.

51 At mid-century, the power of parliaments varied among the German states, as did the extent to which the parliaments represented the traditional estates. Sheehan, "The German States and the European Revolution," in *Revolution and the Meanings of Freedom in the Nineteenth Century*, ed. Isser Woloch (Stanford, CA: Stanford University Press, 1996), 259–60. For the transition in citizenship ideas, see Reidel, "Bürger, Staatsbürger, Bürgertum," 683–87, 702–06; Sheehan, *German History*, 55–71; Nathans, *Politics of Citizenship in Germany*, 37–53; Willibald Steinmetz, "'Speaking Is a Deed for You': Words and Action in the Revolution of 1848," in *Europe in 1848*, ed. Dowe et al., 834.

On French and American models, see Freitag, *Friedrich Hecker*, 52, 111; Horst Dippel, *Germany and the American Revolution, 1770–1800: A Sociohistorical Investigation of Late Eighteenth-Century Political Thinking*, trans. Bernhard A. Uhlendorf (Chapel Hill: University of North Carolina Press, 1977); Dipple, *Die amerikanische Verfassung in Deutschland im 19. Jahrhundert: Das Dilemma von Politik und Staatsrecht* (Goldbach: Keip Verlag, 1994); Günter Moltmann, *Atlantische Blockpolitik im 19. Jahrhundert: Die Vereinigten Staaten und der deutsche Liberalismus während der Revolution von 1848/49* (Düsseldorf: Droste Verlag, 1973); Schurz, *Reminiscences*, 1: 29.

Some scholars argue that there were German theorists attracted to the notion of classical republican citizenship popular in the United States at the time of the Revolution. Freitag, *Friedrich Hecker*, 63–95; Paul Nolte, "Bürgerideal, Gemeinde und Republik: 'Klassischer Republikanismus' in frühen deutschen Liberalismus," *Historische Zeitschrift* 254 (1992): 609–56; Hans Erich Bödecker, "The Concept of the Republic in Eighteenth-Century German Thought," in *Republicanism and Liberalism in America and the German States, 1750–1850*, ed. Jürgen Heideking and James A. Henretta (Cambridge: Cambridge University Press, 2002), 35–52.

52 Constitution of the German Empire (proposed, 1849), sec. 6, art. 1, para. 131, 132.

would be bound to respect "every German's" equality before the law. The constitution enumerated many specific rights, including freedom of speech, freedom of religion, and the freedom to organize politically. In a move that would one day seem significant to immigrants in the United States, the constitution also granted the "non-German speakers of Germany" the right to their own languages.[53] Like the U.S. Constitution, this German constitution did not make the franchise a right of citizenship, but it stipulated that the lower house in the empire's parliament would consist of "representatives of the German *Volk*."[54] In subsequent legislation, the Frankfurt Parliament decreed that an eligible voter was a German man of "good reputation" over the age of twenty-five. A few classes of men, including those who had received public welfare, were excluded, but servants, day laborers, and other men without property would have been enfranchised had this law taken effect.[55] Although the parliament heatedly debated the status of poor German men, there was never any chance that women would become voting citizens. As in France and the United States, the non-voting status of women proved the existence of a second-class form of citizenship.[56]

Plenty of revolutionary leaders were dissatisfied with the parliament's work. August Willich would have liked some concrete recognition of the economic rights of citizens. Along with other socialists, he argued that there would have been no parliament without the sacrifices of workers and peasants. Impoverished Germans deserved more than suffrage in return.[57] Marx and Weydemeyer, who thought Willich and his ilk impractical, resigned themselves early on to a liberal — and in their minds therefore limited — revolution. While Marx always questioned nationalism and patriarchy, he never made his approval of the constitution contingent on their demolition. His main reservations, shared with liberals such as Schurz, Müller, and Hecker, were that the parliamentarians had not declared Germany a

---

53 Ibid., sec. 6, esp. art. 8, para. 188.
54 Ibid., sec. 4, art. 3, para. 93. For a translation and discussion, see Jörg-Detlef Kühne, "Civil Rights and German Constitutional Thought, 1848–1871," in *German and American Constitutional Thought*, ed. Hermann Wellenreuther (Oxford: Berg, 1990), 199–232.
55 Frankfurt Parliament, "Gesetz betreffend die Wahlen der Abgeordneten zum Volkshause," April 12, 1849 (available online at http://www.documentarchiv.de/nzjh/1849/reichswahlgesetz1849.html, accessed Dec. 4, 2012).
56 The Frankfurt Parliament itself had been elected by all "mature independent citizens," but most of the elections were indirect. Sperber, *Rhineland Radicals*, 173; Eyck, *Frankfurt Parliament*, 45–46, 57–61; Reidel, "Bürger, Staatsbürger, Bürgertum," 1: 711–12; Kühne, "Civil Rights and German Constitutional Thought," 199–232. On half-way or "passive" citizenship, see Sheehan, "German States and the European Revolution," 260–61; Bödecker, "Concept of the Republic in Eighteenth-Century German Thought," 36.
57 Easton, *Hegel's First American Followers*, 168–74.

republic and, by temporizing, had given the forces of reaction time to regroup.[58]

In the end, all the wrangling came to nothing. In March 1849, the Frankfurt Parliament offered the crown of a united Germany, excluding Austria, to Friedrich Wilhelm IV of Prussia, but the king had no interest in subjecting himself to constitutional limitations. Instead, he turned his troops on civilians in Berlin and sent military aid to the ousted princes in the Southwest. The volunteer militias that held out longest against Prussian troops in Baden included Schurz, Willich, and both Annekes. When the insurgency finally collapsed in July 1849, they were among the many revolutionaries who, facing prosecution or simply disillusioned, left Germany for good.[59]

A generation of emigrants had lived through this momentous episode in European history. The political refugees most clearly preserved the ideas and emotions of the revolutions, but hundreds of thousands of less politically active Germans also emigrated when nothing was done about the conditions that had triggered the protests in the first place.[60] Socialists and conservatives were aware that liberal nationalists had proffered compelling alternatives to the status quo: a nationalism based on residence, not race or even culture, and a form of citizenship grounded in universal manhood suffrage. In North America, all German-speaking immigrants would reconsider these ideas, not as subjects of divided kingdoms and principalities, but as members of a minority group in an Anglo-American republic.

GERMAN VOLK: FROM NATION TO ETHNICITY

The Revolutions of 1848 certainly influenced how German Americans conceived of citizenship, but so too did their status as newcomers in the United States. Of course, there was no one immigrant experience. Coming from various mostly western German states, immigrant men, women, and children practiced different religions, settled in different places, and held different jobs. Yet German-American families used similar strategies

---

58 Marx explained his position in the pages of the *Neue Rheinische Zeitung*. Extensive excerpts are translated in Marx and Engels, *Collected Works*, 7: 15–445. See also Obermann, *Joseph Weydemeyer: Ein Lebensbild*, 121–69.

59 Anneke, *Memoiren einer Frau aus den badisch-pfälzischen Feldzug* (Newark: [n.p.], 1853); Mathilde Anneke to Franziska Rollmann, [1849], reel 1, fr. 96–98, Mathilde and Fritz Anneke Papers (microfilm), WHS; Schurz, *Reminiscences*, 1: 196–236; Schurz to his Parents and Sisters, July 21, 1849; Schurz to his Friends, July 23, 1849; Schurz to his Parents, July 31, 1849, in *Intimate Letters of Carl Schurz, 1841–1869*, ed. and trans. Joseph Schafer (Madison: State Historical Society of Wisconsin, 1928), 58–74; Easton, *Hegel's First American Followers*, 169.

60 Conzen, "Germans," 406.

to overcome the strain of relocation. Aspiring community leaders could tap and purvey broadly resonant images of rewarding social bonds among immigrants as they consolidated and characterized German Americans as a group. The politics of slavery and black suffrage would soon entwine with ethnic formation, but even the common denominators of German-American self-representation affected the ideological climate that former slaves would face upon emancipation. The festive sociability that filled the German-language public sphere constituted German immigrants as a specifically cultural minority. In the United States, the German *Volk* was not to be a race or a nation; it would be an ethnicity.[61]

In 1848, German-born Americans were already a diverse lot numbering about half a million. When news of the European uprisings reached the United States, the country's best-known German residents greeted the prospect of revolution with excitement.[62] Friedrich Münch, a beloved politician and writer who had settled on a Missouri vineyard during the 1830s, was so moved that he rued ever having abandoned his fatherland.[63] Milwaukee's Germans learned of the revolutions through their newspapers, churches, and *Vereine* and quickly arranged a city-wide display of solidarity.[64] At mass meetings, immigrants often gave touring revolutionaries a warm reception. One such occasion in Cincinnati saw Johann Bernard Stallo, who had emigrated from Oldenburg as a child and was just beginning a career as a jurist and politician, welcome Friedrich Hecker to Ohio.[65] From there, Hecker traveled on to St. Louis, where immigrants were just as eager to see him.[66]

---

61 Arguing that the Forty-Eighters developed an "ethnic" identity, see Nagel, *Von republikanischen Deutschen zu deutsch-amerikanischen Republikanern,* 388–402.

62 Conzen, "Germans," 406; Gustav Koerner, *Memoirs of Gustav Koerner, 1809–1896,* 2 vols. (Cedar Rapids, IA: The Torch Press, 1909), 1: 528–41; Levine, *Spirit of 1848, 83–86;* Wittke, *The German-Language Press in America* ([Lexington]: University of Kentucky Press, 1957), 59–74; Wittke, *Refugees of Revolution,* 29–42, 83–86; Gazley, *American Opinion of German Unification,* 454–58; Kamphoefner, "'Auch unser Deutschland muss einmal frei werden': The Immigrant Civil War Experience as a Mirror on Political Conditions in Germany," in *Transatlantic Images and Perceptions: Germany and America since 1776,* ed. David E. Barclay and Elisabeth Glaser-Schmidt (Cambridge: Cambridge University Press, 1997), 87–107. Emphasizing liberalism before 1848, see Steven Rowan, "German Language Newspapers in St. Louis, 1835–1974," in *The German-American Experience in Missouri: Essays in Commemoration for the Tricentennial of German Immigration to America, 1683–1983,* ed. Howard W. Marshall and James W. Goodrich (Columbia: Missouri Cultural Heritage Center, University of Missouri – Columbia, 1986), 48–49; Conzen, *Immigrant Milwaukee,* 172.

63 William G. Bek, "The Followers of Duden: Friedrich Muench," *Missouri Historical Review* 18 (1924): 428; Friedrich Münch, *Gesammelte Schriften,* ed. Konrad Ries and Carl G. Rothmann (St. Louis: Julius Meyer, 1902), xi–xxiii.

64 Conzen, *Immigrant Milwaukee,* 154–91; Rudolph A. Koss, *Milwaukee* (Milwaukee, WI: Herold, 1871), 263–64; Ernest Bruncken, "The Germans in Wisconsin Politics: I. Until the Rise of the Republican Party," *Parkman Club Publications* 9 (1896): 234–35.

65 Easton, *Hegel's First American Followers,* 23–32.   66 Freitag, *Friedrich Hecker,* 152.

Yet the apparently overwhelming enthusiasm for the revolutions concealed differences that would always complicate the work of interpreting their legacy and constructing German ethnicity. Religion deeply divided German immigrants. About one-third of German Americans were at least nominally Roman Catholic, and the institutions of the Church sheltered some Catholics from other German speakers.[67] The country's first German-language Catholic newspaper, the *Wahrheitsfreund* (Friend of Truth), had appeared in Cincinnati in 1837. Its founder was John Martin Henni, a Swiss-born priest whose appointment as the first bishop of Milwaukee in 1843 inaugurated a long period of German ascendancy among Wisconsin Roman Catholics.[68] In Ohio and Missouri, Germans congregated in "national parishes" led by German-speaking priests within Irish-led diocese and archdiocese. Like their coreligionists to the north, many of them valued the parochial schools, charities, and lay organizations that separated them from non-Catholics.[69] Among Protestant Germans, the orthodox Lutherans of the Missouri Synod also developed a strong institutional base. The relatively small synod, which actually crossed state lines, was known for its theological and political conservatism.[70] Religiously observant immigrants, who associated with fellow believers and cleaved to dogmas of their own, were the least likely to accept liberal nationalism in 1848. Rudolph Koss, an immigrant doctor and early chronicler of German Milwaukee, noted that Protestant pastors in the city had been among the "isolated voices from

67 Conzen, "Immigrant Religion and the Republic: German Catholics in Nineteenth-Century America," *German Historical Institute Bulletin* 35 (2004): 45. It is very difficult to confirm this number, but a Milwaukee priest believed that about one-third of Milwaukee Germans were Catholic in 1852. Anthony Urbanek, Report to Archbishop of Vienna, Edward Milde, 1853, in "Documents: Letter of the Right Reverend John Martin Henni," *Wisconsin Magazine of History* 10 (1926): 89.

68 Peter Leo Johnson, *Crosier on the Frontier: A Life of John Martin Henni* (Madison: State Historical Society of Wisconsin, 1959), 45–48, 56–76. On the *Wahrheitsfreund*, see Karl J. R. Arndt and May E. Olsen, *German-American Newspapers and Periodicals, 1732–1955: History and Bibliography* (Heidelberg: Quelle & Meyer, 1961; reprint, New York: Johnson Reprint Corp., 1965), 457.

69 On Ohio, see Max Burgheim, *Cincinnati in Wort und Bild* (Cincinnati: M. & R. Burgheim, 1888), 241–42; Joseph M. White, "Religion and Community: Cincinnati Germans, 1814–1870" (PhD diss., University of Notre Dame, 1980). On Wisconsin, see Wilhelm Hense-Jensen, *Wisconsin's Deutsch-Amerikaner bis zum Schluß des neunzehnten Jahrhunderts*, 2 vols. (Milwaukee, WI: Verlag der Deutschen Gesellschaft, 1900), 1: 71–95; Steven M. Avella, *In the Richness of the Earth: A History of the Archdiocese of Milwaukee, 1843–1958* (Milwaukee, WI: Marquette University Press, 2002). On Missouri, see William B. Faherty, *The St. Louis German Catholics* (St. Louis: Reedy Press, 2004). More broadly, see Barry, *Catholic Church and German Americans*; Georg Timpe, ed., *Katholisches Deutschthum in den Vereinigten Staaten: Ein Querschnitt* (Freiburg im Breisgau: Herder & Co., 1937); Philip Gleason, *The Conservative Reformers: German-American Catholics and the Social Order* (Notre Dame, IN: University of Notre Dame Press, 1968); Conzen, "German Catholics in America," in *The Encyclopedia of American Catholic History*, ed. Michael Glazier and Thomas T. Shelley (Collegeville, MN: The Liturgical Press, 1997), 571–83.

70 Luebke, "The Immigrant Condition as A Factor Contributing to the Conservatism of The Lutheran Church – Missouri Synod," *Concordia Historical Institute Quarterly* 38 (1965): 19–28.

the reactionary side" during the revolutions. Minimizing the significance of these religious leaders still further, he added that the faithful did not necessarily follow their clergy.[71] Koss, like most secular writers, showed little interest in the German Americans who were wary of the mainstream production of ethnicity.

Some Germans avoided American cities because they wanted their conservative and communal beliefs to be safe from liberal nationalism. As paradoxical as it might seem to move to the United States in the name of tradition, there were people who migrated with the intention of forming tight-knit enclaves in the rural Midwest.[72] A group of parishioners at St. Peter's Cathedral in Cincinnati planned one such community in the early 1830s. These Catholics, who all hailed from the same area in northwestern Germany, pooled their resources to settle in the western part of Ohio. The town they founded, Minster, was known for its insular piety – not its demonstrative German nationalism – well into the twentieth century.[73] The Revolutions of 1848 did not end such initiatives. In 1854, a group of Catholics in Baden nominated a priest to lead them to St. Nazianz, Wisconsin. The spokesmen of German America would never really speak for these small religious settlements.[74] Sometimes editors and politicians appeared to forget that a majority of German immigrants in Wisconsin and Ohio, and a significant minority in Missouri, lived outside the major centers at mid-century.[75] Rural dwellers were not all religious conservatives, but they were generally less liberal than urbanites.[76]

The cities were not monolithic either, and it was there that class most clearly structured the German community. In comparison to native-born and Irish-born workers, German immigrants were strongly represented in the skilled trades such as carpentry, leatherwork, shoemaking, and garment

---

71 Koss, *Milwaukee*, 265.
72 See especially Conzen, *Making Their Own America: Assimilation Theory and the German Peasant Pioneer* (New York: Berg Publishers, 1990); Gjerde, *Minds of the West: Ethnocultural Evolution in the Rural Middle West, 1830–1917* (Chapel Hill: University of North Carolina Press, 1997); Kamphoefner, "The German Agricultural Frontier: Crucible or Cocoon?" *Ethnic Forum* 4, no. 2 (1984): 21–35.
73 Anne Aengenvoort, *Migration, Siedlungsbildung, Akkulturation: Die Auswanderung Nordwestdeutscher nach Ohio, 1830–1914* (Stuttgart: F. Steiner, 1999).
74 Manitowoc Nord-Westen, "Geschichte der Entstehung und Gründung der deutschen Colonie, St. Nazianz," trans. J. J. Schlicher, *Wisconsin Magazine of History* 31 (1947): 85.
75 Louise Phelps Kellogg, "The Story of Wisconsin, 1634–1848: IV. Foreign Immigration in Territorial Times," *Wisconsin Magazine of History* 3 (1920): 321.
76 Rural Missouri Germans might create dense settlements, but they were not all conservative. See Russel L. Gerlach, "Population Origins in Rural Missouri," *Missouri Historical Review* 71 (1975): 1–21; Kamphoefner, *The Westfalians: From Germany to Missouri* (Princeton, NJ: Princeton University Press, 1987); Robert W. Frizzell, *Independent Immigrants: A Settlement of Hanoverian Germans in Western Missouri* (Columbia: University of Missouri Press, 2007).

production.[77] These craftworkers leavened the working-class culture and politics of American towns, leading strikes and forming mutual aid associations.[78] In 1853, for example, Germans coordinated workers in several industries who struck for higher wages in Cincinnati, Dayton, Milwaukee, and many other locations.[79] Unskilled wageworkers, who made up about one-fifth of the German-American workforce, had even more reason to be disgruntled, since they endured lower pay, less predictable hours, and more dangerous workplaces. Their vulnerability made them difficult to organize, but German-born laborers were also an unmistakable presence in the Midwestern city.[80] Class differences were a source of irritation to some of the editors, lawyers, and politicians who became ethnic leaders, but urban areas offered a possible windfall of voters.[81]

Regardless of religion, location, or class, nearly all German immigrant households maintained traditions that eased the wrenching feelings that often attended migration, distinguished the recent arrivals from other Americans, and formed the basis for ethnicity. Germans were much more likely than the Irish to cross the Atlantic with family members, and some of them followed relatives who had moved months or years earlier.[82] Mathilde and Fritz Anneke settled in Milwaukee because one of Mathilde's cousins already lived in the area, and soon her mother, two of her sisters, and Fritz's brother joined them. It was not typical for extended families to live under one roof, but the arrangement allowed the Annekes to leave their children in the care of Mathilde's mother and sisters while they both traveled for their careers. Mathilde wrote that she did not find "heavenly bliss" in all the "domestic cares and work" of "washing, tidying, cleaning, cooking, digging, and

---

77 Levine, *Spirit of 1848*, 60–62; Conzen, *Immigrant Milwaukee*, 95–113; Audrey L. Olson, "St. Louis Germans, 1850–1920: The Nature of an Immigrant Community and Its Relation to the Assimilation Process" (PhD diss., University of Kansas, 1963), 31–36.

78 See generally Keil, ed., *German Workers' Culture*; Stanley Nadel, *Little Germany: Ethnicity, Religion, and Class in New York City 1845–80* (Urbana: University of Illinois Press, 1990); Steven J. Ross, *Workers on the Edge: Work, Leisure, and Politics in Industrializing Cincinnati, 1788–1890* (New York: Columbia University Press, 1985), 172–78; Stanley Nadel, "The German Immigrant Left in the United States," in *The Immigrant Left in the United States*, ed. Paul Buhle and Dan Georgakas (Albany: State University of New York Press, 1996), 45–51; Elliott Shore, Ken Fones-Wolf, and James P. Danky, eds., *The German-American Radical Press: The Shaping of a Left Political Culture, 1850–1940* (Urbana: University of Illinois Press, 1992).

79 Levine, *Spirit of 1848*, 140; Nadel, "German Immigrant Left," 49.

80 Ibid., 62; Conzen, *Immigrant Milwaukee*, 85–90, 99.

81 Obermann, *Joseph Weydemeyer: Ein Lebensbild*, 238–9, 340–52.

82 Conzen, "Germans," 411; Hasia Diner, *Erin's Daughters in America: Irish Immigrant Women in the Nineteenth Century* (Baltimore: Johns Hopkins University Press, 1983), 31. Assessing the scholarship on chain migration, see Kamphoefner, "Chain Migration and Diaspora: The Settlement Patterns of Immigrants from 'Greater Westphalia' across the U.S.A.," in *Die deutsche Präsenz in den USA: The German Presence in the U.S.A.*, ed. Josef Raab and Jan Wirrer (Berlin: LIT Verlag, 2008), 139–63.

weeding."[83] Such chores must have consumed many German-American women, though, for they had high rates of marriage and low rates of paid employment.[84] Most middle-class German-American women supported their husbands from within the home. In cities and large towns, mothers who could not afford to devote themselves exclusively to their own families might take in boarders, and many girls spent a period in domestic service.[85] Farming families also organized along patriarchal lines, but immigrant women were more active farmers than their Yankee neighbors. One Missouri Synod pastor said that his wife "helped energetically with the farm work," and the sight of a German woman plowing a Midwestern field shocked many an Anglo-American observer.[86]

For all the differences among them, immigrant households preserved the German language and European customs. Women shouldered much of the responsibility for converting what had been understood as national traits in Europe into ethnic characteristics in the United States. German Midwesterners believed that women were essential to fostering German culture within their families. Historian Anke Ortlepp has found that the women who joined immigrant organizations in nineteenth-century Milwaukee all accepted the ideal of the *Kulturträgerin* (female bearer of the culture), whether they were middle-class, working-class, socialist, Catholic, or Protestant. German immigrant women believed themselves "the most important means of conveying the crucial cornerstones of German-American identity such as language, values, and cultural attributes."[87] In a country with an Anglo-American majority, the *Kulturträgerin* performed

---

83 Mathilde Anneke to Johanna Weißkirch, July 14, 1857, in Anneke, *Mathilde Franziska Anneke*, ed. Wagner, 88, 75.

84 Conzen, *Immigrant Milwaukee*, 52; Keil, "Die Auswirkung der deutschen Auswanderung auf den amerikanischen Arbeitsmarkt," in *Die deutsche Präsenz*, ed. Raab and Wirrer, 228–29.

85 Conzen, *Immigrant Milwaukee*, 54–55; Silke Wehner-Franco, *Deutsche Dienstmädchen in America, 1850–1914* (Münster: Waxmann, 1994), 2–5.

86 Peter Heinrich Dicke, "Autobiography of Peter Heinrich Dicke: Pastor and Pioneer Missionary," trans. Eleanor Katherine Daib, *Concordia Historical Institute Quarterly* 78 (2005): 152. Gjerde, *Minds of the West*, 135–221, describes rural Midwestern families with particular insight. See also Linda Schelbitzi Pickle, *Contented among Strangers: Rural German-Speaking Women and their Families in the Nineteenth-Century Midwest* (Urbana: University of Illinois Press, 1996); Christiane Harzig, "Gender, Transatlantic Space, and the Presence of German-Speaking People in North America," in *Traveling between Worlds: German-American Encounters*, ed. Thomas Adam and Ruth Gross (College Station: Texas A & M University Press, 2006), 159–68. Focusing on the Anglo-American reaction, see Gjerde, "Prescriptions and Perceptions of Labor and Family among Ethnic Groups in the Nineteenth-Century American Middle West," in *German-American Immigration and Ethnicity in Comparative Perspective*, ed. Wolfgang Helbich and Walter D. Kamphoefner (Madison, WI: Max Kade Institute for German-American Studies, 2004), 117–37.

87 Anke Ortlepp, *"Auf denn, Ihr Schwestern!": Deutschamerikanische Frauenvereine in Milwaukee, Wisconsin, 1844–1914* (Stuttgart: F. Steiner, 2004), 262. See also Monika Blaschke, "Communicating the Old and the New: German Immigrant Women and Their Press in Comparative Perspective around 1900," in *People in Transit: German Migrations in Comparative Perspective*, ed. Dirk Hoerder and

a slightly different role than in Europe. She passed on a foreign language and foreign mores, work that was necessary to the development of ethnicity and ultimately to the immigrant framing of citizenship.

Women introduced their American-born children to the *Muttersprache* that would bind the immigrants to each other and differentiate them from other inhabitants of the United States. One Wisconsin woman, Rose Schuster Taylor, wistfully remembered growing up in Dane County during the 1860s and 1870s. On winter evenings, her mother sang German songs and staged German plays with the children. Taylor's father joined in too, telling German fairy tales and reading the poetry of Heinrich Heine and Johann Wolfgang von Goethe aloud.[88] In nearby Watertown, Margarethe Schurz extended her maternal role by starting what may have been the first kindergarten in the United States. The daughter of prosperous Jewish liberals from Hamburg, Schurz had studied Friedrich Fröbel's theories of educational play before moving to Wisconsin with her husband Carl in the early 1850s. She first taught her own daughter and young relatives and then opened her doors to other families.[89] By rearing children to speak German, such women and countless other mothers laid the groundwork for ethnicity.

German-American commentators assumed that women would also hand down what Jacob Müller termed "German spirit and nature" within the home. With a remarkable degree of unanimity, immigrant leaders believed that Germans brought authentic sociability, warm simplicity, and principled integrity to an austere and individualistic land. Müller, who would become a Republican politician in Cleveland, thought that American life "lacked a spiritual core," and many other liberal refugees at first saw their new home as a country "of humbug and materialism."[90] St. Louis's Heinrich Börnstein said that he preferred "the friendly, cozy tone of a North German home" to the fast-paced acquisitiveness and gluttony he witnessed

Jörg Nagler (Cambridge: Cambridge University Press, 1995), 313–28; Hense-Jensen, *Wisconsin's Deutsch-Amerikaner*, 1: 18–19.

88 H. J. Taylor, "Peter Schuster: Dane County Farmer," *Wisconsin Historical Magazine* 29 (1945): 80–82. See also William Bruce, "Memoirs of William George Bruce," *Wisconsin Magazine of History* 16 (1933): 380–82.

89 Ann Taylor Allen, "American and German Women in the Kindergarten Movement, 1850–1914," in *German Influences on Education in the United States to 1917*, ed. Henry Geitz, Jürgen Heideking, and Jurgen Herbst (Cambridge: Cambridge University Press, 1995), 85–103; Hannah Werwath Swart, *Margarethe Meyer Schurz: A Biography* (Watertown, WI: Watertown Historical Society, 1967); Hans L. Trefousse, *Carl Schurz: A Biography*, 2d ed. (New York: Fordham University Press, 1998), 64–65; Hense-Jensen, *Wisconsin's Deutsch-Amerikaner*, 1: 138.

90 Mueller, *Memories of a Forty-Eighter*, 4; Burgheim, *Cincinnati in Wort und Bild*, 147. See also Trommler, "The Use of History in German-American Politics," in *German Forty-Eighters*, ed. Brancaforte, 279–93.

in the United States.[91] Socialist Forty-Eighters essentially agreed. Joseph Weydemeyer wrote to Marx of his new home: "I don't think there is another place where one encounters the shopkeeper's mentality in more revolting nakedness. Any other aim in life besides making money is considered an absurdity here, and you can see it on every face, on every brick." Weydemeyer believed that although some immigrants were seduced by the pursuit of material gain, many of them shared his contempt for American culture.[92] Lutheran and Catholic leaders may not have much liked Müller, Börnstein, or Weydemeyer, but they were no less worried that American materialism would erode German families and communities.[93]

The spokesmen's apprehensions were themselves part of the project of constructing German ethnicity. Their public pronouncements both expressed and shaped immigrants' private longings. German-American leaders did not simply communicate ethnic identity, they also fashioned it. It pays to remember that public figures had political, economic, and personal reasons for believing that they represented a group of people with common interests. Forty-Eighters and other politicians hoped to promote their various ideologies, an objective that encouraged them to cultivate a bloc of voters among whom German origin was more salient than religion, location, or class. As they went, their beliefs imprinted their views of Germanness. The revolutionaries had to make a living too. They could be found among the proprietors of publications and venues that catered to immigrants who identified ethnically. Heinrich Börnstein, who quickly became a successful editor-cum-politician, also operated a beer hall and, briefly, a German theater company in St. Louis.[94] In most cases, ethnicity also yielded rewards beyond elected office or profit. Being a *Kulturträgerin*, for example, must have brought clubwomen personal satisfaction and a modicum of prestige. Blatant and subtle bids for power accompanied the production of ethnicity, ensuring that it would be contentious and value-laden from the start.

Even the uncontroversial core of German ethnicity was politically consequential. At *Verein* and church gatherings, theatrical performances, and beer gardens, immigrants became an ethnicity. They joined together and

---

91 Boernstein, *Memoirs of a Nobody*, 122, 79–81, 83.

92 Joseph Weydemeyer to Karl Marx and Friedrich Engels, Dec 1, 1851, quoted and trans. in Obermann, *Joseph Weydemeyer: Pioneer of American Socialism* (New York: International Publishers, 1947), 26. (The English version of Obermann's biography is shorter than the later German volume but covers Weydemeyer's involvement in American politics in more detail.) For similar working-class reactions to the United States, see Shore, Fones-Wolf, and Danky, eds., *German-American Radical Press*.

93 Gjerde, *Minds of the West*, 66–70, 257–62; Peterson, *Popular Narratives and Ethnic Identities*, 105.

94 Boernstein, *Memoirs of a Nobody*, 249–52, 254–60.

consecrated the qualities that they agreed made them unique, constituting themselves as a group of Americans bound by voluntary connections and sharing admirable habits. German-American identity was not only culturally constructed; it was constructed as cultural. The immigrants saw themselves as members of an ethnic entity rather than a racial one. Some individuals might occasionally claim that Germans were biologically superior too, but the festive culture of the 1850s and 1860s configured a cultural model of American pluralism.

Numerous events intensified the sense that voluntary attachments and shared rituals held the immigrants together. German Midwesterners could attend the regular meetings of sharpshooting clubs, singing societies (usually male), and other *Vereine*, or treat themselves to a range of rehearsed entertainments, highbrow and low. By the time of the Civil War, Cleveland, Cincinnati, and St. Louis all kept professional German theater companies in the black, and traveling acts and amateur productions graced stages in towns as small as Missouri's Boonville, Lexington, Hannibal, and Cape Girardeau.[95] Yet the most elemental activity through which German Americans constituted themselves as a cultural group was social drinking. Midwestern saloons and public houses functioned as community centers where immigrants bonded with each other and infused their relationships with meaning. Neighborhood bars were primarily male spaces, but at beer gardens women joined men, and children were welcome too.[96] Families, *Vereine*, and church groups relaxed at outdoor establishments during the summer months. These sites of German ethnicity dotted the landscape of cities such as Cincinnati, St. Louis, and Milwaukee. Kathleen Neils Conzen has described how *gemütlich* social gatherings temporarily obscured the everyday distinctions of religion and class and evoked a profound sense of common feeling. She argues that "festive culture drew [German immigrants]

---

95 John H. Kremling, "German Drama on the Cleveland Stage: Performances in German and English from 1850 to the Present" (PhD diss., The Ohio State University, 1976); Peter C. Merrill, *German-American Urban Culture: Writers and Theaters in Early Milwaukee* (Madison, WI: Max Kade Institute for German-American Studies, 2000); Alfred H. Nolle, "The German Drama on the St. Louis Stage" (PhD diss., University of Pennsylvania, 1917); Daniel L. Padberg, "German Ethnic Theater in Missouri: Cultural Assimilation" (PhD diss., Southern Illinois University, 1980), 172.

96 E. D. Kargau, *St. Louis in früheren Jahren: Ein Gedenkbuch für das Deutschthum* (St. Louis: Aug. Wiesbusch & Sohn, 1893), 204–09; Burgheim, *Cincinnati in Wort und Bild*, 147; German-American Biographical Pub. Co., *Cleveland and its Germans*, 39–41; *La Crosse Nord Stern*, May 26, 1860; Hense-Jensen, *Wisconsin's Deutsch-Amerikaner*, 1: 56–69; Conzen, "Ethnicity as Festive Culture: Nineteenth-Century German America on Parade," in *The Invention of Ethnicity*, ed. Werner Sollors (New York: Oxford University Press, 1989), 48; Tom Goyens, *Beer and Revolution: The German Anarchist Movement in New York City, 1880–1914* (Urbana: University of Illinois Press, 2007); Klaus Ensslen, "German-American Working-Class Saloons in Chicago," in *German Workers' Culture*, ed. Keil, 163–76.

to one another and set them apart from other Americans."[97] Festivity in all its forms, Conzen proposes, *was* ethnicity. Although she did not explore the line between ethnicity and race, as immigrants themselves would during the Civil War era, Conzen's insight supports the contention that German Americans became a cultural minority.

Sometimes assertions of dominance and battles for control revealed the different agendas that marked the ethnicity of festive culture. Although the Turnverein was perhaps the most visible ethnic organization in Midwestern cities, some immigrants resented this status. Others tried to sway the group's politics. The first club formed right after Hecker's visit to Cincinnati in 1848, but within weeks, other cities had started their own.[98] Led by disciplined elected committees that scheduled a roster of gymnastics exhibitions, concerts, educational programs, and social occasions, the Turnverein made the heady liberal nationalism of 1848 a mainstay of German-American ethnicity. Secular German Americans could proclaim that the Turnverein was "the center of spiritual [*geistig*] life for citizens of German descent," and no German-American politician could hope to attract the votes of urban Germans without an appearance at his local Turner Hall.[99] Yet the Turners' iteration of German ethnicity excluded many German Americans. The Cincinnati Turnverein was fairly typical in drawing most of its members from ranks of the skilled working class. Merchants and professionals made up a minority, and the unskilled did not join.[100] The humanistic spirit of the *Verein* generally put off religious Germans throughout the region, although some observant Lutherans did become Turners.[101] The Missouri Synod prohibited its members from joining, and many immigrants simply found that religious faith, parish life, and family satisfied their search for meaning and community.[102] Turners manifested German ethnicity without representing all German Americans.

Quarrels within the Turnverein also signaled that different ideological groups vied to shape German ethnicity in North America much as they had fought to direct German nationalism in Europe. During the early 1850s, some Turners saw a chance to challenge free-market liberalism. August

97 Conzen, "Ethnicity as Festive Culture," in *Invention of Ethnicity*, ed. Sollors, 48.
98 Levine, *Spirit of 1848*, 91.
99 Hense-Jensen, *Wisconsin's Deutsch Amerikaner*, 1: 157; *Erinnerung an Milwaukee die Stadt der Zusammenkünfte deutscher Vereine im Jahre 1877* (Milwaukee, WI: Philipp Best Brewing Co., 1877), 55.
100 Levine, *Spirit of 1848*, 91–93; Delores J. Hoyt, *A Strong Mind in A Strong Body: Libraries in the German-American Turner Movement* (New York: Peter Lang, 1999), 24.
101 H. Keller to John Knell, July 6, 1870, box 2, folder 2, John Knell Papers, WHS.
102 Luebke, "Immigrant Condition as a Factor Contributing to the Conservatism of the Lutheran Church – Missouri Synod," 25; Wittke, *Spirit of 1848*, 94–95.

Willich founded a specifically socialist chapter in Milwaukee on one visit, and Joseph Weydemeyer used the *Turn-Zeitung* to spread Marxist doctrine from New York. A national body called the Sozialistische Turnverein even attempted to coordinate all the local clubs.[103] Yet Weydemeyer was disappointed by the response to his work, and the economic program of the "socialist" national committee was vague enough not to offend many economic liberals. It called for "freedom, prosperity, and education for all" and the reconciliation of capital and labor, hardly a Marxist position.[104] The "red flag of socialism" was still enough to prompt liberal Milwaukeeans to start a number of alternative Turner groups.[105] Like Protestant congregations, Turnverein chapters splintered and reconsolidated, severing allegiances to the national league and founding competing umbrella organizations.[106] American politics, like the German revolutions, would divert socialists into liberal campaigns, but not before they tried to claim and define German-American identity for themselves.

The attempts of liberal leaders to crystalize ethnicity and imbue it with their values extended beyond the Turnverein. In May 1852, Milwaukee's Workers Reading and Education Society, an eclectic but essentially liberal organization that attracted Forty-Eighters such as Peter Engelmann and the Annekes, suggested that German religious, social, musical, sporting, and labor groups hold a *Volkfest*. After a committee composed of fifteen lawyers, politicians, and businessmen made careful preparations, the city's Germans put aside their political and religious differences for a day of "cheerfulness and gaiety." Before noon, a veritable "human migration" filled the streets with "countless multitudes of people." At two in the afternoon, speeches kicked off a program of singing, sports demonstrations, and merriment that continued late into the night. The spectacle was nonpartisan, but no one could miss the significance of German-speaking immigrants coalescing behind respectable leaders who bore the banner of liberal nationalism. Tellingly, though, Milwaukee's Germans could not cooperate long enough

103 Easton, *Hegel's First American Followers*, 177; Obermann, *Joseph Weydemeyer: Ein Lebensbild*, 253–55, 274–79.
104 Quoted in Levine, *Spirit of 1848*, 91. See also Hannes Neumann, *Die deutsche Turnbewegung in der Revolution 1848/49 und in der amerikanischen Emigration* (Stuttgart: Karl Hofmann Schorndorf, 1968), 73–88; Eric L. Pumroy and Katja Rampelmann, eds., *Research Guide to the Turner Movement in the United States* (Westport, CT: Greenwood Press, 1996), xviii; German-American Biographical Pub. Co., *Cleveland and its Germans*, 64–65.
105 Koss, *Milwaukee*, 275. On the Milwaukee Turners, see also Conzen, *Immigrant Milwaukee*, 179; Koss, *Milwaukee*, 371, 401–04; Hense-Jensen, *Wisconsin's Deutsch-Amerikaner*, 1: 155–58. On similar developments in St. Louis, see Kargau, *St. Louis in früheren Jahren*, 293–308; Neumann, *Die deutsche Turnbewegung*, 73–88. See also Wagner, "Turner Societies and the Socialist Tradition," in *German Workers' Culture*, 221–40; Hermann Schlüter, *Die Anfänge der deutschen Arbeiterbewegung in Amerika* (Stuttgart: J. H. W. Dietz Nachfolger, 1907), 199–214.
106 Ibid., 208; Nadel, *Little Germany*, 120–21, 128–29.

to make the festival a regular occurrence.[107] The ethnicity that German Americans called into being through theater, drinking, *Vereine*, and *Feste* would be the object of dispute.

Even before immigrants formally discussed cultural pluralism, German ethnicity in the United States had unmistakably diverged from German nationality in Europe. Being German in the American context could not mean striving for a German polity. Whereas the Turnverein had once called Germans to unite across the state boundaries of Central Europe, it now urged immigrants to retain their cultural difference within an existing state. By choosing to honor Thomas Paine as their model citizen, Turners announced that their ethnicity was not in competition with American nationalism. They admired the American revolutionary's cosmopolitanism, secularism, and support for universal manhood suffrage. In Paine, Turners saw a fervent liberal who had appreciated diversity.[108] German culture, they were sure he would have concurred, could complement political loyalty to the American state. It was a point driven home by American flags at folk festivals and beer gardens. One Milwaukee journalist, who grew up learning German from his mother, interpreted this symbol in his memoirs. Immigrants, he wrote, "believed that the American flag was big enough to permit them to enjoy themselves in accordance with their own native customs."[109]

When expressed so broadly, German-American ethnicity resonated for immigrants across religious, geographical, and class lines. Still, its effectiveness did not make it neutral or fixed. Immigrants were always reimagining American Germandom in light of their personal partialities. They would frequently find themselves at odds with each other, but they worked together to construct an ethnicity that was neither national nor racial, but cultural. Constituting themselves ethnically in the public sphere prepared immigrants to argue that the United States was a culturally plural nation. This development would touch African Americans, but before immigrants contemplated how, they would formalize a language of citizenship based on their own interests.

GENDERING OF CITIZENSHIP

CULTURAL PLURALISM German Americans adjusted the liberal
As they became an   ons of 1848 had popularized. Citizenship
nationalism that   69, 433.
                    106–10; Mark O. Kistler, "German-American Liberalism and Thomas
        Quarterly 14 (1962): 81–91; Honeck, *We Are the Revolutionists*, 90; Cleveland
        Nov. 24, Dec. 22, 1852, Feb. 2, 1853; Koss, *Milwaukee*, 275.
107 Ko noirs," 368.
108

still involved the bedrocks of individual rights and national loyalty, but now immigrants maintained that no nation was truly liberal unless it whole-heartedly embraced cultural pluralism. Immigrant newspapers presented this position when they took up drinking and voting rights. During these campaigns, the dynamics of ethnicity helped to gender the citizen. Immigration would leave an impression on the language and law of citizenship well before Reconstruction turned the national debate to the rights of black men and women.

To German-American editors fell the primary responsibility for crafting an explicit language of cultural pluralism. Most of these men were partisan entrepreneurs who were invested in a political party as well as the German-language press. Since the 1830s, the most successful German newspapers had affiliated with the Democrats, an easy choice since in the North the Party of Jackson tailored its politics to immigrant voters.[110] Cincinnati Democrats founded the *Volksblatt* in 1836 because leading Germans in the city considered an existing Whig sheet "an affront to the German name."[111] By 1852, the *Cincinnati Volksfreund* and the *Columbus Westbote* had increased the number of major Democratic papers in Ohio. That year, Müller helped sponsor Cleveland's new *Wächter am Erie*, which early on backed Democratic candidates too.[112] St. Louis boasted the first German-language newspaper west of the Mississippi. Dating to 1835, the *Anzeiger des Westens* had sided with the state's free soil Democrats by the early 1850s.[113] Just northwest of St. Louis, the *St. Charles Demokrat* did likewise when it first appeared in 1852. In 1844, a Milwaukee politician had lured editor Moritz Schöffler away from Jefferson City, Missouri, with promises that Democrats in his growing city would support a German-language newspaper.[114] Milwaukee Whigs countered Schöffler's *Banner* with the *Volksfreund* in 1847, but within five months, it too was supporting the Democrats.[115] Other newspapers came and went,

110 Hense-Jensen, *Wiscon-*
Olsen, *German-American Deutsch-Amerikaner*, 1: 98; Wittke, *German-Language Press*; Arndt and
Ethnic Press in the United Sta..ers; James M. Bergquist, "The German American Press," in *The
Conn.: Greenwood Press, 198? ...istorical Analysis and Handbook*, ed. Sally M. Miller (Westport,
WI: Max Kade Institute for Germ... Henry Geitz, ed. *The German-American Press* (Madison,
America: An Immigrant Press Visualizes ...an Studies, 1992); Peter Conolly-Smith, *Translating
Smithsonian Institution, 2004).* ...ular Culture, 1895–1918* (Washington, DC: The
111 Burgheim, *Cincinnati in Wort und Bild*, 199. ...ular Culture, 1895–1918* (Washington, DC: The
112 German-American Biographical Pub. Co., *Clev...
113 Rowan, "German Language Newspapers," 46–49.
114 Carl Heinz Knoche, "The German Immigrant Press ...mans, 42–44.
University, 1969), 21–26; Moritz Schoeffler to Franz Hue... ...PhD diss., The Ohio State
fler to Franz Huebschmann, Dec. 23, 1847, June 20, 1848; ... 1844; Moritz Schoef-
MCHS. ...bschmann Papers,
115 Arndt and Olsen, *German-American Newspapers*, 694.

and religious periodicals remained popular, but these secular dailies and weeklies in urban Ohio, Missouri, and Wisconsin tackled citizenship law most directly.

Immigrant newspapers were the perfect medium in which to elaborate both German ethnicity and cultural pluralism. They effectively encapsulated the German-language public sphere in print. Most obviously, newspapers publicized a range of German-language activities. The back cover of a standard four-page sheet would usually include columns of advertisements for German-owned businesses and entertainments alongside notices from churches and *Vereine*. In addition to reproducing the fabric of German neighborhoods, newspapers published stories of special interest to immigrants. European news, which crossed the Atlantic by mail until 1866, often filled half a page, and most papers also ran serialized fiction from Germany.[116] Even the typeface bespoke ethnic difference. All German-language publications used a gothic font with barbed letters and bold down-strokes. Even before readers began the all-important editorial, the newspapers announced that German language and culture were worth preserving in the United States.

It is unsurprising that German-American editors became the most passionate and powerful pluralists in the United States. In Europe, the Frankfurt parliamentarians had only grudgingly adopted a purely political (and therefore culturally plural) definition of the German *Volk* after rationalizing that granting citizenship rights to male residents would somehow make them more German. In the United States, this reluctance gave way to an aggressive pluralism. No German-American editor wrote that American citizenship should make Germans more like Anglo-Americans. August Thieme, a Saxon who had briefly argued for a republic in Frankfurt but now edited Cleveland's *Wächter am Erie*, made a standard argument in 1853.[117] The young journalist proclaimed that people did not migrate to the United States, "the meeting place of humanity," in order to "lose themselves in an undifferentiated intermixture." Immigrants were instead to retain their unique characteristics, which in the German case meant *Gemüthlichkeit*, a deeply satisfying conviviality. Thieme thought that the United States "should be a many-voiced but harmonious choir, in which every *Volk* projects its own voice."[118] Newspapers continued to use the word *Volk*

---

116 My impressionistic conclusion is confirmed in Erich Hofacker, *German Literature as Reflected in the German-Language Press of St. Louis Prior to 1898* (St. Louis: Washington University, 1946).

117 German-American Biographical Pub. Co., *Cleveland and its Germans*, 82–83.

118 *Wächter am Erie*, July 16, 1853.

(and sometimes *Nationalität* or simply *Deutschtum*) to refer to Germans, but here the German *Volk* was an ethnic minority in an American state.

Editors did not need a special occasion to hold forth on German *Gemütlichkeit*, but attacks on alcohol consumption and immigrant voting reliably both elicited renewed calls for cultural pluralism and stimulated discussion of citizenship. Thieme's earnest vision of a multiethnic America came in response to a sally by Cleveland's temperance movement. In 1853, there was talk that Ohio should follow the example of Maine and prohibit the sale of intoxicating liquors. Reporting on a meeting in October, the *Wächter am Erie* wrote that German immigrants did not oppose the "Maine Law" because of "love of liquor and intemperance" but "out of higher principles of justice and ethics." As exaggerated as these protestations might seem, immigrants understood social drinking as part of their generous cultural bequest to the United States. To condemn public drinking was, in German-American minds, to repudiate pluralism.

Interestingly, however, German ethnicity was not to be enshrined as a collective right, but as an individual one. The Maine Law, Thieme wrote, "completely abrogated personal freedom, freedom of trade, and the Constitution of the Union."[119] Although Thieme clearly believed noncitizens deserved these rights too, this was the language of citizenship, specifically the liberal nationalist citizenship of individual rights within the nation-state.

Immigrant voting was more closely related to the law of citizenship – and the careers of partisan editors – than social drinking. In Ohio and Missouri, where voters had to be white male citizens over the age of 21 who had lived within the state for at least a year, newspapers beseeched immigrants to naturalize and turn out on election day.[120] In Wisconsin, German immigrants had had the opportunity to debate electoral law when the territory prepared to enter the Union in 1847 and 1848. Moritz Schöffler took temporary leave from the *Banner* to serve in the constitutional convention. The only German American in the body, he managed to pass a provision that allowed immigrant men to vote once they had resided in the state for a year and filed the "first papers" that registered their intention to naturalize.[121] The convention also promised a referendum on African-American voting. In 1849, more Wisconsinites approved of a black suffrage amendment than

119 Ibid., Oct. 11, 1853.
120 Keyssar, *Right to Vote*, 351, 384–85; *Anzeiger des Westens*, Nov. 8, 1851, April 3, 1852, Nov. 13, 1857; *Cincinnati Volksfreund*, Nov. 4, 1852; *Wächter am Erie*, Oct. 11, 1853.
121 Moritz Schoeffler to Franz Huebschmann, Feb. 11, 1844, Dec. 23, 1847, June 20, 1848, box 1, folder 1, Huebschmann Papers, MCHS; Knoche, "German Immigrant Press," 21–26; Wisconsin Constitution (1848), art. 3, sec. 1; Koss, *Milwaukee*, 232; Bruncken, "Germans in Wisconsin Politics: I," 230; Hense-Jensen, *Wisconsin's Deutsch-Amerikaner*, 1: 96–104.

opposed it, but that support only amounted to a total of about 6,800 votes. Since more than 34,000 men had cast votes in the gubernatorial contest held on the same day, the state's Board of Canvassers determined that suffrage had not received a real majority.[122] When the result was invalidated, Wisconsin joined Ohio and Missouri in limiting the franchise by race. The new state had given some white men who were *not* citizens the franchise but denied political rights to citizens who were female or nonwhite.

Although Wisconsin's 1848 constitution technically divorced citizenship from voting, German Americans still thought of the ballot as a citizenship right. Immigrants would mull over the phenomenon of the nonvoting citizen during the 1850s, but they remained untroubled by the anomaly of the voting noncitizen. Friedrich Fratney, editor of Milwaukee's *Volksfreund*, wrote, "The suffrage is the right of the citizens of a republic," adding, "But the more the suffrage is extended, the more will the needs of the people be regarded."[123] Convinced of European men's fitness for citizenship and their loyalty to the United States, German-American politicians had no difficulty moving their focus from naturalization to first papers. Indeed, the emphasis on declaring intent reflected their belief that American citizenship was volitional and ethnically inclusive. According to this view, an immigrant man became American when he made the decision to commit himself to the American polity, not after the passage of time had rendered him more like an *Anglo*-American. Allowing "declarant" aliens to vote was consistent with the implicit messages of German-American festivity.

With its anti-temperance and pro-voting drives, the press made it possible for German-born men to take part in American politics without jeopardizing their identification with the immigrant community. As far as editors were concerned, there was absolutely no conflict between being politically American and culturally German. Political action could actually enhance German culture. The conclusion that men's citizenship protected their right to drink and their right to vote aligned perfectly with the liberal nationalism of the revolutions and the migratory experience, increasing the ideology's relevance.

Nothing in the history of liberal nationalism in Europe or North America predicted that women's suffrage would gain political traction, and it would have been astonishing if large numbers of German immigrants had become

122 Leslie H. Fishel, Jr., "Wisconsin and Negro Suffrage," *Wisconsin Magazine of History* 46 (1963): 185; Michael J. McManus, *Political Abolitionism in Wisconsin, 1840–1861* (Kent, OH: Kent State University Press, 1998), 64–65.
123 Friedrich Fratney, undated pamphlet, [1849–1852], quoted in Bruncken, "Germans in Wisconsin Politics: I," 231.

women's rights activists. Yet the immigrants did more than transplant a German approach to gender or acquiesce to the American status quo. The dominant constructions of ethnicity suggested that women's rights would undermine the immigrant community and endanger pluralism. They branded gender equality anathema to liberal nationalism. German ethnicity, as constituted in public festivity and refined in widely-circulated newspapers, bolstered immigrant men's voting rights, but would impede women who wanted similar opportunities.

Ethnicity could gender citizenship in part because the survival of German culture depended on women's work within the home. German Americans resembled Anglo-Americans in their fear that politics would distract women from their domestic role and destabilize society, but their arguments also contained an ethnic component. German-speaking women were not only likely mothers, but also potential *Kulturträgerinnen*. To many German immigrants, the transformation of gender roles threatened ethnicity itself. If the immigrant home was to be a haven from the individualism and materialism of the United States, German-American women must vigilantly guard it. A woman who wrote to a German-language newspaper in St. Louis described the German wife as alleviating the "concerns and burdens of her husband." She sensed that marriage reduced the Anglo-American woman to a "minor character" who was captive to her husband's "lust for making money."[124] That relationship was nothing to be emulated. A German-language monthly in Cincinnati approvingly quoted an American reporter who reached similar conclusions. "The German," the reporter wrote, "does not regard his wife as a mere ornament like the American." Immigrant women supposedly exhibited the "German traits" of "thrift, honorableness, and active industriousness."[125] Implicated in American superficiality and greed, women's rights seemed to menace German culture.[126]

Women's political activity also posed a more immediate threat to the prevailing mode of German ethnicity. Antebellum feminism emerged among Anglo-American reformers who also advocated abolition and temperance.[127] Many German-American editors, as we shall see, endorsed abolition, but none could abide "the temperance fanaticism of females

124 *Anzeiger des Westens*, May 15, 1859.
125 *Der deutsche Pionier* 5 (1873): 246. See also *Anzeiger des Westens*, Oct. 25, 1851, Oct. 16, 1859; Hense-Jensen, *Wisconsin's Deutsch-Amerikaner*, 18–19; Münch, *Gesammelte Schriften*, 437; Wehner-Franco, *Deutsche Dienstmädchen*, 115–26.
126 On superficiality, see Carl Schurz to Charlotte Voss, Oct. 20, 1852, in *Speeches, Correspondence and Political Papers of Carl Schurz*, ed. Frederic Bancroft, 6 vols. (New York: G. P. Putnam's Sons, 1913), 1: 4.
127 Ellen Carol DuBois, *Feminism and Suffrage: The Emergence of an Independent Women's Movement in America, 1848–1869* (Ithaca, NY: Cornell University Press, 1979), 21–52; Blanche Glassman

[*Weiber*]." Schöffler at the *Wisconsin Banner* was appalled when local "female temperance furies" destroyed liquor supplies – the "property of citizens" – and their "female comrades in folly" asked the legislature to replicate the Maine Law.[128] Anglo-American proponents of temperance and women's suffrage would become more insistent once slavery had been abolished and black men had been enfranchised, but many German Americans already suspected that if Anglo-American women had the chance, they would vote down immigrants' right to drink. They did not see women's suffrage as liberalism in action, but as fanaticism unleashed.[129]

Most immigrants closed ranks against the Anglo-American women who took aim at the cultural pillars of their community. In an 1865 letter to a St. Louis newspaper, "M" (purportedly a woman) defended female immigrants against accusations that they were apathetic to the problems of alcohol abuse. M maintained that German women disliked drunkenness as much as Anglo-Americans, but they believed it could best be combatted from within women's "natural sphere," the home. Agitating for temperance in public would only imperil women's special strengths.[130] Although M made her own public statement anonymously, it could be read as a play for another kind power. Women sought authority through ethnicity. As *Kulturträgerinnen*, they realized that forging German-American identity might be an avenue to female empowerment. Ultimately, however, M only buttressed the position of male editors. Like most German-American women, she abjured political citizenship in the name of ethnic solidarity.

Mathilde Anneke was an exception, a woman who questioned the commonplace that sexual equality would never garner German-American support. Her extraordinary career shows how difficult it was to make German ethnicity conducive to women's suffrage. In March 1852, Anneke published the first issue of the *Deutsche Frauen-Zeitung*, a monthly dedicated to the rights of women. Addressing German readers, Anneke spoke of "the uplift of the woman" and "demanded the social improvement of [the woman's] position, the right to work, and above all, the political right to vote." That summer, she left Milwaukee to make an "agitation tour" from

Hersh, *The Slavery of Sex: Feminist-Abolitionists in America* (Urbana: University of Illinois Press, 1978).

128 *Milwaukee Wisconsin Banner*, Jan. 10, 1855.

129 German historian Michaela Bank blames the "nativism" of Anglo-American feminists for the tension between German immigrants and the American women's rights movement. While she overstates the case, her emphasis on the ethnocultural divide is useful. Bank, *Women of Two Countries: German-American Women, Women's Rights, and Nativism, 1848–1890* (New York: Berghahn Books, 2012).

130 *Westliche Post*, May 4, 1865.

Chicago to Boston and then south through Pennsylvania and back west-ward along the Ohio River.[131] If anyone could have won over German immigrants, it would have been this accomplished woman whom friends described as warm and selfless.[132] Some German-American men did back Anneke. Friedrich Fratney allowed her to use *Volksfreund*'s printing press in Milwaukee, and newspapermen further afield distributed the journal and offered her accommodation on the road. August Thieme advertised the *Frauen-Zeitung* and introduced Anneke in Cleveland. Turners occasionally paid her to speak.[133] There were even a handful of Forty-Eighters on the East Coast who were openly sympathetic to enfranchising women.[134] Some German Americans were prepared to extend the logic of liberal nationalism to include political rights for women.

Anneke was stymied, however, within the German-language public sphere in Ohio, Missouri, and Wisconsin. Many German-American news-papers came out against her, and printers at the *Volksfreund* boycotted the paper, forcing her to move the *Frauen-Zeitung* to Newark and then New York City, where it languished until publication ceased in 1853. Anneke remarked at the time that "it nearly seems as though there was a conspiracy against this paper on the part of men."[135] In spite of her misfortune, Anneke set herself the onerous task of integrating women's suffrage into German-American identity. One example from the postwar period shows how diffi-cult it was to dispel the notion that women's rights were incompatible with German ethnicity. By 1869, Anneke was a fixture in Milwaukee's German community, directing a bilingual girls' school and representing Wiscon-sin at national feminist conventions. When she attended the meeting that founded the National Woman Suffrage Association that year, a group of parents wrote to a German-language newspaper to reassure immigrants that Anneke kept her political opinions out of the classroom.[136] Anneke was a formidable leader, but she retained her standing among German Amer-icans despite her feminism, not because of it. She never could reconcile

131 Anneke, *Mathilde Franziska Anneke*, ed. Wagner, 323.
132 *Amerikanische Turnzeitung*, Jan. 4, 1885.
133 *Wächter am Erie*, Sept. 11, 1852. See also *Columbus Westbote*, March 12, 1852; Koss, *Milwaukee*, 318–19.
134 Nagel, *Von republikanischen Deutschen zu deutsch-amerikanischen Republicanern*, 132; Wittke, *Refugees of Revolution*, 164.
135 Anneke, *Mathilde Franziska Anneke*, ed. Wagner, 317; Koss, *Milwaukee*, 381–83. The demise of the newspaper may not in itself prove much, however, since many publications failed within a couple of years.
136 Hense-Jensen, *Wisconsin's Deutsch-Amerikaner*, 1: 133. See also Annette P. Bus, "Mathilde Anneke and the Suffrage Movement," in *German Forty-Eighters*, ed. Brancaforte, 79–92.

ethnic diversity and women's rights to the satisfaction of most immigrants or native-born suffragists.

Because immigrants tied individual political rights to the merits of a foreign culture and argued that that culture required the self-abnegating service of women, the citizenship claims of German-born men undercut women's status. The ethnicity that German-American women helped build effected their subordination. This gendering was only one part of a German-American approach to citizenship that would become more influential on the eve of the Civil War.

As Jacob Müller wrote later in the century, the turmoil of 1848 and the voyage across the Atlantic conditioned how immigrants participated in the American debate over citizenship. Having failed to win a German citizenship that was based on individual rights and the creation of a nation-state in Europe, immigrants stressed individual rights and cultural diversity in the United States. During the 1850s, Forty-Eighters would reckon with the implications of ethnic pluralism: What did it mean for slavery and the citizenship of black men? Müller himself would join the Republican Party, opposing slavery and championing black suffrage after the war. To propagate an antislavery construction of German ethnicity, however, Müller and his colleagues would have to confront class and religious divisions among German Americans and the issue of race.

2

The "Freedom-Loving German," 1854–1860

On April 18, 1859, Carl Schurz rose to address about two thousand Boston Republicans in historic Faneuil Hall. He had traveled from his home in Wisconsin to tell New Englanders that "True Americanism" required a commitment to equal citizenship, not a "one-sided pride" in Anglo-Saxon ancestry. He heralded American diversity, declaring that the United States was "the *great colony of free humanity*, which has not old England alone, but the *world*, for its mother-country." To this statement of pluralism, Schurz added an antislavery note. The republic could fulfill its "ideal mission" as the world's standard-bearer of progress only if it both welcomed immigrants *and* abolished slavery. The German-American Republican drew a parallel between anti-immigrant sentiment and slavery. He compared the Alien and Sedition Acts of 1798 to the Fugitive Slave Act of 1850, equating the expulsion of foreign-born residents with the recapture of fugitives from bondage. He sought to persuade Republicans in Massachusetts that just as they resisted the spread of slavery, they should reject a proposal that would require immigrant men to wait two additional years after they were naturalized to vote.[1]

Schurz's "True Americanism" speech translated arguments that had developed within the German-language public sphere of the 1850s. German Americans had always maintained that their cultural background should be no impediment to American citizenship, but during the decade before the Civil War, many of them began to link this idea to antislavery politics. Whether they favored prohibiting slavery from new territories or abolishing it immediately, Schurz and most other Forty-Eighters saw antislavery as a natural extension of the liberal nationalism that they had fought for in

---

1 Schurz, "True Americanism," April 18, 1859, in *Speeches, Correspondence and Political Papers of Carl Schurz*, ed. Bancroft, 1: 56, 51.

Europe. Slavery was the ultimate travesty of individual rights, and it fettered national progress. Schurz's socialist colleagues doubted that economic individualism would be the nation's salvation, but they nonetheless saw abolition as a precondition for further change. Most liberal and socialist Forty-Eighters, along with many other immigrant politicians in the Midwest, joined the Republican Party, which formed in 1854 to halt slavery's spread.

The German-born Republicans produced the captivating myth of the "freedom-loving German," an immigrant man who asserted the value of cultural diversity while he took on slavery. This idea was mythic because its significance lay not in Republican vote tallies or Union army enlistments, but in its success as a form of ethnic self-definition. As Republicans practiced German antislavery politics, they mobilized antislavery German ethnicity. This chapter examines how German-American Republicans brought together pluralism and antislavery, two strands of liberalism that would transform their party and, ultimately, the law of citizenship.

German-American Democrats would contest – and thereby mold – Republican ideas in three related ways. The first was economic. Democrats accused the Republican Party, which advocated a national bank and protective tariffs, of representing the special interests of a select group of wealthy Americans. The Democrats' second argument was "ethnocultural," in the terminology of historians.[2] German Americans loyal to the memory of Andrew Jackson pointed out that in states such as Massachusetts, Anglo-American Republicans had connections to the anti-immigrant American, or Know Nothing, Party. How, they asked, could immigrants be expected to vote for a party that included politicians who were unfriendly toward Catholicism and wanted to deny some foreign-born citizens the right to vote? The third Democratic challenge restated the previous two in racial terms. Some German-American Democrats said that since the well-heeled Republicans apparently cared more about African Americans than they did European immigrants, a vote for the Republican Party was tantamount to a betrayal of whiteness.

In response to these Democratic objections, German Republicans would refine their arguments. Economically, German immigrants proved more

---

2 The ethnocultural school of historiography emphasized that confession underpinned political allegiances. See Richard L. McCormick, "Ethno-Cultural Interpretations of Nineteenth-Century Voting Behavior," *Political Science Quarterly* 89 (1974): 351–77; Ronald P. Formisano, "The Invention of the Ethnocultural Interpretation," *Journal of American History* 99 (1994): 453–77; Formisano, *The Birth of Mass Political Parties in Michigan, 1827–1861* (Princeton, NJ: Princeton University Press, 1971); Paul Kleppner, *The Cross of Culture: A Social Analysis of Midwestern Politics, 1850–1900* (New York: The Free Press, 1970). Summarizing the early application of this approach to German-American voting, see the essays in Luebke, ed., *Ethnic Voters and the Election of Lincoln.*

interested in laissez-faire than most members of the Republican Party. They agreed with Democrats that when the government meddled in markets, it disproportionately benefited the well off, but unlike their opponents, they identified slavery as an example of just such interference. Socialist Republicans, who did not idealize free markets, won some personal followers but relatively few ideological converts. Republican German Americans were even more active on the ethnocultural front. Forty-Eighters muted their criticism of the Catholic Church and tried to silence the Anglo-Americans in their party who dabbled in nativism or temperance. It was in the area of race, however, that German immigrants would contribute most to the ideology that Republicans would mine during Reconstruction. By coupling immigrant and African-American rights, as Schurz did in Faneuil Hall, they advanced liberalism and paved the way for a language of citizenship unconstrained by race. Yet as they constructed the freedom-loving German, immigrant Republicans also subtly differentiated themselves from African Americans. They doubled down on the cultural category of ethnicity. German-speaking opponents of slavery did not dwell on the difference between whiteness and blackness, but they would feel out the line between ethnicity and the more biological category of race.

Economic, religious, and racial maneuvering created the Republican notion of the freedom-loving German, but each step in the process was also gendered. German-American antislavery took shape at party conventions, on editorial pages, and in *Verein* meetings, not after Sunday services or at quilting bees. Its masculine quality stood in notable contrast to what historians have described as the more feminine spirit of Anglo-American abolitionism. A German-American approach to gender was therefore part of the package of immigrant ideas that bilingual politicians such as Schurz delivered to English-speaking Republicans. By the start of the Civil War, the myth of the freedom-loving German would convince the majority of them to accept immigrants, and specifically immigrant *men*, as the archetypal new citizens.

ANTISLAVERY AND PARTISANSHIP

Unlike Anglo-American abolitionism with its religious roots, German-American antislavery was always primarily a political affair. The exclusively male world of partisan politics set the parameters for immigrants' combination of antislavery and German ethnicity. The party system was in flux in Ohio, Missouri, and Wisconsin during the 1850s, with conflict over the westward expansion of chattel slavery reconfiguring old alliances. In the unfolding debate, German–American editors and politicians, mediating between American politics and the German community, both voiced and guided immigrant opinion. Before investigating the economic, ethnocultural, and racial dimensions of German-American antislavery, then, it is helpful to plot its evolution.

Antislavery became a credible part of German ethnicity in the Midwest because few immigrants had ever profited directly from the peculiar institution and some German-born leaders had long spoken out against it. Immigrants in Ohio and Wisconsin had no economic stake in slavery, and many of them coveted Western lands for themselves. If slaveholders settled in the West, enslaved labor would outcompete family farms, making the economic independence for which immigrant men hungered more difficult to grasp. When in 1848 the Free Soil Party organized around this supposition, however, most immigrant politicians in Ohio and Wisconsin resisted its allure, remaining Democratic. The Free Soilers did achieve the limited victory of inducing some Democrats, including Milwaukeeans Franz Hübschmann and Friedrich Fratney, to declare a general disapproval of slavery.[3] As Republicans would later remind them, Wisconsin Democrats passed a legislative resolution in 1849 instructing the state's delegation in Washington to oppose any extension of slavery into conquered Mexican territory.[4] That year, Cincinnati's J. B. Stallo endeavored to sell a plan for gradual emancipation to fellow Democrats in Kentucky. The eighteen-year-old Friedrich Hassaurek, fresh from the barricades in Vienna, ridiculed Stallo in the for what he saw as an unacceptably cautious scheme. The confrontation proved only that Forty-Eighters were not the first immigrants to oppose slavery.[5]

In Missouri, antislavery also predated 1848 and the Republican Party, and there it became more closely identified with German ethnicity than in any other state. Slavery was legal in Missouri, but most German-speaking settlers wanted to establish small farms, independent workshops, or their own stores.

---

3 Bruncken, "Germans in Wisconsin Politics: I," 232. The few German Wisconsinites who did support the Free Soil Party were very committed. Hense-Jensen, *Wisconsin's Deutsch-Amerikaner,* 1: 112–13. On Ohio, see Steven E. Maizlish, *The Triumph of Sectionalism: The Transformation of Ohio Politics, 1844–1856* (Kent, Ohio: Kent State University Press, 1983), 117; Levine, *Spirit of 1848,* 150. Hassaurek was also interested in the Free Soil Party, according to an 1888 account. Burgheim, *Cincinnati in Wort und Bild,* 126.

4 Reprinting the 1849 instructions, see the Democratic *Madison Wisconsin-Staats-Zeitung,* Feb. 19, 1855. For Republican references, see *La Crosse Nord Stern,* Oct. 17, 1857; *Wisconsin Demokrat,* Nov. 9, 1854; Schurz, "Political Morals," Nov. 18, 1858, in *Speeches of Carl Schurz,* ed. Schurz (Philadelphia: J. B. Lippincott & Co., 1865), 42; Mathilde Anneke to Fritz Anneke, Sept. 23, 1859, March 31, 1860, in *Mathilde Franziska Anneke,* ed. Wagner, 108, 118.

5 *Cincinnati Deutsche Republikaner,* Aug. 16, 1849 and other clippings in box 2, folder 1, Friedrich Hassaurek Papers, Ohio Historical Society (hereafter OHS).

Even those German Americans who could afford the outlay were unlikely to own slaves.[6] When the question of permitting slavery in the new territories began to split the Democratic Party, German Missourians stood by Thomas Hart Benton, whose moderate free soil inclinations cost him reelection to the Senate in 1850. One of Benton's greatest supporters was Heinrich Börnstein, who edited the *Anzeiger des Westens* in St. Louis. During the free soil Democrat's 1852 run for the House of Representatives, Börnstein announced, "The Germans against everyone, to a man for Benton."[7] He was both following German opinion and guiding German ethnicity. He would not have made such a claim without some foundation, but the editor drew German-American men together around a specific platform. Börnstein's skill as an exponent of antislavery ethnicity can be gauged from the profits and circulation of the *Anzeiger*, which was the largest German-language newspaper in Missouri until the late 1850s.[8]

When the Kansas-Nebraska Act shook American politics in 1854, it tested whether German immigrants were more committed to antislavery or the Democratic Party. The legislation, initiated by Illinois Democrat Stephen A. Douglas, stipulated that Kansas and Nebraska would enter the Union under "popular sovereignty." The white men who settled in these territories would vote on whether to legalize slavery and overturn a congressional prohibition that dated back to the Missouri Compromise of 1820. Incensed Northerners founded the Republican Party. German immigrants had to decide whether it was for them.

A few pioneering Wisconsinites tried to break immigrant ties to the Democratic Party. Karl Röser, a minor Forty-Eighter who edited the *Wisconsin Demokrat* in Manitowoc, wrote that "the sacred rights of the north [sic] have been outraged and the moral sense of its inhabitants insulted." After traveling to Madison for a convention "to effect the formation of the new freedom party," Röser called German Americans around the state to the Republican standard. But the editors of Wisconsin's three largest German newspapers, all steadfastly Democratic, declined to print his invitation.[9]

Milwaukee had no German Republican leader until later in the summer of 1854, when Forty-Eighter Bernhard Domschke arrived from Louisville,

6 Kamphoefner, *Westfalians*, 116–17; Frizzell, *Independent Immigrants*, 89–120. The English-language *St. Louis Missouri Republican* remarked on the low rates of slave ownership among immigrants. Reported in *Wöchentlich Anzeiger des Westens*, April 25, 1858.

7 *Wöchentlich Anzeiger des Westens*, Aug. 7, 1852. See also Oct. 23, Dec. 22, 1851. On Benton's career, see Adam Arenson, *The Great Heart of the Republic: St. Louis and the Cultural Civil War* (Cambridge, MA: Harvard University Press, 2011), 28–46.

8 Boernstein, *Memoirs of a Nobody*, 120, 135.

9 Bruncken, "The Political Activity of Wisconsin Germans, 1854–1860," *Proceedings of the State Historical Society of Wisconsin* 49 (1901): 195; *Wisconsin Demokrat*, July 4, 1854

Kentucky. Friedrich Fratney immediately challenged Domschke to a public debate. In Market Hall, Fratney argued that although the Kansas-Nebraska Act was a mistake, Germans belonged within the Democratic Party. The encounter showcased Democrats' fear that immigrants might be attracted to political antislavery. Seeing Domschke as a competitor, Fratney hoped that even if immigrants did dislike slavery, they would not let it govern their partisan affiliations. A few months later, Domschke took the logical step of founding Milwaukee's first German-language Republican newspaper. He needed Anglo-American financial backing, however, and like the two other German Republican papers in the state, Domschke's *Kosar* did not thrive.[10] By 1856, Carl Schurz had also settled in Wisconsin and entered Republican politics, but he was not particularly successful either.[11] Fritz Anneke lived in the state intermittently without becoming politically active.[12] The cause of antislavery interested Wisconsin Germans, but it led few of their spokesmen into the new party.

In Ohio and Missouri, however, the most prominent German-American politicians and editors joined the Republican Party, staking out the institutional space within which the myth of the freedom-loving German could grow. Deciding against forming their own "progressive" party, German opponents of slavery in the two states mostly endorsed Republican John C. Frémont for the presidency in 1856.[13] In Ohio, J. B. Stallo, Friedrich Hassaurek, and Jacob Müller became Republicans.[14] August Thieme's *Wächter am Erie* and the *Toledo Express* supported Frémont, as did the *Volksblatt* and August Willich's *Deutscher Republikaner* in Cincinnati.[15] Outnumbered by about two to one, Ohio's Democratic editors became increasingly defensive. The *Columbus Westbote* and the *Cincinnati Volksfreund* could attribute German support for Frémont only to "fanatical blindness."[16]

The Republican Party was not politically viable in Missouri, so the antislavery *St. Charles Democrat*, along with two other German-language

10 Ibid., Aug. 17, 1854; Koss, *Milwaukee*, 449–50; Bruncken, "Political Activity of Wisconsin Germans," 195–96; Hense-Jensen, *Wisconsin's Deutsch-Amerikaner*, 1: 171–73.
11 Trefousse, *Carl Schurz*, 61.   12 Schulte, *Fritz Anneke*, 49–63.
13 Levine, *Spirit of 1848*, 102–06; Boernstein, *Memoirs of a Nobody*, 172–81; Mueller, *Memories of a Forty-Eighter*, 33.
14 Timothy C. Day to Hassaurek, June 24, 1856, box 2, folder 3, Hassaurek Papers, OHS; Burgheim, *Cincinnati in Wort und Bild*, 126; *Columbus Westbote*, Feb. 10, 1854; Mueller, *Memories of a Forty-Eighter*, 151; Trefousse, *Carl Schurz*, 59–60.
15 *Toledo Express*, June 13, 1856. A list appeared in *Wöchentlich Anzeiger des Westens*, July 10, 1856. For state-by-state tallies of newspaper affiliations and circulation numbers, see *Wöchentlich Anzeiger des Westens*, Aug 28, 1856. See also Easton, *Hegel's First American Followers*, 190.
16 *Cincinnati Volksfreund*, Oct. 16, 1856. Using a similar tone, see *Columbus Westbote*, Oct. 17, 1856. A respected scholar of the German-American press observed that the editors of the two newspapers thought they were fighting a "lone battle." Wittke, *German-Language Press*, 140.

newspapers, backed Democrat James Buchanan in 1856.[17] Other German-American leaders were undeterred. Friedrich Münch campaigned nationally for the Republicans, and Börnstein was a Frémont man, using the *Anzeiger* to cover Republican events across the Mississippi River in Illinois.[18] It was a start, at least. Efforts to weave antislavery into the fabric of German ethnicity originated in the masculine arenas of electoral politics and the partisan press, but Republicans would have to deal with class, religion, and race to make further headway.

CLASS AND POLITICAL ECONOMY

The Republicans who sought to characterize German Americans as a freedom-loving group quickly learned that the diversity of immigrants' economic interests made their work more difficult. Antislavery could not occupy a central place in German ethnicity if middle-class proprietors and professionals were the only ones to embrace it. Quite aware of the Republican dilemma, German Democratic leaders argued that their adversaries condoned economic policies that served only a minority of Americans. The new party, according to the Democrats, was one of self-interested employers and self-satisfied professionals. Since charges of Republican plutocracy and elitism had the potential to turn working-class whites against African-American citizenship during Reconstruction, it is worth examining how German Republicans reacted during the 1850s. Although a few socialists had their own ideas, liberals were chiefly responsible for the alliance of working-class and middle-class immigrant men in the Republican Party. They solidified German-American antislavery while strengthening economic liberalism and a male-centered approach to citizenship.

To depict antislavery as preoccupation of the privileged, Democrats alleged that the Republican Party was simply a revival of the discredited Whigs. In 1854, Friedrich Fratney explained to immigrants arriving in Milwaukee why Germans had originally gravitated to the Party of Jackson. In the *Banner*, he wrote that since the 1830s, the Democrats had struggled to prevent a national bank from putting public funds to work for private investors. They had fought to lower the protective tariffs that sheltered certain industries from foreign competition but saddled consumers with artificially inflated prices. In short, Democrats had defended ordinary Americans

---

17 *Wöchentlich Anzeiger des Westens*, July 10, Aug. 28, 1856.

18 Marlin T. Tucker, "Political Leadership in the Illinois-Missouri German Community, 1836–1872" (PhD diss., University of Illinois, 1968), 40–44; *Wöchentlich Anzeiger des Westens*, June 26, July 3 and 24, 1856.

against "gentlemen of monopoly and privilege." Unless they were vigilant, Fratney warned, plutocrats would once again control the country.[19] His party had won a mass constituency among urban immigrants with a spirited working-class liberalism, not socialism. All evidence seemed to show that when governments entered the marketplace – be it in Europe or the United States – they favored the rich. German–American Democrats repeated that they were the true liberals, while Republicans stood for unearned privilege. To sustain this contention, politicians realized that they had to distract voters from the Southern Democrats who felt entitled to the labor of people who were enslaved.[20] It would not be easy to portray Republicans as economic predators until after emancipation.

As long as slavery survived, the German Republicans courting German workingmen called their attention to the manifest absurdity of associating the institution with laissez-faire. Nowhere was Democratic inconsistency clearer than in Missouri. There, slavery perverted the labor market, impinging on immigrant men's ambitions of economic independence. The real gentlemen of monopoly and privilege, Börnstein averred in 1858, were the slaveholders. In what became a refrain, the paper compared slavery to the "system of nobility" that Germans had been familiar with in Europe, asserting that "small property in land and rational agriculture is in conflict with aristocratic exploitation."[21] The analogy emphasized that slaveholders used the state and federal governments to create a legal environment in which they could exploit African-American labor. In Europe, limiting inherited power and government regulation promised to ease economic distress. In Missouri, ending the government-sanctioned slave system might generate real opportunities. Some urban wageworkers, rural laborers, and tenant farmers perhaps thought that it was unlikely that such steps would be sufficient to achieve economic justice, but until a free market for labor

19 *Wisconsin Banner*, Sept. 27, 1854. See also *Cincinnati Volksfreund*, Oct. 6, 1860; *Fremont Courier*, June 9, 1859. Later newspapers provide more detailed arguments against protectionism. See *Anzeiger des Westens Wochen-Blatt*, Nov. 22, 1866; *Cincinnati Volksfreund*, Feb. 2, 1867; *Columbus Westbote*, April 27, 1865, July 23, 1868. On hard money, see *Cincinnati Volksfreund*, July 22, 1868; *Columbus Westbote*, Feb. 20, 1868; *Fremont Courier*, July 18, 1868; *Anzeiger des Westens Wochen-Blatt*, Sept. 20, 1866. More generally, see also *Columbus Westbote*, Oct. 29, 1868; *Anzeiger des Westens Wochen-Blatt*, Jan. 21, 1866; *Cincinnati Volksfreund*, Nov. 3, 1868; *Fremont Courier*, Oct. 3, 1867, Aug. 27, 1868.
20 On the earlier antislavery impulse among Northern Democrats, see Jonathan H. Earle, *Jacksonian Antislavery and the Politics of Free Soil* (Chapel Hill: University of North Carolina Press, 2004); Sean Wilentz, "Slavery, Antislavery, and Jacksonian Democracy," in *The Market Revolution in America: Social, Political, and Religious Expressions, 1800–1880*, ed. Melvyn Stokes and Stephen Conway (Charlottesville: University Press of Virginia, 1996), 202–23.
21 *Wöchentlich Anzeiger des Westens*, April 25, 1858. For further examples, see Kamphoefner, "Auch unser Deutschland muss einmal frei werden," 87–107; *Wächter am Erie*, March 16, April 27, 1853, Feb. 1 and 11, 1860.

was instituted, the possibility remained. Republican politicians described German immigrants as "free laborers" and the backbone of "the solid middle [*Mittlestand*]," imagining them all allied against the illiberal institution of slavery.[22]

Republican leaders made slightly different arguments to working-class immigrants further north. From Manitowoc, Wisconsin, Karl Röser composed a useful formulation of the liberal consensus among the small number of German Republicans in his state. Fending off an early barrage of accusations that his party neglected the concerns of white workers, Röser explained why ending slavery would actually help them: "If human rights and the rights of the people are recognized in the great association, the state, then as a consequence of this social equality of rights, workers' rights will be too." He complicated matters by referring to four different kinds of rights, but Röser's main point was that legal equality for black Americans would secure, not detract from, the citizenship of members of other groups. The rest of the piece made it clear that Röser believed that the government would not need to do anything more than end slavery and establish "an equality of rights" before the law to create a fair economy. Although he identified himself as a "social democrat," he wrote that "communists' favorite theories . . . are totally alien to the mighty movements of the age."[23] While the "slave power" tampered with the labor market, Röser could offer antislavery as an all-purpose salve.

In Cincinnati, Hassaurek became famous not for engaging with Democrats' arguments, but for matching their rabble-rousing style of working-class politics. Dead set against slavery from the start, Hassaurek rattled Ohio with speeches that scorned organized religion.[24] His *Hochwächter* newspaper promised to speak for the "younger" element of the German migration, and he seemed to delight in offending venerable politicians.[25] Hassaurek supported strikes during the early 1850s, but he believed that abolition should mark the extent of government action on behalf of wageworkers, or so he wrote in a "philosophical dissertation" he completed during the war and in letters to English-speaking Republicans later in the decade.[26] Instead of socialism, he served up the sort of vigorous urban politicking at which Democrats were so skilled. Hassaurek was one of the men who ensured that Cincinnati would boast a solid contingent of German-born working-class Republicans.

22 *Wöchentlich Anzeiger des Westens*, Oct. 25, 1851.   23 *Wisconsin Demokrat*, Aug. 17, 1854.
24 Burgheim, *Cincinnati in Wort und Bild*, 126–27; *Columbus Westbote*, Feb. 10 and 24, 1852.
25 Burgheim, *Cincinnati in Wort und Bild*, 137; Wittke, "Friedrich Hassaurek," 4.
26 Levine, *Spirit of 1848*, 140; folders 3 and 7, box 2, Hassaurek Papers, OHS.

Like Hassaurek, most German Republican leaders countered Democrats without negating the liberal premise of their opponents' arguments. Staunch economic liberalism recommended these politicians to the immigrants who had leaned Democratic and distinguished them from the majority of native-born Republicans. In 1852, Thieme described Whig economic policies as "conservative, monopolizing, narrow-hearted, and plutocratic" in the *Wächter am Erie*. He never reconsidered his position, even when he joined the party that inherited those policies.[27] Before the Civil War, a newspaper registered its commitment to laissez-faire in its coverage of tariffs and plans for a central bank, and German Republican sheets in Ohio, Missouri, and Wisconsin disparaged both. Börnstein at the *Anzeiger des Westens* recoiled at a rumor that attempts were afoot to start a new party to champion protective tariffs and a national bank.[28] Domschke reprinted an editorial against the tariff from Missouri's *St. Charles Democrat* in his latest Milwaukee newspaper.[29] Adding to the din, Schurz assured a Madison, Wisconsin, crowd that the tariff question had "been settled by compromises," and the national bank had "been put upon the shelf of history."[30] Although most English-speaking Republicans approved of tariffs and the bank, their free labor ideology was broad enough to include politicians who did not.[31] German Republicans depended on this latitude to carve out a niche where immigrants could come together despite their class differences.

If most German Republicans responded to Democratic attacks by flaunting their own liberal credentials, a handful of Forty-Eighters introduced socialism into the new party. Disagreements between liberals and socialists

27 *Wächter am Erie*, Aug. 9, 1852. See also April 27, 1853. German Republican opposition to tariffs was presented or reported in *Cincinnati Volksfreund*, Dec. 18, 1867, July 25, 1868; *Wächter am Erie*, Nov. 7, 1867; *St. Charles Democrat*, Feb. 7, 1867; *Westliche Post*, March 5, 1868. Germans divided over tariffs in Europe, but free trade ideas were ascendant in universities before 1848 and among the Forty-Eighters who migrated to the United States. Ivo Nikolai Lambi, *Free Trade and Protection in Germany, 1868–1879* (Wiesbaden: Franz Steiner Verlag, 1963), 4, 7; Wittke, *Refugees of Revolution*, 256; Freitag, *Friedrich Hecker*, 20; Trefousse, *Carl Schurz*, 182.
    Hard money German Republicans included Gustav Körner, Carl Schurz, Emil Preetorius, and Friedrich Hassaurek. See *Westliche Post*, Jan. 7, 1867; *Wächter am Erie*, Nov. 23, 1867; Koerner, *Memoirs*, 2: 583; Trefousse, *Carl Schurz*, 182; Hassaurek to Rutherford B. Hayes, Sept. 15, 1875, and other letters, box 2, folder 10, Hassaurek Papers, OHS. See also Irwin Unger, *The Greenback Era: A Social and Political History of American Finance, 1865–1879* (Princeton, NJ: Princeton University Press, 1964), 134, 276; Wittke, *German-American Press*, 160–61.
28 *Wöchentlich Anzeiger des Westens*, Nov. 22, 1857.
29 *Atlas*, Oct. 13, 1860. Domschke's *Korsar* had failed by early 1856, and his *Milwaukee Journal* appeared for only a few months before the *Atlas* began publication in November 1856. Koss, *Milwaukee*, 455.
30 Schurz, speech at Madison, Oct. 16, 1857, quoted in *Madison Daily State Journal*, Oct. 19, 1857, Schurz Papers, WHS. Hense-Jensen, *Wisconsin's Deutsch-Amerikaner*, 1: 176. See also similar analysis in Bruncken, "Germans in Wisconsin Politics: I," 206.
31 Foner, *Free Soil, Free Labor, Free Men*, 11–39, 168–75; Tuchinsky, *Horace Greeley's* New-York Tribune. On working-class Republicanism, see also Mark A. Lause, *Young America: Land, Labor, and the Republican Community* (Urbana: University of Illinois Press, 2005).

over political economy were sometimes antagonistic, but they also widened German antislavery. Joseph Weydemeyer, who corresponded almost weekly with Marx and Engels from New York, had no patience for the liberal orthodoxies of low tariffs and a private banking system. He even scoffed at the idea that universal manhood suffrage would be a "panacea for healing the ills of the world."[32] During the early 1850s, he took slavery much more seriously. He analyzed the institution in the pages of the *Turn-Zeitung*, and his Amerikanische Arbeiterbund heavily criticized the Kansas-Nebraska Act. The group resolved to "protest most emphatically against both white and black slavery."[33] The mention of "white slavery" was a nod to the belief that the end of bound labor would not in itself inaugurate a model society. For Marxists, abolition was to be but a stage in the progression of history. Industrialization and the political rise of the working class would prefigure a more thoroughgoing transformation of work. As had been true in 1848, socialists endorsed as critical intermediate steps measures that liberals considered ends in themselves. The Arbeiterbund's statement also revealed how easy it would be for socialists to equate the adversities that white workers and black slaves faced, although Weydemeyer usually avoided that trap. He decided to prioritize antislavery and support the Republicans. As his admiring biographer put it, "There was no longer any time to argue against petty-bourgeois individualistic attitudes, for events in the United States were pressing for vital decisions."[34]

Weydemeyer's presence in the Republican Party increased its ideological breadth, but other German-American socialists did more to enlarge its working-class constituency. Until 1857, Weydemeyer worked on the East Coast, where he complained about how few immigrants appreciated his economic analysis.[35] Meanwhile in Cincinnati, August Willich exhibited the charisma that would endear him to his troops during the Civil War. He decried slavery at public events and from the pages of the *Republikaner*. Like Weydemeyer, he saw human bondage through the prism of class conflict. He dreamed of a "social republic" in which human relationships would be rescued from the degradation of economic exploitation.[36]

---

32 *New York Turn-Zeitung*, Feb. 1, 1852, quoted and trans. in Obermann, *Joseph Weydemeyer: Pioneer of American Socialism*, 46; Obermann, *Joseph Weydemeyer: Ein Lebensbild*, 231–94; Hal Draper, "Joseph Weydemeyer's 'Dictatorship of the Proletariat,'" *Labor History* 3 (1962): 208–13.

33 Quoted in Hermann Schlüter, *Lincoln, Labor, and Slavery: A Chapter from the Social History of America* (New York: Socialist Literature Co., 1913), 75–76; Obermann, *Joseph Weydemeyer: Pioneer of American Socialism*, 78–81; Obermann, *Joseph Weydemeyer: Ein Lebensbild*, 335–37; Nadel, *Little Germany*, 128–29.

34 Obermann, *Joseph Weydemeyer: Pioneer of American Socialism*, 86.

35 Obermann, *Joseph Weydemeyer: Ein Lebensbild*, 274, 340.

36 Honeck, *We Are the Revolutionists*, 94–98; Easton, *Hegel's First American Followers*, 180–90.

Predictably, Weydemeyer called his former comrade naive.[37] For the Marx-ist Weydemeyer, socialism was distinct from liberalism, its inherently flawed precursor. For Willich, socialism was an elevated form of liberalism (he used the term "republicanism") brokered with a camaraderie not unlike the spirit of German-American festivity. When Willich stressed the centrality of abolition to his socialist vision, he did the Republican Party a great service.

Socialists and liberals would work together in the *Vereine* that assisted Republican newspapers and committees in inducting working-class German Americans into the antislavery movement. When Weydemeyer moved to Milwaukee in 1857, he found a small but vibrant leftist scene where German-speaking socialists and liberals exchanged ideas. The Work-ers' Reading and Education Society included Milwaukee's "most solid Germans," but a range of men mapped different routes to economic justice in its formal debates. Franz Hübschmann was liberal in outlook, Fritz Anneke had imbibed Cologne's workingmen's culture (although he never identified as a socialist in the United States), and Wilhelm Weitling was a Magdeburg-born socialist whose utopianism earned him Marx's contempt.[38] The Turnverein, which was almost uniformly antislavery in the Midwest, brought men of various economic philosophies together under the rubric of "universal human freedom."[39] Socialists participated but did not usually dominate. When Weydemeyer told Milwaukee Turners that free trade was a distraction from workers' real goals, they reacted so negatively that he quit Wisconsin and headed south to Chicago.[40] Such friction indi-cated that real ideological differences remained among the immigrants who opposed slavery. It was also evidence that they continued to rub shoulders.

Women occasionally participated in organizations such as the Turnverein, but they played a minor role in the institutions that bridged class divides to form immigrant antislavery before the Civil War.[41] In fact, *Vereine*, like political parties, hardened the masculine cast of the German-American

37 Obermann, *Joseph Weydemeyer: Ein Lebensbild*, 287–94.
38 Koss, *Milwaukee*, 337, 313. *New York Times*, Jan. 27, 1871; Zucker, ed. *Forty-Eighters*, 353; Schulte, *Fritz Anneke*, 52. On the membership of left-leaning organizations, see Levine, *Spirit of 1848*, 124–25; Hense-Jensen, *Wisconsin's Deutsch-Amerikaner*, 1: 157. For discussion agreeing that socialism was not widespread in Milwaukee before the Civil War, see Hense-Jensen, *Wisconsin's Deutsch-Amerikaner*, 1: 80–81; *Erinnerung an Milwaukee*, 54–55.
39 Quoted in Burgheim, *Cincinnati in Wort und Bild*, 156.
40 Obermann, *Joseph Weydemeyer: Ein Lebensbild*, 352.
41 Female auxiliaries would multiply following the war. Anneke, *Mathilde Franziscka Anneke*, ed. Wagner, 75–76; Koss, *Milwaukee*, 318–19, 336–37, 399–404. On Anneke and the Turners, see Theodore Mueller, "The Milwaukee Turners through the Century," June 13, 1953, box 1, folder 1, Milwaukee Turners Records, 1852–1944, WHS Milwaukee Area Research Center (hereafter WHS-MARC).

movement. The immigrant left was not as receptive to women's activism as the networks of Anglo-American abolitionism.[42] Numerous historians have documented that church groups initiated native-born women into writing, speaking, fundraising, and petitioning for the abolition of slavery. These experiences led some female abolitionists to question the abrogation of their own rights, and a few even began to demand equal citizenship, including the franchise, for themselves.[43] During the late 1850s, Anglo-American antislavery became more partisan and masculine too, but Republicans did not replace what German Americans sometimes derided as the sentimental culture of abolitionism; they co-opted it. The anecdote about Abraham Lincoln attributing the Civil War to Harriet Beecher Stowe's abolitionist novel, *Uncle Tom's Cabin*, may be apocryphal, but scholars have shown his party's continuing ties to the cultural world that Stowe represented.[44]

The tension between the religious, feminized tone of Anglo-American abolitionism and the secular, masculine ethos of German-American antislavery hung over Mathilde Anneke's work in Milwaukee. A proponent of women's suffrage by the early 1850s, Anneke turned to English-speaking women for fellowship. She developed a passionate friendship with the Connecticut-born Mary Booth, whose husband, Sherman, orchestrated the 1854 jailbreak of Joshua Glover, a man who had fled enslavement in Missouri. A federal court enraged Wisconsinites by convicting Sherman Booth of defying the Fugitive Slave Act. In a separate incident, he was tried for illicit sexual contact with a fourteen-year-old employee. During the second court case, Anneke lived with Mary, supporting her emotionally

42 A working-class antislavery movement had appeared among Jacksonian workingmen that somewhat resembled the German-American movement. See Wilentz, "Slavery, Antislavery, and Jacksonian Democracy," 202–23.

43 DuBois, *Feminism and Suffrage*, 21–52; Hersh, *Slavery of Sex*; Julie Roy Jeffrey, *The Great Silent Army of Abolitionism: Ordinary Women in the Antislavery Movement* (Chapel Hill: University of North Carolina Press, 1998); Jean Fagan Yellin, *Women and Sisters: The Antislavery Feminists in American Culture* (New Haven, CT: Yale University Press, 1989); Stacey M. Robertson, *Hearts Beating for Liberty: Women Abolitionists in the Old Northwest* (Chapel Hill: University of North Carolina Press, 2010), esp. 183–200; Chris Dixon, *Perfecting the Family: Antislavery Marriages in Nineteenth-Century America* (Amherst: University of Massachusetts Press, 1997); Susan Zaeske, *Signatures of Citizenship: Petitioning, Antislavery, and Women's Political Identity* (Chapel Hill: University of North Carolina Press, 2003), 145–72.

44 Daniel R. Vollaro, "Lincoln, Stowe, and the 'Little Woman/Great War' Story: The Making, and Breaking, of a Great American Anecdote," *Journal of the Abraham Lincoln Association* 30, no. 1 (2009): 18–34; David Grant, "Uncle Tom's Cabin and the Triumph of Republican Rhetoric," *New England Quarterly* 71 (1999): 429–48; Rebecca Edwards, *Angels in the Machinery: Gender in Party Politics from the Civil War to the Progressive Era* (New York: Oxford University Press, 1997), 27–35; Michael B. Pierson, *Free Hearts and Free Homes: Gender and American Antislavery Politics* (Chapel Hill: University of North Carolina Press, 2003), 22–23, 165–90; Melanie Gustafson, *Women and the Republican Party, 1854–1924* (Urbana: University of Illinois Press, 2001), 7–33.

and carrying messages and food to Sherman in prison.[45] Anneke had no time for the Booths' temperance, and she never severed her connections to other Forty-Eighters, but she cherished aspects of Yankee reform culture.[46] While ethnicity and language – she never was entirely comfortable speaking English – drew her back to the antislavery of the Turnverein, gender and her relationship to Mary pulled her toward the abolitionism of the Booths.

The masculine political culture of German-American antislavery spanned economic ideologies and class boundaries. To win the votes of workers, German Republicans usually made the essentially liberal argument that eliminating slavery and other governmental sources of inequality would make the American economy just, but they couched that argument in populist terms. A handful of socialist immigrants decided to adopt the strategy that they had used in 1848: cooperation with liberals. In German Europe, they had concluded that establishing a republic would be the first in a sequence of reforms that would free workers from the humiliation and suffering of wage labor. Abolition functioned similarly in the United States. By focusing on immediate objectives, socialists again augmented liberalism. Liberal and socialist leaders who had made common cause against monarchy in German Europe, now filed into the Republican Party to do battle with slavery. Although many German immigrants remained faithful Democrats, Republicans in the Midwest had surmounted class divides, at least for the time being. They would still, however, have to contend with the religious differences among themselves and the religious biases of their native-born colleagues.

NEGOTIATING ETHNOCULTURAL OBSTACLES

Most German-American antislavery leaders were secular humanists, but if they were to shape German ethnicity, they could not ignore the power of faith.[47] Religion divided immigrants and permeated American politics. The Republican Party was, as Eric Foner puts it, "an expression of the hopes and fears of northern native-born Protestants."[48] Republicans always fared best

---

45 Diane S. Butler, "The Public Life and Private Affairs of Sherman M. Booth," *Wisconsin Magazine of History* 82 (1999): 166–97; McManus, *Political Abolitionism in Wisconsin*, 87–90; Honeck, *We Are the Revolutionists*, 104–36.

46 Butler, "Public Life and Private Affairs of Sherman M. Booth," 168.

47 On the organized "freethinker" movement, see Katja Rampelmann, *Im Licht der Vernunft: Die Geschichte des deutsch-amerikansichen* Freidenker-Almanachs *von 1878 bis 1901* (Wiesbaden: Franz Steiner Verlag, 2003). The work of Mischa Honeck and Daniel Nagel insightfully addresses how religious and cultural tensions affected Forty-Eighters. Honeck, *We Are the Revolutionists*; Nagel, *Von republikanischen Deutschen zu deutsch-amerikanischen Republikanern*, 325–402.

48 Foner, *Free Soil, Free Labor, Free Men*, 227.

in the Northeast, where English-speaking abolitionists regarded slavery as a sin. Many of those same Yankees distrusted German and Irish immigrants, especially Catholics, which gave Democrats another opportunity to present African Americans and German Americans as born enemies. The whole situation forced German Republicans to examine their own religious prejudices and to remonstrate with the Anglo-Americans who were using their shared party as a vehicle for a Protestant crusade.

Not an election would pass without Democrats charging that Republicans were reviving the nativism of the Know Nothings.[49] During the reordering that followed the Kansas-Nebraska Act, the Know Nothing Party had won a host of congressional and state races. It showed well in the North, where its candidates campaigned to stop slavery's westering advance *and* restrict immigrants' right to vote and Catholics' right to hold office. In Massachusetts and some other states, Republicans allied with Know Nothings. Ohioans elected Republican Salmon P. Chase governor in 1855 at the head of a slate that included Know Nothings, although Chase personally rejected nativism.[50] In Wisconsin that year, the Know Nothings told their supporters to vote the Republican ticket. Although the state's Republican platform censured anti-immigrant organizations, the nativists took credit for Republican victories. They were pleased that Röser lost his bid for the office of state treasurer. He polled far behind most of the party's American-born nominees.[51] Watching these machinations, Democrats had good reason to question whether the Republican Party was a suitable political home for German immigrants.

Some German Democrats also suspected that German Republicans, especially the Forty-Eighters, harbored anti-Catholic prejudice. If this were true, how could they expect churchgoers to warm to the idea of the freedom-loving German? Forty-Eighters' anticlericalism often did lapse into a provocative denunciation of all things Roman Catholic. In 1853, for example, Hassaurek urged non-Catholic Germans to protest the visit of Gaetano Bedini, a papal envoy. The young editor, who himself had received

---

49 *Cincinnati Volksfreund*, Oct. 16, 1856.
50 Maizlish, *Triumph of Sectionalism*, 202–17. Historians who emphasize the importance of Anglo-Protestantism in the Republican Party include Michael F. Holt, *Forging a Majority: The Formation of the Republican Party in Pittsburgh, 1848–1860* (New Haven, CT: Yale University Press, 1969); and William E. Gienapp, *The Origins of the Republican Party, 1852–1856* (New York: Oxford University Press, 1987). In contrast, Tyler Anbinder maintains that although anti-immigrant sentiment was significant, slavery was the decisive factor in the party realignment of the decade. Anbinder, *Nativism and Slavery: The Northern Know Nothings and the Politics of the 1850's* (New York: Oxford University Press, 1992).
51 William F. Thompson, ed., *The History of Wisconsin*, vol. 2, *The Civil War Era, 1848–1873*, by Richard N. Current (Madison: State Historical Society of Wisconsin, 1976), 226–27; Joseph Schaefer, "Know Nothingism in Wisconsin," *Wisconsin Magazine of History* 9 (1925): 12–18.

a Catholic education from Piarist brothers in Vienna, had legitimate concerns that the ambassador had some connection to the executions of Italian nationalists, but his incendiary rhetoric stirred up an anti-Catholic frenzy. When Bedini arrived in Cincinnati, 1,200 men, women, and children rioted, causing one death.[52] In light of such violence, an Anglo-American acquaintance later wrote to Hassaurek that German Republicans agreed with "nine-tenths" of the message of the Know Nothings.[53]

The Bedini riot was an extreme case, but anti-Catholicism was common among German-American Republicans. In St. Louis, Börnstein filled the *Anzeiger* with invective against "the doings of the fanatical Roman priesthood" and published a German-language novel featuring a Jesuit plot in America's heartland.[54] Milwaukee's secular press was also critical of the Roman Catholic hierarchy. One Wisconsin priest worried to the Archbishop of Vienna that German-American Catholics might fall prey to the propaganda of the "false apostles of liberty."[55] Schurz evinced a measured anti-Catholicism. When he addressed Faneuil Hall in 1859, he claimed that Catholicism "nourished principles which are hardly in accordance with the doctrines of true democracy."[56] By impugning the Catholic Church in this way, German Republicans undermined their own ability to control the meaning of ethnicity in a religiously diverse immigrant community.

Yet even the most impassioned Forty-Eighter related to religion differently than a native-born Protestant. Many émigrés had grown up among Catholics. Schurz remembered his Catholic hometown, Libnar, fondly, although he had rejected the dogma of the Church and the "superstition" of folk Catholicism at an early age.[57] Arnold Krekel, who edited the *St. Charles Demokrat* in Missouri, had been brought up Catholic, and his siblings remained in the fold. J. B. Stallo had even trained for the priesthood as a young man, and he taught at Jesuit colleges in New York and Cincinnati during the 1840s.[58] Unlike most Anglo-Americans, German-American

52 John T. McGreevy, *Catholicism and American Freedom: A History* (New York: W. W. Norton, 2003), 25; White, "Religion and Community," 34–49; Levine, *Spirit of 1848*, 188–91; Wittke, "Friedrich Hassaurek," 2; *Columbus Westbote*, Feb. 10, 1854.

53 Timothy C. Day to Hassaurek, Washington, DC, March 25, 1856, box 2, folder 3, Hassaurek Papers, OHS. Historian Steven Rowan similarly argues that freethinker Henry Börnstein "split the difference" with nativists. Steven Rowan, "Introduction," in *Memoirs of a Nobody*, 19.

54 *Wöchentlich Anzeiger des Westens*, Dec. 27, 1851; Heinrich Börnstein, *Die Geheimnisse von St. Louis* (Cassel: H. Hotop, 1851); Koss, *Milwaukee*, 433–34.

55 Anthony Urbanek, Report to the Archbishop of Vienna, Edward Milde, 1853, in "Documents: Letter of the Right Reverend John Martin Henni," trans. Peter Leo Johnson, *Wisconsin Magazine of History* 10 (1926): 80–94, esp. 93.

56 Schurz, "True Americanism," 1: 60.

57 Schurz, *Reminiscences*, 1: 30–38; Schurz, "True Americanism," 1: 60.

58 Kamphoefner, "German-Americans and Civil War Politics," 240; Easton, *Hegel's First American Followers*, 28–32.

Republicans were close to Catholics. Their main fear was that religious bodies would exert undue political influence. In this respect, however, Anglo-American Protestantism seemed a greater threat than the Catholic Church. Protestants were already passing their religious values into law, in places prohibiting alcohol consumption and Sunday amusements.[59] Protestantism also underpinned the attempts of the Know Nothings to limit the political rights of immigrants and Catholics. Secular German Americans did not hold the same worldview as Protestant Anglo-Americans.

In fact, Know Nothing activity prompted many German-born Forty-Eighters to reevaluate how they discussed religion in public. Because the connection between anti-Catholicism and nativism was so strong, Republicans who pilloried Catholicism risked alienating *all* immigrants. After 1854, immigrant Republicans deliberately softened the language they used to refer to the Church. The *Anzeiger* became more precise in its criticisms, objecting specifically to "fanatical priests' papers" and speculating that "nine-tenths of our Catholic countrymen share our standpoint in this respect."[60] Later in the decade, a German-born confidant of Abraham Lincoln warned him not to rely on Friedrich Hecker, who "cannot conciliate opponents, and amongst Catholicks [sic] and even orthodox Protestants he is considered as the very Anti-Christ."[61] Writing of Milwaukee in 1854, Rudolph Koss noted, "The battle between the Republicans and the Democrats had begun, and religious controversies receded into the background."[62] German anti-slavery depended on this shift.

While German Republicans tried to relieve the religious strains among immigrants, they pleaded with Anglo-Americans in their party to disavow anti-immigrant sentiment. This work constituted one of the immigrants' most important contributions to Republican thinking about citizenship.[63] Although many native-born Republicans were not nativists in the first place, it was the prospect of votes from the Germans of the Midwest that made them incorporate immigration into their ideology.[64] Without German Americans, Republicans would not have seen immigrants as a positive good for the United States. With German Americans, they could not

---

59 See for example *Wöchentlich Anzeiger des Westens*, Aug. 5, 1854.
60 Ibid.
61 Gustav Koerner to Abraham Lincoln, July 17, 1858, Abraham Lincoln Papers, Library of Congress (hereafter LOC), quoted in Tucker, "Political Leadership in the Illinois-Missouri German Community," 218.
62 Koss, *Milwaukee*, 457.
63 Arguing that opposing nativism was German immigrants' greatest addition to the Republican Party, see Bergquist, "The Mid-Nineteenth-Century Slavery Crisis and the German Americans," in *States of Progress: Germans and Blacks in America over 300 Years*, ed. Randall M. Miller (Philadelphia: The German Society of Pennsylvania, 1989), 55–71.
64 Foner, *Free Soil, Free Labor, Free Men*, 237.

help but entertain the idea that naturalized men were the archetypal new citizens.

Republicans' success in overcoming nativism and recruiting immigrants varied from state to state. In Massachusetts, Know Nothings in the legislature rounded up enough Republican support in 1858 to propose the ballot measure that occasioned Schurz's address on "True Americanism." The referendum passed all the same, but turnout was just 17 percent, and it met with a chorus of disapproval from Republicans around the country.[65] Nativism was generally less pronounced in the Midwest, but the Republican Party in Schurz's home state of Wisconsin never outgrew its Yankee roots. When Republicans nominated Schurz for lieutenant governor in 1857, he lost whereas other Republican candidates won. One Wisconsinite wrote to Schurz, "I am mortified that the result is not as it should be." The writer attributed the outcome to "prejudices of birth and creed," but found consolation in the fact that most Republicans had not split their votes.[66] Two years later, when Republicans did not nominate Schurz for the governorship, immigrants thought they detected a conspiracy to check the progress of the "Liberal progressive German element."[67] One German delegate from Grant County identified "a 'native' ellement [sic] at that convention of controlling importance," and Germans in the Manitowoc delegation drafted a long statement of indignation.[68] Röser boycotted the party's final choice, incumbent Alexander Randall, but Schurz decided to earn Republicans' gratitude by stumping for Randall.[69] If Wisconsin had been typical, Schurz's career would have been uncertain and his pro-immigrant antislavery would have been untenable.

Germans were more successful in flushing nativism out of the Republican Party in Ohio. Although Yankee abolitionism fed Republicanism there too, especially in the northeastern part of the state, Cincinnati Germans acted as a counterweight. As early as 1855, Hassaurek helped reassure Salmon Chase that German votes could compensate for any loss of nativist support, and Republicans began to distance themselves publicly from the

65 Dale Baum, "Know-Nothingism and the Republican Majority in Massachusetts: The Political Realignment of the 1850s," *Journal of American History* 64 (1978): 973–74.

66 Louis P. Harvey to Schurz, Dec. 20, 1857, reel 1, fr. 119, Carl Schurz Papers (microfilm), LOC, Washington, DC.

67 John Erdebrink to Schurz, June 22, 1859, reel 1, fr. 248, Schurz Papers, LOC; *Wisconsin Demokrat*, Sept. 30, 1859; John E. to Schurz, Aug. 22, 1859, reel 1, Schurz Papers, LOC. This time Schurz declined the indignity of taking second position on the ticket.

68 M. K. Young to Schurz, Sept. 20, 1859, reel 1, fr. 262, Schurz Papers, LOC.

69 *Wisconsin Demokrat*, Oct. 7, 1859. In response to a *Westliche Post* editorial, Röser's paper said that developments in Wisconsin were not as bad as those in the East. On Schurz, see Trefousse, *Carl Schurz*, 77; Jacob Tschudy to F. Lindemann, Sept. 17, 1859, reel 1, fr. 257–59, Schurz Papers, LOC.

Know Nothings.[70] Still, Ohio was less hospitable to German antislavery than Missouri.

Republicans had never fraternized with Know Nothings in Missouri. The party was an outgrowth of free soil Democracy. In 1851, Thomas Hart Benton had cemented his ties to German immigrants by reprimanding the legislature for restricting alcohol sales.[71] Based on the ensuing skirmish, Börnstein hazarded that regular Democrats might "make an alliance with the Know Nothings and take away Germans' right to vote."[72] Further north, the idea of any Democrats cooperating with nativists would have sounded preposterous, but with proslavery Democrats lashing out at antislavery Germans, the allegation almost seemed plausible. Missouri Republicans were strongly anti-nativist because of the German role in the antebellum party. These conditions provided the best-case scenario for German-American antislavery before the Civil War.[73] Working-class and middle-class immigrants had united against slavery, Forty-Eighters had not antagonized all Catholics, and Know Nothings had not tainted the Republican Party. Antislavery ethnicity, in the guise of the freedom-loving German, would flourish in Missouri.

ANTISLAVERY ETHNICITY

Having described the Republican Party as elitist and hostile to immigrants, some Democrats concluded that it was insufficiently dedicated to the white race. German-American Republican reactions to Democratic race-baiting demand detailed attention because they would affect the rewriting of citizenship law following the Civil War. Although some antislavery immigrants agreed that it was imperative to guard the boundary between blackness and whiteness, most of them considered universal human rights a much higher priority. Nearly as importantly, all German Republicans linked antislavery to immigrant rights and constructed their aversion to slavery as an ethnic one. With these peculiarities, they added a crucial dimension to the American language of citizenship. As German–American Republicans questioned

---

70 For evidence of specific attempts to neutralize nativism and attract the German vote, see Salmon P. Chase to Hassaurek, Columbus, Ohio, April 7, 1857, box 2, folder 5, Hassaurek Papers, OHS; Timothy C. Day to Murat Halstead, Washington, DC, Jan. 29, 1857, box 1, folder 1, Murat Halstead Papers, Cincinnati Historical Society (hereafter CHS). Chase's focus had always been antislavery, so he needed little persuasion. Foner, *Free Soil, Free Labor, Free Men*, 249; Maizlish, *Triumph of Sectionalism*, 220–24.
71 *Wöchentlich Anzeiger des Westens*, Dec. 22, 1851, May 22, 1852, June 17, 1854.
72 Ibid., April 24, 1856.
73 Kamphoefner, "Missouri Germans and the Cause of Union and Freedom," *Missouri Historical Review* 106 (2012): 11–36.

the salience of the difference between black and white, they would inadvertently reinforce the distinction between race and ethnicity.

When Republicans condemned slavery and consorted with nativists, they threatened white privilege as Democrats understood it. For decades, the Democratic Party had appealed to whiteness to build a national coalition that included slaveholders in the South and immigrants in the North. By offering working-class men from Ireland and Germany a place in a white man's nation, Democrats gave them a psychological stake in the preservation of whiteness. Their party entrenched the racial boundaries that made the United States a *Herrenvolk* democracy, a democracy for members of the master race.[74]

Although German Democratic newspapers were more likely to defend German ethnicity than a generic whiteness, their editorials did sometimes indict Republicans for racial treachery. The editor of Ohio's *Fremont Courier*, referring to the disfranchisement of immigrants in Massachusetts, asked, "Who gives Negroes rights that they deny white citizens born in Europe?" Not content to leave readers to answer the question themselves, the paper fingered the culprits as "the black Republicans."[75] The ubiquitous epithet provided the simplest expression of the idea that white Republicans were race traitors. The *Columbus Westbote* quoted an "ultra-black Republican paper" as saying, "The Negroes are just as entitled to vote as anyone, and in respect to ability, reasoning, and discernment, they stand above the great majority of Irishmen and Germans and other immigrant citizens."[76] Since Republicans would willingly sacrifice the rights of immigrant Germans to the demands of black Americans, the paper argued, white men must organize by race. Similar comments appeared in Cincinnati's *Volksfreund*, Milwaukee's *Banner und Volksfreund* (formed from an 1855 merger), and Green Bay's *Banner*.[77] They all occasionally recast economic and ethnocultural insecurities as matters of race.

A handful of antislavery Germans took the bait, claiming that one of the advantages of abolition was that it would protect the sanctity of whiteness. Although this was a minority view, it merits attention as a path not taken,

---

74 George M. Fredrickson, *White Supremacy: A Comparative Study in American and South African History* (New York: Oxford University Press, 1981), 61, 84, 90–94, 322; Roediger, *Wages of Whiteness*, 59–60; Alexander Saxton, *The Rise and Fall of the White Republic: Class Politics and Mass Culture in Nineteenth Century America* (London: Verso, 1990); Ignatiev, *How the Irish Became White*, 127–61; Jean H. Baker, *Affairs of Party: The Political Culture of Northern Democrats in the Mid-Nineteenth Century* (Ithaca, NY: Cornell University Press, 1983), 212–58.
75 *Fremont Courier*, June 9, 1859.   76 *Columbus Westbote*, Oct. 17, 1856.
77 *Banner und Volksfreund*, Sept. 2, 1857; *Green Bay Banner*, April 15, 1859; *Cincinnati Volksfreund*, June 1, 20, 1856; *Columbus Westbote*, Sept. 29, 1854, March 24, 1859, Oct. 18, 1860. Ridiculing such ploys, see *Toledo Express*, June 2, 1856.

a racial alternative to the ethnic ideal of the freedom-loving German. One Ohio immigrant privately told Hassaurek that he wanted "Detestable Slave-holding Aristocrats, Contemptible Would be Aristocrats, and Cowardly Niggers" to leave the United States for Cuba, thus ridding the country of "3 nuisances at once."[78] No antislavery politician was so crude in public, but the editor of Wisconsin's *La Crosse Nord Stern* wrote in 1857 that he wished that slaves would be freed, educated, and sent to Africa "to maintain the purity of the races."[79] At that point, the editor still had not signed on to the Republican campaign, but the comment showed that antipathy for slavery was not incompatible with white supremacy. Börnstein's *Anzeiger des Westens*, a Republican paper that infrequently promoted antislavery in the name of whiteness, provided the odd example too. "Above all," the editors once wrote, "it is the white workers, it is the free white population of Missouri, that must be emancipated from the Slave Power, the slave oli-garchy, the slavery-aristocracy."[80] They positioned themselves as the *white* Republicans. It was a stance all Republican editors could have taken.

Yet it was rare for German Republicans to resort to race to justify anti-slavery. As natural as it would have been for the newcomers to cling to whiteness, there were also reasons for them to focus on the humanity they shared with blacks. In Missouri, some immigrants interacted with African Americans. Henry Clay Bruce, who had once been enslaved, commented in his memoirs that the German population around Brunswick, in the central part of the state, had earned the suspicion with which local slave-holders regarded them: "They were opposed to slavery and when they had an opportunity to tell a slave so, without his master's knowledge, they often did it." Bruce suggested that some immigrant Germans and enslaved African Americans could become quite close, saying, "Slaves never betrayed a friend; they would stand severe punishment rather than give away a white friend who favored freedom for all."[81] Circumstantial evidence of mean-ingful interracial relationships surfaced in 1858, when the slaveholders of Warrenton believed that immigrants had helped a man flee bondage. Two Anglo-Americans were charged with facilitating the escape, but several Germans, including one subscriber to the *Anzeiger*, were accused of com-plicity. After holding a meeting, the native-born residents of the settlement

78 Louis Krouskopf to Hassaurek, March 1860, box 2, folder 6, Hassaurek Papers, OHS.
79 *La Crosse Nord Stern*, Aug. 22, 1857. Bernhard Domschke reprinted an article that proposed coloniz-ing former slaves to Africa as a practical solution to the extraordinary prejudice African Americans faced in the United States. *Atlas*, April 20, 1859.
80 *Wöchentlich Anzeiger des Westens*, June 13, 1858. See also April 25, 1858.
81 H. C. Bruce, *The New Man: Twenty-Nine Years A Slave, Twenty-Nine Years A Free Man* (York, PA: P. Anstadt & Sons, 1895; reprint, New York: Negro Universities Press, 1969), 90–91.

west of St. Louis threatened to run ten German families out of town and destroy their property. It was only by enlisting the help of the county sheriff that the immigrants managed to remain in their homes. The hysteria gave immigrants cause to feel that they had just as much in common with enslaved blacks as they did with slaveholding whites.[82]

Even the vast majority of antislavery Germans who did not know African Americans personally were unlikely to explain themselves in the language of whiteness. German Republicans packed their editorials with the same liberal vocabulary that Forty-Eighters had introduced in Europe and all immigrants used in the United States. While native-born opponents of slavery also spoke of human rights, German Americans' transnational perspective and immigrant experience added weight to such references. In 1851, Börnstein reprinted an editorial arguing that if the United States recognized the "inviolable, sacrosanct nature of innate human rights," slavery must be abolished.[83] In states that were already "free," editors proceeded to tackle other forms of racial oppression. In 1854, Thieme at Cleveland's *Wächter am Erie* editorialized against the treatment of black abolitionist Frederick Douglass at a free soil convention. "Colored men may stand behind the table in the land of freedom," Thieme observed, "but not sit at it."[84] Indignant at the result of the 1857 *Dred Scott* case, the editor of the *Toledo Express* complained that the Supreme Court had rendered the Declaration of Independence's dictum that "all men are created equal" a lie.[85] With the election of 1860 nearing, Bernhard Domschke's new newspaper in Milwaukee, the *Atlas*, inquired why the Democrats believed that popular sovereignty meant "that a lighter colored people had the right to rob darker colored people of their human rights."[86] German Republicans were more likely to ask that African Americans be treated according to the universal laws of liberalism than to insist on the racial distance between the two groups.

Even before the Civil War, some German Republicans in Wisconsin believed that fidelity to universal principles meant that black men should vote. Yankee lawmakers instigated a new referendum on the issue in 1857, but few Republican politicians devoted much energy to its passage. The wavering editor at the *Nord Stern* asked why neither Carl Schurz nor Alexander Randall "had the courage to defend the consequence of their principles, voting rights for Negroes." The *Nord Stern* itself was against

82 *Wöchentlich Anzeiger des Westens*, May 16, 1858.
83 Ibid., Oct. 25, 1851. See also Nov. 29, 1851, Jan. 24, March 28, Feb. 7, 1858.
84 *Wächter am Erie*, Aug. 14, 1852. See also Sept. 11, 1852, Jan. 15, Feb. 23, 1853.
85 *Toledo Express*, March 19, 1857. See also *Atlas*, March 21, 1857.
86 *Atlas*, Oct. 13, 1860. See also March 14, 1857, Feb. 15, 1859; *Wisconsin Demokrat*, April 22, 1858.

African-American suffrage. "Not in principle," the editor insisted, "but in current practical achievability."[87] He added, however, that two German-language newspapers, Domschke's *Atlas* and Röser's *Demokrat*, recommended that readers vote "yes" in the referendum.[88] Black suffrage went down in defeat, 45,157 to 31,964, with only about two-thirds of Republicans in favor.[89] The number of German Wisconsinites who voted Republican was so small that it is difficult to determine whether they bucked the overall trend. In other states, German Republicans avoided grappling with suffrage until after emancipation.

What set German Republicans apart from other white Midwesterners was their ethnic claim that German immigrants understood freedom better than most Americans. They did not subscribe to one view of race, but they were all actively forming ethnicity. German-American Republicanism conveyed distinctive ideas about citizenship because it connected antislavery to immigrant rights through the myth of the freedom-loving German. Schurz was far from alone in this. In the first issue of the St. Louis *Westliche Post* in 1857, the editors notified readers that they revered the two great causes of freedom: antislavery and immigrant rights. Transforming Missouri "into a flourishing free state," they wrote, was inseparable from championing the interests of the "adoptive population" and encouraging the "political and social influence of the German element." The *Westliche Post* reasoned that immigrant-friendly policies would attract more free settlers, who in turn would discourage slavery.[90] Across town, Börnstein seconded this German-American exceptionalism in 1859, criticizing an Anglo-Missourian who debated the slavery question "not, like we Germans, primarily from the humanitarian point of view, but from the idea of utility."[91] On the eve of the war, his *Anzeiger* printed a piece claiming that Germans held a unique "mission" in the "present crisis" because they were "filled with more intensive concepts of freedom, with more expansive notions of humanity than most peoples of the earth." Börnstein believed that "the German is an opponent of slavery, and the German is always unfailingly there when free

---

87 *La Crosse Nord Stern*, Aug. 22, Oct. 8, 1857.

88 Ibid., Oct. 8, Aug. 22, 1857. On Röser, see *Oshkosh Deutsche Zeitung*, Oct. 17, 1857.

89 McManus, *Political Abolitionism in Wisconsin*, 150–57, esp. 156.

90 *Westliche Post*, Sept. 27, 1857, trans. in Steven Rowan, *Germans for a Free Missouri: Translations from the St. Louis Radical Press, 1857–1862* (Columbia: University of Missouri Press, 1983), 50–51. For similar arguments about the connection between protecting immigrants and restricting slavery, see *St. Charles Demokrat*, April 10, 1862, trans. in Anita M. Mallinckrodt, *What They Thought, Vol. 2, Missouri's German Immigrants Assess Their World* (Augusta, Missouri: Mallinckrodt Communications and Research, 1995), 4–6.

91 *Anzeiger des Westens*, April 17, 1859, quoted and trans. in Kamphoefner, "St. Louis Germans and the Republican Party, 1848–1860," *Mid-America: An Historical Review* 57, no. 2 (1975): 82.

labor is being defended, through law and the Constitution, against the pressure and dominance of slavery and the despotic principles of government it brings with it."[92] This was an exaggeration, even in Missouri, but immigrant leaders around the Midwest found it a useful one.

The Republican line that Germans were ethnically predisposed to hate slavery struck a chord in the German-language public sphere. Unlike some Irish Americans, German Americans celebrated ethnic pluralism, not white supremacy, in their popular culture. Even German Democrats did not join the Irish immigrants who honed their sense of whiteness at blackface minstrel shows, in which white men played foolish, self-indulgent, and subservient black characters.[93] Although blackface was also used in antislavery productions, minstrelsy usually brought working-class men together to revel in their common whiteness at the expense of African Americans.[94] Few German immigrants frequented such events. In one sample of forty-three performers working in 1838, seven were born outside of the United States, none of them in German lands.[95] Even at the height of blackface's popularity in the1860s, shows were not advertised in German-language newspapers. Neither were they standard fare at the numerous German-language entertainment venues in Midwestern cities.[96] In 1883, an immigrant wrote to a

---

92 *Anzeiger des Westens*, Dec. 17, 1860, trans. in Rowan, *Germans for a Free Missouri*, 147.

93 Several works make passing reference to German immigrant involvement in Civil War era minstrelsy: Kazal, *Becoming Old Stock*, 114, 323; Roediger, *Wages of Whiteness*, 118; Alan W. C. Green, "'Jim Crow', 'Zip Coon': The Northern Origins of Negro Minstrelsy," *Massachusetts Review* 11 (1970): 393. Ultimately, all these claims can be traced back to a 1930s monograph, Carl Wittke's *Tambo and Bones*. Wittke identified two German-born men in an extensive prosopography including scores of performers. Wittke, the son of German immigrants and an historian of German immigration, was well equipped to present more proof of a German-American role in blackface had it existed. Wittke, *Tambo and Bones: A History of the American Minstrel Stage* (Durham, NC: Duke University Press, 1930), 233, 236.

94 Baker, *Affairs of Party*, 213. David Roediger argues the potentially subversive class messages of blackface were funneled into racial rather than class solidarity. Roediger, *Wages of Whiteness*, 127. Emphasizing the class-based subversion of blackface, see Wilentz, *Chants Democratic: New York City and the Rise of the American Working Class, 1788–1850* (New York: Oxford University Press, 1984), 259; William F. Stowe and David Grimsted, "White-Black Humor," *Journal of Ethnic Studies* 3 (1975): 80–83. For the relationship between blackface and the Democratic Party, see Baker, *Affairs of Party*, 237; Saxton, "Blackface Minstrelsy and Jacksonian Ideology," *American Quarterly* 27 (1975): 19–23; Robert C. Toll, *Blacking Up: The Minstrel Show in Nineteenth-Century America* (New York: Oxford University Press, 1974), 65–97. Other scholars stress that the racial content of blackface was ambivalent and fluid. See Eric Lott, *Love and Theft: Blackface Minstrelsy and the American Working Class* (New York: Oxford University Press, 1993), 15–37; Mark E. Neeley, Jr., *The Boundaries of American Political Culture in the Civil War Era* (Chapel Hill: University of North Carolina Press, 2005), 97–127; William J. Mahar, *Behind the Burnt Cork Mask: Early Blackface Minstrelsy and Antebellum American Popular Culture* (Urbana: University of Illinois Press, 1999).

95 Saxton, "Blackface Minstrelsy and Jacksonian Ideology," 7.

96 It is difficult to prove the absence of German-language blackface in the United States during the 1860s and 1870s, but my extensive reading of German-language newspapers did not reveal any advertisements or reports of performances. Studies of German-American theater do not mention it, although they identify the staging of burlesques and vaudeville-style shows. Nolle, "German Drama

Milwaukee newspaper to ask – rhetorically – whether "citizens of German origin" had to attend "Minstrel Shows" in order to be good Americans. Using the English-language term for the American art form, he maintained that it was still as foreign to German Americans as "Camp Meetings" and "women's crusades."[97] Much later, a memoirist in the city described the taste for blackface as something that second-generation German Americans acquired only once they had assimilated.[98] Since German Americans had their own festive culture, German Republicans did not have to compete with an entertainment that other immigrants used to shore up their whiteness.

As uninterested as German-American proponents of antislavery were in blackface, they were also wary of the religious, sentimental, and feminized trappings of Anglo-American abolitionism. Mathilde Anneke, from her liminal position between German-American Republicans and native-born abolitionists, understood the cultural divide between her *Landsmänner* and authors such as Harriet Beecher Stowe. Together with Mary Booth, Anneke would spend the war years in Switzerland, where the two women collaborated on several pieces of antislavery fiction for German-language newspapers.[99] In "Die Sclaven-Auction," a Dutch immigrant's son and a Republican politician teamed up to rescue an enslaved woman from the buyers who leered at her on the auction block in Alexandria, Virginia. In some respects, "Die Sclaven-Auction" was unlike German-American antislavery culture as a whole. Its adjective-laden style – one scholar has called it "kitsch" – bore little resemblance to the masculine and militaristic cadences of newspaper editorials, partisan electioneering, and Turner pageantry. Yet Anneke and Booth were sensitive to their German-speaking audience. The story completely lacked the religious imagery of *Uncle Tom's*

on the St. Louis Stage," 77–81; Kremling, "German Drama on the Cleveland Stage," 190–93; Merrill, *German-American Urban Culture*, 25–32.

97 *Der deutsche Pionier* 15 (1883): 130–31. The piece appeared in an English-language newspaper before being translated in the *Milwaukee Seebote* and reprinted in Cincinnati's *Der deutsche Pionier*.

98 Bruce, "Memoirs of William George Bruce," 12. For other indications that German-American performers began to stage blackface in German-American venues only toward the end of the century, see Klaus Ensslen, "German-American Working-Class Saloons in Chicago: Their Special Function in an Ethnic and Class-Specific Cultural Context," in *German Workers' Culture*, ed. Keil, 173, 175; Christine Heiss, "Popular and Working-Class German Theater in Chicago, 1870 to 1910" in *German Workers' Culture*, ed. Keil, 188–90; Berndt Ostendorf, "'The Diluted Second Generation': German Americans in Music 1870 to 1920," in *German Workers' Culture*, ed. Keil, 279; Kazal, *Becoming Old Stock*, 113–14.

99 Anneke, "Die Sclaven-Auction: Ein Bild aus dem amerikanischen Leben," in *Die gebrochenen Ketten: Erzählungen, Reportagen und Reden, 1861–1873*, ed. Maria Wagner (Stuttgart: Hans-Dieter Heinz Akademischer Verlag, 1983), 27–48; Wagner, "Mathilde Anneke's Stories of Slavery in the German-American Press," *MELUS* 6 (1979): 14. On the writing of the stories, see Honeck, *We Are the Revolutionists*, 125–33.

Cabin, concluding prosaically with the young black woman working land in New York State with her husband. Anneke also had her Dutch-American protagonist commend the Republican character for his support of immigrants.[100] With one foot in Anglo-American abolitionism and the other in German-American antislavery, Anneke once more highlighted the difference between the two.

Rather than emulate Irish Americans or Anglo-Americans, German Republicans added antislavery to rituals of ethnicity that they shared with other German-speaking Americans, giving cultural heft to the notional figure of the freedom-loving German. Following a campaign event in the "entirely German" town of Augusta, Missouri, Friedrich Münch described how the Republicans evoked the spirit of 1848 and manipulated the festive culture of German America. When the hall reserved for an evening of German speeches was crammed full, townspeople crowded at the doors and windows. Afterwards, members of the local Turnverein paraded with flags and lanterns in streets glowing by the light of eight bonfires. A German band played as locals toasted one of the heroes of 1848, Italian Giuseppe Garibaldi. When the people of Augusta dispersed, Münch supposed they would vote Republican and fight to retain "our German way of life here, for only Germans can enjoy themselves in such a way by putting thought, heart, and hand to a cause they support." He echoed New York Republican William H. Seward's statement that Missouri was "Germanizing itself to make itself free."[101] Here was a forceful answer to Democrats' race-baiting: German Americans proud of their ethnic difference who stood firm against slavery. German Republicans tried to influence politics through ethnicity and shape ethnicity through politics.

Occupying the same German-language public sphere as Republicans, German Democrats acknowledged the power of antislavery ethnicity. In a backhanded move, they conceded its popularity when they said that Republicans were not in fact sincere in their disdain for the peculiar institution. Following the Kansas-Nebraska Act, the *Columbus Westbote* wrote that Republicans were "just professional politicians and unprincipled office seekers [who] are now using this issue as a hobbyhorse because they can't find a better one at the moment."[102] The editor implied that if the Republicans had been serious about staunching slavery, they might deserve German-American support. Before the presidential election of 1856, the *Westbote* chastised immigrants who were deceived by the cry of "Negro freedom"

---

100 Anneke, "Die Sclaven-Auction," 37.
101 *Anzeiger des Westens*, Oct. 22, 1860, trans. in Mallinckrodt, *From Knights to Pioneers*, 303–04.
102 *Columbus Westbote*, Sept. 29, 1854.

because "who is so blind that he cannot see that the leaders of the so-called black Republican Party are perpetrating a dreadful humbug with the slavery issue?"[103] The *Cincinnati Volksfreund* concurred in its commentary on the Republicans' 1860 convention: "The slavery issue is surely totally suited to pull one over on the people, and here you usually find right in the fore-ground those politicians who are as indifferent to the Negro as they are to the man in the moon."[104] As Democratic editors rushed to deny that Republicans were genuinely interested in African Americans, they con-firmed that the antislavery construction of German ethnicity held some appeal to their readers.

From Wisconsin, where Republicans won few German votes, came the strongest evidence that German Democrats too were drawn to antislavery. In an 1856 editorial headed "Republican Humbuggery," the *Banner und Volksfreund* complained that Republicans exploited the public uproar on occasions such as the passage of the Kansas-Nebraska Act.[105] A year later, it editorialized that the "Know Nothing-Republicans" were waging a polit-ical war against the South "under the pretext of humanity and the cloak of antislavery."[106] Rather than always argue against antislavery, Wiscon-sin Democrats often questioned Republicans' sincerity. Calling slavery the Republican "hobbyhorse," a Madison newspaper repeated that Democrats in the state had never liked it.[107] The editor of the *Oshkosh Deutsche Zeitung* wrote that Republicans "use a generally admirable humanity as a mere pre-tence [sic]" and proclaimed himself no friend of slavery.[108] Such a reaction vindicated the Republican decision to rely on an antislavery version of German ethnicity instead of peddling whiteness.

The exact implications of the freedom-loving German for American citizenship would only later become certain, but already two competing tendencies were emerging. The myth suggested both the desirability of equality among men and the superiority of German ethnicity. On the one hand, men such as Schurz, who promoted immigrant men's voting as they denounced slavery, inevitably found themselves likening ethnicity and race. During Wisconsin's 1857 referendum on suffrage, Domschke at the *Atlas* wrote, "We are decidedly hostile to any proscription of people on the basis of place of birth, religion, or color."[109] He presented race alongside ethnicity and religion as an illegitimate basis for discrimination. Two years

---

103 Ibid., Aug. 1, 1856. See also April 21, 1859.   104 *Cincinnati Volksfreund*, April 21, 1859.
105 *Banner und Volksfreund*, June 11, 1856. Also describing Republicans' resort to antislavery as a "humbug," see *Watertown Weltbürger und Anzeiger Vereinigtes Wochenblatt*, June 26, 1858.
106 *Banner und Volksfreund*, Sept. 2, 1857.   107 *Wisconsin-Staats-Zeitung*, Feb. 19, 1855.
108 *Oshkosh Deutsche Zeitung*, Oct. 13, 1857.   109 *Atlas*, Oct. 17, 1857.

later, the *Atlas* reported that Michigan's German Republicans had held a mass meeting in defense of voting rights for naturalized immigrant men. "That all people are born free and equal and have equal political rights" rang out from the Detroit gathering.[110] The logic of immigrant antislavery was already beginning to suggest that African Americans could follow immigrant men and become voting citizens.

The freedom-loving German, however, also said that he was better than other Americans. All of the cultural work that surrounded the myth ingrained the distinction between ethnicity, which was cultural and malleable, and race, which represented a more fundamental sort of difference and a more rational reason to exclude individuals from full citizenship. German Republicans did something less obvious than retreating into whiteness. They built up ethnicity as a category that contrasted with race. Being "freedom-loving," clearly a cultural attribute, became part of the German ethnicity that immigrants were already defining and expressing culturally. German Americans did not think of themselves as individuals belonging to a different race than African Americans, but as members of a completely different type of group. Instead of counterposing whiteness and blackness, this mode of self-definition set the category of ethnicity in implicit opposition to race. The most outspoken critics of racial hierarchy in the antebellum North − individuals such as Domschke − would have vehemently disagreed that their understanding of being German subtly conflicted with their commitment to political citizenship for African Americans. Whatever their personal intent, however, German-American Republicans were all part of a movement that increased the conceptual distance between ethnicity and race, a fact that would undercut their work for African-American citizenship during Reconstruction.

TRANSFORMING THE REPUBLICAN PARTY

By the late 1850s, antislavery German Americans had perfected their arguments and were set to transform the Republican Party. The future of slavery was the public issue of the day. It overshadowed economic and ethnocultural concerns. Many immigrants remained Democrats, but not because German Midwesterners voted along class lines. Among the Forty-Eighters, socialists had united with liberals under the aegis of free labor, deciding to wait until slavery was abolished to push for further economic reform or revolution.

110 Ibid., April 21, 1859.

Religion was trickier. Catholics never streamed into the Republican Party, but German Republicans no longer attacked Catholicism as viciously as they once had. They directed their ire instead towards nativism. Antislavery was now inextricable from the leading, although not unchallenged, form of German ethnicity in the Midwest. Instead of cleaving to race, Republicans focused on ethnicity. Since they still thought of American pluralism in cultural terms, this orientation left the relationship between race and citizenship unclear. They were unequivocal, however, about gender. From Republican speeches and editorials to working-class rallies and small-town celebrations, their antislavery was noticeably masculine.

Returning to Schurz's "True Americanism" speech in 1859, we can see how German Republicans communicated these ideas to the rest of the party. Battling for the voting rights of immigrant men, Schurz depicted the American nation as an entity that evolved as it welcomed new groups of people. "It is true," he observed, "the Anglo-Saxon establishes and maintains his ascendancy, but without absolutely absorbing the other national elements. They modify each other, and their peculiar characteristics are to be blended together by the all-assimilating power of freedom." He added that "every people, every creed, every class of society has contributed its share to that wonderful mixture out of which is to grow the greatest nation of the new world."[111] Religion and class were not valid grounds for exclusion in Schurz's mind, and different "nations" and "peoples" enhanced American life. Significantly, Schurz did not advocate *racial* pluralism, and when he enumerated the cultural gifts of different peoples, African Americans were completely absent. This was an ethnic schema with an antislavery twist: slavery had to end because freedom was the force that allowed different groups of Americans to live in harmony. Above all, Schurz wanted the Republican Party to be palatable to a spectrum of immigrant men.

And he was thinking of men. Schurz brought German-American gender politics to New England. He told Bostonians that "the title of manhood is the title to citizenship." With this casual dismissal of titles of nobility, the Wisconsin politician emphasized that women were not fit for full citizenship, a point with which the men and women in his Boston audience did not unanimously agree. Gerrit Smith, who had helped arrange for Schurz to speak in Massachusetts, was the cousin of women's rights leader Elizabeth Cady Stanton and backed women's suffrage.[112] (He was also the model for

111 Schurz, "True Americanism," 1: 54, 63.
112 John Stauffer, *The Black Hearts of Men: Radical Abolitionists and the Transformation of Race* (Cambridge, MA: Harvard University Press, 2002), 210–18.

the Republican politician in Mathilde Anneke's "Die Sclaven-Auction.")
Brimming with Yankee abolitionism, Smith and Stanton critiqued women's
exclusion from political citizenship. Their feminism was never about to
become a Republican staple, but it would inform its own set of proposals
for citizenship during Reconstruction. Schurz well knew that he was an
ambassador to such people from the German Midwest.[113] As such, he
wanted to persuade Bostonians that immigrant men were the typical new
American citizens and American citizenship conferred the right to vote on
men.

Schurz and other German Americans reaped the rewards of their work
at the Republican national convention of 1860. Although relatively few
German immigrants were official delegates, they flocked to Chicago anyway. Röser, Domschke, and Schurz came down from Wisconsin, and
Jacob Müller, Thieme, Stallo, and Hassaurek traveled from Ohio. Friedrich
Münch, Arnold Krekel, Carl Dänzer, and Carl Bernays were there from
Missouri, and Joseph Weydemeyer was also in attendance.[114] Many of these
men attended a preconvention meeting at the Deutsches Haus Hotel, at
which it was agreed that German Republicans would support any candidate who pledged himself to antislavery, anti-nativism, and homestead
grants for Western settlers.[115] Schurz, who formally represented Wisconsin, took these priorities to the convention's platform committee, where
he reminded other Republicans of the importance of German-born voters.
The fourteenth article of the final platform declared,

The Republican party is opposed to any change in our naturalization laws, or any
state legislation by which the rights of citizens hitherto accorded to immigrants
from foreign lands shall be abridged or impaired; and in favor of giving a full
and efficient protection to the rights of all classes of citizens, whether native or
naturalized, both at home and abroad.[116]

This plank was nothing new to the party's surprise nominee. Abraham
Lincoln had already cultivated relationships with German Illinoisans, buying
a half share in Springfield's German-language newspaper and renouncing the

113 Schurz, "True Americanism," 57.
114 It is unclear exactly who attended the meeting at the Deutsches Haus, but a list compiled from
     newspaper reports appears in F. I. Herriott, "The German Conference in the Deutsches Haus,
     Chicago, May 14–15, 1860," *Transactions of the Illinois State Historical Society* 35 (1928): 159–84.
     For official delegates, see Republican National Convention, *Proceedings of the Republican National
     Convention Held at Chicago, May 16, 17, and 18, 1860* (Albany: Weed Parsons and Company, 1860),
     146–53.
115 Bergquist, "The Forty-Eighters and the Republican Convention of 1860," in *German Forty-Eighters*,
     ed. Brancaforte, 141–56.
116 For Schurz's comments, see Republican National Convention, *Proceedings*, 92.

Massachusetts amendment.[117] Lincoln and the Republican Party officially ratified the position of German immigrants on American citizenship.

The Illinoisan still did not poll uniformly well around the Midwest. Most German Missourians did support Lincoln in 1860.[118] At least 80 percent of the German voters in St. Louis were for him, and since about half of them were nominal Catholics, Lincoln must have won many Catholic votes.[119] (August Willich later remarked that not *all* Catholics were "dumm"; those in Missouri had voted to elect Lincoln.[120]) St. Louis gave a plurality of its votes to Lincoln, but only the heavily Swiss and German county of Gasconade granted him a majority.[121] Overall, Northern Democrat Stephen Douglas won more votes in Missouri than any other candidate. Lincoln ran a distant fourth behind Constitutional Unionist John Bell and Southern Democrat John C. Breckinridge.

The free state of Ohio went for Lincoln in 1860, but its German-born residents were less Republican than German Missourians. Germans in rural Ohio strongly supported Douglas, but in some small towns they were moving away from the Democratic Party.[122] Immigrants started Republican clubs and requested German campaign speakers. Letters from German-born Republicans in locales such as Zanesville, Marion, Springfield, Chillicothe, and Dayton convinced Hassaurek and the chair of the state's Republican Committee that "the conversion of the Germans to the Republican faith is only a question of time."[123] There was something to the preelection hype. The Democratic *Fremont Courier* later reported disapprovingly that many German-American workers in Cleveland, Toledo, and Sandusky had voted Republican during the early 1860s.[124] German immigrants in Cincinnati supported Lincoln on election day. Contemporaries concluded as much, and four of the city's five most German wards yielded Lincoln substantial

117 Lincoln sold the paper once he was safely nominated. Harold Holzer, *Lincoln President-Elect: Abraham Lincoln and the Great Secession Winter, 1860–1861* (New York: Simon and Schuster, 2008), 149. For Lincoln's view of the platform, see *Wisconsin Demokrat*, May 1, 1860.

118 For a survey of immigrant voting in 1860, see Luebke, ed., *Ethnic Voters and the Election of Lincoln*. Kamphoefner, "German-Americans and Civil War Politics," provides the most rigorous and comprehensive evaluation of this literature.

119 Appendix, Table 3; Kamphoefner, "St. Louis Germans and the Republican Party," 69–88.

120 *Cincinnati Volksfreund*, Aug. 31, 1866.

121 U.S. Census Bureau, Population Schedule of the Eight Census of the United States 1860, manuscript returns for Gasconade County, Missouri; Dean Burnham, *Presidential Ballots, 1836–1892* (Baltimore: Johns Hopkins University Press, 1995), 578.

122 Thomas J. Kelso, "The German-American Vote in the Election of 1860: The Case of Indiana with Supporting Data from Ohio" (PhD diss., Ball State University, 1968).

123 William T. Bascon to Hassaurek, Sept. 19, 1860, and other letters in box 2, folder 6, Hassaurek Papers, OHS.

124 *Fremont Courier*, Aug. 13, 1868.

majorities.[125] In the Queen City too, some German Catholics must have gone Republican.[126] State-wide, however, Democrats probably held onto a slight lead among German voters.[127]

One historian has written, "Lincoln would have won in Wisconsin if all German votes had been given to Douglas, as doubtless five sixths of them were."[128] Milwaukee Germans stayed largely Democratic, but Republicans made a few gains in other areas.[129] Before the election, the editor of the *La Crosse Nord Stern* wrote to Schurz that although most local Germans were Democrats, "a not insignificant number are now sitting on the fence."[130] Another La Crosse Republican was more optimistic: "We have made a breach into the German ranks here & we wish to storm the camp."[131] According to a party operative, there were also German voters who would give Republican speeches a fair hearing in Manitowoc, Sheboygan, Monroe, and Sauk City, and historians have located pockets of German Protestants who voted Republican.[132] Revealingly, however, although Schurz's Wisconsin colleagues begged him to help out at home, he put his energy into states where he could expect to be of more use to the party.[133]

After Lincoln's election, German Republicans took stock. One of Hassaurek's correspondents congratulated him on his role in the "conversion of the Germans," and Schurz told his wife that the president-elect had named him "foremost of all" among his campaigners.[134] In Ohio and Missouri, Republicans were now the august leaders of the German-language public sphere. Wisconsin lagged behind, but German Republicans there had pushed the Democrats to come out against slavery. Nationally, German Midwesterners had reshaped the party that brought Lincoln to power. By connecting antislavery to the voting rights of immigrant men, they had

---

125 Appendix, Tables 1 and 2; Levine, *Spirit of 1848*, 252; Kamphoefner, "German-Americans and Civil War Politics," 241.

126 White, "Religion and Community," 47–51.

127 Kamphoefner, "German-Americans and Civil War Politics."

128 Joseph Schafer, "Who Elected Lincoln?" *American Historical Review* 47 (1941): 60.

129 Appendix, Table 4.

130 John Ulrich to Schurz, Sept. 8, 1860, reel 1, fr. 422, Schurz Papers, LOC. The paper threw its support to Lincoln after Northern Democrats nominated Douglas. *La Crosse Nord Stern*, July 28, 1860.

131 Norman Eastman to Schurz, Sept. 13, 1860, reel 1, fr. 443, Schurz Papers, LOC.

132 Horace Rublee to Schurz, Oct. 12, 1859, reel 1, fr. 269, Schurz Papers, LOC; Schafer, "Who Elected Lincoln?" 56–57.

133 Wisconsin State Republican Central Committee to Schurz, Aug. 27, 1860; Horace Rublee to Schurz, Sept. 20, 1860; Louis P. Harvey to Schurz, Oct. 11, 1860, reel 1, fr. 377–78, 464, 496, Schurz Papers, LOC.

134 Guido Ilges to Hassaurek, Nov. 27, 1860, box 2, folder 6, Hassaurek Papers, OHS; Schurz to Margarethe Schurz, Oct. 2, 1860, in *Intimate Letters*, ed. and trans. Schafer, 226.

publicized a language of citizenship based on their own experiences. The immigrant man, German Republicans said, was the archetypal American citizen. They had yet to resolve how that would affect citizenship law, but four years of warfare would leave the myth of the freedom-loving German more potent than ever.

3

Black Suffrage as a German Cause in Missouri, 1865

On January 15, 1865, German immigrants gathered in the St. Louis Turner Hall to celebrate. Four days earlier, Missouri had finally passed an ordinance emancipating the people still enslaved in the state. A mixture of relief and exultation coursed through the crowd of men waiting expectantly for the evening's speeches. Emil Preetorius, a Forty-Eighter who edited the *Westliche Post*, used the moment to make a particularly portentous address. After tracing the abolition of slavery in Missouri back to the Turners' campaign for democratic reform in German Europe, Preetorius looked to the future. The immigrants' next task, he said, would be to enfranchise African-American men. Speaking in his native tongue, Preetorius told the assembly that "the great principle of freedom and equality" required that the convention revising Missouri's constitution consider such a move. "Distinctions based on color or race" contravened the "principles of the Declaration of Independence" and must go. The ricocheting applause that greeted his words led Preetorius to write that "the Radical *Deutschtum* of St. Louis" had "taken a firm position on the two highly important questions of Reconstruction and voting rights."[1]

As the Civil War was entering its final months in 1865, men such as Preetorius suddenly claimed African-American suffrage as a German-American cause. Missourians were rewriting their state constitution at the time, giving Forty-Eighters and other German Republicans the opportunity to practice the arguments that they would make around the country after the war's formal conclusion in April. The Midwestern state made for a good testing ground because many Americans believed that it represented the sectional ordeal in microcosm. A German-born journalist visiting from Illinois observed that Missouri "became typical of all the struggles of the Union."

1 *Westliche Post*, Jan. 17, 1865.

It was "the first of the border states that was wrested from the iron grasp of secession, and all the turmoil and battles that still lay ahead for the United States made their first appearance here."[2] Some of those same features, however, also made Missouri somewhat anomalous. As a slave state that had remained in the Union, it was reconstructed from within, not by Congress. When Missouri Unionists discussed the rights of the freed people, they did not have to weigh state control against federal power. Instead, they could concentrate on the equally fraught questions of whether American citizenship necessarily entailed voting rights *in Missouri* and whether it should be racially inclusive. Would black men become full citizens like naturalized men or would they obtain the second-class status of all American women?

When a group of black veterans petitioned the Missouri convention to permit African Americans to vote, German-American leaders were poised to back them up.[3] Like Preetorius, most German Missourians would have described themselves as "Radicals," the name adopted by the Unionists in the state who had fought to abolish slavery. In 1865, the most important of these immigrant Radicals decided that the same liberal nationalist principles that had driven them to oppose slavery bound them to pursue race-neutral suffrage law. This chapter describes how ethnicity functioned within their movement. German Radical leaders aimed, they said, to dismantle the legal barrier between race and ethnicity. They sometimes likened themselves to the freed people. They always portrayed respect for immigrants and tolerance of African Americans as two parts of the same liberal impulse. Yet as the Turner Hall meeting attested, the struggle for black suffrage, like the anti-slavery crusade, became an ethnic one. Whatever their ostensible message, politicians built on an essentially cultural form of identification when they appealed to voters in the public sphere. Despite the ambitious goal specified by men such as Preetorius, the political culture of German-American Radicalism continued to represent ethnicity and race as meaningfully different categories. In the end, the new constitution would not enfranchise black men, but the debates would reveal the unusual reasoning and idiosyncratic political style that German-born supporters of African-American suffrage would bring to Reconstruction. Ethnicity both fueled German Radicalism and constrained it.

---

2 *St. Charles Demokrat*, April 13, 1865.
3 Missouri Constitutional Convention, *Journal of the Missouri State Convention Held at the City of St. Louis, January 6-April 10, 1865* (St. Louis: Missouri Democrat, 1865), 53; Margaret L. Dwight, "*Black Suffrage in Missouri, 1865–1877*" (PhD diss., University of Missouri – Columbia, 1978), 43–68; Aaron Astor, *Rebels on the Border: Civil War, Emancipation, and the Reconstruction of Kentucky and Missouri* (Baton Rouge: Louisiana State University Press, 2012), 211–12.

ANTISLAVERY ETHNICITY IN WARTIME

Although forged in the antebellum years, the opinions that German-American Republicans shared during the Missouri constitutional convention of 1865 hardened during the Civil War. What had begun as a war for national preservation became a war against slavery, strengthening the hand of the liberal nationalists who believed that the survival of the United States depended on implementing human rights and vice versa. Some immigrants resented the Northern war effort, and many of the hundreds of thousands of German-born Union soldiers were not motivated by the abstractions of nation or freedom, but combat and wartime politics did steel antislavery German ethnicity.[4]

Nationalistic and antislavery fervor spread more slowly among German Americans in Ohio and Wisconsin than it did in Missouri. Some Republicans certainly rushed to put their politics into action after the firing on Fort Sumter. On April 17, 1861, J. B. Stallo was among the speakers at the Cincinnati Turner Hall calling immigrants to enlist. By the following evening, the ranks of the "German" Ninth Ohio Infantry Regiment were filled, mainly by Turners. Later that year, one of their number, August Willich, left to command an Indiana regiment that would achieve considerable success.[5] In Wisconsin, as one immigrant recalled, "When Lincoln called citizens to arms to defend the Union, the Turners were there to heed the call with great enthusiasm."[6] The Milwaukee Turnverein immediately made preparations to quarter recruits, furnish a flag, and excuse enlistees from membership dues.[7] One confirmed Republican, Bernhard Domschke, waited until 1862 to leave the *Milwaukee Herold* (a paper with more promise than the *Korsar* or *Atlas* before it) and join the Northern forces.[8] Carl Schurz donned a uniform that year too, although he could hardly be called a

4 Helbich, "German-Born Union Soldiers: Motivation, Ethnicity, and 'Americanization,'" in *German-American Immigration and Ethnicity*, ed. Helbich and Kamphoefner, 295–325. See the letters in Kamphoefner and Helbich, eds., *Germans in the Civil War: The Letters They Wrote Home*, trans. Susan Carter Vogel (Chapel Hill: University of North Carolina Press, 2006). On German immigrant service, see also Martin Öfele, *German-Speaking Officers in the United States Colored Troops, 1863–1867* (Gainesville: University of Florida Press, 2004).

5 Wittke, "The Ninth Ohio Volunteers," *Ohio Archeological and Historical Quarterly* 35 (1926): 409–10; Honeck, *We Are the Revolutionists*, 99. Cleveland's Turners contributed on a less dramatic scale. German-American Biographical Pub. Co., *Cleveland and Its Germans*, 93–94.

6 George Brosius, *Fifty Years Devoted to the Cause of Physical Culture, 1864–1914* (Milwaukee, WI: Germania Publishing Co., 1914), 12.

7 Recording Secretary of the Milwaukee Turnverein, Minutes, Apr. 18 and 26, May 3, June 17, 1861, box 5, vol. 14, Milwaukee Turners Records, WHS-MARC.

8 J. J. Schlicher, "Bernhard Domschke: II: The Editor and the Man," *Wisconsin Magazine of History* 29 (1945): 451–52. Fritz Anneke also had an ill-fated and short-lived career as a Union officer. Schulte, *Fritz Anneke*, 66, 72–81.

Wisconsinite after 1860. After a brief stint as American minister in Spain he returned to the United States to serve as a brigadier general.[9] There were new leaders too. Three of the Salomon brothers from Manitowoc served with distinction in the army, and a fourth, Eduard Salomon, was elected lieutenant governor on the Republican ticket in 1861.[10]

German-born Democrats, a majority in Ohio and Wisconsin, begrudged the boost the war gave Republicans. Some of them responded by becoming War Democrats. One Clevelander reported that he − "like most Germans" − went into coalition with the Republicans.[11] In Milwaukee, Moritz Schöffler's imposing *Banner und Volksfreund* hailed Lincoln's inaugural speech, broadcast the president's call for troops, and referred to secessionists as "traitors" and "fire-eaters."[12] The *Watertown Weltbürger* in central Wisconsin and the *Fremont Courier* in northwestern Ohio followed suit, but more tentatively, while the *Columbus Westbote, Cincinnati Volksfreund*, and *Milwaukee Seebote* deprecated war plans despite secession.[13] These editors repeated the Democratic slogan, "The Union as it was, the Constitution as it is, and the Negroes where they are."[14] More distressing to Republicans was a destructive draft riot among German-speaking Luxembourgers in Ozaukee County, Wisconsin, in the autumn of 1862. *Seebote* editor Peter V. Deuster, an Aachen-born Catholic who had immigrated as a teenager in the 1830s, egged the protestors on. Writing right after Lincoln had announced the preliminary Emancipation Proclamation, Deuster warned European immigrants that "abolitionists" wanted to "annihilate" them "to make room for the Negro."[15] In later years, few immigrants would want to remember such racist dissent, but it represented a real countercurrent in German ethnicity.

By 1865, most Democrats conceded the hegemony of Republicans' liberal nationalism among German Americans. They had learned how coercive a force wartime patriotism could be. Democrats who felt that violent

---

9 Trefousse, *Carl Schurz*, 98–119.

10 Louis Falge, ed., *History of Manitowoc County, Wisconsin*, 2 vols. (Chicago: Goodspeed Historical Association), 1: 255; Herman Salomon, "The Civil War Diary of Herman Salomon," *Wisconsin Magazine of History* 10 (1926): 205–10.

11 German-American Biographical Pub. Co., *Cleveland and its Germans*, 85.

12 *Wisconsin Banner und Volksfreund*, Jan. 6, March 6 and 7, Apr. 16, 19, and 20, May 11 and 12, 1861.

13 *Fremont Courier*, May 2, 1861; *Watertown Weltbürger*, Apr. 20, 1861. The *Sheboygan National Demokrat* vacillated. See May 18 and 29, June 29, July 20, 1861.

14 *Columbus Westbote*, Aug. 28, 1862.

15 *Seebote*, Oct. 25, 1862, quoted and trans. in Frank L. Klement, "Catholics as Copperheads during the Civil War," *Catholic Historical Review*, 80 (1994): 45; Klement, "Deuster as a Democratic Dissenter During the Civil War: A Case Study of a Copperhead," *Transactions of the Wisconsin Academy of Sciences, Arts and Letters* 55 (1966): 21–38; Lawrence H. Larsen, "Draft Riot in Wisconsin, 1862," *Civil War History* 7 (1961): 421–23.

opposition to the draft reflected poorly on the German community casti-gated Peter Deuster.[16] The editor of the *Seebote* also realized that abolitionist Forty-Eighters led German America now more than ever. After several days of post-riot posturing, he yielded to Eduard Salomon, who had become Wisconsin governor upon the sudden death of his predecessor. One of Salomon's duties was to oversee conscription in the state. By the time that drafting commenced in Milwaukee, Deuster had temporarily abandoned racist vitriol and was counseling calm.[17] The ascent of Republican lead-ers and ideas was replayed on a national scale as military leaders such as Schurz stood up for immigrant soldiers. In refuting aspersions cast on the honor of German-American troops, they sealed their position as ethnic heroes. A Union defeat at Chancellorsville, Virginia, in 1863 provided the best example.[18] All of the Democratic newspapers that published Schurz's angry defense of his men increased his power to define what it was to be German American. When the last Democratic and Catholic holdouts resigned themselves to emancipation, some of them gestured to the Repub-lican myth of the freedom-loving German.[19] The editor of the *Cincinnati Volksfreund* backed the Thirteenth Amendment in January 1865 specifi-cally because he thought that German immigrants believed slavery to be "a moral, social, and political evil."[20]

Missouri, the embattled epicenter of German-American antislavery, fig-ured prominently in the Republican construction of ethnicity. During the winter of 1860–1861, governor-elect Claiborne Fox Jackson had maneu-vered to lead his state out of the Union.[21] As Jackson mobilized state militia and called for secessionist volunteers, German immigrants drilled boldly in the streets of St. Louis, preparing to keep Missouri loyal by force. "To Arms!" the *Anzeiger* called in April 1861, and Heinrich Börnstein did not limit himself to written exhortation.[22] Along with Franz Sigel, who was then superintendent of St. Louis schools, and Francis P. (Frank) Blair, Jr.,

---

16 *Watertown Weltbürger*, Nov. 11, 1862; *Banner und Volksfreund*, Nov. 14, 1862.

17 *Seebote*, Nov. 18, 19, 20, and 28, 1862; *Banner und Volksfreund*, Nov. 13, 1862.

18 Christian B. Keller, *Chancellorsville and the Germans: Nativism, Ethnicity, and Civil War Memory* (New York: Fordham University Press, 2007).

19 *Seebote*, Jan. 24, 1865. For earlier converts see *Banner und Volksfreund*, Sep. 27, 1862; *Watertown Weltbürger*, Sep. 27, 1862. Representing the archdiocese of Cincinnati, see *Wahrheitsfreund*, May 10, 1865. A German scholar of American Catholicism, Michael Hochgeschwender, has found that the antislavery prelates garnered the most support among middle-class, German-speaking Catholics in large cities. Hochgeschwender, *Wahrheit, Einheit, Ordnung: Die Sklavenfrage und der amerikanische Katholizismus, 1835–1870* (Paderborn: Ferdinand Schöningh, 2006), 356–89.

20 *Cincinnati Volksfreund*, Jan. 15, 1865.

21 William E. Parrish, ed., *A History of Missouri*, vol. 3, *1860–1875*, by Parrish (Columbia: University of Missouri Press, 1973), 6, 8–10.

22 *Anzeiger des Westens*, April 19, 1861, trans. in Rowan, *Germans for a Free Missouri*, 180.

a native-born Democrat-turned-Republican from an influential political family, he organized the Unionist Home Guards.[23] Both the *Anzeiger* and the *Westliche Post* were keen to note that in this "second American revolution," Forty-Eighters would once again take up arms for nation and liberty.[24] With universal principles and ethnic pride on the line, it did not take long for violence to erupt.

What occurred on May 10, 1861, would provide a rallying point for Republicans who argued that there was a German position on American citizenship in 1865. Anticipating that militiamen loyal to Governor Jackson would seize the federal arsenal in St. Louis, U.S. Army Captain Nathaniel Lyon went on the offensive. He supplemented his regular troops with recruits from the local German community, including Börnstein, Sigel, and a substantial number of Turners. With this new contingent, in which German immigrants outnumbered regulars four to one, Lyon surrounded and captured the secessionists who had assembled at Camp Jackson. But that was not the end of the incident. As Lyon's men marched their prisoners through St. Louis, Jackson's supporters heckled the Unionists with anti-German slurs. Discipline was already crumbling when a shot scattered the crowd. The gunfight that followed left some thirty people dead.[25] Despite the tragic outcome, German Americans were proud to have shown themselves more devoted to the United States than the native-born citizens of Missouri. In the retelling, the "Camp Jackson Affair" became the most powerful symbol of the freedom-loving German.

When the Civil War began in earnest, German Missourians earned a reputation for opposing slavery as ferociously as they supported the Union. After Federal troops quickly sent Jackson's administration into exile, Conservative Unionists, who hoped that slavery would outlast the war, tried to govern the state. They had to contend with Confederates (about one-third of the Missourians who took up arms fought for secession) and Radical Unionists.[26] German immigrants made up a large fraction of the antislavery opposition. In June 1862, between 60 and 70 of the 178 representatives at a Radical convention in Jefferson City were German-born, and the

---

23 Engle, *Yankee Dutchman*, 51; William E. Parrish, *Frank Blair: Lincoln's Conservative* (Columbia: University of Missouri Press, 1998).

24 *Anzeiger des Westens*, April 27, 1861, trans. in Rowan, *Germans for a Free Missouri*, 187.

25 Accounts of the affair appeared in the *Anzeiger* and the *Westliche Post* as well as various reports and memoirs. For useful narratives, see Parrish, *History of Missouri*, 3: 11–14; Burton, *Melting Pot Soldiers*, 38–41; Arenson, *Great Heart of the Republic*, 217. For the composition of the forces, see Andreas Dorpalen, "The German Element and the Issues of the Civil War," in *Ethnic Voters and the Election of Lincoln*, ed. Luebke, 78.

26 James M. McPherson, *Battle Cry of Freedom: The Civil War Era* (New York: Oxford University Press, 1988), 293.

following year, a similar meeting passed a resolution of "heartfelt gratitude" to the Germans.[27] Immigrants helped elect a Radical governor, Thomas C. Fletcher, in 1864. German Missourians obviously worked with Anglo-American Radicals, but not always harmoniously. Radical German Americans had an especially antagonistic relationship with Charles D. Drake, a St. Louis politician who had not voted for Lincoln in 1860 and did not speak out against slavery until 1861. Making matters worse, Drake was a former Know Nothing. He was repulsed by public alcohol consumption and Sunday recreations.[28] Missouri's wartime politics only further convinced German immigrants that their long-standing aversion to slavery and their abiding interest in cultural pluralism set them apart.

The course of the war also increased German Missourians' sympathy for the enslaved. When Confederate regulars and secessionist guerillas targeted immigrants, they set German Americans against all that the Confederacy represented.[29] According to a Frenchman who traveled in the border state during the war, the pervasive violence ensured that "everyone is an extremist; between the radical abolitionists and the friends of the South there is no moderate Unionist middle ground." Apparently unaware of all the Conservative Unionists, the sojourner interpreted Missouri's Civil War as a conflict between recent German immigrants and the descendants of older "Anglo-French families." He described a scene on board a Mississippi steamer in which a group of "stubborn" German immigrants bore witness for emancipation in an argument with two plantation owners and some "adventurers."[30]

Personal letters also showed that fighting the Confederacy heightened the sensitivity of German Americans to the depredations of slavery. From Franklin County, southwest of St. Louis, Karl Frick informed relatives in Europe that the slaves were "driven by white men with whips in their hands and often terribly mistreated and also poorly fed and so there are black families with 4 to 5 children where the mother and father are torn apart and sold thousands of miles away." Traitorous slaveholders, Frick told

27 Jörg Nagler, *Fremont contra Lincoln: Die deutsch-amerikanische Opposition in der republikanischen Partei während des amerikanischen Bürgerkrieg* (Frankfurt am Main: Peter Lang, 1984), 90, 139.

28 William Parrish, *Missouri under Radical Rule, 1865–1870* (Columbia: University of Missouri Press, 1965), 5; Charles D. Drake, Manuscript Autobiography (1879), 176l, Western Historical Manuscript Collection – Columbia (hereafter WHMC – Columbia), Missouri.

29 Frizzell, *Independent Immigrants*, 89–121; Michael Fellman, *Inside War: The Guerrilla Conflict in Missouri during the American Civil War* (New York: Oxford University Press, 1989), 70–71, 181.

30 Ernest Duvergier de Hauranne, *A Frenchman in Lincoln's America*, trans. and ed. Ralph H. Bowen (Chicago: R. R. Donnelley & Sons Company, 1974), 308, 305, 312. This contemporary observation is in sharp contrast with scholarship that emphasizes the dominance of Conservative Unionism in the state. See for example Astor, *Rebels on the Border*.

his family, "don't want to set their slaves free and just want to exploit other humans, that is blacks, because they don't regard them as human beings."[31] Trying to make sense of the destructive war, Frick described disunion as the last resort of men who sneered at human rights. Secessionists, immigrants concluded, had turned on the American nation and the liberal principles for which it stood.

As the war dragged on, German Radicals' support for African Americans and frustration with other Missouri Unionists occasionally interrupted national politics. Criticizing Lincoln's slowness to come around to emancipation, these immigrants became a real irritant to the Lincoln administration. The discord emerged during the first year of the hostilities when General John C. Frémont tried to free people who were held in slavery by disloyal Missourians. German Republicans already admired Frémont, partly because of his choice of German-born lieutenants such as Sigel and Joseph Weydemeyer (who had followed the general west from New York in July 1861). They welcomed the confiscation orders.[32] When Lincoln sided with Missouri Conservatives, who now included Frank Blair, and countermanded Frémont, German Missourians were livid. Their protests so alarmed Blair's brother, U.S. Postmaster General Montgomery Blair, that he warned Lincoln that Missouri's Germans were "revolutionists, not reformers" and were "evidently" forming an alliance with the secessionists.[33] They were not, of course, but they did favor emancipation. Lincoln's 1863 proclamation did not mollify them, for it had no effect on slavery in loyal states. That year, a delegation of Missouri Radicals, including Emil Preetorius and several other German Americans, headed to Washington to make their case to the president in person. Lincoln, unwilling to alienate Conservatives, refused to see them.[34] Rebuffed, some German Radicals begged Frémont to challenge Lincoln for the Republican nomination in 1864. The *Westliche Post* was the most significant newspaper to participate in this bid, but other German-language papers in the Midwest flirted with the idea too. Frémont wisely withdrew his candidacy before the national convention, but Missouri delegates cast the only votes against Lincoln in the opening round of balloting.[35]

Although the Frémont nomination ended ignominiously, Radical leaders had linked German ethnicity and African-American rights in Missouri.

---

31 Quoted in Kamphoefner and Helbich, eds., *Germans in the Civil War*, 347–48, 353–55.
32 Obermann, *Joseph Weydemeyer: Ein Lebensbild*, 374; Engle, *Yankee Dutchman*, 67, 86–89.
33 Montgomery Blair to Abraham Lincoln, Feb. 18, 1863, Lincoln Papers, LOC, quoted in Nagler, *Fremont contra Lincoln*, 112.
34 By January 1863, only one German-language newspaper in the state did not support immediate emancipation. Nagler, *Fremont contra Lincoln*, 141.
35 Ibid., 208–50; Honeck, *We Are the Revolutionists*, 161–68.

Even rank-and-file immigrants gave Conservative Unionism a wide berth, as evidenced in their reaction to Forty-Eighter Carl Dänzer's abrupt turn to the right. During 1863, Dänzer resurrected the *Anzeiger* – temporarily known as the *Neuer Anzeiger* – as a Conservative newspaper.[36] Although he assumed that emancipation was a fait accompli, Dänzer was highly critical of the president's decision to make it a war aim. In 1864, the *Neuer Anzeiger* endorsed the Democratic presidential nominee, General George B. McClellan. It featured stories typical of the Democratic press: warnings against governmental overreach, heartfelt calls for peace, and racial scaremongering. Commenting on the recruitment of African-American soldiers, Dänzer declared it ludicrous that "in several months our long-time tobacco-planting and housebroken black house pets [will be] transformed into musket carriers and soldiers of freedom for Uncle Sam."[37] To top it off, Dänzer slighted the recognized leaders of St. Louis *Deutschtum* and abandoned references to "German" ideals. In return, most German Americans shunned his newspaper and his politics. As late as 1868, the *Anzeiger* only claimed to represent 30 percent of German-speaking voters in Missouri; its competitors estimated the proportion at 10 percent.[38] Such failures confirm that after a series of interactions with Confederates, Conservative Unionists, African Americans, and Lincoln's government, German immigrants were among the white Missourians most interested in racial equality. In their name, a few determined leaders would attempt to enfranchise black men.

RACE, ETHNICITY, AND VOTING CITIZENSHIP FOR MEN

Facing the dilemmas that would soon confront the entire United States, the delegates who arrived in St. Louis in January 1865 began to draft a constitution to protect the rights of the freed people and guarantee the safety of all Unionists. During nearly three months of deliberations, German Radicals would lobby for the extension of American citizenship, maintaining that the law should treat race no differently than ethnicity. Yet this simple proposal belied the immigrants' more nuanced contribution to Reconstruction. In the heated exchange over who deserved which rights, it would become clear how the ethnic form of German-American Radicalism could undercut Radical leaders' avowed objective. Immigrant politicking continued to construct ethnicity differently than race. At times, politicians seemed to

36 Boernstein, *Memoirs of a Nobody*, 373–75, 383–85; *Neuer Anzeiger des Westens Wochen-Blatt*, Aug. 5 and 11, Sept. 1, 1863, June 4, Sept. 23, 1864.
37 Ibid., Dec. 12, 1863.
38 *Anzeiger des Westens Wochen-Blatt*, April 23, 1868.

believe that the very fact that immigrants were prepared to compare race and ethnicity was proof that they belonged to a sort of group that had a special role in American life.

The German-American Radicals' campaign took shape while Anglo-American Radicals and Conservatives competed for control of Missouri. Only eight German-born men were among the Missouri Unionists elected to reframe the constitution, and one of them, Arnold Krekel, held the largely procedural position of convention president.[39] Charles Drake, who led the English-speaking Radicals, dominated the sixty-six-man body, guiding debate in the Committee of the Whole and drafting resolutions behind the scenes.[40] With the cooperation of Radical delegates from the rural districts most riven by violence, Drake pushed through the infamous "ironclad oath." This section of the constitution, which overrode previous amnesties, required potential voters and certain professionals to swear that they had never even voiced sympathy for the rebellion.[41] It immediately led indignant Conservatives, even those who had forsworn secession, to tag the constitution a "Draconian Code," a play on Drake's name that branded his handiwork as authoritarian.[42]

Conservative Unionists comprised only about a quarter of the delegates, but they claimed to speak for a much larger portion of the state, including Confederates who had not taken part in elections but would eventually have to reenter Missouri politics. Conservative politicians outside the convention, such as Frank Blair and Edward Bates, Lincoln's first attorney general, vehemently opposed Drake's plan for voter registration, and they also began to air their attitudes toward African-American citizenship. All but four members of the convention voted to abolish slavery, but most of the Conservatives hoped to restrict African Americans' access to the courts, public education, and the ballot box.[43]

39 On Krekel's role, see *Mississippi Blätter*, Jan. 8, 1865, Jan. 15, 1865; *Westliche Post*, Jan. 19, 1865; *St. Charles Demokrat*, Jan. 12, 1865; *Wächter am Erie*, Jan. 14, 1865.
40 Missouri Constitutional Convention, *Journal*; Parrish, *Missouri under Radical Rule*; David D. March, "The Campaign for the Ratification of the Constitution of 1865," *Missouri Historical Review* 47 (1953): 223–32.
41 Martha Kohl, "Enforcing a Vision of Community: The Role of the Test Oath in Missouri's Reconstruction," *Civil War History* 40 (1994): 292–307; Parrish, *Missouri under Radical Rule*, 61–75; Harold M. Hyman, *The Era of the Oath: Northern Loyalty Tests during the Civil War and Reconstruction* (Philadelphia: University of Pennsylvania Press, 1954), 110–14.
42 Parrish, *Missouri under Radical Rule*, 28; Drake, Autobiography, 1091. Historians largely adopted the Conservative characterization of the convention. Fred DeArmond, "Reconstruction in Missouri," *Missouri Historical Review* 61 (1967): 364–77. Parrish's 1965 work, although more even handed, portrayed the Radicals as to some extent "fanatical" and "vindictive." Parrish, *Missouri under Radical Rule*, 25–26, 14, 50.
43 For a first-hand Conservative account, see William F. Switzler, "Constitutional Conventions in Missouri, 1865–1875," *Missouri Historical Review* 1 (1907): 109–20.

Although Anglo-American Radicals and Conservatives fought bitterly over the ironclad oath, they nearly all shared a view of American citizenship that justified the disfranchisement of black men in Missouri. They could easily cite the time-honored traditions of withholding suffrage from some citizens and excluding African Americans from membership in the imagined national community. German Americans who wanted to institute race-neutral voting policies were up against decades of legal precedent and an established Anglo-American language of citizenship. While there were commonalities between the development of citizenship in the United States and in German Europe, the peculiarities of American law shaped Reconstruction, in Missouri and nationally. An outline of the American background is therefore necessary to make sense of the Radical German challenge.

Between national independence and the Civil War, Americans had tried to balance two strains of citizenship, both of which had roots in Europe. One was "republican." Many of the American revolutionaries, immersed in classical republican political theory, believed that citizenship should be exclusive to a relatively small number of men but should confer extensive rights of political participation. The republican citizen also bore significant duties, most importantly to perform military service. In fact, he resembled the *Bürger* of the self-governing European towns. According to republican theory, a citizen was a man whose landed wealth assured both his independence from outside influences and his interest in the good of the whole.[44] Many people within a given polity could never attain such a status.

Yet Americans inherited a second tradition of citizenship, which was more inclusive but carried minimal rights or duties. Although they preferred not to dwell on it, the relationship between monarch and subject informed Americans' understanding of the bond between state and citizen. After winning independence from Britain, national and state governments had taken on functions, such as taxation and defense, that the Crown had previously performed. In some contexts, Americans would see citizenship as a status analogous to Prussian *Staatsbürgerschaft*, which required only the payment of taxes in return for protection from foreign threats.

By 1865, Americans had devoted years of jurisprudence to reconciling republican citizenship (active yet exclusive) with imperial citizenship

---

44 Bernard Bailyn, *The Ideological Origins of the American Revolution*, enlarged ed. (Cambridge, MA: Belknap Press of Harvard University Press, 1992); Gordon S. Wood, *The Creation of the American Republic, 1776–1787* (Chapel Hill: University of North Carolina Press, 1969); Wood, *The Radicalism of the American Revolution* (New York: Vintage Books, 1991).

(inclusive yet passive). Unlike the Forty-Eighters, the American revolutionaries had managed to win their independence and found a republic, unleashing new demands for active citizenship. The most successful of the early initiatives came from unpropertied men. They argued that if the legitimacy of the government was to rest on the consent of the governed, men without property must participate in politics too. Historians have identified this "liberal" position with philosophers such as John Locke and publicists such as Thomas Paine.[45] Following the Revolution, working-class white men reminded other Americans of their military service and proposed that their independence – and therefore their citizenship – rested on their mastery of their own labor and their authority as heads of household.[46] Although they argued in the republican language of military service and independence, poor men promoted liberalism. By the 1850s, Americans were familiar with an active *and* inclusive language of citizenship, and most states had no property requirements for voting.[47]

Perhaps surprisingly, as more white men clamored for voting citizenship, they developed the arguments that Missourians could use to deny it to black men. With citizenship broadening, white men had come under new pressure to explain why women and African Americans should not vote. As in German Europe, women were excluded from the franchise on the grounds that they were naturally dependent on men. Jurists knew, however, that women's membership in the nation-state afforded them some civil protections, such as freedom of speech, and meant that they had to perform some duties, such as the payment of taxes. The practical and theoretical solution to this impasse was a form of second-class, passive citizenship. By 1865, women's citizenship had become, in historian Nancy Cott's words, "a touchstone to justify less-than-participatory citizenship."[48] Women's status was a powerful alternative to the model of citizenship represented by naturalized immigrant men. Conservatives could argue that the immigrant man might be archetypal, but there were other kinds of American citizen. They saw no reason that black men should not become non-voting citizens like women.

---

45 Keyssar, *Right to Vote*, 9–17; Smith, "American Creed," 229–31; Heater, *Brief History of Citizenship*, 50–57, 65–79; Chilton Williamson, *American Suffrage: From Property to Democracy, 1760–1860* (Princeton, NJ: Princeton University Press, 1960), 10–12, 62–75.
46 Keyssar, *Right to Vote*, 42–52. In an investigation of state constitutions during the Revolutionary Era, historian Marc W. Kruman found that Americans described suffrage as "a natural right more than a privilege." Kruman, *Between Authority and Liberty: State Constitution Making in Revolutionary America* (Chapel Hill: University of North Carolina Press, 1997), 94, 97.
47 Keyssar, *Right to Vote*, 26–32.
48 Cott, "Marriage and Women's Citizenship," 1451; Kerber, "Paradox of Women's Citizenship in the Early Republic."

When Americans debated black men's place in Missouri in 1865, they were also addressing how racial understandings of the American nation would be encoded in law. Just as the Frankfurt parliamentarians had argued over what tied Germans together in 1848, Americans worked to pin-point what made them a community. Republicanism and liberalism were undoubtedly important, but the nation that the Founders had imagined was also Protestant, English-speaking, and white.[49] During the 1830s and 1840s, the Democratic Party had assailed the idea that the United States was primarily an Anglo-Protestant land. It had increased the salience of whiteness. Many states explicitly excluded black men from voting for the first time during the Jacksonian period.[50]

In a technical sense, state-level decisions did not pertain to national citizenship, but state and national citizenship could not be rhetorically or legally disentangled. Supreme Court Chief Justice Roger Taney underlined this fact when he denied American citizenship to Dred Scott in 1857. Blacks, the judge ruled in *Scott v. Sandford*, "were not intended to be embraced in this new political family, which the Constitution brought into existence, but were intended to be excluded from it."[51] Taney presented ample evidence that the framers of the Constitution had not viewed African Americans as their equals. How, he asked, could the Founding Fathers have intended to bestow United States citizenship on black Americans when they had accepted slavery? The chief justice maintained that they had not meant to grant national citizenship to people who did not receive citizenship from individual states. Although Taney was incorrect about the status of African Americans in some states at the time that the American Constitution was ratified, his ruling showed that state and national citizenship were conceptually and judicially interdependent and that racial prejudice affected how judges interpreted both.[52]

While Taney excluded African Americans from American citizenship altogether, Missouri Conservatives thought that black men shared the passive, second-class status held by women. American jurists often detached

---

49 Smith, "American Creed," 232–40; Fredrickson, *The Black Image in the White Mind: The Debate over Afro-American Character and Destiny* (New York: Harper & Row, 1971); Reginald Horsman, *Race and Manifest Destiny: The Origins of American Racial Anglo-Saxonism* (Cambridge, MA: Harvard University Press, 1981); Saxton, *Rise and Fall of the White Republic.*

50 Keyssar, *Right to Vote,* 55–59.

51 Benjamin C. Howard, ed., *Report of the Decision of the Supreme Court of the United States, and the Opinions of the Judges Thereof, in the Case of Dred Scott versus John F. Sandford* (Washington, DC: Cornelius Wendell, 1857), 12.

52 Paul Finkelman, *An Imperfect Union: Slavery, Federalism, and Comity* (Chapel Hill: University of North Carolina Press, 1981); Don E. Fehrenbacher, *The Dred Scott Case: Its Significance in American Law and Politics* (New York: Oxford University Press, 1978).

the right to vote from black men's citizenship. Edward Bates recalled his experience in Lincoln's cabinet. As attorney general, he had surveyed court decisions regarding citizenship and determined that although emancipation brought African Americans national citizenship, that status did not in itself bear any particular set of rights.[53] As voting had always been the preserve of the states, it was particularly difficult to conclude that political participation was a right of American citizenship. Other leading Conservatives such as Frank Blair also emphatically rejected the idea that the freedmen possessed the right to vote, even if they were citizens.[54] The small minority of Missouri Germans who identified as Conservative must have agreed. Dänzer wrote in the *Anzeiger des Westens* that voting was neither a "human right" nor a "citizenship right." He pointed to Northern states such as Ohio and Wisconsin that did not allow free African-American men to exercise the franchise. The editor added for good measure that the "Negro race" had never "proved its ability for self-rule."[55] In 1865, Conservative Missourians could draw on nearly a century of history to counter both the notion that American citizenship included voting rights and what Bates called "the absurd theory of the exact equality of men."[56]

Although the Anglo-American Radical delegates to the Missouri convention did not agree with every one of the Conservatives' dismissive views of African Americans, most of them had the same basic understanding of citizenship as the Conservatives: there were active and passive citizens, and black men belonged to the latter group. Drake and many other Republicans around the country distinguished between the civil and political rights of citizens. Civil rights included legal protections of life, liberty, and property.[57] All citizens, according to the Radical majority in the Missouri convention, possessed them.[58] Most Radicals believed that the political rights of active citizenship, on the other hand, could be withheld at the discretion of the existing electorate. Drake was certain that citizenship did not always involve voting rights; minors and women were citizens yet denied the franchise. The Radical leader also believed that African-American suffrage would hurt his chances of getting the constitution ratified.[59] U.S. Senator

---

53 Cott, "Marriage and Women's Citizenship," 1445; Wang, *Trial of Democracy*, 8.
54 Dwight, "Black Suffrage in Missouri," 33–39; Parrish, *Frank Blair*, 221–23.
55 *Anzeiger des Westens Wochen-Blatt*, Jan. 20, 1865.
56 Edward Bates, *The Diary of Edward Bates, 1859–1866*, ed. Howard K. Beale (Washington, DC: U.S. Government Printing Office, 1933; reprint, New York: Da Capo Press, 1971), 445.
57 Foner, *Free Soil, Free Labor, Free Men*, 261–67.
58 Some of Drake's followers also supported efforts to instate race-neutral suffrage qualifications. See Missouri Constitutional Convention, *Journal*, 20–21, 26, 147–48.
59 Dwight, "Black Suffrage in Missouri," 40; Parrish, *Missouri under Radical Rule*, 117.

Benjamin Gratz Brown was the only native-born, white Missourian of any note to concur with German Radicals that "freedom and the franchise" were "inseparable."[60]

In Missouri, German Americans launched the strongest assault on the established wisdom that citizenship came in active and passive forms and that African Americans were not fit to vote. The Revolutions of 1848 and their own naturalization – both ultimately liberal nationalist affairs – taught prominent Radicals that all men, regardless of race, should enjoy the same type of citizenship. As their antebellum and wartime politics predicted, Radical newspaper editors, convention delegates, and leaders at mass meetings used ethnicity to further their cause. The public movement for black suffrage also reinvigorated and reconstituted ethnicity, the consequences of which Radicals could not completely control.

Emil Preetorius did the most to associate German ethnicity with race-neutral male citizenship in print. By 1865, his *Westliche Post* was more profitable than any other German-language newspaper in Missouri, Illinois, or Ohio, reporting annual revenues from advertising and subscriptions of about $150,000. Nine thousand copies of each issue circulated, and Preetorius judged the actual readership at about twenty thousand. He could expect to exert some influence over German Missourians.[61] Preetorius was also instrumental in convening the meeting in Turner Hall on January 15, 1865. An editorial headed "Onward!" had announced it in that morning's *Post*. Over the days that followed, he called on the constitutional convention to recognize "the spirit of progress" and strike the word "white" from voting qualifications. The editor wrote that it was essential that prejudice on the basis of "race, creed, or color" not be written into law. Preetorius entreated his German-American readers to see African-American suffrage as a fitting culmination to the enthusiasm that had carried their own community through the war.[62]

The Turner Hall meeting itself set the ethnic terms of the German-American movement for black voting rights. The interdependence of ethnicity and politics was never clearer than at a rousing Turner celebration. Georg Hillgärtner, a Forty-Eighter lawyer and journalist, felt at home in this

---

60 *Westliche Post*, Jan. 6, 1865; Norma L. Peterson, *Freedom and Franchise: The Political Career of B. Gratz Brown* (Columbia: University of Missouri Press, 1965), 143.

61 The revenue figures are from a survey by the *Cincinnati Commercial* that was reported in *Westliche Post*, Feb. 9, 1866. For circulation, see *Westliche Post*, April 11, 1865. See also Harvey Saalberg, "The *Westliche Post* of St. Louis: A Daily Newspaper for German-Americans, 1857–1938" (PhD diss., University of Missouri, 1967), 140. Preetorius became sole editor in April 1865. *Westliche Post*, April 12, 1865.

62 *Mississippi Blätter*, Jan. 15, 1865.

milieu. His speech that evening emphasized the centrality of the franchise to the exercise of citizenship, asking, "Is he a free man who is muzzled on account of his skin color? Or is that a free state – let alone the *most* free state – whose people's hands are bound in regard to the election of their custodians and lawmakers?"[63] Arnold Krekel, president of the constitutional convention, also spoke, pronouncing it "laughable" that "skin color" should deprive any male citizen of his right to vote. In fact, even the possibility of a "Negro president or governor" held no "horror" for him. Krekel felt that he voiced the "principles" of his audience.[64] He was right. The meeting elected a committee to relay its support for African-American suffrage to the convention.[65] One man who was there that night recounted in the *Post* that the "warm and emotionally uplifting" evening had inspired him to "stand true to the full principle of freedom, also to the full accomplishment of the same – to the end."[66] Radical leaders had deftly engaged the full potential of German ethnicity.

Meanwhile, German-born convention delegates, who followed newspaper editorials and immigrant meetings, fortified the new pro-suffrage ethnicity by communicating it to English-speaking Missourians. Georg Husmann represented Gasconade County, the only county in the state to have cast a majority of its votes for Lincoln in 1860. A small, heavily bearded man who spoke unaccented English, Husmann and his neighbors keenly felt their vulnerability to secessionist violence. (He wrote to Governor Fletcher in April 1865 to request a replacement for the cannon lost in a secessionist raid.[67]) The noted viticulturist sat on the convention's committee for the executive with his quieter colleague Georg Thilenius, from Cape Girardeau. When they reported back to the whole body, the two German Americans told the other delegates that they could not accept using the word "white" to describe qualified candidates for governor. They protested any distinction in original law "between white, black, red, or brown." "We hold," they said, "that we were not sent here to pander to a prejudice which may unfortunately exist, but to deal equal justice to all, without regard to color."[68] In an interview with the *Westliche Post*, Husmann stressed that he was not a lone crusader, but the spokesman for an immigrant community.

63 *Westliche Post*, Jan. 17, 1865; Zucker, ed., *Forty-Eighters*, 305.
64 *Westliche Post*, Jan. 19, 1865.
65 Missouri Constitutional Convention, *Journal*, 59.
66 *Westliche Post*, Jan. 17, 1865.
67 H. D. Hooker, "George Husmann," *Missouri Historical Review* 23 (1929): 353–60; Georg Husmann to Thomas Fletcher, April 12, 1865, box 1, folder 15, Records of Governor Thomas Clement Fletcher, Missouri State Archives (hereafter MSA), Jefferson City.
68 Missouri Constitutional Convention, *Journal*, 48.

A meeting of his constituents in Hermann had charged him with persisting until Missouri's constitution was a "model document."[69]

Another immigrant who said that he brought German ideas of American citizenship to the convention became Charles Drake's chief opponent. Isidor Bush had fled Vienna following the Revolutions of 1848, but he was not one of St. Louis's more famous Forty-Eighters. Since the beginning of the war, he had risen rapidly from Jewish community leader to state legislator.[70] Bush shook up the convention in February 1865, when he helped lead a protest of Drake's leadership. Twenty-six delegates who wanted to revoke the convention's power to overhaul the constitution threatened futilely to resign.[71] Then in March, Bush took the floor to argue that voting rights for "colored" men were a "necessary, unavoidable, logical consequence of freedom." Apologizing for his "dialect," he proclaimed that voting was not a privilege, but "the right of everyone who lives in the civil society of a free government." To him, separating passive from active citizenship was simply a pretext for codifying racism. This Prague-born Jew made a point of attributing this conclusion to his "German way of thinking."[72] A remarkable variety of minor politicians tied black suffrage to German ethnicity.

Perhaps it was inevitable that when immigrant men conveyed the lessons of 1848 and naturalization – framed as ethnicity – they ran into trouble rationalizing the place of women. If the Radicals believed that voting was automatically a citizenship right for African-American men, Dänzer asked in the *Anzeiger*, how did they explain women's status as nonvoting citizens?[73] In the United States, Conservatives could use women's less-than-participatory citizenship to negate the proposition that naturalized men's voting citizenship was normative. Immigrants such as Bush were ill equipped to respond. With somewhat tortuous reasoning, he stated that citizenship included the franchise, but three groups of people did not qualify for either: residents without the necessary intellectual capacity (such as minors), enemies of public well-being (such as secessionists), and residents lacking an "interest" in civil society. At first it seemed that Bush believed that all women fell into this final excluded group. When pressed by other delegates, however, Bush

69 *Westliche Post*, Jan. 18, 1865.

70 Dwight, "Black Suffrage in Missouri," 23; Nagler, *Fremont contra Lincoln*, 90; Walter Ehrlich, "Isidor Bush," in *The Dictionary of Missouri Biography*, ed. Lawrence O. Christensen et al. (Columbia: University of Missouri Press, 1999), 138–40; Zucker, ed., *Forty-Eighters*, 283.

71 Missouri Constitutional Convention, *Journal*, 89; Parrish, *Missouri under Radical Rule*, 21; Drake, Autobiography, 1061.

72 Bush's speech was reported in the March 25, 1865 *Westliche Post*.

73 *Anzeiger des Westens Wochen-Blatt*, Feb. 10, 1865.

said that women who received no financial support from men and "carried the burdens and duties of citizens" should be able to vote. He found himself arguing that Missouri should recognize the citizenship of unmarried women who demonstrated independent decision making and held a stake in the community. They should have the right to exercise the franchise. Never clarifying how to judge whether single women met these qualifications, he made it plain that he believed marriage stripped women of citizenship altogether. Bush had no problem with gender distinctions, but he did not want to condone a second-class, non-voting form of American citizenship. He therefore squeezed women into one of two awkwardly defined categories: married noncitizens or unmarried full citizens.[74] This improvised solution never reappeared in the German-language public sphere.

Most German Radicals simply ignored gender, an omission that contrasts tellingly with their attention to race. Although German Americans were hardly alone in blocking women's suffrage, Missouri's leading native-born white proponent of black suffrage, Senator Brown, had supported enfranchising women since his election in 1863.[75] German Radicals' blend of liberal nationalism and ethnic solidarity kindled African-American men's hopes that they might win the vote, but as Mathilde Anneke could have foretold, the same forces conspired against women. Economic dependence disqualified them from citizenship, and German ethnicity added another hurdle. Immigrant women's role as *Kulturträgerinnen* militated against their involvement in politics, and German-American antislavery was at odds with the feminized culture of Anglo-American abolitionism. Radicals who offered immigrant men's citizenship as a model for the freedmen left gender largely unexamined.

German immigrants wrestled with race much more openly, but there too they were often confounded. When supporters of African-American suffrage tried to underscore the similarities between race and ethnicity, they came up against the generally accepted line between biology and culture. Preetorius unwittingly summed up the conundrum in a simple statement in the *Westliche Post*. "Differences of race [*Race*] and color," he wrote, "should be as unimportant as those of belief or descent."[76] "Race" and "color" apparently were similar but not synonymous categories. Why use two separate words if they had identical meanings? If Preetorius really believed that race was not just a matter of color, it would follow that race denoted smaller groups: the French race, the English race, the Irish race, and

74 *Westliche Post*, March 25, 1865.   75 Peterson, *Freedom and Franchise*, 163–64.
76 *Westliche Post*, Jan. 20, 1865.

so on. Perhaps Germans constituted a race. The structure of the sentence, however, suggests an alternative reading. German immigrants were probably to be understood as members of a group marked by "descent," which Preetorius paired with the unmistakably cultural and malleable "belief." The editor evidently thought it obvious that men could not be robbed of citizenship based on descent. Indeed, that assumption formed the premise of his remark. Race was an invalid basis for exclusion because ethnicity undisputedly was. The logic of Preetorius's comparison relied on race and ethnicity being defined differently. Even in likening the two, Radicals had to distinguish between them.

In his comment, Preetorius reflected the language and law of his new home, but German Radicals were not bystanders in the effort to pin down race, color, and descent in the United States. These terms acquired meaning as Europeans settled alongside Americans of English and African ancestry. German immigrants had helped invent ethnicity through their redefinition of the German *Volk*. In Missouri, antislavery and black suffrage were facets of the ethnic project. Preetorius, Krekel, Husmann, and Bush repeatedly used familiar German-American rituals and imagery to convince immigrants to support African Americans. Part instinct and part strategy, this politics played on cultural commonalities among immigrants as much as shared humanity with the freed people. It consolidated group identity more than it stimulated intergroup empathy. One of Krekel's appeals was representative. "The immigrating German," he told the January 15 meeting in Turner Hall, "is the only one who is not biased by prejudice against the Negro."[77] For the immigrants who were drinking in the festive atmosphere, German superiority was likely the most resounding message of the evening. It seemed natural to reaffirm the cultural foundation of German identity in America. Leaders of German-Missourian public opinion professed a desire to do away with the line between race and ethnicity, but the explicitly ethnic cast of their politics also sustained and elaborated that divide.

The difficulty of comparing race and ethnicity in the American context was most obvious when the German-born promoters of African-American political rights tried to influence immigrants in the public sphere. Radical politicians leapt at every chance to equate African-American and immigrant rights. They charged Conservatives with the same sort of "prejudice" that the Know Nothings had directed at newcomers during the 1850s. Isidor Bush said that only "fear and prejudice" blocked the passage of black men's

---

77 Ibid., Jan. 19, 1865. See also Feb. 17, 1865.

voting rights.[78] The *St. Charles Demokrat* editorialized that "prejudice and narrow-heartedness" hampered considerations for the "colored people."[79] More precise parallels, however, would betray the fact that Radicals had constructed African Americans and immigrants as members of different kinds of collectivities.

Disputes over the perennial controversies of immigrant drinking and immigrant representation exposed the tensions between race and ethnicity. Immigrants cried ethnic discrimination when Charles Drake inserted a "morality clause" into the draft constitution.[80] Missouri's declaration of rights already included religious freedom, but Drake qualified it: "The liberty of conscience hereby secured shall not be so construed as to excuse acts of licentiousness, nor to justify practices inconsistent with the good order, peace, or safety of the State, or with the rights of others."[81] German Americans worried that this caveat was designed to aid Anglo-Protestants who planned to interfere with their prized custom of social drinking. Irate, Preetorius wrote in the *Westliche Post* that Drake was making religious tests "requirements for citizenship [*bürgerliche*] and civil [*staatliche*] rights."[82] The editor could not pass up the opportunity to bring in African-American rights. He implied that ethnic and racial prejudice were of a piece, forecasting that "racial intolerance" would triumph in partnership with religious chauvinism. Both tendencies, Preetorius emphasized, ran contrary to "enlightened Radicalism."[83] After a number of public meetings, St. Louis immigrants put this argument to the convention in a formal petition.[84] An out-of-state contributor to the *Westliche Post* also connected immigrant and black rights at the time, hoping that "in Missouri, religious freedom as well as the emancipation of the slaves and their absorption into the citizenry of this state will achieve a complete victory over the machinations of fanatics and reactionaries."[85] With Drake playing the perfect foil, German Radicals said that Anglo-Americans harassed immigrants just as they persecuted African Americans.

The leap from the drinking rights of immigrants to the voting rights of black men was both perfectly understandable and patently absurd. Drake's insult reminded immigrants how much they valued German festive culture

78 Ibid., March 25, 1865.
79 *St. Charles Demokrat*, Jan. 26, March 2, April 27, 1865. For nearly identical phrasing, see *Westliche Post*, March 25, 1865.
80 Ibid., Feb. 28, 1865.
81 Missouri Constitutional Convention, *Journal*, 256, 81–82.
82 *Mississippi Blätter*, Feb. 19, 1865.   83 *Westliche Post*, Jan. 24, 1865.
84 Ibid., Feb. 18, 21 and 22, 1865; *Mississippi Blätter*, Feb. 19, 1865; *St. Charles Demokrat*, March 2, 1865.
85 *Mississippi Blätter*, Feb. 19, 1865.

and how much they depended on American pluralism. To suggest, however, that the challenges that immigrants and African Americans faced were anything near equivalent was to misrepresent Civil War-era Missouri. As black Missourians tasted freedom and demanded citizenship rights, Confederate guerrillas stepped up their sometimes fatal attacks.[86] The economic legacy of slavery would unfold more slowly and more insidiously, but it was already evident that the right to a glass of beer was not high on African Americans' list of concerns. The lens of the immigrant experience had distorted German Americans' outlook on citizenship. At one point, Preetorius taunted that since Drake was preparing to legislate morality, he might as well restrict voting to men who were white *and* native-born.[87] It was another illogical extrapolation. Foreign-born citizens would not lose the franchise in 1860s Missouri, mostly because decades of European immigration had already shaped American law. As the Democratic Party's whole character and the Republican Party's 1860 platform proved, native-born Americans did not see ethnicity as they saw race.

Drake could not preclude naturalized men from voting citizenship, but he did dilute immigrant representation in the state legislature, which provoked renewed allegations of prejudice. The provision in question stipulated that the state's most populous counties elect their representatives to the Missouri House from geographically compact districts. At-large elections for county delegates had given German-American votes substantial weight in St. Louis's aggregated returns. Drake's new plan meant that the immigrants would decide elections only in the districts where they were most heavily concentrated.[88] The Anglo-American leader also tried to prevent the extension of suffrage to unnaturalized men. In both cases, German Radicals made much of Drake's "bigotry." In addition to using similar vocabulary in their arguments for immigrant and African-American voting, some Radicals went out of their way to relate the two. Husmann implausibly argued that Drake opposed alien voting in order to stop African Americans voting in the future. He said that immigrants would support race-neutral political rights because "every immigrant" is for "citizenship rights for all."[89] Drake let German Americans liken racial and ethnic discrimination all over again.

86 Parrish, *Missouri under Radical Rule*, 106–07; Fellman, *Inside War*, 231–42; Astor, *Rebels on the Border*, 121–45.

87 *Westliche Post*, Jan. 24, 1865.

88 Missouri Constitutional Convention, *Journal*, 262. For a report of the convention debate, see *Mississippi Blätter*, Feb. 19, 1865. For further discussion, see *Westliche Post*, March 16, April 12 and 13, June 6, 1865.

89 Husmann was paraphrased. *Westliche Post*, March 29, 1865.

When the convention did in fact give the right to vote to aliens who had filed their first papers, it was precisely because German Missourians had so successfully defined themselves as members of a group quite unlike African Americans. Delegates pandered to German-American exceptionalism. German men had arrived in the United States sure that they were ready to be full citizens. Their newspapers presented naturalization as a formality, a symbol of the decision to join the American polity. Yet Missouri Radicals could not spell out this belief because it contradicted their public position. To state that unnaturalized immigrant men had a *right* to vote would have undermined their argument that voting attended national citizenship. To assert that it was simply in Missouri's best interests for resident aliens to vote would have been to jettison the individual *rights* at liberalism's core. In a bind, German-American Radicals held their tongues. They refrained from abandoning male equality or ethnic superiority.[90] Ethnicity had a momentum of its own that complicated its use as a medium for pro-suffrage politics.

In debating drinking and voting, advocates of black suffrage used ethnicity to court their constituents without realizing that it stood as a counterpoint to race. Oblivious, they tried to redefine race as a more embedded form of ethnicity. Friedrich Münch had laid out the thinking behind this idea during the war. He had described blacks as a "lower race" but rejected the possibility of biological inferiority, blaming instead systematic exploitation and the ban on educating slaves.[91] It followed that race was not, in fact, fixed and biological, but changeable and cultural. While it is certainly relevant that immigrants believed that the ethnic characteristics of German Americans were positive and the racial characteristics of African American were negative, where German Radical leaders differed from most whites in their state was on the issue of malleability.[92] German Radicals commonly maintained that although African Americans were deficient in many respects, they could change. If Conservatives saw racial characteristics as an insurmountable obstacle to African-American citizenship, German Radicals saw them as a hindrance that could be overcome with the passage of time.

When German Radicals discussed educating the freed people, they showed that their racial ideas were not only sometimes at odds with their

---

90 An English-born delegate first raised the idea, but Bush introduced the measure that finally passed. Missouri Constitutional Convention, *Journal*, 193, 201. On the negligible response, see *St. Charles Demokrat*, April 13, 1865; Parrish, *Missouri under Radical Rule*, 30.

91 *St. Charles Demokrat*, June 5, 1862, trans. in Mallinckrodt, *What They Thought*, 2: 19.

92 Kate Masur found that Anglo-American reformers in Washington, DC, also held a malleable view of race. Masur, *Example for All the Land*, 52–53.

ethnic politics; those ideas also masked personal ambivalence about African Americans. German immigrants were great champions of education. After emancipation, Münch lost no time in introducing a bill "For the Education of Negro Children" to the Missouri legislature, and the following year, Krekel joined the board of the Lincoln Institute, which members of the 62nd U.S. Colored Infantry Regiment founded to serve African Americans.[93] The *Westliche Post* published several essays on compulsory schooling. The contributors exuded confidence in the power of public education, especially for African Americans. One writer argued that since African Americans were "eager to learn" and "able to learn," their education would go a long way to dispelling prejudice.[94] Still, the conviction that race did not render African Americans incapable of improvement often came with a sense of urgency regarding the current state of the freed people. If African Americans were to become citizens, they would have to be "educated to be intelligent and good people."[95] Preetorius himself put it most baldly, admitting, "We consider the mass of Negroes now still totally incapable of exercising the franchise."[96] It would "require a long and hard struggle on the part of the Radical friends of freedom before the last traces of [slavery] in political and social relations are eliminated."[97] According to the leaders of German Radicalism, African Americans could change, but they must.

One policy reflected both German Radicals' skeptical assessment of African Americans and the faith they placed in education – literacy tests for voters. Such requirements, German Radical leaders genuinely hoped, would facilitate race-neutral suffrage. Preetorius, for example, thought that voters should be judged on "their service and talent, education and patriotism," not their race.[98] Nonetheless, Radicals first floated the literacy qualification as one that would apply to black voters alone. Bush, for all his lofty rhetoric, proposed that African-American men be able to vote only after the lapse of eleven years and if they were literate and "of good moral character."[99] In a plan that attracted more coverage (and anticipated President Lincoln's cautious musings on Louisiana several weeks later), Krekel suggested that the legislature conduct a referendum on whether to enfranchise "persons of color" who had lived in Missouri at the time of emancipation and had

---

93 *St. Charles Demokrat*, Feb. 2, 1865; Parrish, *Missouri under Radical Rule*, 128–30; *Eighth Annual Report of the Superintendent of Public Schools of the State of Missouri* (Jefferson City: Reagan & Carter, State Printers, 1874), 128–31.

94 *Westliche Post*, Jan. 28, 1865.   95 Ibid., Feb. 10, 3, and 11, 1865.

96 Ibid., Jan. 15, 1865.   97 *Mississippi Blätter*, Jan. 15, 1865.

98 Ibid., Jan. 15, 1865.   99 *Westliche Post*, March 25, 1865.

either passed a literacy test or served in the Union army.[100] In the convention, Husmann praised the speech of Reverend W. G. Eliot, who outlined a program that included a literacy test for all voters and a comprehensive system of childhood education and evening classes for adults.[101] The *Westliche Post* never stamped its imprimatur on any one of these options, but they all aligned with Preetorius's understanding of race and his doubts about African Americans.[102]

The Radical determination to transform African Americans echoed the approach of Forty-Eighters to German Jews. As in 1848, universal manhood suffrage and similar liberal policies were to lead the nation toward perfection. Although many of the Frankfurt parliamentarians had been anti-Semitic, they had settled on the idea that according Jews citizenship rights would advance the German nation. Germany would progress, they believed, because if it were true to the highest of ideals, it could incorporate the supposedly backward Jews into the national community. Since discrimination seemed to have retarded the development of both black Americans and Jewish Germans, liberals assumed that equal citizenship would uplift both groups. Such reasoning allowed the supporters of universal manhood suffrage to hold quite different views of the freedom-loving German and the recently freed African American. German-American Radicals could argue that black men should follow immigrant men into full citizenship, not because the people who had been enslaved could improve the United States, but because the nation, if truly liberal, could improve them.

Believing that they presented a coherent and consistent liberal nationalism, Radical German leaders failed to see the ways in which the United States differed from German Europe. African Americans sought full membership in a community where race and ethnicity were distinct, partly as a result of immigrants' ongoing justifications of their own citizenship. The argument that race was only a more intense type of ethnicity could not surmount the prejudices of Anglo-Americans or, indeed, of most German Americans. In it, there remained much Conservatives could use. Carl Dänzer at the *Anzeiger* was heartened when Preetorius mentioned how

---

100 Missouri Constitutional Convention, *Journal*, 186–87; Abraham Lincoln, speech delivered April 11, 1865, in *The Collected Works of Abraham Lincoln*, ed. Roy P. Basler, 9 vols. (New Brunswick, NJ: Rutgers University Press, 1953–1955), 8: 399–405.
101 Missouri Constitutional Convention, *Journal*, 53; *Westliche Post*, Jan. 25–27, 1865.
102 *Westliche Post*, March 30, 1865. The final constitution would have required literacy of all new Missouri voters after 1876, but the whole document would be replaced before then. Missouri Constitutional Convention, *Journal*, 261; Keyssar, *Right to Vote*, 377.

long he thought it would take to reclaim African Americans from the cultural and intellectual deprivations of slavery.[103] He probably also noticed that literacy tests could both satisfy Radical principles and limit black voting. Most fundamentally, the Radicals who rallied the support of "freedom-loving Germans" had done as much to reify ethnicity as to conflate it with race.[104] These subtleties did not dictate the final form of Missouri's 1865 constitution, for African-American suffrage never stood a chance, but they would surface again in the national debate in coming years.

THE DILEMMA OF RATIFICATION

On April 8, 1865, the day before Lee surrendered to Grant at Appomattox Court House, the convention in Missouri approved the document it had spent the previous months drafting. Drake had engineered a working majority – thirty-eight of the fifty-one delegates present – without winning over any of the German Americans. Arnold Krekel, as presiding officer, did not vote, although he was first person to engross the new constitution with his signature.[105] Missouri's fundamental law would still provide for two tiers of citizenship and reserve political rights for white men. To the displeasure of immigrants, it also reduced German-American representation in the state legislature while allowing that body to regulate alcohol sales and consumption. The immigrants had mixed feelings about the most polarizing part of the proposed constitution, the section ordering that voters must swear that they had always been loyal to the United States in word and deed.

In the battle over ratification, German-American Radicals were caught between Drake and the Conservatives. They could neither unreservedly endorse Drake's constitution, which was far from liberal, nor comfortably side with Conservatives, whose loyalty to the nation was suspect and antipathy toward blacks beyond question. As German immigrants weighed their options, dismaying acts of violence strengthened Drake's case that only extreme measures would head off a secessionist resurgence. A week after the convention had finished its work, Missourians were stunned to learn of Lincoln's assassination. Closer to home, former Confederates regularly terrorized African Americans and sporadically victimized German

---

103 *Anzeiger des Westens Wochen-Blatt*, Feb. 10, 1865.
104 Historians have largely overlooked the growing distaste for blatant racism and biological thinking in Northern circles, but historian Kate Masur explores how it could coexist with arguments that the freed people were culturally deficient. Masur, *Example for All the Land*, 53, 190–01, 198, 255–56.
105 Missouri Constitutional Convention, *Journal*, 247.

Americans.[106] In June, Krekel was describing the details of the constitution when his makeshift stage was set alight.[107] No Unionist could casually dismiss the security concerns behind the ironclad oath.

German Radicals reached various compromises on the question of ratification. A few German-speaking leaders believed that assenting to the imperfect constitution was the best way to ensure Unionist government. Krekel calculated that black suffrage had no shot at success whatsoever unless immigrants cooperated with Drake's Anglo-American Radicals. The *St. Charles Demokrat* took its cue from Krekel, who had founded the paper years earlier.[108] *Demokrat* editorials argued that prejudiced and treacherous Missourians would rule the state unless the constitution was ratified.[109] A second group of German-American delegates, which included Isidor Bush and five others, came to the opposite conclusion. With five Anglo-Americans, they penned an open letter recommending a "no" vote in June. The missive's primary complaint was that the ironclad oath might strip the vote from some patriotic men.[110] Among the signers were German Americans who wanted black suffrage but preferred the risks of Conservative rule to the certainties of Drake's constitution.[111]

The most influential German Radicals, however, refused to work with either the Conservatives or Drake. These men held that the freedom-loving German, who appreciated racial equality, would die for the United States, and tenaciously defended cultural pluralism, could steer an independent course through Missouri politics. Two of the German Americans whose names had appeared on the largely Conservative open letter publicly disassociated themselves from it. Anton P. Nixdorf of Miller County said that his name had been added without permission.[112] Georg Husmann, a more strenuous opponent of Conservatism, made a point of condemning the constitution because it prohibited African-American men from voting. He cared little about the rights of Confederate sympathizers. The constitution, he said categorically, was "not radical enough."[113] In a private letter to Governor Fletcher, Husmann listed Krekel and Senator Brown among "our weak kneed [R]adical friends" who would vote for the constitution

106 Parrish, *Missouri under Radical Rule*, 106–07; Fellman, *Inside War*, 231–42; Astor, *Rebels on the Border*, 138–43.
107 *St. Charles Demokrat*, June 8, 1865.
108 Drake, Autobiography, 1161; *Westliche Post*, April 15, 1865; *St. Charles Demokrat*, April 13, 1865.
109 Ibid., April 27, May 4, 11, and 18, 1865.   110 *Westliche Post*, April 15, 1865.
111 Ibid., April 12 and 23, 1865.   112 Ibid., April 27, 1865.
113 Ibid., May 13, 1865; Drake, Autobiography, 1083–84.

despite its being "repugnant to every principle" they held. Emil Preetorius he pronounced "doubtful."[114]

Although Preetorius opposed the document in principle, the editor vacillated on ratification. The *Westliche Post* published an array of opinion pieces for and against the constitution. Its editorials wavered back and forth. On election day, June 6, Preetorius reasserted the arguments that he had first made in the Turner Hall nearly six months earlier. It took several paragraphs for him to reach the matter of ratification itself. Nothing, he stated on behalf of the editorial staff, could move them "to endorse with our votes a constitution which does not do justice to freedom of belief or the equality of all people, and which contains a districting division detrimental to the influence to which *Deutschtum* is entitled." But should German immigrants forsake the Radicals for the Conservatives? "No one believes," the editorial ran, "that the Conservative anti-constitutionalists are serious about the progressive ideas they now profess. They will show their true face soon enough after the election, and those Radical anti-constitutionalists who seek to substitute the old Radicals with their new allies will soon find themselves bitterly disappointed." For now, Preetorius accepted that his readers would "vote according to their consciences" on the constitution.[115]

The independence that the *Westliche Post* encouraged nearly scuttled the Radical coalition. Across the state, Unionists ratified the constitution by a narrow margin of only 1,862 of a total of 85,478 votes cast. Radicals would have received a stronger mandate if it were not for German immigrants. Although rural Unionists (along with soldiers fighting for the North) were the Missourians most likely to vote in the affirmative, the minority of Missouri Germans who lived outside St. Louis were divided.[116] At one extreme, 98 percent of eligible electors in Freedom Township, Lafayette County voted for the document that promised to neutralize local secessionists.[117] More typically, the constitution reached only about 27 percent support in Husmann's Roark Township, in Gasconade County, and 31 percent in Krekel's St. Charles County.[118] Although the latter's small

114 Husmann to Thomas Fletcher, May 5, 1865, box 1, folder 16, Records of Governor Thomas Clement Fletcher, MSA. Fire damage obscured part of the signature, but the letter is in Husmann's hand.

115 *Westliche Post*, June 6, 1865.

116 Parrish, *Missouri under Radical Rule*, 48. Voters were white male citizens (and immigrant men who had formally declared their intention to become citizens) who took the ironclad oath. Parrish, *Missouri under Radical Rule*, 44–45.

117 Frizzell, *Independent Immigrants*, 142.

118 Office of the Secretary of State, Elections Division, Election Returns, 1846–1992, box 10, folder 10, MSA; *St. Charles Demokrat*, June 15, 1865.

German settlements of Augusta and New Melle were heavily pro-constitution, that result apparently was not indicative of sentiment in the county as a whole.[119] The impression that immigrants were generally averse to the constitution originated, of course, in St. Louis. There it netted about a third of the vote in the German wards and across the city.[120]

The debacle proved once more the practical difficulties of enacting immigrant Radicalism. As early as January 1865, a few visionaries had rehearsed the argument that the status of naturalized male immigrants – not that of native-born women – provided a template for the freedmen. They disavowed exclusion based on race and second-class citizenship for men. Yet the same German pride that suffused immigrants' language of citizenship also hobbled their ability to erase the discursive distinction – let alone the legal line – between race and ethnicity. Organizing as an immigrant bloc also had more concrete consequences. German-American Radicals divided the coalition of white Missourians who were at least minimally receptive to African-American overtures. Indeed, their tentative alliance with Conservatives prefigured the Liberal Republican movement that would sweep Republicans out of government in the state within five years. Before then, German-American Radical Republicans, complete with all the rhetorical power, conceptual limitations, and political liabilities of their approach to American citizenship, would enter the debate over national Reconstruction.

119 Ibid.
120 Parrish, *Missouri under Radical Rule*, 46; *Westliche Post*, June 8, 1865.

4

Principle Rising, 1865–1869

Carl Schurz became one of the most sought-after public speakers in the postbellum United States. Equally masterful in German and English, he rivaled Franz Sigel as the most famous German-born American and Ralph Waldo Emerson as the most expensive speaker in the American Literary Bureau's stable of lecturers.[1] In 1867, after years serving the Union cause as a diplomat, brigadier general, and itinerant politician, Schurz settled down in Missouri to take up co-editorship and part-ownership of the *Westliche Post.*[2] As the instantly recognized leader of St. Louis Germans, he was the perfect choice to welcome Philip H. Sheridan to the city that September. Schurz, flanked by Union veterans, told the Irish-American general:

You see before you Americans, white or black, proud that their country calls them son. You see Irishmen, proud that their ancestors called the Green Isle their home. You see Germans, French, Scandinavians, English, Hungarians, Poles, Bohemians, Italians, Spanish, proud to be united with you through the bond of common citizenship and enthusiastic zeal for a great common concern, proud to have fought with you, and always prepared to fight with you again.

It was Schurz at his most predictable, lauding naturalized citizens and awkwardly including African Americans in a pluralist model designed for European immigrants. But he had a new battle in mind. He was marshaling his troops for the largely political campaign of reconstructing the states of the former Confederacy. The success of this endeavor, Schurz told Sheridan and the former soldiers, would hinge on whether the United States honored the "civil and political rights of all of its citizens."[3] He was calling for the enfranchisement of black men, the fight that, with slavery abolished, had become the centerpiece of Radical Republicanism.

1 C. M. Bresford to Schurz, Aug. 26, 1871, reel 6, fr. 133, Schurz Papers, LOC.
2 Trefousse, *Carl Schurz*, 115–17, 162–63.   3 *Woechentlich Westliche Post*, Sept. 11, 1867.

Schurz's brand of immigrant Radicalism would gain strength among German-American Republicans between 1865 and 1869, imprinting itself upon Reconstruction. Schurz made a liberal nationalist case for African-American suffrage. Armed with the franchise, black men would assure the region's loyalty to the United States and introduce a free labor regime to the South. Even Marxist Joseph Weydemeyer, who believed that working for wages would not bring African Americans true freedom, accepted the liberal's prescription for the immediate reconstruction of the Southern economy. More broadly, of course, universal manhood suffrage expressed the principle of male equality within the nation-state. Most Radicals, whatever their nativity, accepted Schurz's liberal nationalism, but his status as a new citizen and transnational actor lent it an aura of universality and transcendence.

"Principle" became the faithful standby of German Republican rhetoric during the late 1860s. Akin to the myth of the freedom-loving German, what I call the "politics of principle" did not depend on the personal intentions of individual politicians. Public and group-centered, it served as the Radicals' construction of ethnicity and politics during the postwar years. The politics of principle flattered German Americans and minimized the differences among them. This chapter tracks its rising appeal to immigrants who were already in the Republican orbit. My argument follows a sequence of events: Schurz's report on Southern states directly following the war, a Wisconsin ballot measure on African-American suffrage in 1865, a similar referendum in Ohio two years later, the presidential election of 1868, and the congressional debate over the Fifteenth Amendment in 1869.

The Radicals would not carry suffrage referenda in Wisconsin, Ohio, or Missouri, and the Fifteenth Amendment would not be powerful enough to protect the rights of African Americans in the South. Rather than interpret these failures as a simple renunciation of Radical principles, however, I propose that they reflect the subtleties of principle-based politics. Immigrant leaders who imagined a racially egalitarian order were not hypocrites, but most of them never engaged the freed people themselves. In public, Radicals were preoccupied with German Americans – their belief in the abstraction of liberal nationalism and their willingness to draw parallels between male immigrants and the freedmen. "Principle" relegated black rights to an abstract realm, enabling Radicals to woo voters by simultaneously spurning racial prejudice and skeptically appraising African Americans. German Radicalism's weakness, then, derived from the same source as its strength. The immigrants' ideas of racial justice were grounded in a sense of themselves, not in a true appreciation of the injustice done African Americans.

This dynamic would shackle the implementation of race-neutral citizenship while liberal nationalism dominated in the late 1860s and make it vulnerable to changes in immigrants' self-perceptions when liberal nationalism faltered after 1870.

PLANS FOR RECONSTRUCTION, 1865

During 1865, Schurz set out the liberal nationalist reasoning that would lead the whole Republican Party toward the Fifteenth Amendment. As a relentless Radical, he had petitioned Lincoln for emancipation from the front lines, rejoicing when the nationalist war finally became a liberal one too. With the president's assassination, Schurz feared that Lincoln's achievements would be squandered. Andrew Johnson, the Tennessee Unionist who assumed the presidency, seemed to Schurz to be suborning violence and treason in the defeated South. Intending to build Reconstruction on a liberal nationalist foundation, Schurz set out that summer to investigate.[4]

In letters to President Johnson, a document submitted to the Senate, and editorials in leading newspapers, Schurz reported that intransigent Southern whites were still a threat to national peace and unity. He related, for example, that a Union army commander in Atlanta had informed him that soldiers and freed people could not venture safely beyond the immediate reach of the garrison. Black Unionists were at particular risk. After interviewing African Americans who sought treatment for bullet wounds, Schurz wrote north that such attacks were calculated to "keep the negroes where they belonged." He made a point of observing that most Southern whites were not only hostile toward individuals who were loyal to the Union, they also showed "*an utter absence of national feeling*" (his emphasis).[5] Security concerns – *national* security concerns – increased the attraction of black suffrage, an essentially liberal policy. Schurz saw enfranchising black men as the best way to protect the integrity of the Union without indefinite federal intervention. He used the actions of defiant white Southerners to persuade Northerners that defending black rights would serve the national interest. In 1865, as in 1848, liberalism and nationalism proved mutually reinforcing.

Schurz also argued that the ballot would equip African Americans to defend free labor. In a letter to his wife, Margarethe, from Jackson, Mississippi, he wrote, "The negroes are unjustly accused of not wishing to work. They are the only people here who do work. I have not seen one white

---

4 Trefousse, *Carl Schurz*, 115–17, 150–55.
5 Carl Schurz, *Report on the Condition of the South* (Senate Executive Documents, 39th Cong., 1st sess., no. 2, 1865; reprint, New York: Arno Press, 1969), 18, 13.

man in the fields. Strangely enough, only the negroes have money; they are the only persons who do not shrink from remunerative labor."[6] His formal report to the Senate included the case of a Georgia planter who would not relinquish the habits of slavery. The Georgian had told Schurz "most seriously" that "one of his negroes had shown himself certainly unfit for freedom because he impudently refused to submit to a whipping."[7] While former slaveholders continued to use violent punishment, the freed people seemed ready to work for fair wages. With formal political power, Schurz hoped, they could control the conditions of their labor. He wrote that if African-American men were enfranchised, they would remake the South in the image of the North. In his mind, granting black men the vote would not only protect the nation, it would inaugurate a liberal economy.

Scholars have noted that Schurz's liberalism was incompatible with the reallocation of land to the freed people, a policy that might have transformed the Southern economy more fundamentally.[8] African Americans certainly aspired to own the land they had toiled in bondage, and a few immigrants flirted with redistribution during 1865, but reallocation never became a clear alternative to Schurz's Radicalism among German-American Republicans.[9] Socialists, while not opposed to the idea, had other priorities. Karl Marx, who had followed the Civil War closely from England, never set much store in rural smallholding. Enlarging the propertied classes interested him less than preparing the working class for revolution. Clues to Marx's ambitions for Reconstruction appeared in published letters he wrote first to Lincoln and then to Johnson on behalf of the International Workingmen's Association (IWA), which had formed in London in 1864. The "First International," as it was later known, recommended to both presidents that they capitalize on the accomplishments of the war and initiate "a new era

---

6 Schurz to Margarethe Schurz, Aug. 27, 1865, in *Speeches, Correspondence and Political Papers of Carl Schurz,* ed. Bancroft, 1: 269.

7 Schurz, *Report on the Condition of the South,* 17.

8 Emphasizing Schurz's economic ideas, see Richardson, *Death of Reconstruction,* 17–20; Richard A. Gerber, "Carl Schurz's Journey from Radical to Liberal Republicanism: A Problem in Ideological Consistency," *Mid-America* 82 (2000): 71–99. Historians since W. E. B. Du Bois have interpreted the rejection of land reallocation as an indication of "the limits of Radical ideology" more generally. Foner, *Reconstruction,* 237; Du Bois, *Black Reconstruction,* 601–06.

9 Foner, *Reconstruction,* 102–10, 309–11; Litwack, *Been in the Storm So Long,* 398–404; Hahn, *Nation under Our Feet,* 129–59; Foner, "Thaddeus Stevens, Confiscation, and Reconstruction," in *Politics and Ideology in the Age of the Civil War,* ed. Foner (New York: Oxford University Press, 1980), 128–49. For rather casual references to land redistribution in the German-language press, see *Milwaukee Herold,* May 6, 1865; *Sauk City Pionier am Wisconsin,* July 1, 1865. For a German-American supporter of such a plan in Chicago, see John Jentz and Richard Schneirov, *Chicago in the Age of Capital: Class, Politics, and Democracy during the Civil War and Reconstruction* (Urbana: University of Illinois Press, 2012), 76.

in the emancipation of labor."[10] Marx and his colleagues anticipated that the wage system would soon be supplanted by freer working relationships. It was the commitment to further change – not a fixation on land – that distinguished Marxist plans from liberal nationalist ones in 1865.

For Marxists, Reconstruction was one point on the continuum of economic history, so their short-term proposals did not conflict with Schurz's arguments. Joseph Weydemeyer, still working to hasten the revolution, was disseminating his ideas to a much smaller audience in 1865. The colonel had stayed on in St. Louis after his assignment in the city during the final years of the war. While Schurz was traversing the Deep South, Weydemeyer was talking up the IWA, preparing to stand for election as county auditor, and writing periodically for the *Westliche Post*.[11] In a series of essays published in September, he referred to land reallocation, but only as an auxiliary to the franchise. "Along with the right to vote," he wrote, "we should also give the freedman the means to defend it and adequate property so he has the independence to excise the right to vote freely."[12] Weydemeyer's aim, like Schurz's, was to find Southerners whose support for his political and economic agenda would make prolonged military occupation unnecessary. Quickly dismissing "slaveholders" and "white trash" (he used the English term in quotation marks), he looked to African Americans as the agents of "free labor," "civilization," and "progress."[13] In contrast to Schurz, however, Weydemeyer wanted to build up industrial capitalism only in order to take it down. Industry "oppresses and exploits" the worker, he believed, but "only through its progressive development can he destroy the form of exploitation itself."[14] The Marxist counterpoint shows that Schurz's economic theory was distinct yet compatible, for a time, with other ideologies.

Yet Schurz's motives were no more narrowly economic than they were shallowly nationalistic. To liberals, economic growth and national power complemented equal male citizenship. In his *Report on the Condition of the South*, Schurz made a multifaceted argument, focusing on the "effect of the extension of the franchise to the colored people upon the development of free labor and upon the security of human rights in the South." He chose not to restate the "moral merits" of suffrage, but he did declare that the freedman could be "an intelligent, reliable and efficient free laborer" *and*

---

10 Karl Marx, "Address from the Workingmen's International Association to President Johnson," May 13, 1865; Marx to Abraham Lincoln, Dec. 23, 1864, in *Collected Works*, 20: 100, 19–20.

11 Obermann, *Joseph Weydemeyer: Ein Lebensbild*, 387–90.

12 *Westliche Post*, Sept. 1, 1865. See also Sept. 8 and 14, 1865.

13 Ibid., Sept. 13, 1865.   14 Ibid., Sept. 14, 1865.

"a good and useful citizen."[15] For him, Radicalism was as Eric Foner has described it, "first and foremost a civic ideology, grounded in a definition of American citizenship."[16]

Guided by the principles of national unity, economic liberalism, and equal citizenship for men, Schurz pitched suffrage to a general audience in the North. Significantly, he wrote in English and coordinated with Charles Sumner of Massachusetts, the Senate's leading Radical.[17] Sumner submitted Schurz's report to the Congress and saw to it that more than one hundred thousand copies were printed.[18] It was altogether fitting that Schurz should make the liberal nationalist argument for black suffrage. He was a Forty-Eighter who had fought for a liberal German nation before transferring his allegiance to the United States in return for citizenship rights. Schurz had no doubt that nation-states defended individual rights and individual rights strengthened nation-states. There was no need to choose between the two. His report was a reminder that the nationalist and economic imperatives of the postwar years worked in tandem to advance African-American rights. In 1865, nationalism still promoted liberalism.

SUFFRAGE IN WISCONSIN AND OHIO, 1865 AND 1867

As the debate over the status of black men in the South began, German-American Radicals also set out to revise citizenship law in the North. In Wisconsin and Ohio, Radicals could pursue a politics of principle untouched by the exigencies of loyalty and free labor. Indeed, politicians could better gauge the racial attitudes of immigrant voters in states where slavery had never found official sanction. Historians typically read failed referenda as evidence that Radicalism repelled most Northerners, but the discussion in the German-language public sphere suggests a more nuanced interpretation.[19] Although there were always large numbers of immigrant

---

15 Schurz, *Report on the Condition of the South*, 44, 21.
16 Foner, *Reconstruction*, 233. See also Foner, "Reconstruction Revisited," *Reviews in American History* 10, no. 4 (1982): 82–100.
17 Schurz to G. L. Stearns, Aug. 29, 1865; Schurz to Charles Sumner, Oct. 17 and 24, Nov. 13, 1865; Charles Sumner to Schurz, Nov. 15, Dec. 25, 1865, reel 3, fr. 98–99, 128–30, 227–28, 263–66, 273–74, Schurz Papers, LOC. Some letters have also been published in vol. 1, *Speeches, Correspondence and Political Papers of Carl Schurz*, ed. Bancroft.
18 Trefousse, *Carl Schurz*, 159.
19 For studies that focus on voter racism, see Parrish, *Missouri under Radical Rule*; James C. Mohr, ed., *Radical Republicans in the North: State Politics during Reconstruction* (Baltimore: Johns Hopkins University Press, 1976); Schwalm, *Emancipation's Diaspora*, 182. For a broad presentation of Republican prejudice, see Woodward, "Seeds of Failure in Radical Race Policy," 125–47. William Gillette argued that when Northern Republicans did promote black suffrage, they were motivated by the simple desire to profit from black votes. Gillette, *Right to Vote*. Felice Bonadio similarly maintained

Democrats who did not like the idea of black suffrage, and some immigrant Republicans resisted it too, Radicalism would spread among leading German-born Republicans and gain widespread respectability. Referenda in Wisconsin in 1865 and Ohio in 1867 illustrate this point. In Wisconsin, the small group of German Republicans was keen on black suffrage from the start, while in Ohio, the larger German Republican community became Radical more gradually.

By April 1865, when native-born Wisconsin legislators proposed a referendum on African-American suffrage, the war had thinned German Republican ranks.[20] After twenty months in Confederate prison camps, Bernhard Domschke returned to Milwaukee to edit the *Herold*, but his health never would recover.[21] Domschke's onetime colleague Fritz Anneke had jumped from post to post in the army until a military court convicted him of insubordination and desertion in 1863. Desperate for work, Anneke took a job at Carl Dänzer's Democratic *Anzeiger des Westens* in St. Louis.[22] He never again lived with Mathilde, who returned to Milwaukee from Switzerland in 1865 to open a private girls' school.[23] Eduard Salomon had also moved to Wisconsin's largest city after his term as acting governor was up. He practiced law and stayed active in Republican circles, but he never became a commanding political figure.[24]

Few in number, German Republican leaders in Wisconsin were firm on suffrage. They could not present theirs as the position of German Wisconsinites, the majority of whom voted Democratic, but they experimented in Radical politics. In 1865, Domschke wrote in the *Herold* that enfranchising black men in Wisconsin was as natural as emancipation.[25] Salomon worked back channels to stop the Johnson faction from controlling the state Republican convention that year. For governor, he supported Lucius Fairchild, whom he considered "all right on the Negro question nationally and in the

that Ohio Republicans adopted the "black hobby" of African-American suffrage to gain an edge in contested counties. Bonadio, *North of Reconstruction: Ohio Politics, 1865–1870* (New York: New York University Press, 1970), 92–106. Robert D. Sawrey identifies a wider range of motives, including the hope of avoiding hypocrisy. Sawrey, *Dubious Victory: The Reconstruction Debate in Ohio* (Lexington: University Press of Kentucky, 1992), 101. Michael Les Benedict is unusual in suggesting suffrage could work in Republicans' favor despite white voters' racism. Benedict, "Politics of Reconstruction," 80; Benedict, *Compromise of Principle*, 326. Many historians observe that Republicans feared racial equality was a losing issue, especially after electoral defeats in 1867. See Benedict, "The Rout of Radicalism: Republicans and the Election of 1867," *Civil War History* 18 (1972): 334–44. On Ohio, see Sawrey, *Dubious Victory*, 115–19.

20 Fishel, "Wisconsin and Negro Suffrage," 189.
21 Schlicher, "Bernhard Domschke: II," 451–52; *Herold*, June 3, 1865.
22 Schulte, *Fritz Anneke*, 66, 72–81, 87.
23 Hense-Jensen, *Wisconsin's Deutsch-Amerikaner*, 1: 224.
24 Falge, ed., *History of Manitowoc County, Wisconsin*, 1: 255.
25 *Herold*, Sept. 23, 1865.

state."[26] According to Salomon's opponents at the *Milwaukee Seebote*, German "do-gooders" attended a daylong black suffrage convention a month before the November referendum.[27] Since African Americans presided over the "mass meeting," this was a rare instance of German immigrants interacting with black Radicals. The German Americans present affirmed the meeting's resolutions, one of which stated, "That we believe that the fundamental principles of republicanism requires [sic] that government should be by the consent of the governed; that those who pay taxes and fight to support the government should have a voice in its administration, and on these grounds we claim the amendment to our state constitution to secure equal and impartial suffrage."[28] Although self-evidently a product of the American-African experience, this was the same basis on which Germans had demanded rights in the European revolutions and attained them in the United States.

Yet in the fall of 1865 some Wisconsin Republicans worried that liberal principles could hurt them at the polls. Universal manhood suffrage might drive voters into the Democratic camp. This uncertainty hinted at the complexity of racial politics in the Civil War era North. Although Republicans in the legislature had introduced the referendum, the party did not include a suffrage plank on its state platform. Wisconsin Radicals sought Lucius Fairchild's personal assurances that he was for the ballot measure. One resident of Wautoma wrote, "I will not vote for *any man*, if I know it, who is not openly in favor of the equally [sic] of all men (without regard to color) *before the law, including the elective franchise*. North and South."[29] In reply, Fairchild reiterated that he would vote for suffrage himself and he urged others to do the same, but he would not provide a written statement to that effect. Democratic newspapers would manipulate it, he thought. Fairchild told a confidant, "All persons know that I am in favor of negro suffrage in this state. The opposition want [sic] it on paper, so that they can make an argument against us on the strength of it."[30] Some Republicans agreed that Fairchild should steer clear of the issue, reporting that voters, especially returning soldiers, did not favor enfranchising African Americans.[31] If white men opposed black suffrage, perhaps they would retaliate against Republicans for suggesting it.

---

26 Eduard Salomon to Moses M. Davis, July 28, 1865, Moses M. Davis Papers, WHS, quoted in Fishel, "Wisconsin and Negro Suffrage," 190; *Seebote*, March 14, 1866.
27 *Seebote*, Oct. 18, 1865. See also *Banner und Volksfreund*, Oct. 11, 1865.
28 *Milwaukee Daily Sentinel*, Oct. 10, 1865.
29 W. E. Webb to Lucius Fairchild, Oct. 5, 1865, box 17, folder 1, Lucius Fairchild Papers, WHS.
30 Lucius Fairchild to William E. Smith, Oct. 11, 1865, box 52, Letterbook, 1865–1867, 268, Fairchild Papers, WHS.
31 See correspondence in box 16, folder 5, Fairchild Papers, WHS.

Some Radicals, however, speculated that African-American rights were not a political liability, but a potential boon. Byron Paine, a native-born lawyer, observed that Lincoln had cajoled the electorate into accepting the abolition of slavery and the enlistment of former slaves. Those decisions, rather than cost the Republican Party, now defined it.[32] The Republican *Milwaukee Sentinel* editorialized that if politicians in Washington, DC, had backed African-American suffrage, Connecticut voters would have passed it by a majority of ten thousand in a recent referendum.[33] Several weeks before Wisconsinites went to the polls, a man from Mineral Point wrote to Fairchild, "I am almost sorry we dodged the question, & I believe with a proper canvass, we could have carried it through."[34] Whether or not he was right, some Radicals suspected that universal manhood suffrage resonated with many Americans at some level.

Although Wisconsin voters denied African Americans political citizenship in November 1865, Radicals were not completely discouraged. The measure won about 46 percent support, while Fairchild garnered more than 54 percent, only a few percent shy of Lincoln's tally in 1860.[35] There were two reasons for hope in these numbers. First, most Republicans had voted to remove racial qualifications for voting from the state constitution. Equally importantly, however, black suffrage had not alienated men from the party. Domschke sounded cheered by the results. Republicans had done better than they had expected in Milwaukee. The defeat of African-American suffrage, he thought, meant only that the "resolution of the issue was pushed back a little."[36] Perhaps Domschke was reacting to the fact that the polling disparity between the suffrage measure and Fairchild was narrower in Milwaukee's German wards than in the state as a whole.[37] He believed that German Republicans in Wisconsin admired the principled stand of the Radicals even when they would not all vote directly for black suffrage. His party potentially benefited from the vague ideal of universal manhood suffrage without quite getting all immigrant Republicans to vote "yes."

Over the next few years, developments in the state of Ohio would support Domschke's hunch that if Radicals stood by their principles, public

32 *Milwaukee Daily Sentinel*, Sept. 1, 1865.   33 Ibid., Oct. 13, 1865.
34 J. F. Allan to Lucius Fairchild, Oct. 19, 1865, box 17, folder 1, Fairchild Papers, WHS.
35 Frank M. Stewart and E. W. Young, eds., *The Legislative Manual of the State of Wisconsin*, 5th ed. (Madison, WI: William J. Park, State Printer, 1866), 198.
36 *Herold*, Nov. 11, 1865. Just five months later, one of the men who had attended the October meeting, Ezekiel Gillespie, engaged Byron Paine and his partners to mount a legal challenge to his rejection from the polls. The state's highest court ruled in his favor. Judges determined that the 1849 referendum had been illegally invalidated. Schwalm, *Emancipation's Diaspora*, 183.
37 Appendix, Table 4. Both the suffrage measure and Fairchild did very poorly in Milwaukee.

opinion would swing in their direction. In the Buckeye State, the large German Republican community gravitated toward Radicalism during the latter half of the 1860s. Analyzing Friedrich Hassaurek's circuitous political journey casts light on the path of Republican politics. By 1866, Hassaurek was no longer the militant abolitionist he had been before the war. During the conflict, while his contemporaries had marched on Southern whites and argued with moderate Republicans, the Forty-Eighter had manned a diplomatic post in Ecuador. Most German-American Republicans had become more committed to black rights during Lincoln's presidency, but Hassaurek returned to Cincinnati having lost his activist streak. In personal letters, he agreed with correspondents who referred sneeringly to the Republicans who supported African-American suffrage as "Reds" and "Radicalissimi."[38] His years living abroad had distanced Hassaurek literally and figuratively from the German-American community, tightening instead his relationships with native-born politicians.[39] Yet his stature among Ohio's Anglo-American Republicans still rested on his influence among German immigrants.[40] Conscious that he had to reestablish his German-American credentials, Hassaurek bought a portion of the largest of Cincinnati's German-language newspapers, the *Volksblatt*.[41]

From the editor's chair at his new newspaper, Hassaurek flung himself into an unsuccessful effort to make Ohio's Republican Germans more conservative in 1866 and 1867. President Johnson was now in open conflict with the congressional Republicans who had passed the Civil Rights Act of 1866, which guaranteed the freed people's right to enter into contracts and receive the protection of the courts. Later that year, Congress proposed the Fourteenth Amendment to write these provisions into the Constitution. The amendment finally overturned *Dred Scott*. For the first time, the Constitution would define national citizenship as a status based on birth or naturalization, and states would be prohibited from abridging "the

---

38 E. Lee to Hassaurek, June 8, 1868; C. N. Riotte to Hassaurek, April 9, 1868, box 1, folder 5, Hassaurek Papers, OHS. Remarking on the transition, see Wittke, "Friedrich Hassaurek," 2; Levine, *Spirit of 1848*, 264; *Columbus Westbote*, April 19, 1866.

39 Silas Tressadeau to William Henry Smith, March 13, 1866, box 2, folder 2, William Henry Smith Papers, OHS. Hassaurek's associates and correspondents included Senator John Sherman, future president Rutherford B. Hayes, Congressman James Ashley, and local Republicans Murat Halstead and Donn Piatt.

40 His Anglo-American Republican correspondents often asked for favorable billing in his newspaper. See for example James Ashley to Hassaurek, Sept. 15, 1868, box 2, folder 8, Hassaurek Papers, OHS. Republicans saw him as a representative of the "German element." See for example W. Howells to William Henry Smith, May 7, 1867, box 2, folder 4, Smith Papers, OHS. For Hassaurek's assumptions about the conservative leanings of German immigrants, see C. N. Riotte to Hassaurek, April 9, 1868, box 1, folder 5, Hassaurek Papers, OHS.

41 Wittke, "Friedrich Hassaurek," 12.

privileges or immunities of citizens of the United States." To Radicals, both immigrant and native-born, all of these things were reassuringly liberal, but Hassaurek at first argued that they would bring too great a federal intrusion into state affairs. He sided with Johnson, who blocked Congress at every turn and angled to form a new party.[42] When Hassaurek saw that no such party was feasible, he allied with conservative and moderate Republicans to keep black suffrage off the platform in Ohio.[43] The Republican legislature outmaneuvered this group, giving Ohio men the chance to vote on the question of enfranchisement anyway in 1867. Radicals were already besting Hassaurek in state and national politics.

Within the German-American community, Radicals fended off attacks from the conservative Hassaurek even more effectively. When August Willich, who by then was best known as a Radical general, entered the race for auditor of Cincinnati's Hamilton County in 1866, Hassaurek conspicuously declined to give him the *Volksblatt*'s blessing.[44] Out of public view, Hassaurek also tried to negotiate the purchase of Cleveland's *Wächter am Erie* in order to dislodge its longtime editor and owner, the Radical August Thieme.[45] Willich won the election, and Thieme refused to sell his paper. A pattern had been set. Pro-suffrage German leaders who identified with the majority in Congress repeatedly trounced Hassaurek. He had miscalculated the mood of German Republicans and the trajectory of postwar politics.

Realizing that his conservatism was not palatable to German-born Republicans, Hassaurek finally corrected his course. A month before Ohio's 1867 referendum, Hassaurek adopted the Radical rhetoric of Schurz, Domschke, Willich, and Thieme. He began to speak of the "necessity of universal suffrage." In a two-hour speech before German Republicans in Cleveland, he argued that Johnson and the Democrats had abetted the "aristocrats of the South," who still despised the Union and "strove to maintain slavery under another name." Hassaurek referred to the principles of nationalism and liberalism as they had appeared in Schurz's *Report*. Like the German-born

---

42 The *Volksblatt* from this period has not survived, but other Cincinnati papers and the *Westliche Post* covered its positions. *Cincinnati Commercial*, March 13, 1866; *Westliche Post*, March 10, 24, and 30, Sept. 11, 1866.

43 J. D. Cox to Hassaurek, May 13, 1867; Rufus Spalding to Hassaurek, Dec. 1867, box 2, folder 8, Hassaurek Papers, OHS. In 1868, Hassaurek drafted a version of the Ohio Republican platform that spoke of Reconstruction only in generalities. See Rutherford B. Hayes to Hassaurek, Feb. 14 and 19, 1868, box 2, folder 10; William H. West to Hassaurek, Feb. 14, 1868; S. J. Critfield to Hassaurek, Feb. 18, 1868, box 2, folder 8, Hassaurek Papers, OHS.

44 The *Westliche Post* supported Willich and described Hassaurek as a "wirepuller." *Westliche Post*, Aug. 7, 1866. See also *Cincinnati Volksfreund*, Oct. 14, 1866.

45 Rufus Spalding to Hassaurek, Jan. 29, Feb. 4, 1868, box 2, folder 8; Louis Smithnight to Hassaurek, Feb. 18, 1868; August Thieme to Hassaurek, Feb. 8, 1868, box 1, folder 5, Hassaurek Papers, OHS.

Radicals, Hassaurek also compared immigrants and African Americans. He explained that the United States was "'a free nation,' that is a nation the laws of which grant equal political rights to whites or blacks, immigrants or native-born."[46] The experience of the immigrant man was an emblem for the principle of male equality, which Hassaurek was now prepared to extend to African Americans. Apparently, the Forty-Eighter now believed that German Republicans would be receptive to the argument that black men's citizenship should mirror their own.

Hassaurek engaged in the politics of principle cynically, a fact that only makes him a better guide to the opinions of German Republicans. He used Radical language because he thought it would appeal to his constituents, not because it expressed his own instincts. In private, a fellow Republican wrote to Hassaurek agreeing that Congress was acting unwisely: "If a nigger gets his throat sque[e]zed . . . a law is pen[n]ed that niggers' throats must not be squeezed."[47] It was the unabashed crudeness of a man certain that the message's recipient shared his views. In public, Hassaurek often said that he was a Republican chiefly because Democrats were traitorous, barbarous, and financially irresponsible.[48] He would not have spoken in idealistic, Radical terms to German crowds if he had not reckoned it advantageous.

Like Domschke, Hassaurek did not measure Radicalism's utility according to the success of suffrage referenda. Ohioans turned down black suffrage. Replicating returns in Wisconsin exactly, only 46 percent of Ohio voters wanted to eliminate the word "white" from voting law.[49] In contrast to the Badger State, however, some German Republican neighborhoods cast majorities for African-American suffrage. More than 50 percent of voters supported the amendment in two of Cleveland's five most heavily German wards and three of Cincinnati's.[50] In the two years since Wisconsin's referendum, Radicalism seemed only to have grown stronger among German immigrants. From the two campaigns, Radical leaders had learned that black suffrage played well among those German Americans who already voted Republican. The tide of liberal nationalism would eventually turn, but in 1867, it was still bearing the Republicans toward black suffrage.

---

46 *Wächter am Erie*, Sept. 13, 1867. Hassaurek's Democratic opponents noted his shift. *Cincinnati Volksfreund*, Sept. 30 and 31, Oct. 7, 1867.
47 E. Lee to Hassaurek, March 11, 1868, box 1, folder 5, Hassaurek Papers, OHS.
48 *Cincinnati Commercial*, Sept. 27, Oct. 11, 1867.   49 Sawrey, *Dubious Victory*, 115–16.
50 Appendix, Tables 1 and 2.

CLASS, POLITICAL ECONOMY, AND RADICAL MOMENTUM, 1865–1868

Hassaurek's reorientation was part of a larger trend in German Republican circles around the Midwest. Radicalism was on the rise. Schurz's plan for national Reconstruction was neatly converging with the arguments for suffrage that Radicals were making in individual states. Yet Republicans confronted some of the same dilemmas as they had during the 1850s. For the politics of principle to become an ethnic movement, German-American Republicans had to address differences among themselves on political economy and prevent working-class defections. As had been true before the war, socialists both widened the Republican Party's ideological scope and supported liberal measures in the short term, while less programmatic working-class leaders probably did more to increase its constituency. Black suffrage would postpone the internal conflict over economic philosophy one last time, becoming the one issue that could hold German Republicans together and carry them into the presidential election of 1868.

By June 1865, German-born Republicans in Ohio, Missouri, and Wisconsin were off to a strong start. The most engaged politicians were quick to abandon Johnson and flock to African-American suffrage. Editors at the *Wächter am Erie*, the *Westliche Post*, the *St. Charles Demokrat*, and the *Milwaukee Herold* made the arguments that would soon prevail among German Republicans.[51] Each of the four papers had criticized Johnson's Southern policy before Congress issued Schurz's report. The *St. Charles Demokrat* maintained that the president was ignoring the principle for which "the people fought, suffered, and finally triumphed."[52] With the tension between Johnson and the Congress mounting, its editor insisted that the North had battled all along for the "re-shaping of the South according to the spirit of freedom, human rights, and real democracy."[53] Countless editorials and numerous public meetings asked that Congress follow Schurz's recommendations.[54] General Sigel used his popularity as wartime hero to campaign against Johnson and for the Republican candidates who wanted

---

51 *Westliche Post*, Jan. 26, 1865; *Wächter am Erie*, March 29, April 12, 1865; *St. Charles Demokrat*, July 6 and 20, Aug. 10, Sept. 14, 1865; *Herold*, Jan 21, 1865.
52 *St. Charles Demokrat*, Oct. 12, 1865.   53 Ibid., April 11, 1867.
54 *Herold*, May 20, 1865; *Westliche Post*, June 22, July 12, Aug. 23 and 24, Sept. 29, 1865. On public meetings, see *Wächter am Erie*, May 31, 1865; *St. Charles Demokrat*, Dec. 7, 1865; *Westliche Post*, Jan. 20, 1866. Union military commemorations often included pleas for black suffrage. See *Westliche Post*, May 11, 1866, May 22, 1867, May 11, 1868; *St. Charles Demokrat*, Aug. 9 and 16, 1866, Aug. 13, 1868.

to enfranchise the freedmen. The reconstituted national Turnerbund also entered the fray on the side of the Radicals.[55]

Despite all the Radical activity, German-American Republicans worried about urban workingmen leaving the party. Since before the war, Forty-Eighters had led a coalition that included immigrants from various occupational backgrounds who ascribed to a range of economic philosophies. Many working-class immigrants had remained Democratic, but Republicans had attracted a sizable number to antislavery free labor ideology. Since emancipation, however, white working-class immigrants in the North had begun to remind politicians that their interests were not the same as those of proprietors and professionals. As the end of slavery forced Americans to revisit the question of whether wage labor was really free labor, urban workers brought their own grievances to the attention of the wider public. Joseph Weydemeyer reflected on these stirrings in 1865. He wrote in the *Westliche Post* that white workers had made enormous sacrifices for the Union. They had served in the military and withstood staggering inflation, while speculators and contractors had reaped large profits. Weydemeyer went on to refer to the "tremendous" examples of white working-class mobilization in "recent years."[56] A range of workers, some of whom wanted to improve the wage system and others who wanted to abolish it, escalated their protests for an eight-hour workday after the war ended. Coordinated strike action peaked in Northern cities and St. Louis during 1867, while independent workingmen's parties formed to press for other concessions.[57]

In 1865, Weydemeyer feared that the white worker might turn on the African American. The Marxist detected that "he is beginning again to look with envy at the 'eternal Negro,' who still dominates public interest."[58] But Weydemeyer preached solidarity. In "the great struggle between labor and monopolistic capital," he wrote, the more allies that labor secured, the better. "Where, then, to find these comrades in the South when not among the workers themselves, regardless of what ancestry determines their skin

---

55 Engle, *Yankee Dutchman*, 212–17; *Wächter am Erie*, Sept. 28, 1868; *Westliche Post*, Oct. 31, 1865, Jan. 25, 1866; *St. Charles Demokrat*, Oct. 10, 1868; *Herold*, Jan. 21, 1865; *Seebote*, March 28, 1866; Pumroy and Rampelmann, eds., *Research Guide to the Turner Movement*, xx.

56 *Westliche Post*, Sept. 14, 1865.

57 Montgomery, *Beyond Equality*; Richardson, *Death of Reconstruction*, 64–65; Richardson, *West from Appomattox*, 64–66; Foner, *Reconstruction*, 475–88; Quigley, *Second Founding*; Beckert, *Monied Metropolis*; Richard Schneirov, *Labor and Urban Politics: Class Conflict and the Origins of Modern Liberalism in Chicago, 1864–97* (Urbana: University of Illinois Press, 1998), 17–68; Jentz and Schneirov, *Chicago in the Age of Capital*, 81–116.

58 *Westliche Post*, Sept. 14, 1865.

color?" Weydemeyer asked the question in one installment of a three-part essay, "On the Negro Suffrage Question."[59]

While some immigrants may have seen African Americans as partners in the socialist struggle, more of them probably took the liberal line that slavery would live on until black men could vote. Schurz and many other Republicans argued that white workers were still at a competitive disadvantage to those who labored under coercive laws and systematic violence. In 1865, these Radicals noticed that emancipation had not created contractual labor relations but a grotesque caricature of them.[60] If the vote made African Americans truly economically independent, most Republicans believed, all wage work would be elevated. The "worker question" and the "Negro question," wrote Thieme in the *Wächter am Erie*, were one and the same.[61] Socialist and liberal arguments coincided again.

Yet some dogmatically liberal Radicals exploited black suffrage cynically to stave off class-based infighting among Republicans. While Weydemeyer saw the enfranchisement of African-American men as a harbinger of the socialist revolution, Emil Preetorius saw it as an *alternative* to any more economic change. Preetorius contracted Weydemeyer to write for the *Westliche Post*, but his own editorials paired pleas for voting rights with admonitions against working-class protest. Reacting to the eight-hour-day movement, he denounced "demagogues" who promised "state aid." Such men, Preetorius wrote, failed to comprehend the private nature of the employment contract.[62] He redirected laborers' anger toward the white Southerners who despised free labor.[63] When working-class St. Louisans elected Weydemeyer city auditor later in 1865, Preetorius told himself that they had followed his advice to focus on Reconstruction in the South.[64] Like antislavery, manhood suffrage did not bring the ideological differences between Weydemeyer and Preetorius to the fore. As long as white Southerners defied the labor contract, Radicals of different stripes could make African-American suffrage their first priority.

Local elections in St. Louis and Cincinnati provided evidence – albeit circumstantial – that the policy of race-neutral manhood suffrage helped Republicans retain the votes of German-born urban workers. When third parties courted working-class German Republicans, Radicals used calls for

59 Ibid.
60 Ibid., Nov. 1, 21, and 30, 1865, Jan. 12, 1866; *Wächter am Erie*, Aug. 9, Sept. 2, 1865.
61 *Wächter am Erie*, Sept. 2, 1865. Most German Republicans argued that the vote would give African Americans economic independence. See *Herold*, Aug. 5, 1865; *Woechentlich Westliche Post*, Oct. 30, 1867; *Wächter am Erie*, June 28, 1865; *St. Charles Demokrat*, April 11, 1867, April 9, 1868.
62 *Westliche Post*, Oct. 7, 1865.   63 Ibid., Sept. 6 and 7, 1865.
64 Ibid., Nov. 8, 10, and 30, 1865.

equal citizenship to hold off large-scale defections. During the St. Louis municipal elections in the spring of 1865, the *Westliche Post* beat back a serious challenge by the Independent Workingmen's ticket. Printing a special edition of his paper, Preetorius sought to discredit the new party as a Conservative front.[65] If German-speaking workers understood that the party was anti-black, he believed, they could not support it. When the Workingmen lost the mayoral race, Preetorius took it to mean that working-class St. Louisans subordinated their immediate economic interests to the higher ideal of male equality.[66] The politics of principle likely deferred class-based schisms.

In Cincinnati, Republicans had less luck, but their opponents triumphed only after neutralizing the issues of Reconstruction. Conservative forces engineered the election of a Workingmen's candidate, Samuel F. Cary, to Congress in 1867. In order to win the votes of German Republicans, however, they carefully ignored the raging citizenship debates. In fact, Cary's nomination itself showed that national politics was already frustrating Democrats. They did not run their own candidate because the reputation of the Democratic Party had been marred, especially among the city's Germans, by its association with the white South. They realized that there was a group of German-born, working-class Republicans who would sooner vote for a Workingmen's candidate than for a Democrat. The *Cincinnati Volksfreund* was one newspaper that upheld the pretense that Cary was independent of the Democrats.[67] While questions of race and citizenship dominated politics during the late 1860s, Republicans were still competitive among the working-class immigrants who had joined the Party of Lincoln before the war. Universal manhood suffrage could draw immigrants with different economic experiences together.

A speech by August Willich shows exactly how Radicals sustained the Republicans' cross-class coalition. Before the 1868 election, Willich headlined a German mass meeting in Cleveland at which both Eduard Salomon and Jacob Müller spoke. The "celebrated warrior" described "the workers of all lands" rising up against the "rule of a privileged class" and for "free labor," but made no mention of revolutionizing wage work. He presented enfranchising black men as the capstone of German Americans' global mission to create nation-states governed by male citizens. Germans had first

65 Roediger, "Racism, Reconstruction, and the Labor Press: The Rise and Fall of the *St. Louis Daily Press*, 1864–1866," *Science and Society* 42 (1978): 159, 163–64; *Mississippi Blätter*, April 2, 1865; *Westliche Post*, April 3 and 4, 1865.
66 Roediger, "Racism, Reconstruction, and the Labor Press," 168.
67 Ross, *Workers on the Edge*, 202–03; *Cincinnati Volksfreund*, Sept. 23, Oct. 5, 1867.

rallied "to the principle that all people are born equal" in "the wars for freedom in the old fatherland," Willich said. He believed that by voting Republican, German Americans would "continue to act for the dominance of the German spirit, in accordance with complete freedom."[68] During the 1860s, Radicals such as Willich used African-American suffrage to fashion a powerful German-American politics of principle that forestalled divisions over political economy and revitalized their working-class following.

THE POWER OF PRINCIPLE

Anyone who had followed German-American Republicanism over the years could see that Willich had turned to well-established themes. The Radical used the language of liberal nationalism and ethnicity, reminding immigrants that they had a unique perspective on American citizenship. By the late 1860s, German Radicals argued that black men should be afforded the same opportunities as male immigrants and likened race and ethnicity. Where would immigrants be, Schurz asked in 1867, without the vote? They would still be called "Dutchmen," not "our German friends."[69] The remark emphasized the fundamental similarities between immigrants and African Americans, implying that black men should be able to vote because immigrant men were. Like leading German Missourians in 1865, German-speaking Radicals around the country intimated that racial groupings were as cultural as they were biological. Stories of education in the South told Radicals that all peoples had the capacity to learn.[70] As was also true in Missouri, however, German Radicals nonetheless distinguished between race and ethnicity, never surrendering the German pride that fostered the notion that ethnicity was a different sort of category than race. That self-assurance could not be extricated from the pursuit of politics in the German-language public sphere. Between 1865 and 1869, German Radicals used the same formula that had made black suffrage "German" in Missouri.

As Reconstruction took shape, however, a new theme, "principle," crystallized. Of course, speaking of abstract ideals was neither new to the postwar period nor exclusive to immigrants, but it was particularly important in the political culture of German-American Republicanism during early Reconstruction. Radical editors repeated that Republicans could amass German votes through "a firm insistence on principles," including, "granting voting

68 *Wächter am Erie*, Sept. 29, 1868.   69 Ibid., Oct. 5, 1867.
70 *St. Charles Demokrat*, Oct. 3, 1867; *Wächter am Erie*, Sept. 12 and 23, 1867; *Westliche Post*, Jan. 12, Feb. 6, 1866, Sept. 12, 1867.

rights to all loyal citizens without distinction of race, color, or ancestry."[71] Yet despite the altruism and optimism of the Radicals, principle would also perform the strange role of reconciling their belief in equal rights for men with their sometimes negative analyses of African Americans.

Ubiquitous in the press, the word "principle" anchored German-language arguments for black suffrage.[72] "The principle of freedom" had compelled German immigrants to become Republicans, according to the *Milwaukee Herold*. Now they must see their work through to completion.[73] A *Westliche Post* editorial agreed, describing how German Republicans had moved from antislavery to black suffrage:

The Germans have stood from the beginning as a strongly principled element in the Republican Party. Keeping its great objective firmly in sight, they consistently marched in the most advanced columns. With few exceptions, they have not been blinded by the benefits of the spoils of power, but have practiced a free, independent critique whenever the party threatens to become untrue or unworthy of its great goal. So they have become a moral power, and have, in the course of events, exercised a powerful influence.... This influence is as necessary today as it ever was.[74]

Principle threaded German-American Republicanism into a coherent narrative, linking Radicals to the tradition of liberal nationalism, proclaiming their ongoing relevance, and compelling future action.

Principle was popular in the public sphere in large part because it signified German ethnic superiority. In Schurz's polished speeches, during the ambitious referenda campaigns, and at rowdy working-class rallies, German immigrants suggested that universal manhood suffrage said more about German immigrants than it did about African Americans. When they inveighed against prejudice, they were crafting their own image as much as identifying with African Americans. Overt racism earned Radicals' self-righteous scorn. It was irrational, crass, and spiteful, traits they did not want pinned on German Americans. Radical politicians lampooned German Democrats who said that the United States was a "white man's country."[75] They were appalled by German-speaking editors who used the word "nigger."[76] In

---

71 *St. Charles Demokrat*, Nov. 4, 1867.
72 Ibid., Dec. 6 and 13, 1866; *Westliche Post*, Jan. 21, 1866, Nov. 3, 1868. For disavowals of vindictiveness, see *Wächter am Erie*, April 12, 1865; *Westliche Post*, Nov. 21, 1865. Also mentioning principle, see *Woechentlich Westliche Post*, Oct. 23, 1867.
73 *Herold*, Oct. 10, 1867.   74 *Woechentlich Westliche Post*, May 8, 1867.
75 *Wächter am Erie*, Sept. 21, 1867.
76 Ibid., Nov. 7, 1867, Sept. 5, 1868; *Westliche Post*, Aug. 4, 1865, Jan. 19, 1866, June 9, Sept. 18, 1868; *St. Charles Demokrat*, Oct. 22, 1868; *Herold*, May 12, 1869.

their own articles, Radicals used "Negro" (*Neger*) and sometimes "colored man" (*Farbiger*), "black man" (*Schwarzer*), or their female equivalents. Only Democratic "demagogues," according to the *Westliche Post*, stooped to racism, and those immigrants who succumbed to it would "demonstrate their own pitiful deficiency."[77] Racism was antithetical to principle. German Americans were superior, Radicals said during the late 1860s, insofar as they spurned the former and professed the latter.

The same German-language Radical newspapers that criticized racism at length sometimes printed dismissive characterizations of African Americans. Readers must have been left wondering whether the principle of male equality was such an abstraction as to bear no relation to the real freedmen. Editors usually depicted African Americans as nascent free laborers or victims of violence in the far-off South.[78] Even in Missouri, Radicals bypassed evidence that blacks were mobilizing against great odds within their own state. From 1865 to 1868, neither the *Westliche Post* nor the *St. Charles Demokrat* ran a lead editorial on racial violence in Missouri. The editors probably did not want to tar their state as dangerous and backward, but that would not explain why they also overlooked inspiring news that black Missourians were organizing politically, building schools and churches, and striving for economic independence.[79] When the black politician Charles H. Tandy spoke in St. Charles, the *Demokrat* praised him as articulate and well educated, but the newspaper lingered over Tandy's point that African Americans must cultivate their "spirits" and "characters" to make themselves "worthy" of citizenship.[80] Such condescension highlighted black shortcomings.

How could the leaders of German-American Radicalism both disparage real African Americans and ardently disavow racism? Uplift provides part of the answer. Radicals believed that the freed people could better themselves. But principle was equally important, even to individual Radicals. As a secular faith, principle transcended the contingencies of real life. Individual Radical spokesmen may have seen themselves as principled precisely because they resolutely defended black men's right to vote *despite* what they

---

77 *Woechentlich Westliche Post*, Oct. 30, 1867. For a similar rejection of Democratic race politics, see *St. Charles Demokrat*, Oct. 22, 1868.
78 See for example *St. Charles Demokrat*, Feb. 7, 1867.
79 For evidence this represented a significant oversight, see Parrish, *Missouri under Radical Rule*, 106–10; Fellman, "Emancipation in Missouri," *Missouri Historical Review* 83 (1988): 36–56; John S. Hughs, "Lafayette County in the Aftermath of Slavery, 1861–1870," *Missouri Historical Review* 75 (1980): 51–63; Astor, *Rebels on the Border*, 146–67; Gary R. Kremer, *James Milton Turner: The Public Life of a Post-Civil War Black Leader* (Columbia: University of Missouri Press, 1991), 17–39.
80 *St. Charles Demokrat*, Oct. 3, 1867. Although the *Demokrat* spelled his name "Tendy," the speaker was probably St. Louis's C. H. Tandy. Parrish, *Missouri under Radical Rule*, 303.

considered proof of African-American inferiority. They gave the impression that although deep down they believed that black Americans were poorly prepared for citizenship, German immigrants were generous and self-controlled enough to stifle these feelings. Principle could have been especially meaningful to men who struggled to suppress their own personal prejudices. It demanded a greater emotional sacrifice. There is evidence that key figures felt all the more virtuous in supporting suffrage because they thought so little of African Americans. Principle bridged the space between ideal and reality. German–American Radicals were men of firm principles, but for some of them, those principles coexisted with reservations about the freed people.

Carl Schurz had always severed the principle of equality from his perceptions of African Americans. He differed from his native-born friends in the abolitionist movement in this respect. One of them, Gerrit Smith, had wrestled with his own prejudice and embarked on a deeply spiritual journey to identify more closely with black men. Most other Anglo-American abolitionists substituted sympathy for empathy, but aligning politics with personal emotions was still important to them.[81] Schurz, in contrast, had eschewed "philanthropic" motives for emancipation and interacted with few African Americans before the war.[82] In 1860, he wrote with derision of a "darkey" employed at a hotel in Toledo, Ohio.[83] As he traveled the South in 1865, he had begun to admire the work ethic of African Americans, but he was quite taken aback to meet a black man to whom he felt a real connection. In New Orleans, Schurz came upon an "old gentleman," who was "dressed with the simple elegance of the cosmopolitan person of taste, and was so fluent and versatile in conversation that [Schurz] was forced to recognize in him a man of more than ordinary talent and varied experience." The Radical politician wrote to Margarethe of how surprised he was to learn that this man was in fact one of Louisiana's many "free colored" citizens: "There is no country of the world, save this, in which he would not be received as a gentleman of the upper class."[84] Behind Schurz's indignation lurked the belief that light-skinned *gens de couleur* should not be lumped together with other people of African ancestry. He found the encounter remarkable because his regard for this individual contrasted with

81 Stauffer, *Black Hearts of Men.*
82 Schurz to Gottfried Kinkel, Jan. 23, 1855, in *Speeches, Correspondence and Political Papers of Carl Schurz*, ed. Bancroft, 1: 16.
83 Schurz to Margarethe Schurz, Jan. 29, 1860, in *Intimate Letters*, ed. and trans. Schafer, 240.
84 Schurz to Margarethe Schurz, Sept. 2, 1865, in *Intimate Letters*, ed. and trans. Schafer, 351. For similar descriptions of distinguished African Americans, see *Westliche Post*, Jan. 20 and 21, 1866; *Woechentlich Westliche Post*, July 31, 1867.

his feelings about the freedmen as a group. Black men of education, poise, wealth, and standing confirmed that race did not render African Americans inherently incapable, justifying a liberalism grounded in the equality of men. In casting them as exceptions, however, German Radicals proved their low opinion of the African-American community as a whole.

Schurz's remove from African Americans was typical of the German Radicals in Ohio, Missouri, and Wisconsin. Willich had appeared alongside black abolitionist Peter H. Clark at antislavery events in antebellum Cincinnati, and Arnold Krekel must have worked with black educators on the board of Missouri's Lincoln Institute after the war.[85] Of the editors active during Reconstruction, however, only Domschke engaged forthrightly with local blacks instead of trafficking in generalities and the exceptions that reinforced them.[86] Most of the time Radicals held black men at arm's length.

The strange relationship between race and principle in the thinking of well-known German-American Radicals helps explain why ordinary immigrant Republicans could find black suffrage admirable in the abstract but misguided in practice. The correspondence of a German-speaking Union corporal from Illinois, Henry A. Kircher, provides some indication of what the public made of Radical politics. Kircher, who had crossed the Mississippi to Missouri in 1861 to volunteer for an overwhelmingly German regiment, wrote to his father in 1863 to explain why he would not like to fight next to black soldiers.[87] He was not disposed either to be a slave driver, or to have his "blood" "mix" with that of African Americans. "I am still not far enough advanced in civilization," he confessed, "that I don't make a difference between white and black anymore."[88] The last comment must have owed something to Kircher's exposure to German Radicals. He was aware that such men would have described his racial views as backward. Instead of entirely discounting the Radical position, however, Kircher gently mocked it. He painted Radicals as willfully blind to things that seemed commonsensical to him. The politics of principle encouraged doubts about how ideals related to reality. The disjuncture between Kircher's loyalty to Radical leaders and his private prejudice can hardly have been unusual.[89]

---

85 Honeck, *We Are the Revolutionists*, 90–98.   86 *Herold*, July 8, 1865.

87 Kircher also spent a few months in an Illinois regiment. Henry A. Kircher, *A German in the Yankee Fatherland: The Civil War Letters of Henry A. Kircher*, ed. Earl J. Hess (Kent, OH: Kent State University Press, 1983), 6–7.

88 Henry A. Kircher to His Father, April 19, 1863, box 3, Engelmann-Kircher Family Papers, Abraham Lincoln Presidential Library and Museum, Springfield, Illinois. My translation is more literal than the published one. Kircher, *A German in the Yankee Fatherland*, ed. Hess, 92.

89 Ibid., 52, 76.

He was just the sort of German-American Republican who might applaud the principle of race-neutral citizenship when it was incorporated into a larger plan for Reconstruction and yet vote against suffrage when it showed up on the ballot.

Some Radical leaders knew that the word "principle" disconnected universal manhood suffrage from the *practice* of black voting and used that fact to reach men like Kircher. Before Ohio's 1867 referendum, Senator Benjamin Wade had informed voters that the proposed constitutional amendment would be "of no practical significance" given the state's small black population. Thieme at the *Wächter am Erie* agreed, stating that the question was, rather, of "great significance in principle."[90] The implicit message to Cleveland Germans was that they could safely vote for this "thing of honor" because it would not have any substantive effect.[91] Some wavering readers of the *Wächter* must have taken Thieme's advice, voting for black suffrage because they believed it was the right thing to do and because they felt that amending Ohio's constitution would change very little. Yet critics of the amendment surely noticed that by dividing principle from practice, Wade and Thieme essentially admitted that the public had reason to object to black men exercising political power. Radicalism emerged as an ideology of citizenship that was consistent, but nonetheless accommodated harmful racial stereotypes. Since the original argument came from Wade, a Massachusetts-born Radical, German immigrants clearly were not alone.

Usually, Radical leaders could speak in grand terms that did not let on that principle masked tensions within their worldview. This was especially true when national Reconstruction, not state law, was at stake. Given violence in the South, most Northerners argued that African-American citizenship would safeguard the nation and serve economic liberalism. Black suffrage was subsumed in a vast program for the whole country. Schurz, always a great rhetorician, told white Americans to accept black suffrage not for the sake of African Americans, but out of idealism. At the Southern Loyalist Convention in 1866, he said that "this Republic will have achieved true glory and secured lasting peace only when she metes out impartial justice to all her children."[92] In this case, Schurz used paternal imagery, not the fraternal language of male equality, but principle worked as before. White voters

90 *Wächter am Erie*, Sept. 12, 1867. See also a similar comment by Weydemeyer on Missouri. *Westliche Post*, Sept. 1, 1865.
91 Ibid., Oct. 5, 1867.
92 Schurz, "Logical Results of the War," Sept. 8, 1866, in *Speeches, Correspondence and Political Papers of Carl Schurz*, ed. Bancroft, 1: 403–04.

did not need to look too far into African-American political participation. The liberal nationalist principle of black suffrage was what mattered.

In the end, misgivings about the freed people hung over Radical politics. German immigrants demonstrated that white Americans could simultaneously rebuke explicit racism and feel superior to African Americans. But the politics of principle was not a sham. Neither insincere nor uncommitted, German-American Radicals were caught up in immigrants' understanding of themselves and their assumptions about world history. Why not speak to the idealism of well-meaning whites? This strategy would make the Fifteenth Amendment possible, but it was not a particularly solid foundation for African-American political power.

ENACTING PRINCIPLE, 1868–1869

As the end of the decade neared, Carl Schurz sensed that a constitutional amendment prohibiting racial discrimination in the administration of the franchise might be within reach. Aiming to subdue the white South, Congress had passed the Reconstruction Act of 1867 prescribing that former Confederate states enfranchise African-American men before reassuming their regular status within the Union. Johnson's veto only deepened Republicans' determination. German-American Republicans, as new citizens with a transnational perspective, allied with native-born Radicals. Both groups held that the United States must outlaw racial qualifications for voting altogether if it was to live up to its liberal values. Schurz's career charts German Radicalism's final rise during the years before the Fifteenth Amendment. The former general would see German Radicalism crest during 1869 and into 1870, leaving its mark – abstract and gendered – on the U.S. Constitution.

Schurz's power continued to derive from his role as an envoy between the German-language public sphere and English-speaking politicians. He conducted immigrants into the party, and in return, he expected his native-born colleagues to hear German Americans out. After 1867, when Schurz bought a share of the *Westliche Post* and moved to St. Louis, he became even more influential. Editing the *Post* with Preetorius suited his political ambitions perfectly, as his subsequent climb in the Republican Party bore out. In 1868, English-speaking Republicans honored Schurz by making him the temporary chair at their national convention in Chicago. On the second day of the meeting, Schurz moved to endorse the principles of the Declaration of Independence and offer mercy to former Confederates in proportion to their loyalty. The uncontroversial resolutions won the convention's unanimous approval. (In contrast, Friedrich Hassaurek's appearance in Chicago ended in humiliation. Hecklers cut his dull speech short.)[93] That year, neither the Republican Party nor its presidential nominee, Ulysses S. Grant, formally backed a suffrage amendment. Even in 1868, not all Republicans appreciated that principle could pay.

Regardless of the party's platform, the presidential election proved that Radicalism was ascendant among German Republican leaders. Signing on to black suffrage at this point were J. B. Stallo, Gustav Körner, Friedrich Hecker, and the editors of the *Illinois Staatszeitung* and the *New Yorker Abendpost*.[94] Around the country, German-American voters greeted Republican campaigners no less enthusiastically than they had in past years. Traveling to stump for Grant, Schurz wrote, "Even in '60 the spirit was not better."[95] Diverse audiences – from "the critical New York Germans" who attended a speech at Cooper Union, to the residents of rural Missouri, where Schurz found himself spending the night in a cart – hailed him.[96] The liberal nationalist energy of 1848 and the Civil War was not yet spent.

Polling results from Ohio and Missouri – although not Wisconsin – showed that Schurz was right that Republicans had held onto their German-American support. All of Cincinnati's five most heavily German wards backed Grant slightly more strongly than they had Lincoln in 1860, and four gave Grant wider margins of victory than he enjoyed in the city as a whole. (He lost in the fifth.)[97] In Cleveland, Grant won majorities in four of the five German wards. "It does the *Deutschtum* in Cleveland particular credit," Thieme commented in the *Wächter am Erie*, "that in this election, by a very large majority, it stood on the side of right, honesty, justice, and Grant."[98] Republican editors tended to exaggerate, but they had not lost votes since 1860. Missourians who had taken the ironclad oath also threw their state behind the Republican candidate, and four of St. Louis's five most heavily German wards were keener to elect Grant than they had been to send Lincoln to the White House in 1860.[99] The *Westliche Post* interpreted this as proof of Radical hegemony, asserting that the votes of St. Louis Germans had seen to it that "all citizens of this great land may compete with each other on the path of progress."[100] There was less to crow about in Wisconsin.

93 *Cincinnati Commercial*, May 22 and 23, 1868; *Cincinnati Volksfreund*, May 22 and 23, 1868.
94 *Westliche Post*, Sept. 5, 1865; Freitag, *Friedrich Hecker*, 305; Koerner, *Memoirs*, 2: 458, 481–82; Wittke, *German-Language Press*, 155; *Westliche Post*, March 10, 1866.
95 Schurz to Emil Preetorius, Sept. 9, 1868, reel 3, fr. 524, Schurz Papers, LOC.
96 Schurz to Margarethe Schurz, Sept. 7, 1868, in *Intimate Letters*, ed. and trans. Schafer, 446; Schurz to Emil Preetorius, Sept. 30, 1868, reel 3, fr. 525, Schurz Papers, LOC.
97 Appendix, Table 2.   98 *Wächter am Erie*, Nov. 4, 1868.
99 Appendix, Table 1.   100 *Westliche Post,* Nov. 4, 1868.

Although Grant won the state, Milwaukee's German wards cast even fewer votes for him than they had for Lincoln.[101] But Wisconsin had never been a German Republican stronghold. Overall, German Americans who were already Republicans had stood by their Radical leaders. Black suffrage, rather than put off the immigrants, had kept them in the Republican Party.

If the politics of principle had helped elect Republican candidates, it was not enough to induce all German Republicans to vote directly to enfranchise black men. Schurz had come to see that many immigrants welcomed speeches deploring racial bias and then cast ballots against African-American suffrage. Before the 1868 election, he had braced himself to "fight through the negro suffrage matter. . . . There are still many prejudices to overcome among the Germans."[102] Most German immigrants in Schurz's adopted state of Missouri respected him, but they still separated the principle of black suffrage from its practice. Although German-born state legislators had assisted in placing the measure on the ballot, their *Landsmänner* actually seem to have been less likely than other Missouri Republicans to support it. With 43 percent of the vote, African-American suffrage was defeated in 1868.[103] St. Louis's first and second wards gave about 35 and 22 percent of their votes (respectively) to suffrage, but about 72 and 66 percent to Grant.[104]

The immigrant Radicalism that Schurz and other politicians touted on the campaign trail was not strong enough to pass state referenda, but it contributed to the environment in which congressional Republicans proposed the Fifteenth Amendment after Grant's election. Immigrant men embodied the possibilities of liberal nationalism. Speaking as newcomers who understood the dangers of unrepresentative government, German-American Radicals explained that the freedmen must, like themselves, become voting citizens. No other group was so well positioned to argue that race and ethnicity were equally illegitimate grounds for discrimination.

Other Republicans, after chasing the German vote in the Midwest, were beginning to grasp how the immigrant story could be useful. They were assimilating the arguments and sentiments contained in Schurz's "True Americanism" speech, the commemorations of the Camp Jackson affair, and the *Report on the Condition of the South*. Frederick Douglass, for example,

---

101 Appendix, Table 4.
102 Schurz to Margarethe Schurz, May 11, 1868, in *Intimate Letters*, ed. and trans. Schafer, 435.
103 Dwight, "Black Suffrage in Missouri," 52–53, 56.
104 Appendix, Table 3; Dwight, "Black Suffrage in Missouri," 97–100; Office of the Secretary of State, Elections Division, Election Returns, box 12, folder 3, MSA; *Westliche Post*, Nov. 5, 1868; *St. Charles Demokrat*, Nov. 19, 1868.

discussed African Americans and Chinese immigrants alongside the people arriving from Europe when he spoke of "our composite nationality." Defending new immigrants in 1869, he said, "We shall mould [sic] them all, each after his kind, into Americans; Indian and Celt, negro and Saxon, Latin and Teuton, Mongolian and Caucasian, Jew and gentile, all shall here bow to the same law, speak the same language, support the same government, enjoy the same liberty, vibrate with the same national enthusiasm, and seek the same national ends."[105] Although German Republicans did not think that a common language was a prerequisite for national communion, Douglass's vision was largely theirs: a liberal nation composed of different peoples. German immigrants had shown Republicans that equal citizenship was workable without cultural uniformity. Douglass blurred the accepted line between culture and biology to include race in that model. German immigrants had helped create a Republican Party that could write the Fifteenth Amendment.

In patterning African-American citizenship after the immigrant experience, Republicans decided to still deny about one-half of Americans the right to vote. Unswayed by the argument for women's suffrage, the immigrants persisted in thinking that female voting conflicted with inclusive male citizenship. Susan B. Anthony had once hoped that Schurz would be an ally to women's suffragists. In 1865, she invited him to give a speech on the benefits of recognizing equal citizenship regardless of "race or color, sect or sex." There is no sign that Schurz even replied to her letter. He was a lifelong opponent of women's equality.[106] With few exceptions, prominent German Americans in Ohio, Missouri, and Wisconsin found the "agitation for women's rights" more or less "distasteful." The Democratic *Cincinnati Volksfreund* wrote that it "originated with Puritans and temperance advocates and with females [*Weibern*] of every sort from Massachusetts and Maine who are angry that men cannot bear children."[107] Mathilde Anneke pleaded

---

105 Frederick Douglass, "Our Composite Nationality," Dec. 7, 1869, in *The Frederick Douglass Papers, Series One: Speeches, Debates, and Interviews*, ed. John W. Blassingame and John R. McKivigan, 5 vols. (New Haven, CT: Yale University Press, 1991), 4: 259. See also the comments of Massachusetts Congressman George S. Boutwell quoted in Samito, *Becoming American under Fire*, 218–19.

106 Susan B. Anthony to Schurz, Dec. 30, 1865, reel 3, fr. 275–77, Schurz Papers, LOC; Trefousse, *Carl Schurz*, 264.

107 *Cincinnati Volksfreund*, Feb. 20, 1869. See also *Columbus Westbote*, Feb. 25, 1869; *St. Charles Demokrat*, Feb. 11 and 18, April 22, 1869, March 3, May 12, 1870; *Westliche Post Wochen-Blatt*, Feb. 10 and 17, Nov. 3, Dec. 1, 1869, May 4, June 13, 1870; *Anzeiger des Westens*, May 6, July 1, 1869. Showing the importance of Missouri developments, several lengthy Ohio and Wisconsin stories referred specifically to the state. *Columbus Westbote*, March 4, 1869; *Cincinnati Volksfreund*, April 15, 1869; *Herold Wöchentliche Ausgabe*, Feb. 26, 1869. For an important study of the women's suffrage movement during Reconstruction, see Faye E. Dudden, *Fighting Chance: The Struggle over Woman Suffrage and Black Suffrage in Reconstruction America* (New York: Oxford University Press, 2011).

with Anglo-Americans not to hitch women's suffrage to temperance, a tactic she labeled "suicidal," but she had limited success, and the strain between the newcomers and the feminists did not abate.[108] Anneke finally joined Anthony and Elizabeth Cady Stanton in opposing the ratification of the Fifteenth Amendment unless it outlawed gender discrimination.[109] The Fifteenth Amendment was the culmination of the Forty-Eighters' liberal nationalism, and it did not include women's right to vote.

Although German-American Radicals had no part in the framing of the Fifteenth Amendment (there were no German-born congressmen at the time[110]), the amendment used their abstract language, which would make its implementation difficult. Instead of granting black men the franchise, it authorized the federal government to intervene if a state denied or abridged the right of citizens to vote because of "race, color, or previous condition of servitude." This wording took account of the constitutional precedent of allowing states to determine voter qualifications. Washington would step in only when states acted unconstitutionally.[111] Prohibiting discrimination – instead of aiding African Americans directly – was also congruent with the German Republican politics of principle. Always most troubled by the blight of legal prejudice, German Republicans were happy to leave the practical details of administration to others. Congress would later follow up with legislation, but the political climate would change markedly before the laws came before the courts. German Republicans were satisfied that the amendment kept the federal government at a distance from the business of voting, and within a few years, they would be challenging the enforcement of the most impressive legal achievement of Reconstruction.[112]

Yet in 1869, German-American Radicals still sounded exuberant. When the Missouri legislature chose Schurz to represent the state in the Senate, he saw it as a vindication of the politics of principle. The senator-elect used his acceptance speech to condemn discrimination and link citizenship rights for immigrants and black men once more. "You have demonstrated before the world," he told an audience in Jefferson City, "that the people of Missouri have overcome the prejudice and narrow-hearted perspective that so easily tarnish the judgment of politicians, and that Missouri opens the

---

108 Undated draft [c. 1869–1872], in *Mathilde Franziska Anneke*, ed. Wagner, 339.

109 DuBois, *Feminism and Suffrage*, 162–202; Mathilde to Fritz, June 1869, in *Mathilde Franziska Anneke*, ed. Wagner, 351.

110 Gustavus A. Finkelnburg, a Republican from St. Louis, began his term in the House the month after the amendment passed Congress. United States Congress, *Biographical Directory of the United States Congress, 1774–2005* (Washington, DC: U.S. Government Printing Office, 2005), 178–82, 1052.

111 Benedict, "Preserving the Constitution"; Maltz, *Civil Rights, the Constitution, and Congress*.

112 *Westliche Post Wochen-Blatt*, July 28, 1869; *St. Charles Demokrat*, July 15, 1869.

gates wide for all those who have the courage, the purpose and the ability to contribute to the completion of the great tasks of this land." Clarifying that he was not just referring to immigrants, he said that "the worker of every race and color [should] possess political rights."[113] Schurz had practiced a politics that took naturalized male immigrants to be both archetypal and normative new citizens. When he likened race and ethnicity, he offered up full citizenship to black men. Meanwhile, he had learned that immigrants found universal manhood suffrage more inspiring when it was kept apart from the quotidian reality of race in the United States. German–American Radicals had defined principle, elevated and abstract, so that it had very little to do with African Americans. Ushered into office by the liberal nationalism of the 1860s, Schurz arrived in Washington just as Congress was about to pass the Fifteenth Amendment.[114]

---

113 *Woechentlich Westliche Post*, Jan. 27, 1869.
114 Schurz to Margarethe Schurz, Jan. 24, 1869, in *Intimate Letters*, ed. and trans. Schafer, 467.

5

Wendepunkt: *The Franco-Prussian War,*
1870–1871

Sweltering temperatures could not stop local Germans from packing into the Sandusky courthouse to demonstrate their solidarity with Prussia and its allies in August 1870. Immigrants in the Ohio town were determined that they "not lag behind any city in the republic" in showing their "loyalty and devotion to the threatened – but therefore all the more ardently loved – Fatherland."[1] Although France had gone on the offensive in July following a diplomatic slight, Prussian Prime Minister Otto von Bismarck actually sought just such an opportunity to consolidate his kingdom's rising power. Within a few months, the Germans would capture Louis Napoleon III, besiege Paris, and found an empire.[2] Excited by the prospect of the new Reich, Sandusky Germans had planned a ceremony of stirring music and speeches, inviting guests from as far away as Detroit and Cleveland. August Thieme, a veteran of the unsuccessful campaign for German unification in 1848 and the editor of Cleveland's Radical *Wächter am Erie*, was one of the visitors who heralded the momentous news from Europe. Unable to hold back his enthusiasm, he proclaimed, "The patriotic fervor in Sandusky is a match for the hundred-degree heat."[3]

The outpouring of German-American pride during the Franco-Prussian War of 1870 and 1871 would mark what the *Cincinnati Volksfreund* called "the turning point [*Wendepunkt*] in the political and social course of the German element in the United States."[4] A wave of euphoria swept through German America. From small-town courthouses to urban parks in Cincinnati, St. Louis, and Milwaukee, tens of thousands of immigrants attended

---

1 *Wächter am Erie*, Aug. 5, 1870.
2 Geoffrey Wawro, *The Franco-Prussian War: The German Conquest of France in 1870–1871* (Cambridge: Cambridge University Press, 2003), 16–40.
3 *Wächter am Erie*, Aug. 5, 1870.   4 *Cincinnati Volksfreund*, April 14, 1871.

"sympathy" meetings as the fighting began.[5] They took to the streets again after September 2, when the German alliance scored a quick victory over the French at Sedan, and they followed each battle until France finally capitulated and Germany formally unified in 1871. Armed conflict focused the German-language public sphere on Prussia's unification of Germany. The process of unification was an incremental one that had edged into German-American news columns during the 1860s, but it only now dominated editorials, peppered private correspondence, and precipitated mass demonstrations. Like the editor of the *Volksfreund*, historians have noticed that the Franco-Prussian War and German unification moved German Americans, but they have not analyzed the impact on Reconstruction.[6] These events were bound, however, to modify how German immigrants approached American citizenship. During the 1860s, the thwarted liberalism of 1848 had guided German-American politics. When Forty-Eighters such as Thieme supported black suffrage, they had argued that black men could join the national community and that governments must guarantee equal male citizenship. In 1870, the war exposed German Americans to a new German nationalism. It came with an alternative definition of the *Volk* and a different role for the state.

The first change to erode the foundations of German-American Radicalism was in immigrants' descriptions of the German *Volk*. The willingness of German-American Republicans to recognize black men as full citizens had grown out of a largely cultural understanding of the German *Volk*. In 1848, the revolutionaries had imagined the *Volk* as a cultural and political

---

5 America's largest German-language newspaper claimed from New York that it would be impossible to report all the sympathy meetings. *Wochenblatt der New-Yorker Staats-Zeitung*, July 23, 1870. There were elaborately planned gatherings in cities from New Orleans to Boston, spontaneous neighborhood celebrations, and smaller events in towns such as Toledo and Dayton in Ohio, Jefferson City, La Grange, and St. Joseph in Missouri, and Wausau in Wisconsin. *Westliche Post*, Aug. 1, 2, 8, and 9, Oct. 19, 1870; *Cincinnati Commercial*, July 20, 1870; *Seebote Wöchentliche Ausgabe*, Aug. 22, 1870; *Banner und Volksfreund*, Aug. 19 and 28, 1870. See also Heike Bungert, "Der Deutsch-Französische Krieg im Spiegel der Wohltätigkeitsbazare und Feiern deutscher und französischer Migranten in den USA, 1870/71," in *Deutschland – Frankreich – Nordamerika: Transfers, Imaginationen, Beziehungen*, ed. Chantal Metzger and Hartmut Kaelble (Stuttgart: Franz Steiner Verlag, 2006), 152–70.

6 The *Volksfreund*'s "tuning point" hinged on increased German-American self-confidence and greater Anglo-American recognition. My argument is more ambitious. On the Forty-Eighters and unification, see Wittke, *Refugees of Revolution*, 355; Levine, *Spirit of 1848*, 264–65; Gazley, *American Opinion of German Unification*, 500. Two historians have identified the 1870s as a period when German Americans cast off American values. They provided unsystematic investigations of German-American opinion and failed to recognize the ways in which the United States itself was changing after the Civil War. Guido Dobbert, "German-Americans between New and Old Fatherland, 1870–1914," *American Quarterly* 19 (1967): 669; Dobbert, "The Disintegration of an Immigrant Community: The Cincinnati Germans, 1870–1920" (PhD diss., University of Chicago, 1965), 4; John H. Hawgood, *The Tragedy of German-America: The Germans in the United States of America during the Nineteenth Century – And After* (New York: G. P. Putnam's Sons, 1940), 279.

entity that could evolve and incorporate new groups as long as the nation-state was true to liberal ideals. In the United States, the German *Volk* had become a purely cultural group, an ethnicity, within a plural nation. Both of these examples had inspired – however problematically – Radicals to work to enfranchise African-American men. The Franco-Prussian War gave rise to a more *essentialist* notion of *Volk*. Its members were believed to share more innate, perhaps biological, characteristics. The boundaries of the newly imagined *Volk* were less permeable. Any change in its make-up would happen only very slowly. German-American editors and politicians repeated that the German *Volk* was naturally suited to self-rule and destined for greatness, while the degraded French were not. These propositions called into question the wisdom of expecting that any man could become a worthy citizen.

The European war altered how the immigrants thought about American citizenship in a second way. It made them rethink the political institutions that gave it meaning. Most of the immigrants, having learned to associate the formation and preservation of nation-states with an expansion of individual rights, assumed that the German Empire would enact the liberal nationalism of 1848 and the Civil War. If the nation-state was the bastion of citizenship rights, then surely a unified Germany would develop liberal institutions. Yet in 1870, most Germans in North America, like most Germans in Europe, found themselves adjusting to accommodate Bismarck. Critics of the Prussian prime minister, mostly socialists, were sidelined on both continents. The task of defending Bismarck demanded greater concessions of German Americans after Napoleon III was taken prisoner. The immigrants had to justify supporting a nascent German empire waging war on a French republic. Unable to claim that Germany was exemplary in its regard for citizenship, they turned to less liberal measures of a government's merit, including the success of its educational system, the efficiency of its military, and the honesty of its bureaucrats. Although some German Americans would later offer scathing critiques of the Reich, for the duration of the war against the despised French, immigrants who were optimistic about Germany's future took the same less-than-liberal course followed by the nationalists in Europe who supported Bismarck.[7]

With the *Wendepunkt* of 1870, then, German Americans did not perform an ideological about-face. They did profoundly reorient ethnicity and

---

7 Hans Trefousse concluded that the immigrant community possessed "a healthy skepticism about conditions in the new Reich." His own evidence showed, however, that criticism of Bismarck's empire developed slowly as the memory of the war receded. Trefousse, "The German-American Immigrants and the Newly Founded Reich," in *America and the Germans*, ed. Trommler and McVeigh, 1: 173.

politics in the public sphere. Immigrants would shift their emphasis and reorder their priorities when it came to matters that had proven critical to citizenship law during the 1860s: the *Volk* and the state. This chapter shows how deeply the Franco-Prussian War affected German–American public life and describes how this communal experience prepared German immigrants to disconnect nationalism from liberalism and retreat from Republican Reconstruction.

TO PRUSSIA'S SIDE

The Franco-Prussian War began just as German-born Republicans and Democrats in the United States were hoping to put the Civil War behind them and find common ground. Some Democrats, having witnessed the Republicans use the cause of black suffrage to retain German votes, decided to bow to the inevitability of the Fifteenth Amendment. Concluding that race-baiting was not an effective campaign tactic, notable German-speaking Democrats in Wisconsin and Ohio were leaders in their party's "New Departure." Peter V. Deuster, the astute Democratic politician who edited the *Milwaukee Seebote*, was one. On June 2, 1869, he argued that "the Democracy must unreservedly accept Negro suffrage – indeed universal suffrage in the broadest sense of the word – if it wants to win over the masses." Deuster was, he added, thinking especially of the German immigrant masses.[8] A week later, the *Seebote* ran a blueprint for Democratic reform that included "universal suffrage for all citizens of the United States."[9] While there were German–American Democrats who were skeptical, Deuster could report that most of his colleagues concurred that his platform gave "clear expression to the views of German Democrats in the Northwest."[10] Even in St. Louis, where Carl Dänzer editorialized against Deuster's plan, the *Westliche Post* observed that the Democracy was "beginning to cast off the state sovereignty doctrine and the anti-nigger doctrine like a snake its skin."[11] Democrats wanted to move beyond the racial politics of the 1860s.

German–American Republicans were also tiring of Reconstruction. "With the Fifteenth Amendment on its way to ratification," the *St. Charles*

---

8 *Seebote Wöchentliche Ausgabe*, June 2, 1869.   9 Ibid., June 9, 1869.
10 Ibid., Aug. 4, 1869. See also Aug. 11, 1869; *Cincinnati Volksfreund*, Aug. 19 and 20, 1869; *Watertown Weltbürger*, July 3, 1869.
11 *Westliche Post Wochen-Blatt*, July 28, 1869. On Dänzer, see *Seebote Wöchentliche Ausgabe*, Nov. 5, 1868.

Demokrat wrote in the summer of 1869, "the Republican Party is entering a new phase. . . . The heroic age of Republicanism is over."[12] August Thieme no longer devoted much space in the *Wächter* to racial justice, and even Carl Schurz signaled that black suffrage was not the priority for him that it had once been. The new senator voted for only one of the five acts that Congress passed to implement the Fifteenth Amendment. In May 1870, he explained that he backed the first "force bill" because he "and thousands of children from [his] native land" had come to the United States to "enjoy the blessings of liberty and self-government" and African Americans deserved similar opportunities. In the same speech, Schurz made it quite clear that his belief in limited government might override his commitment to African-American rights in the future.[13] As the senator sidled away from Radical Reconstruction, his newspaper in St. Louis pondered which new issues would replace "those that the Republican Party has finally helped to victory."[14]

Many of the subjects that did dominate editorials during 1869 found German-American Democrats and Republicans in accord, even before the European war began. German politicians in both parties united in denunciation of protective tariffs and inflationary monetary policies, renewing their commitment to laissez-faire. Socialists, as we shall see, were deserting mainstream politics. Their departure left Democratic and Republican editors to count free trade and "hard money" among their most urgent concerns.[15] The reorganization of the women's suffrage movement, which coincided with a burst of temperance activity, also rankled immigrants during 1869. In opposing "Temperenzlerei," which they took to be an ethnocultural attack, German Republicans had more in common with German-born Democrats than their Yankee colleagues.[16] German immigrants agreed once more as the Grant administration began to earn a reputation for nepotism and malfeasance. They anticipated that they would play a special role in preventing political corruption in the United States. Schurz used his

12 *St. Charles Demokrat*, July 15, 1869.
13 Schurz, "The Enforcement of the Fifteenth Amendment," May 19, 1870, in *Speeches, Correspondence and Political Papers of Carl Schurz*, ed. Bancroft, 1: 484–509.
14 *Westliche Post Wochen-Blatt*, July 28, 1869.
15 On the German-American consensus on free trade and hard money, see *Wächter am Erie*, May 4, 1870; *Mississippi Blätter*, May 8, 1870. See also *Wochenblatt der New-Yorker Staats-Zeitung*, Oct. 28, 1869, June 10, 1871. In Ohio, German Democrats reluctantly accepted an inflationary plank in the state platform. *Cincinnati Volksfreund*, June 7, 1871. On Schurz and free trade, see J. B. Stallo to Schurz, May 10, 1869; Francis Lieber to Schurz, Dec. 11 and 30, 1869, reel 4, fr. 16–19, 225–26, 276–77, Schurz Papers, LOC.
16 See for example *Cincinnati Volksfreund*, April 13, July 27, Aug. 3 and 4, 1869; *Westliche Post*, June 15, July 21, Aug. 4, 1869; *Seebote Wöchentliche Ausgabe*, Sept. 1, 1869.

maiden speech in the Senate to advocate civil service reform, a topic he had not emphasized since the 1850s.[17] Many observers could see that German Americans were approaching consensus on economic, ethnocultural, and administrative questions. "How everything changes," the Democratic *Cincinnati Volksfreund* noted as it surveyed the political landscape in 1869.[18] With German-American politics stalled, immigrants stood ready to unite in a nationwide movement with its own consequences for black citizenship, but they needed some impetus.

In 1870, German Americans had known for some years that Europe was changing too. Schurz gave a lecture in the late 1860s to explain Germany's "new era" to Americans. Since the end of the reactionary 1850s, Schurz said, the middle class had expanded, nationalist organizations had revived, and public education had flourished. Many states were allowing Germans to travel, work, and trade more freely. "In the progressive movement of civilization no nation on earth can claim preeminence over the German," he extolled.[19] The senator minimized the compromises that opposition politicians had made along the way. Although he acknowledged the authoritarian bent of Prime Minister Bismarck, he did not detail how self-identified liberals had come to consent to his leadership.[20] In 1862, the Prussian parliament had refused King Wilhelm I legislation to cement his hold on the army. To break the stalemate, the king had dissolved the body and appointed Bismarck prime minister. Bismarck ruled without a legislature until 1866. When Prussia was in the middle of fighting Austria, its rival for dominance in German Europe, the kingdom's liberal nationalists had relented. Most of Bismarck's one-time opponents voted to legitimize the actions he had taken over the previous four years.[21] Other German politicians made similar calculations as Prussia annexed several small German states and drew others into the North German Confederation, the forerunner to the Reich of 1871. Liberals in the North German Reichstag opted, as historian James J.

17 *Congressional Globe*, 42st Cong., 2nd sess., 155–56 (March 19, 1869).
18 *Cincinnati Volksfreund*, Aug. 21, 1869.
19 Schurz, "Lecture on Germany," typescript speech [c. 1867–1869], p. 1, box 1, folder 7, Schurz Papers, WHS. On the substance of these developments, see Sheehan, *German Liberalism*, 79–118; Wolfgang J. Mommsen, *Das Ringen um den nationalen Staat: Die Gründung und der innere Ausbau des Deutschen Reiches unter Otto von Bismarck, 1850 bis 1890* (Berlin: Propyläen Verlag, 1993), 103–20; Shlomo Na'aman, *Der Deutsche Nationalverein: Die politische Konstituierung des deutschen Bürgertums, 1859–1867* (Düsseldorf: Droste, 1987).
20 Schurz, "Lecture on Germany," 23.
21 Sheehan, *German Liberalism*, 123–40; Gordon A. Craig, *The Politics of the Prussian Army, 1640–1945* (New York: Oxford University Press, 1955), 174–79; Otto Pflanze, *Bismarck and the Development of Germany*, vol. 1, *The Period of Unification, 1815–1871* (Princeton: Princeton University Press, 1990), 164–233; Wolfram Siemann, *Gesellschaft im Aufbruch: Deutschland, 1849–1871* (Frankfurt am Main: Suhrkamp Verlag, 1990), 200–31.

Sheehan puts it, to support "the Bismarckian state as the instrument and guardian of national unity."[22]

After the settlement with Bismarck, German "liberalism" diverged from the politics that Schurz had known as a revolutionary in 1848 and practiced as a Radical Republican during the 1860s. Germany's Liberal National Party, which formed in 1867, institutionalized cooperation with the Prussian regime. Even members of the Progressive Party voted for most of Bismarck's initiatives in the Reichstag.[23] With working-class Germans only slowly entering parliamentary politics, members of both of these parties saw German progress chiefly in terms of economic growth, cultural prestige, foreign recognition, and the inclusion of the southern German states in a Prussian-led union. They still planned reforms, arguing that the elected representatives of the *Volk* should exercise more control over government, especially the military, but they hoped that they could achieve their own goals in alliance with the powerful Bismarck. Behind this belief lay an optimism that the united German *Volk* and the inexorable forces of history would overpower Prussian militarism and the prime minister's authoritarianism.[24] The new strategy did not constitute a wholesale betrayal of liberal ideals, but it did change the liberal agenda. As one German historian wrote, liberals moved their focus "from freedom and justice to unity, order, and power."[25] The Franco-Prussian War, when it came, would ratify the trends of the 1860s.

Like his contemporaries who had stayed in Europe, Schurz believed that the North German Confederation was not "the United Germany the German patriots have so long been dreaming of," but he also felt that a Prussian-led state could not long "remain a despotism."[26] An audience with Bismarck in January 1868 increased his personal faith in the direction of German nationalism. Europe's rising statesman honored the former student exile with an invitation to his residence in Berlin. Over Rhenish wine and Cuban cigars, Bismarck solicited Schurz's opinions on German and American politics and offered him a frank assessment of international affairs. The Bismarck of Schurz's memoirs banters genially about republican government. He impresses the German-American politician with his pragmatism despite never conceding any ground. When Schurz discussed the encounter

22 Sheehan, *German Liberalism*, 134.   23 Siemann, *Gesellschaft im Aufbruch*, 250–57.

24 Sheehan, *German Liberalism*, 123–35; Dieter Langewiesche, *Liberalism in Germany*, trans. Christiane Banerji (Princeton: Princeton University Press, 2000), 91–101; Andreas Biefang, *Politisches Bürgerthum in Deutschland, 1857–1868: Nationale Organisationen und Eliten* (Düsseldorf: Droste Verlag, 1994), 298, 357–430.

25 Nipperdey, *Germany from Napoleon to Bismarck*, 714.

26 Schurz, "Lecture on Germany," 34, 40.

with veterans of 1848 living in Berlin, he agreed that although Bismarck was not to be entirely trusted, this was the man to unite Germany.[27] Back in the United States, immigrants reeling from the news of the "Brüderkampf" (fratricidal conflict) between Protestant Prussia and Catholic Austria were more cautious. Most German Americans seemed indifferent to Bismarck's ambitions for Europe until the war between Prussia and France claimed the headlines in July 1870.[28]

"War at Last," announced *The New York Times* on July 16.[29] As one contributor to the *Westliche Post* noted, the new transatlantic telegraph connection made it easier for Americans to "experience such a magnificent spectacle."[30] The cable had already relayed details of the diplomatic power play over the designs of a nephew of Wilhelm I on the Spanish throne. Once the fighting began, it fed the American appetite for news of what the *Cincinnati Volksfreund* called "the greatest event of the century."[31] Ohio Governor Rutherford B. Hayes received a letter from an associate in New York informing him that "the war telegrams make immense excitement here as much as our own war."[32] A German living in St. Louis wrote to a friend in Milwaukee that "the war news is so plentiful and stimulating of late that you can scarcely catch your breath anymore."[33] The burgeoning urban dailies competed to cover the war, printing battle maps, experimenting with bold headlines, and supplementing war correspondence with late-breaking telegraph reports. Murat Halstead, the *Cincinnati Commercial* editor who happened to be vacationing in Europe at the onset of hostilities, rushed to provide firsthand commentary. Snubbed by the French, he traveled with the Prussian army and mailed exclusive dispatches back to Ohio.[34] The editors of minor papers could not provide such exclusive coverage, but the news reached smaller communities all the same. At home in Green

27 Schurz, *Reminiscences*, 3: 265–80. After the initial visit, Bismarck invited Schurz back to dine the following evening.

28 Gazley, *American Opinion of German Unification*, 468–82; Wittke, *German-Language Press*, 165. See for example *Fremont Courier*, April 12, 1866; *Anzeiger des Westens Wochen-Blatt*, April 19, May 10, July 5 and 26, 1866; *St. Charles Demokrat*, July 5, 1866. Among the more optimistic papers were *Columbus Westbote*, June 22, Aug. 2, 1866; *Herold Wöchentliche Ausgabe*, June 15, 1866. Horrified by Prussia's victory was the Catholic *Wahrheitsfreund*, Aug. 1, 1866.

29 *New York Times*, July 16, 1870.   30 *Westliche Post*, Sept. 16, 1870.

31 *Cincinnati Volksfreund*, Aug. 10, 1870.

32 J. A. Joel to Rutherford B. Hayes, Aug. 25, 1870, reel 19, fr. 385, Rutherford B. Hayes Papers (microfilm), Library of Rutherford B. Hayes Presidential Center (hereafter HPC), Fremont, Ohio.

33 B. Fackelheim to John Knell, Aug. 10, 1870, box 2, folder 2, Knell Papers, WHS.

34 Murat Halstead to Mary Banks Halstead, Aug. 28, 1870, box 3, folder 27, Murat Halstead Papers, CHS; *Cincinnati Volksfreund*, Sept. 1, 1870; Donald Walter Curl, "An American Reporter and the Franco-Prussian War," *Journalism Quarterly* 49 (1972): 480–88. On the newspaper coverage, see Katz, *From Appomattox to Montmartre*, 63–66; Mark W. Summers, *The Press Gang: Newspapers and Politics, 1865–1878* (Chapel Hill: University of North Carolina Press, 1994).

Bay, Wisconsin, Senator Timothy O. Howe learned the outcome of one significant battle from a telegram update on a Saturday evening.[35]

From the outset, American politicians were divided over the European war. President Grant remarked to the American minister to France, Elihu B. Washburne, "Every unreconstructed rebel sympathizes with France, without exception, while the loyal element is almost as universally the other way."[36] Republicans were grateful that Prussia, unlike France, had restrained itself from trading with the Confederate states during the Civil War. Democrats were appreciative of the role the French had played in American independence.[37] The religious leanings of the parties compounded the effect of their sectional affiliations and foreign policies.[38] Democratic editors generally acknowledged that Napoleon III had brought the war upon himself, but they nevertheless sympathized with the largely Catholic French people.[39] In letters to Cincinnati's Archbishop John Purcell, an Ohio priest described the war as one between French Catholics and Prussian Protestants. Naturally, he identified with the French.[40] From New York, one of Governor Hayes's correspondents wrote that "the mass hope the Germans will win, but the Irish or Roman Catholics hope France will win."[41] Hayes himself, a Methodist and a Republican, was visiting Milwaukee when he told a relative, "How good the news of Prussia flogging Napoleon."[42]

The German-American community displayed few such partisan and religious divisions. The Democratic and pro-Catholic *Fremont Courier* could report on the August meeting in Sandusky with as much elation as Thieme's Republican and anticlerical *Wächter*.[43] Like their coreligionists in the southern German states of Baden, Württemberg, and Bavaria, German-American Catholics fell into line behind Prussia. They strongly objected to the suggestion that France and Germany were fighting a religious war.[44] Catholic organs and newspapers with a large Catholic readership claimed, "The

35 Timothy O. Howe to Charles Sumner, Sept. 4, 1870, box 2, folder 1, Howe Papers, WHS.
36 Ulysses S. Grant to Elihu B. Washburne, Aug. 22, 1870, in *The Papers of Ulysses S. Grant*, ed. John Y. Simon, 32 vols. (Carbondale: Southern Illinois University Press, 1967–2012), 20: 254–59.
37 *Cincinnati Enquirer*, July 30, 1870; *New York World*, July 16 and 17, 1870.
38 *Cleveland Leader*, July 22, 1870; Gazley, *American Opinion of German Unification*, 320–424. For a breakdown of newspaper positions, see *Cincinnati Enquirer*, July 23, 1870.
39 *Cincinnati Enquirer*, Aug. 17, 1870; *Wochenblatt der New-Yorker Staats-Zeitung*, Aug. 27, 1870.
40 John N. Thisse to John Purcell, Aug. 18, 1870, box 22, Thisse to Purcell, March 5, 1871, box 26, Archbishop John Baptist Purcell Papers, Archives of the Archdiocese of Cincinnati (hereafter AAC).
41 J. A. Joel to Hayes, Aug. 25, 1870, reel 19, fr. 385, Hayes Papers, HPC.
42 Hayes to His Uncle, Aug. 8, 1870, reel 171, fr. 928, Hayes Papers, HPC.
43 *Fremont Courier*, Aug. 11, 1870.
44 *Wahrheitsfreund*, July 27, Sept. 7, 1870; *Fremont Courier*, July 21, Aug. 4 and 18, 1870; *Cincinnati Volksfreund*, Aug. 22, 1870. On the enthusiasm of Catholics in Germany for the new Reich up until mid-1871, see Rebecca Ayako Bennette, *Fighting for the Soul of Germany: The Catholic Struggle for Inclusion after Unification* (Cambridge, MA: Harvard University Press, 2012), 22–26.

Catholic Church is more free and happy in Prussia, than she is in France."[45] Although more restrained in its support of Prussia than his secular colleagues, the editor of the *Wahrheitsfreund* wrote that he was pleased that "the best times of German history have returned, and the same self-sacrificing enthusiasm and devotion to the Fatherland, which flared up with such force in 1813, is now erupting again."[46] After Peter Deuster decided that the French were responsible for the war, his *Seebote* cheered on Prussia as loudly as any paper, noting that Austrian public opinion was with "Germany."[47] Within the Catholic Church, German Americans sparred with their Irish-born brethren. A Missouri lawyer traveling in South Carolina wrote to a colleague that "our Gallic and Tutonic [sic] citizens are disposed to reherse [sic] the war in miniature."[48] Back in St. Louis, a mixed German-Irish parish in St. Louis split when a priest offered an invocation to the Prussian army. To the north in Cincinnati, Archbishop Purcell tried to remain neutral, but some German immigrants found this insufficient. One lodged a formal protest.[49] Although there is no evidence in the documentary record, it is difficult to imagine that the Diocese of Milwaukee escaped such conflict.

German Americans who dissented from the ethnic consensus were relegated to a marginal position within the German-language public sphere. Some socialists, for example, were skeptical of Germany's militarized nationalism. One German-American group in New York stated that "the interests of workers demand a fraternity of workers of all lands for the overthrow of all monarchs," concluding that Prussia was no more worthy of support than France.[50] Adolf Douai, who edited the socialist *New York Arbeiter-Union*, told a Steinway Hall audience that "as a social reformer" he could not consider patriotism the "highest" sentiment. But his hesitance only slightly blunted the symbolism of him taking the stage with Senator Schurz and a host of eminent German Americans at the mass meeting on July 22, 1870. Douai knew the draw of ethnic loyalty, telling German Americans, "There will be no individual who is not filled with a sense of his faithfulness to the old Fatherland."[51] Indeed, socialists stood with Democrats and Republicans, Catholics and Protestants at demonstrations and fundraisers throughout the

---

45 *Fremont Courier*, Aug. 11, 1870; *Wahrheitsfreund*, Sept. 7, 1870; *Cincinnati Volksfreund*, Aug. 2, 1870. For reviews of the Catholic press on the war, see *Cincinnati Volksfreund*, Aug. 26, 1870.
46 *Wahrheitsfreund*, July 27, 1870.   47 *Seebote Wöchentliche Ausgabe*, Aug. 10, 1870.
48 R. K. Charles to John Darby, Aug. 9, 1870, box 4, John Fletcher Darby Papers, MHS.
49 J. N. Adelrich Benziger, sworn statement, Feb. 10, 1871, Purcell Papers, AAC; William B. Faherty, *The St. Louis German Catholics* (St. Louis: Reedy Press, 2004), 57; *Cincinnati Volksfreund*, Aug. 22, 1870.
50 *Wochenblatt der New-Yorker Staats-Zeitung*, Aug. 6, 1870.
51 Ibid., July 23, 1870; Justine Davis Randers-Pehrson, *Adolf Douai, 1819–1888: The Turbulent Life of a German Forty-Eighter in the Homeland and in the United States* (New York: Peter Lang, 2000).

country, and newspapers commented on how few socialists questioned the war.[52] No protests materialized in Cincinnati, St. Louis, or Milwaukee. Former Ohio socialist August Willich, who was visiting Germany after the conclusion of his term as Hamilton County auditor, even offered his services to the Prussian army. The sixty-year-old was declined, but his eagerness to fight was indicative of the mood among working-class Cincinnatians.[53] Anglo-American eyewitnesses reported that the residents of the Over-the-Rhine neighborhood seemed to back Prussia unanimously.[54] In New York, workers apparently cancelled their subscriptions to the *Arbeiter-Union* when Douai became more critical of Prussia.[55] By letting the publication fold, German Americans denied one of the empire's socialist opponents a public voice and upheld the wartime version of German ethnicity.

The mainstream press censured other immigrants who deviated from the German-American line on the war. After a few days of military engagements, a small Wisconsin newspaper predicted that "the petty spite against Prussia that still exists here and there in individuals" would yield to the "general solidarity."[56] Republican and Democratic newspapers rebuked the contrarian Carl Reemelin, a German Cincinnatian who editorialized for the French cause in an English-language newspaper. Friedrich Hassaurek wrote, "Reemelin scratches himself critically behind the ear, distorts his face shrewdly, and finally comes to the conclusion that he, Carl Reemelin, cannot right now 'loftily and enthusiastically neigh and stomp,' but would rather fall to the rear."[57] Even Reemelin, however, saw fit to use a pseudonym. Groups of immigrants appeared more threatening than eccentric individuals. A Milwaukee meeting criticized "those of our German brothers whose position in regard to their [specific German] states makes it impossible for them to fight for the German cause."[58] The only sign that immigrants were acting on such loyalties came when 300 Hanoverians reportedly volunteered for the French army in Chicago. Newspapers condemned the move, once again trying to stifle dissent.[59] Letters between the Annekes indicate that some German Americans chose to keep their true feelings about the war private. Although Fritz partook of the general belief that "through unity

52 *Wochenblatt der New-Yorker Staats-Zeitung*, Aug. 6, 1870.

53 Easton, *Hegel's First American Followers*, 199.   54 *Cincinnati Commercial*, July 16, 1870.

55 *Cincinnati Volksfreund*, Aug. 3, 1870; *Herold Wöchentliche Ausgabe*, June 20, 1870.

56 *La Crosse Nord Stern*, July 22, 1870.

57 *Cincinnati Volksblatt* quoted in *Seebote Wöchentliche Ausgabe*, Aug. 29, 1870; Charles Reemelin, *The Life of Charles Reemelin* (Cincinnati: Weier & Daiker, 1892). Boston's radical Forty-Eighter, Karl Heinzen, was also ostracized for resisting the general enthusiasm. Wittke, *Refugees of Revolution*, 255–56.

58 *Sauk City Pionier*, July 30, 1870.

59 *Cincinnati Volksfreund*, July 25, 1870; *New Philadelphia Deutsche Beobachter*, Aug. 11, 1870.

comes freedom," Mathilde rejoined that "the bloodletting of the people" would only be "to the advantage of the tyrants." Tellingly, she did not make this view public.[60] During 1870, there was no place for judicious treatments of war in the German-American community.

On the whole, women did not challenge male bellicosity. In fact, it was during this war that German-language newspapers disclosed the first widespread female involvement in organizing celebrations and raising funds. Milwaukee women – except Mathilde Anneke, of course – were particularly active. They formed the Patriotic Ladies Aid Association, with a female president, executive committee, and ward representatives. The organization held a concert and a four-day fair to collect money for the widows and orphans of German soldiers.[61] Women in La Crosse, Cincinnati, and St. Louis undertook similar enterprises, and one woman in St. Louis addressed a large crowd at a public meeting.[62] That immigrant women first assumed such prominence at specifically German-American events demonstrates the importance of ethnicity to their experience of gender. It also shows that the Franco-Prussian War unified the German community more than the Civil War had. Taking on the French brought German Americans together across the divisions of party, class, religion, and gender. This phenomenon could not help but influence the politics of citizenship.

With the rest of the world, German Americans were surprised when on September 2, 1870, after only six weeks of fighting, German forces won a decisive battle at the French town of Sedan. The Germans captured Napoleon III and were well on their way to winning the war. In the United States, celebrations of victory replaced expressions of sympathy. German St. Louisans had the good fortune to have planned a large fair for Sunday, September 4. An estimated 10,000 to 25,000 men, women, and children, all just learning of Sedan, crowded into Concordia Park for the "unity festival" (*Verbrüderungsfest*). With a women's committee selling refreshments and local brewers pouring free beer, the event raised over $20,000.[63] It

---

60 Fritz to Mathilde, July 21, 1870, in *Mathilde Franziska Anneke*, ed. Wagner, 287; Mathilde to Fritz, July 29, 1870, reel 3, fr. 632, Anneke Papers, WHS. For similar privately expressed ideas, see Freitag, *Friedrich Hecker*, 363–85; Wittke, *Refugees of Revolution*, 255–56; *Wochenblatt der New-Yorker Staats-Zeitung*, July 23, 1870; *Cincinnati Volksfreund*, Aug. 3, 1870.

61 *Banner und Volksfreund*, Sept. 6, 8, 15, and 16, Oct. 19, 21, and 29, Nov. 2, 16, and 17, 1870; Hense-Jensen, *Wisconsin's Deutsch-Amerikaner*, 1: 229. Some German women had joined their native-born sisters in similar activities during the Civil War, but immigrants did not take the initiative. Klement, "Milwaukee Women and the Civil War," *Historical Messenger* 21 (1965): 9–14.

62 *La Crosse Nord Stern*, Nov. 4, 1870; *Cincinnati Volksfreund*, Aug. 26, 1870; *Westliche Post*, Aug. 20, 1870; *Mississippi Blätter*, Sept. 25, 1870.

63 *Westliche Post*, Sept. 5, 1870; *Anzeiger des Westens*, Sept. 5, 1870; *New York Times*, Sept. 5, 1870.

was the sort of occasion that made its way into letters and memoirs. In 1893, a German American remembered that the parade of church groups, Turnvereine, singing societies, and lodges was "down to the present day, the largest that has been seen here."[64] Cincinnati Germans also marked the Battle of Sedan in fine fashion with bonfires, music, artillery salvos, and fireworks, but they were less forthcoming with donations.[65] Cleveland and Milwaukee Germans sent a steady flow of funds to help victims of the war, but were less demonstrative.[66]

For all the jubilation, peace did not come with Napoleon III's surrender. France's interim government hastily declared the state a republic and resolved to continue fighting. The German armies laid siege to Paris and held out for the Third French Republic to cede Alsace and Lorraine. Prussia maintained that the annexation of these contested regions, which were inhabited by both French- and German-speakers, was a point of national security.[67] It was at this juncture that the central committee of the North American arm of the International Workingmen's Association, which was largely German American and located in New York, came out strongly against Prussia.[68] Anglo-Americans began to turn against the Germans too. Days after Sedan, the *New York World* declared that France "courageously holds aloft the banner of free institutions and places itself in the van of a great republican movement in Europe."[69] Republicans were now more inclined to agree with the Democratic newspaper.[70]

Most German Americans, however, were unimpressed by what they regarded as the chimera of French republicanism, believing that Germans

64 Kargau, *St. Louis in früheren Jahren*, 209. An Anglo-American wrote to his father that it was a "grand affair." James H. Rollins to James S. Rollins, Sept. 5, 1870, folder 106, Rollins Papers, WHMC – Columbia. See also A. Rühl to Louis Benecke, Sept. 13, 1870, folder 721, Benecke Papers, WHMC – Columbia.

65 *Cincinnati Commercial*, Sept. 8, 1870. See also *Cincinnati Volksfreund*, Sept. 8, 1870; Anton Eichhoff, *In der neuen Heimath: Geschichtliche Mittheilung über die deutschen Einwanderer in allen Theilen der Union* (New York: E. Steiger & Co., 1884), 300.

66 *Wächter am Erie*, July 21, 1870; *Cleveland Leader*, Aug. 9, 15, 29, and 30, Sept. 3 and 15, 1870; *Seebote Wöchentliche Ausgabe*, Sept. 5 and 12, 1870; *Banner und Volksfreund*, Sept. 6, 7, and 8, 1870.

67 Wawro, *Franco-Prussian War*, 230.

68 North American Federal Council of the IWA, "Resolutions Submitted to Anti-War-Meeting" [Sept. 1870], reel 1, fr. 1102, IWA Papers, WHS.

69 *New York World*, Sept. 6, 1870.

70 On the swing in public opinion, see *Cincinnati Enquirer*, Sept. 9, 1870, Jan. 23 and 31, 1871; *New York Tribune*, Sept. 7, 1870; *Chicago Tribune*, Sept. 7, 1870; *Cincinnati Commercial*, Sept. 8, 1870; *St. Charles Demokrat*, Oct. 6, 1870; *Westliche Post*, Sept. 14 and 20, 1870; *Cincinnati Volksfreund*, Sept. 20, 1870; *Wächter am Erie*, Sept. 5, 1870. See also Francis Lieber to Hamilton Fish, Sept. 17, 1870, vol. 72, Hamilton Fish Papers, LOC. Some Republican papers were still skeptical of France: *The Nation*, Sept. 15, 22, and 29, 1870; *Cleveland Leader*, Sept. 5, 6, 7, and 9, 1870; *Milwaukee Daily Sentinel*, Sept. 7 and 9, 1870.

were dying because the French were too stubborn to admit defeat.[71] German immigrants remained anxious about friends and relatives who were serving in Europe. One man in central Missouri wrote to a friend, "My 5th army corps at home, in which I have a number of brothers and cousins and a great many friends, has been holding out very bravely everywhere, though it has also suffered dreadful losses, but I still don't know if members of my family are among them. I haven't received a letter from home in over a month."[72] Immigrants who did hear from their loved ones learned the toll of German nationalism. A Wisconsinite got word that his family was "lucky during the war," but the message included the news that five acquaintances had been killed or wounded.[73] Another letter, which was designed to reassure its recipient that "there is probably nothing to worry about on account of the war," described trainloads of wounded Germans and imprisoned Frenchmen passing through a town in central Germany.[74] Casualties kept mounting until long after the results of the war were apparent. In January 1871, Wilhelm I became the emperor of the new German Empire and Paris finally fell to Prussian bombardment. When formal peace negotiations between the belligerents concluded in May, the war had confirmed the *Westliche Post*'s verdict that "no strike was made by the brave armies beyond the Ocean without its effect also being felt here."[75]

REVISITING THE GERMAN VOLK

Having brought Germans immigrants together, the Franco-Prussian War promoted a less liberal language of citizenship. Central to this change was a new conception of the German *Volk*. German Americans had never doubted that they were superior, but from 1848 to 1870, they had seen culture as the main factor that set them apart. The liberalism of the Forty-Eighters and the Radical Republicans had included a cultural understanding of the characteristics that Germans shared, which implied that the boundaries and nature of the *Volk* were not fixed. In 1848, the revolutionaries had

---

71 *Cincinnati Volksfreund*, Sept. 19, 1870; *St. Charles Demokrat*, Sept. 22, 1870; *Westliche Post*, Sept. 14, 1870; *Wächter am Erie*, Sept. 6, 1870; *New Philadelphia Deutsche Beobachter*, Sept. 15, 1870; *Banner und Volksfreund*, Sept. 7 and 8, 1870. Even the Catholic *Wahrheitsfreund* supported the annexation of Alsace and Lorraine to the German Empire, remarkably arguing that Catholics in the area wanted German rule. *Wahrheitsfreund*, Nov. 30, 1870.
72 Theodore Boehm to Louis Benecke, Sept. 28, 1870, folder 722, Benecke Papers, WHMC – Columbia. See similar concern in Fritz Herzberg to Louis Benecke, Aug. 11, 1870, folder 721, Benecke Papers, WHMC – Columbia.
73 Johann Heinrich Dücker to Peter and Claus Dücker, April 14, 1871, Duecker Family Papers, WHS.
74 Concordia Martini to Louis Martini, Nov. 7, 1870, box 3, folder 11, Germans in the United States Collection, WHS.
75 *Westliche Post*, Dec. 13, 1870.

imagined the German *Volk* as a cultural and political grouping that incorporated various peoples and refined itself over time. In the United States, even the most racist immigrants had reinterpreted the *Volk* as an ethnic group, a cultural minority in a plural nation. German-American Radicals had applied the lessons of 1848 and migration to African Americans, arguing that racial minorities should not be excluded – bounded off – from the community of citizens, in part because race was cultural and changeable like ethnicity. Although Radicals had not in the end dissolved the distinction between African Americans' race and their own ethnicity, the most influential German-American leaders had insisted that no man should be denied citizenship on the basis of race or ethnicity since no group was biologically incapable of learning the skills of citizenship. The notion of a culturally defined German *Volk*, passed down from 1848, had motivated the German-American Republicans working on black suffrage during the 1860s.

The German nationalism of 1870, however, rested on elite and popular claims that the German *Volk* was *essentially* predisposed to greatness. When Germans in Europe contrasted themselves to the French, they suggested that innate differences among *Völker* determined the fate of different states. For some Europeans, Prussia's victory was a confirmation of the theory expounded by early nineteenth-century German scholars such as Barthold Georg Niebuhr: world history was a struggle between races.[76] Bismarck, for example, interpreted Prussia's success as a triumph of the German race.[77] This line of thinking was not as biological as the racial theorizing of the late nineteenth century. Time remained an important variable in the more racial constructions of peoplehood circulating in 1870. "Superior" groups such as the Germans were more "advanced"; "inferior" ones such as the French lagged "behind."[78] Yet Germans referred to more clearly bounded groups with more deeply seated traits that varied less over time. Immigrants would find it difficult to reconcile these new ideas with the racial politics of the American nation. Within the United States, it still made sense for immigrants to see themselves as an ethnicity, a cultural subgroup of the white race. It would be an oversimplification, and a confusing one at that, to say that German Americans redefined the German *Volk* as a "race," but

76 Ivan Hannaford, *Race: The History of an Idea in the West* (Washington, DC: The Woodrow Wilson Center Press, 1996), 235–50.

77 Ibid., 287–315.

78 Ibid., 274–76. See also Vick, *Defining Germany*, 20–22; Reinhart Koselleck, "Volk, Nation, Nationalismus, Masse," 7: 380–89; Werner Conze, "Rasse," in *Geschichtliche Grundbegriffe*, ed. Brunner, Conze, and Koselleck, 5: 148–57.

the new essentialism was more racial than the old approach. The German-American public sphere would become more fertile ground for arguments that it would be futile to try to surmount the differences in status that existed among groups of people.

The conflict in Europe influenced racial thought in North America because immigrants viewed it as a *Volkskrieg*, a clash between the French and German *Völker*.[79] While some Anglo-Americans dismissed the war as a spat between Napoleon III and Bismarck, the immigrants emphasized that "all of Germany stands on the side of Prussia," and they immediately recognized that this alliance would lead to the unification of the German states (with the exception of Austria) and the reshaping of Europe.[80] Thieme wrote in the *Wächter am Erie*, "The day of the great, long-predicted decision has come – the struggle not between dynasties but between two *Völker* is erupting. The deep-rooted antipathy between Romandom and Germandom demands a bloody resolution."[81] The *St. Charles Demokrat* asked, "Whom does Germany wage war against?" Not Napoleon III alone, the editor wrote, but the French *Volk*. The two *Völker* would vie for control of Europe.[82] The *Watertown Weltbürger* also used the designation *Volkskrieg*, declaring that the Prussian army "is truly the *Volk* in arms."[83] Consistent with these characterizations, German-language newspapers pointedly called the conflagration "the German-French War." At stake, editors maintained, was the future of the whole German *Volk*, not just Prussia.[84]

A few commentators even spoke of a "race war." While this description was controversial, it revealed the seriousness of the challenge to the culturally demarcated *Volk* and the liberalism of 1848. The Democratic editor of the *New-Yorker Staats-Zeitung* projected that the war would continue until it was clear "whether the Germanic or the Latin race [*Race*] henceforth would be the leader in the affairs of nations [*Völkerleben*]." German Americans seldom used the word "race." When they did, they usually were referring to the differences between whites and blacks, not among European groups. Before 1870, immigrants habitually called themselves a German minority in an Anglo-Saxon land, only on scattered occasions speaking of a Germanic race that included the English. The New York newspaper, which was

---

79   *Westliche Post*, Aug. 29, 1870. In the English-language press, Democrats were most likely to see the war primarily as one fought between monarchs. See *Cincinnati Enquirer*, July 29, 1870; *New York World*, July 20, 1870; *Chicago Tribune*, July 18, 1870; *Springfield (Mass.) Daily Republican*, July 16, 1870; *Cleveland Leader*, July 23, Aug. 8, 1870; *The Nation*, July 14, 1870.
80   *Sauk City Pionier am Wisconsin*, July 23, 1870.   81   *Wächter am Erie*, July 16, 1870.
82   *St. Charles Demokrat*, Aug. 4, 1870.
83   *Watertown Weltbürger*, Aug 6, 1870. See also *Illinois Staatszeitung*, Jan. 2, 1871.
84   *Cincinnati Volksfreund*, Aug. 31, 1870.

experimenting with contested terms and unfamiliar ideas, did not even use the German spelling of "race."[85] The *Staats-Zeitung* argued that the English had fought the French and Spanish (who all belonged to the Latin race) over the Americas in the eighteenth century and the Germans and English had fought the French during the Napoleonic Wars of the early nineteenth century. Now, the Germans and the French were at it again. In the *Staats-Zeitung's* analysis, the boundaries between the races were somewhat porous. The piece ascribed what strength France did possess to an infusion of Germanic blood.[86] Still, it carefully grouped European peoples into larger white races, which was uncommon. It was the most extreme example of the essentialist thinking that appeared during the European war.

Another Democratic editor shot down the ideas of the *New-Yorker Staats-Zeitung*, showing in the process that German Americans were struggling to make sense of the racial fallout from the war. Dänzer at the *Anzeiger* thought that talk of a "Germanic race" was ridiculous. As a practical matter, he believed that theorizing about Germanic, Latin, and Slavic races played into the hands of the French, who were trying to form an alliance with Spain, Italy, and Portugal. It would not help Germany to elevate the conflict to the level of race war. Yet Dänzer had more fundamental objections. He disagreed with the "outdated classification of the *Völker* of Europe, which are increasingly all jumbled up by our industrial century, into three great race-groups."[87] This editor was uncomfortable with the proliferation of categories based on competing biological, cultural, and political criteria. Dänzer must have realized that the *Staats-Zeitung's* taxonomy was incongruent with the established language of citizenship in the United States. The binary of white and black was of paramount importance to him, and German Americans were already unquestioned members of the white race. Immigrants also valued the cultural peculiarity of their *Volk* (separate from the English) and their political affiliation with the American nation. It was difficult enough to sustain stable definitions of race, *Volk*, and nation in the American context. What would German Americans gain from conceiving of a new race that included the Germans and the English?[88]

85 Schurz made a fleeting reference to different "branches" of the "good old Germanic stock" in an 1858 speech. Schurz, "Political Morals," 50. On the variation and change in how races were delimited and denoted, see Hannaford, *Race*, 235–76; Kazal, *Becoming Old Stock*, 118–29; Jacobson, *Whiteness of a Different Color*, 39–90; Bruce Baum, *The Rise and Fall of the Caucasian Race: A Political History of Racial Identity* (New York: New York University Press, 2006), 118–61.

86 *Wochenblatt der New-Yorker Staats-Zeitung*, July 23, 1870.

87 *Anzeiger des Westens*, July 25, 1870.

88 Russell Kazal describes how the calculations of German immigrants changed once Southern and Eastern Europeans began arriving in the United States later in the century. Kazal, *Becoming Old Stock*.

Dänzer proposed another meaning for the German *Volk*, one that was entirely out of step with German-American public opinion in 1870. He soberly judged that "tribes distinguished by [differences in] intellectual life and other characteristics [*Volksindividualitäten*]" were coming together as "a political organism of shared material interests." The interests of states, he wrote, had nothing to do with "blood ties to the tribes that founded this or that empire a millennium ago."[89] Although most German Americans would have agreed with Dänzer that the German Empire was a political union and the German *Volk* itself was made up of different tribes, his dispassionate sketch of the German *Volk* as a group of people with common interests did not capture the spirit of 1870 and 1871.[90] Like the *Staats-Zeitung*, the *Anzeiger* was an outlier. Between the two, the German-American public sphere filled with emotional displays of essentialist German solidarity.

In their celebrations, Germans in the United States communicated the idea that a set of inherited characteristics bound them to Germans in Europe. This position built on the preexisting structure of German-American ethnicity, of course. Schurz had cheerfully generalized about immigrant groups in his "True Americanism" speech in 1859. At that time, however, he was telling Americans not to fear the differences among Europeans because they were only cultural. Against the backdrop of the Franco-Prussian War, the commonalities among Germans seemed to run deeper. When Cincinnatians marked the Battle of Sedan, J. B. Stallo, now a judge, told the animated crowd, "We can proudly say that the customs and instincts of the German *Volk* have always been to free self-determination." Although he was careful not to gloat at the humiliation of the French, Stallo believed that "for the French, there is no difference between freedom and anarchy."[91] He alluded to culture and institutions, but Stallo also spoke of unchanging German "instincts." In contrasting the French and the Germans in the shadow of Sedan, Stallo conjured up essential and enduring difference. He saw that difference as immensely important; it mapped the course of history.

Indeed, the contrast between the Germans and the French was vital to the redefinition of the German *Volk*. In 1870, when German Americans reveled in German identity, they often denigrated non-Germans, producing

---

89 *Anzeiger des Westens*, July 25, 1870.
90 For references to various German tribes (*Stämme*), see *Banner und Volksfreund*, July 22, 1870; *Wächter am Erie*, April 11, 1870.
91 *Cincinnati Volksfreund*, Sept. 8, 1870. Francis Lieber also blended character and governance when he told Hamilton Fish that all France's "king-less governments had been democratic despotisms" because "the French have never respected what civil liberty is." Francis Lieber to Hamilton Fish, Sept. 17, 1870, vol. 72, Hamilton Fish Papers, LOC.

an explicit hierarchy of *Völker* and vesting it with great significance. Politicians and editors said that the French people were not fit for self-rule. At the New York meeting in Steinway Hall, former Wisconsin governor Eduard Salomon blamed the Franco-Prussian War on "the backwardness of the French *Volk* itself, which, despite its much-praised civilization, still languishes in medieval bands."[92] Emil Rothe, a Democrat who had just moved from Wisconsin to Cincinnati to edit the *Volksfreund*, was more reasonable.[93] He voiced a widely held belief when he wrote that since the Napoleonic Wars "the French peasant has essentially remained as he was then, ignorant in the highest degree, but the German masses have advanced in general education."[94] The word Rothe used for education, "Bildung," connoted character, cultivation, and even breeding. Schooling alone, in Rothe's mind, could not soon overcome the deficiencies of the French. Germans lifted themselves higher by demeaning their enemy.

Based on the German rout of the French, immigrants decided that the qualities of different *Völker* could preordain history. In 1848, it had seemed for a time that all European peoples were rising up together against their rulers, but in 1870, either France or Germany would win. The supposed attributes of a *Volk* thus took on more explanatory power. If the German-American public sphere was to be believed, inherited characteristics drove world events, governing which nations would rise and which would fall. The *St. Charles Demokrat* was sure in August 1870 that somehow the "more peace loving character" and "deeper *Bildung*" of the Germans would see them to victory.[95] In this rendering, military and political developments manifested the relative strengths of different *Völker*. Causation was not the primary interest of the editor of the *Nord Stern* in La Crosse, Wisconsin, but he wrote that it was well known that "the German *Volk* stands at the pinnacle of progress, enlightenment, intelligence, morality, and justice, that a victory for Germany would mean a victory for progress."[96] When success was imminent, Schurz's *Westliche Post* ran an editorial saying that it would give "the [German] nation an external position of power that corresponded to its moral and spiritual [*geistig*] greatness."[97]

92 *Wochenblatt der New-Yorker Staats-Zeitung*, July 23, 1870.

93 On Rothe's life and career, see *Emil Rothe: Sein Charakter, eine Leben und Wirken* [Cincinnati, 1895], box 1, Fick Pamphlet Collection, German-Americana Collection, University of Cincinnati.

94 *Cincinnati Volksfreund*, July 19, 1870. For similar arguments, see *Watertown Weltbürger*, Aug. 6, 1870; *Wächter am Erie*, April 11 and 20, 1870; *Banner und Volksfreund*, July 25, 1870; *Cincinnati Volksfreund*, Aug. 9, 1870. At one point, Rothe attributed the failings of the French "spirit" ("Geist") to the Napoleon III's "crazy government system" ("verrüchten Regierungssystems"). *Cincinnati Volksfreund*, July 21, 1870. See also Aug. 9, 1870.

95 *St. Charles Demokrat*, Aug. 4, 1870.   96 *La Crosse Nord Stern*, July 22, 1870.

97 *Westliche Post*, Sept. 5, 1870.

The cumulative effect of the new descriptions of the Germans and the French was to suggest that the essential nature of *Völker* inscribed the contours of history. There were continuities in German-American thinking from before 1870. The immigrants' estimations of the French resembled German Democrats' views of African Americans following the Civil War. Even Republicans had occasionally wondered whether the slavery had left African Americans unready for citizenship. From 1865 to 1869, however, the most successful public arguments had come from Radicals who had stressed that all people would be able to improve themselves if the laws restricting some groups were overturned. German Radicals did not completely recant this position in 1870, but they now indicated that they thought that uplift would be wasted on the French. Whereas they had once harbored the condescending belief that institutions could change people, they now saw the dominance of certain peoples as inevitable. Belaboring the principle of equality among men at this point would have seemed quaint or naive. When German Republicans revisited universal manhood suffrage, it would be in a new ideological environment.

REEVALUATING THE GERMAN STATE

As German Americans reconceptualized the German *Volk*, they also reevaluated German political institutions, a second wartime initiative that would touch American citizenship. Citizens belonged to national communities, but the rights of membership were as relevant as the fact of membership. States enumerated and enforced citizenship's guarantees. They established the bodies that would represent citizens. In 1870 and 1871, two new states formed for the consideration of German Americans, the Third French Republic and the German Empire. Of course, the immigrants were passionate partisans, and their prejudices about the French and German *Völker* colored how they surveyed the respective governments. Comparing France and Germany before the guns stilled, German immigrants turned from the representative functions of government and the constitutional protection of rights to the institutions of public education, armed force, and general administration. This new preoccupation was not necessarily sinister, but it is striking that individual rights did not now consume the German-American community as they had up until Congress proposed the Fifteenth Amendment.

A heavy dose of wishful thinking eased German Americans into defending the illiberal institutions of the new Reich. Like Germans in Europe, the immigrants did not wait to learn the details before averring that the empire would be nothing like Kingdom of Prussia. The *St. Charles Demokrat* assured readers that Germany's central administration would be strong enough to neutralize the aristocracy. The newspaper counseled patience, adding, "As soon as the German *Volk* feels the need for a republic, it will also know to achieve it."[98] The editor of the Democratic *Cincinnati Volksfreund*, displeased with the American president and Congress, emphasized that the empire would not be *too* centralized. The federal structure of the emerging polity, Emil Rothe believed, would ensure that states could safeguard "German freedom."[99] He also wrote that if the imperial parliament (Reichstag) represented popular will, the emperor would have no choice but to "handle it very carefully."[100] The arguments in the *Demokrat* and the *Volksfreund* were mutually exclusive, but editors at both papers trusted that Germans would create a praiseworthy state. Schurz simply informed the U.S. secretary of state that in spite of Prussia's "monarchical form of government[,] it will also turn out to be the most progressive power, steadily progressive."[101] Such statements were so common that the *Watertown Weltbürger* joked that German Americans seemed to think that Germany would become a republic and elect Franz Sigel president.[102] In later years, more immigrants would adopt the *Weltbürger*'s cynical tone, but well into 1871, most of them exuded an uncritical optimism.

So confident were German Americans in the empire that they joined the politicians in Germany who were compromising their own liberal nationalism. The liberal nationalism of 1848 and the Civil War had held that promoting individual rights strengthened nation-states and that strengthening nation-states promoted individual rights. There was no room in such a theory to disengage means from ends. Even rationalizing that Bismarck's realpolitik was regrettably the most practical way to unite Germany vitiated the Forty-Eighters' fundamental precept that a reciprocal relationship existed between nation-states and individual rights. Untethering liberalism from nationalism gutted the ideology that had dominated the 1860s.

In the German-American speeches and editorials of 1870, immigrants sacrificed individual rights to national greatness. Rothe's *Cincinnati Volksfreund* reprinted an article from Chicago that commended Bismarck's maxim that the great challenges facing Germany would be resolved not "by speeches and majority decisions . . . but by iron and blood." The famous

98 *St. Charles Demokrat*, Dec. 1, 1870.   99 *Cincinnati Volksfreund*, Oct. 29, 1870.
100 Ibid., Nov. 21, 1870.
101 Schurz to Hamilton Fish, Sept. 10, 1870, in *Speeches, Correspondence and Political Papers of Carl Schurz*, ed. Bancroft, 1: 519–20.
102 *Watertown Weltbürger*, Aug. 27, 1870.

prophesy, made in the heat of the standoff between the Prussian prime minister and parliament in 1862, encapsulated the new German nationalism, and Rothe swallowed it: "[The Forty-Eighters'] youthful dream of a united Germany has become a living, tangible reality – perhaps by other means than they had in mind – perhaps under a different tricolor than the black, red, and gold, but what difference does that make?"[103] The *Seebote* picked up the thread. Deuster wrote, "For history as such, for the political development of the German nation, it really makes no difference whether the emperor will be crowned by the German *Volk* or by the German princes. The main thing is that by this action the unity of Germany is finally secured."[104] German Americans were prepared to subordinate their longing for German freedom to their excitement for German unity.

Once German immigrants accepted Bismarck as the architect of a unified Germany, they were drawn down a path that led away from liberal nationalism. In September 1870, Prussia's adversary became a republic, leaving German Americans to argue that it was possible for monarchies to provide better government than republics. There was reason enough to doubt the Third Republic. After its defeat at Prussian hands in 1871, the Paris Commune would shake the new administration, and the reaction against it would return the country to bloody turmoil.[105] Many Americans worried about the new French government. But German immigrants refused to confer on it any legitimacy at all. It was a "sleight of hand" performed for a gullible international audience, reported the *St. Charles Demokrat*.[106] This was not a real republic, Thieme at the *Wächter am Erie* repeated; it did not emanate from the people.[107] The *Westliche Post* chided Americans for their naïve attraction to the word "republic." The editors asked how anyone could fail to see "that a republic born of madness has only a desperately small chance of survival."[108] Joining the chorus, a speaker at a St. Louis fundraising event jeered at French efforts: "Prayers of necessity are not devotion, and a republican form of state forced upon a *Volk* that has degenerated into slavery is not a republic." She intoned, "Germany is today, without bearing

103 The *Volksfreund* paraphrased Bismarck's famous statement. *Cincinnati Volksfreund*, Aug. 11, 1870. For explicit support of German unification under Prussian control, see *Cincinnati Volksfreund*, July 18, Aug. 10, Oct. 29, 1870; *Fremont Courier*, Dec. 1, 1870; *St. Charles Demokrat*, July 21, 1870; *Westliche Post*, Aug. 29, 1870; *Anzeiger des Westens*, July 18, 1870; *Wächter am Erie*, July 19, 1870; *Illinois Staatszeitung*, Jan. 22, 1871. For a statement from the Turnerbund, see *Westliche Post*, Aug. 2, 1870.
104 *Seebote Wöchentliche Ausgabe*, Dec. 12, 1870.
105 Adeptly describing the Commune and the American reaction, see Katz, *From Appomattox to Montmartre*.
106 *St. Charles Demokrat*, Sept. 22, 1870.   107 *Wächter am Erie*, Sept. 6, 1870.
108 *Westliche Post*, Sept. 14, 1870. See also Sept. 28, 1870; *Fremont Courier*, Sept. 25, 1870; *Seebote Wöchentliche Ausgabe*, March 6, 1871.

the name, closer in reality to the concept of the true essence of a free state than Paris with all its republicanism."[109] Although German immigrants still measured states against some of the old standards of good government, the simple mid-century taxonomy that separated conservative monarchies from liberal republics was gone.

To back up their position that Germany, with its aristocracy and its emperor, was superior to France, a republic, some German-American editors referenced its constitution. By late 1870, they could see that the princes of the southern German states, including Baden, Bavaria, and Württemberg, would join an empire much like the North German Confederation. Perusing the document under which the Reich would operate, the editors of the *Westliche Post* noted, "In some respects the constitution of Germany is more democratic than the Constitution of the United States."[110] Editors Carl Schurz and Emil Preetorius were willing to tolerate an arrangement that was far less liberal than that outlined in the stillborn constitution of 1849. King Wilhelm would become emperor, Prime Minister Bismarck would become chancellor, and members of the nobility would retain many of their existing privileges in the member states. Under the constitution, the chancellor wielded significant power. He headed the government, which initiated legislation, allocated funds, and directed the extensive administrative functions of the state. The government, not the Reichstag, oversaw the army, in which all young men were compelled to serve for a period of time.[111]

In a very selective reading of the constitution, the *Westliche Post* specifically cited citizenship law as one of its strengths. The citizens – the *Post* termed them *Bürger* – of each German state would become citizens of the Reich. Schurz and Preetorius must have been thinking of the Fourteenth Amendment in the American Constitution when they added that the constitution decreed that every German state must recognize the rights of all *Bürger*.[112] This misleading observation ignored the fact that the relevant constitutional articles and associated legislation referred not to national citizens, but to "members of the empire" (*Reichsangehörige*), who did not enjoy the protection of a bill of rights. Reflecting a more race-based conception of citizenship, the constitution also established that this status could be transmitted by descent outside of Germany's borders.[113] Although there

109 *Mississippi Blätter*, Sept. 25, 1870.   110 Ibid., Dec. 18, 1870.

111 Craig, *Politics of the Prussian Army*, 217–20; Pflanze, *Bismarck and the Development of Germany*, 1: 490–506; Ernst Rudolf Huber, *Deutsche Verfassungsgeschichte seit 1789*, 8 vols. (Stuttgart: W. Kohlhammer, 1957–1991), 3: 745–65, 809–22; Sheehan, *German Liberalism*, 130–32.

112 *Mississippi Blätter*, Dec. 18, 1870.

113 Constitution of the German Empire (1871), Article 3; Der Norddeutsche Bund, "Gesetz über die Erwerbung und den Verlust der Bundes- und Staatsangehörigkeit," June 1, 1870. The citizenship

were plentiful examples of illiberalism, all adult male *Reichsangehörige* could vote for the Reichstag, as a few German-speaking editors informed their readers. The immigrant leaders knew, they said, that the imperial parliament would become ever more important.[114] German Americans had not totally abandoned the ideal of participatory citizenship for men. They clutched at certain aspects of the German constitution to explain their acquiescence to others.

On the whole, however, the immigrants did not discuss citizenship law and representative institutions at the height of the convulsions in Europe. They trumpeted the empire's schools, armies, and civil service, all of which had less to do with nineteenth-century liberalism's individual rights. Stallo told Cincinnatians, "No republic can be made overnight merely by pro-claiming it; it must be developed slowly and gradually within a *Volk*, in its minor institutions, in its everyday actions and intentions."[115] The judge set great store in the German *Volk*, but he also credited "minor institutions" with Germany's achievements. Narrowing in on one in particular, the *St. Charles Demokrat* wrote that any country claiming to be a "civilized nation," must educate its children. That France had fallen short was appar-ent from the illiterate soldiers filling German prison camps.[116] The Prussian system, on the other hand, rated "far above the American," according to a recent report.[117] The *Seebote*, which usually disagreed with the *Demokrat*, also held up German education as a model for the United States.[118] The idea was not entirely new to English-speaking Americans. As early as the 1840s, Massachusetts educator Horace Mann had praised Prussia's provision of free and compulsory public elementary schooling and its national net-work of graded secondary and tertiary institutions.[119] Perhaps Prussia's feats on the battlefield were a testament to the caliber of its system of education.

The Prussian army was also irrefutably impressive, and it was hardly liberal. Every German-language orator and editor marveled at the Prus-sian war machine. One newspaperman in Ohio summed up the general

---

law of the North German Confederation was adapted to apply to the *Reich* in 1871. Huber, ed., *Dokumente zur deutschen Verfassungsgeschichte*, 5 vols. (Stuttgart: W. Kohlhammer Verlag, 1961–1966), 2: 290, 249–53; Brubaker, *Citizenship and Nationhood in France and Germany*.

114 *St. Charles Demokrat*, July 21, 1870; *Wächter am Erie*, March 28, 1871; *Watertown Weltbürger*, Feb. 4, 1871.

115 *Cincinnati Volksfreund*, Sept. 8, 1870.   116 *St. Charles Demokrat*, Jan. 26, 1871.

117 Ibid., Dec. 15, 1870.   118 *Seebote Wöchentliche Ausgabe*, Jan. 23, 1871.

119 Horace Mann, *Report of an Educational Tour in Germany, and Parts of Great Britain and Ireland* (London: Simkin, Marshall, and Company, 1846); John A. Walz, *German Influence in American Education and Culture* (Philadelphia: Carl Schurz Memorial Foundation, 1936), 7–46; Daniel Fallon, "German Influences on American Education," in *The German-American Encounter: Conflict and Cooperation between Two Cultures, 1800–2000*, ed. Frank Trommler and Elliott Shore (New York: Berghahn Books, 2001), 77–87.

awe when he wrote, "It is difficult to imagine a more complete military organization."[120] But by 1871, a Cleveland immigrant wanted to clarify that it was not Prussian *militarism* that beguiled German Americans, and the *Illinois Staatszeitung* was warning German politicians not to let the army be a tool of the emperor.[121] No editor, however, recalled the crisis between Wilhelm I and his parliament over the military during the mid-1860s. Emil Rothe was alone in believing that a standing army with mandatory military training was necessarily "a republican institution and purveyor of culture" among the German masses.[122] Most immigrants settled for preening at the efficiency and order of German regiments, which they contrasted with the waste and politicking they had perceived in the Union army.[123] Although German Americans did not welcome authoritarian militarism, their rhetoric placed institutional effectiveness ahead of individual rights and representation.

To immigrants proud of Prussian educational and military infrastructure, the kingdom's tradition of administrative probity was another counterweight to the new Germany's shortcomings in citizenship law. Democrats and Republicans alike compared President Grant's civil service unfavorably with the Prussian bureaucracy. "Corruption, special interest legislation, and privileges," Rothe lamented in the *Volksfreund*, "characterize our public life in such a conspicuous way that we must blush when we hold up our current state of affairs, republican in name only, as an example for other *Völker* to imitate."[124] He was frustrated that Republicans – "utopians, who themselves have no regard for any constitution" – tried to present the United States – "where we unfortunately face corruption and lack political character at every step" – as "the yardstick of all politics."[125] Cincinnati's maverick Republican Friedrich Hassaurek was also annoyed that Americans feigned to have "the best government under the sun."[126] The *St. Charles Demokrat* chimed in with an example of how the United States might learn from Germany. There were more constraints on the German emperor, the longwinded editor maintained, than on the American president. He wrote that the emperor "cannot, like the president of the United States, hire and suddenly fire thousands of officials according to mere whim. Rather, his

120 *New Philadelphia Deutsche Beobachter*, Aug, 25, 1870.
121 *Wächter am Erie*, April 11, 1871; *Illinois Staatszeitung*, Jan. 7, 1871.
122 *Cincinnati Volksfreund*, Feb. 13, 1871.
123 See for example *Cincinnati Volksfreund*, Sept. 29, 1870. On Civil War corruption, see Helbich, "German-Born Union Soldiers: Motivation, Ethnicity, and 'Americanization,'" in *German-American Immigration and Ethnicity*, ed. Helbich and Kamphoefner, 295–325.
124 *Cincinnati Volksfreund*, Feb. 6, 1871.
125 Ibid., Aug. 25, Sept. 14, 1870. See also *Watertown Weltbürger*, Aug. 6, 1870.
126 *Westliche Post*, Oct. 20, 1870.

hands are absolutely bound by law and custom. Even if he just wanted to drive the poorest gate engraver or highway toll collector, who was guilty of nothing, from office on mere whim, a cry of indignation would go out through the land and teach him that the era of patriarchal despotism was long gone."[127] The Franco-Prussian War ushered in a new era of transnational comparisons.

The lure of great educational systems and armies – and streamlined administration in general – did not set German Americans off on a *Sonderweg* (special path) to fascism. The immigrants hit on some real weaknesses in American government, and they did so at a time when the citizenship controversy of the 1860s seemed largely settled. The Franco-Prussian War did lend credence to the idea that successful countries needed clean and efficient bureaucracies more than they needed effective representative institutions or a rigorous regime of citizen rights. German Americans' less liberal ideas of *Volk* also stood out. But such reconsiderations did not contradict other changes in American politics in the early 1870s, and they were not the immigrants' alone.[128]

A growing group of self-styled native-born "reformers" shared the German-American response to German unification. The same Anglo-American Republicans who were beginning to obsess about ridding the United States of corruption, demagoguery, and fiscal irresponsibility believed that the German people were superior to the French and admired German institutions. The reform-minded Murat Halstead at the *Cincinnati Commercial* gratified German Americans by writing from Europe that "every hour that I have been on German soil has increased my estimate of the German nation. They have the brain and muscle, and the country, to take undisputed hereafter the first place among the powers of Europe."[129] It was another reformist periodical, *The Nation*, that led the English-language

---

127 *St. Charles Demokrat*, March 9, 1871.
128 Historian George M. Fredrickson wrote in 1965 of a shift among Northern intellectuals during the Civil War era from individualism to institutionalism. Fredrickson referred to disciples of German philosopher Georg Hegel and to Berlin-born theorist Francis Lieber, who had immigrated to the United States during the 1820s. Lieber corresponded with Schurz, but generally moved in Anglo-American circles. Despite the German connections, however, Fredrickson focused on Anglo-American thought. Discussing changing interpretations of the American Revolution, he wrote, "The universalist theory of national origins, as put forth by an ante-bellum historian like George Bancroft, had made the American revolution not only the fruit of a specific historical tradition, but also a creed of liberty for all mankind. This view was beginning to give way to the particularist approach of 'Anglo-Saxonism.'" Fredrickson's argument coincides with mine, but addresses the slower and more general effects of the Civil War. Fredrickson, *The Inner Civil War: Northern Intellectuals and the Crisis of the Union* (New York: Harper and Row, 1965), 146.
129 *Cincinnati Commercial*, Aug. 31, 1870. For the German-American reaction to these and other observations, see *Cincinnati Volksfreund*, Aug. 23, Sept. 1, 1870; *Watertown Weltbürger*, Sept. 3, 1870.

press in explaining the differences between the French and the Germans as essentialist ones. In an issue of the weekly that appeared in August 1870, editor E. L. Godkin vaunted the skill, efficiency, and physical strength of the German soldier and published a letter flattering the German *Volk*.[130] The correspondent was Forty-Eighter Friedrich Kapp, a former resident of New York who had returned to his native Prussia for good earlier that year. Kapp described the German people taking up arms to save themselves from "the infuriated hordes of duped Frenchmen." Americans, he pressed *The Nation*'s readers, must support the Germans in the "war between the Teutonic and Latin races."[131] Together, Kapp and Godkin introduced stock German-American ideas of the Franco-Prussian War to English-speaking Americans.

Godkin went further, though, elaborating on the ideas of *Volk* and state that would lead him to prioritize reform over African-American citizenship. In accord with the German-language press, he ascribed Prussia's rise to its state apparatus, not its reverence for citizenship rights, and ruminated what the United States should take from recent European history. *The Nation* explained that Germany was seeing "the result of sixty years of patient training, of contentment with slow gains, of respect for knowledge and for discipline, of close attention to the education of children, and of constant remembrance that a man is bound to labor for the state no less in his home than in the ranks of the army." Riveted, Godkin observed, "The lesson is full of instruction for all of us as well as for France."[132] While patronizing the "sentimental" Americans gulled by the French Republic, he delighted in the unification of Germany: "We look on [France's] decline, terrible and full of suffering as the process is, and the rise of Germany and of German habits of thought into supremacy, as one of the greatest gains humanity has made."[133] Godkin's ideological agreement with German immigrants foreshadowed the political alliance that would remake Reconstruction over the next few years.

Although German Ohioans, Missourians, and Wisconsinites knew that they stood at a *Wendepunkt* in 1870, a turning point is meaningful only in light of what went before and what would come after. Before August Thieme had arrived in Sandusky to exhort German immigrants to see Prussia's cause as their own, he had labored for a German republic in

---

130 *The Nation*, Aug. 11, 1870. See also William M. Armstrong, *E. L. Godkin and American Foreign Policy, 1865–1900* (New York: Bookman Associates, 1957), 112–13.

131 *The Nation*, Aug. 11, 1870. Friedrich Kapp, *Vom radikalen Frühsozialisten des Vormärz zum liberalen Parteipolitiker des Bismarckreichs: Briefe 1843–1884*, ed. Hans-Ulrich Wehler (Frankfurt am Main: Insel Verlag, 1969).

132 *The Nation*, Aug. 25, 1870.   133 Ibid., Sept. 29, 1870.

1848 and universal manhood suffrage from 1865 and 1869. Although he continued to favor African-American men's right to full citizenship in 1870, he became impatient with the Republican Party after the Fifteenth Amendment passed Congress. It must have been with relief that Thieme turned to the news coming from Germany. Calling the conflict a war between *Völker*, he reproached German Americans who did not support Prussia and found fault with the French people and their new republic.[134] He could not share Godkin's respect for the Prussian army, but with the other German Ohioans in that Sandusky courthouse, he was full of expectations for the German *Volk* and the German Empire. He and many other German Americans would ride these currents out of the Republican Party and into a coalition that advocated, among other things, the return of Southern government to white hands.

---

134 Zucker, ed., *Forty-Eighters*, 348; *Wächter am Erie*, Sept. 5 and 6, 1870; Wittke, *Refugees of Revolution*, 350–51, 356–58.

6

The Liberal Republican Transition, 1870–1872

In 1870, with Missouri's gubernatorial election looming, the *Westliche Post* called on its readers to emulate their counterparts across the Atlantic. Observing that Germans in Europe were in the throes of founding an awe-inspiring country, Carl Schurz's newspaper asked Germans in America, "We . . . who have rested for years on the laurels of the great Union victory, in which we assumed a glorious role, can we say the same of ourselves?"[1] Where the *Post* cajoled, the *St. Charles Demokrat* urged. "Show that the Germans can decide battles not only on the other side of the Ocean!" ran an early November editorial.[2] Editors at the *Post* and the *Demokrat* had previously invoked the spirit of 1848 and the myth of the freedom-loving German to elect Republicans and instate African-American suffrage. With France all but vanquished and the union of German states about to be consummated, the leaders of German-American public opinion had a new reason to induce immigrants to act "over here as over there."[3] They wanted Missourians to vote for the Liberal Republican Party, which subordinated questions of African-American rights to free trade, civil service reform, and reconciliation between Northern and Southern whites.

The new political movement, which grew from its Missouri roots to contest the presidential election of 1872, saw to it that the arc of Republican Reconstruction began to curve downward. The three major groups of Americans who constructed the Liberal Republican Party are therefore especially relevant to historians' efforts to explain white Northerners' fading commitment to African Americans. The first group, reform intellectuals in the mold of *The Nation*'s E. L. Godkin and the *Chicago Tribune*'s

1 *Mississippi Blätter*, Oct. 30, 1870. 2 *St. Charles Demokrat*, Nov. 3, 1870.
3 *Mississippi Blätter*, Oct. 30, 1870.

Horace White, became less sympathetic to the black laborers of the agricultural South as they became apprehensive of a swelling proletariat in the industrializing North. For them, ending Republican Reconstruction was just one part of an agenda of government retrenchment, laissez-faire economics, and civil service reform.[4] The second source of contributors to Liberal Republicanism was the Democratic community in the border states. Democrats worked behind the scenes in the hope that healing the rift between white Unionists and Confederates would speed their own return to political power, something that they knew would come at the expense of African Americans.[5] Democrats' cynicism did nothing to diminish their importance, as leaders and constituents, to the new party.

The motives of the third large group of Liberal Republicans, German Americans, are less well understood, despite Schurz's recognized role as one of the party's masterminds.[6] In 1872, the senator said that German immigrants "had joined it in Masse [sic]" and "in some Western states they

---

4 Foner, *Reconstruction*, 488–99. Foner builds on John G. Sproat, *"The Best Men": Liberal Reformers in the Gilded Age* (New York: Oxford University Press, 1968), 1–44. With similar interpretations, see Richardson, *Death of Reconstruction*, 102–04; Richardson, *West from Appomattox*, 121–47; Cohen, *Reconstruction of American Liberalism*, 119–22.

5 Blight, *Race and Reunion*, 122–29; Gillette, *Retreat from Reconstruction*, 57–61; Michael Perman, *The Road to Redemption: Southern Politics, 1869–1879* (Chapel Hill: University of North Carolina Press, 1984), 108–31; Burg, "Amnesty, Civil Rights, and the Meaning of Liberal Republicanism"; Jacqueline Balk and Ari Hoogenboom, "The Origins of Border State Liberal Republicanism," in *Radicalism, Racism, and Party Realignment: The Border States during Reconstruction*, ed. Richard O. Curry (Baltimore: Johns Hopkins Press, 1969), 220–44.

  Focusing on the ideology of twenty-three leaders, Andrew L. Slap argues that the Liberals were motivated by classical republicanism until the "movement" became a "party" in May 1872. Slap, *The Doom of Reconstruction: The Liberal Republicans in the Civil War Era* (New York: Fordham University Press, 2006). By minimizing the salience of race in the 1872 election and distinguishing between the ideological movement and the calculating party, Slap in some ways harks back to Earle D. Ross, *The Liberal Republican Movement* (New York: H. Holt and Company, 1919). On the earlier historiography, see Patrick W. Riddleberger, "The Radicals' Abandonment of the Negro during Reconstruction," *Journal of Negro History* 45, no. 2 (1960): 88–102; Richard A. Gerber, "The Liberals of 1872 in Historiographical Perspective," *Journal of American History* 62 (1975): 40–75; James M. McPherson, "Grant or Greeley: The Abolitionist Dilemma in the Election of 1872," *American Historical Review* 71 (1965): 43–61.

6 For an exception, see Nagler, "Deutschamerikaner und das *Liberal Republican Movement*, 1872," 415–38. Nagler's analysis does not delve into the ideology of German-American Liberals or situate the movement in a broader context. Most historians who recognize the role of German Americans have explained it by emphasizing Schurz's leadership, pointing to German Americans' ethnocultural interests, or describing the economic principles that German-American and native-born Liberals shared. Gerber, "Carl Schurz's Journey from Radical to Liberal Republicanism," 71–99; Slap, *Doom of Reconstruction*, 1–24; Parrish, *Missouri under Radical Rule*, 228–34, 287–313; Thomas Barclay, *The Liberal Republican Movement in Missouri, 1865–1871* (Columbia: State Historical Society of Missouri, 1926), 162, 219, 272; Kleppner, *Cross of Culture*, 111; Michael E. McGerr, "The Meaning of Liberal Republicanism: The Case of Ohio," *Civil War History* 28 (1982): 310. One monograph observes in passing how the European and American trends "dovetailed." See Honeck, *We Are the Revolutionists*, 185.

formed the whole backbone of the movement."[7] Unlike native-born reform intellectuals, German Americans constituted a large group of swing voters without whom the Republican Party was "surely doomed," at least according to weighty politicians such as Wisconsin's Cadwallader Washburn.[8] Beyond mere numbers, immigrants could cite their wartime service and postwar Radicalism to deflect accusations of disloyalty and racial prejudice. German Americans – not reform intellectuals or border state Democrats – made the Liberal Republicans a plausible third party.

Dealing with Liberal Republicanism among German Americans, this chapter uncovers the specific steps by which former Republicans sacrificed African-American rights to other priorities. Ethnicity, including the new images of the German *Volk* and German institutions that spread during the Franco-Prussian War, was at work throughout the process. In the movement's initial stages in Missouri, Liberal Republicans echoed German liberals' capitulation to Bismarck in Europe. Like the Forty-Eighters who accepted that the blood-and-iron chancellor would oversee German unification, the Liberal Republicans largely let former Confederates set the terms of American reconciliation. The most prominent Liberal politicians were former Radical Republicans, but by emphasizing reunion, they passed the initiative on matters of race to their onetime opponents. If Liberal Republicans in Schurz's home state could still credibly vaunt themselves as the proponents of race-neutral male citizenship in 1870, they increasingly had to adopt a willful ignorance in order to overlook the white supremacy of Democrats once the movement went national. As a more rigid racial hierarchy entered Liberal Republican discourse, so too did admiring depictions of Germany's administrative institutions. German-born Liberal Republicans admonished Americans to follow Prussia's example and professionalize their civil service. Civil service reformers often discounted citizen rights and sometimes questioned whether it had been wise to enfranchise black men in the first place.

Collectively, these modifications amounted to an overhaul of the liberal nationalism that had until recently predominated in the German-American public sphere. By arguing that the North and South would only reunite when Northern Republicans stopped guarding the citizenship of black Southerners, Liberals set national unity in conflict with the enforcement of rights. While Germans were disassociating liberalism from nationalism in Europe, Liberal Republicans were conducting a similar operation. Despite

7 Schurz to Horace Greeley, May 6, 1872, reel 7, fr. 603, 607, Schurz Papers, LOC.
8 Cadwallader C. Washburn to Elihu B. Washburne, Dec. 25, 1870, quoted in Grant, *Papers of Ulysses S. Grant*, ed. Simon, 21: 83.

its name, Liberal Republicanism stood for a less liberal nationalism, one that prized reunion and reform, not the voting rights of men.

GERMAN MISSOURIANS AND THE QUESTION OF LIBERAL REPUBLICAN CONSISTENCY, 1870

German Americans first made Liberal Republicanism their own in Missouri. There they rehearsed the party's appeals to German ethnicity and fine-tuned its allusions to the upheavals in Europe. Just as importantly, the Missouri campaign of 1870 helped German-American Republicans smoothly extricate themselves from Reconstruction by providing cover for the argument that African-American suffrage was entirely compatible with reconciliation and reform. Unlike states under federal control, Missouri still prohibited former Confederates from exercising the franchise. Lifting the ironclad oath and allowing more white men to vote, as Liberal Republicans advocated, would not necessarily endanger the rights of black Missourians. The immigrant Republicans who joined the Liberal Republican Party could protest their consistency toward white and black voters. The elections of fall 1870, however, began to teach Liberals what was involved in chasing the votes of former Confederates, the strategy that would determine the party's place in national politics.

German Missourians could reasonably argue that Liberal Republicanism represented the liberal nationalism that they had cherished all along. The formation of the new party, the *Westliche Post* pointed out, was only the latest episode in a long history of "disharmony between the German Republicans and Mr. Drake and his special friends and followers."[9] Schurz and Charles Drake, who now dueled in the Senate, led two Republican factions that differed substantively on policy. Schurz favored hard money and free trade as well as noninterference with alcohol consumption, while Drake preferred unsecured greenbacks, protective tariffs, and the tight regulation of intoxicating beverages.[10] Since the 1865 constitutional convention, Missouri's German politicians had tried to enfranchise black men and had tolerated the disfranchisement of disloyal white men only as a temporary expedient. The German-born lawmaker Gustavus A. Finkelnburg recommended to the legislature that it strike race-based voting restrictions *and* the ironclad oath from the state constitution in 1865, and Schurz had

---

9 *Westliche Post*, Oct. 1, 1870.
10 Trefousse, *Carl Schurz*, 182–96; Barclay, *Liberal Republican Movement in Missouri*, 150–82; Parrish, *Missouri under Radical Rule*, 268–99; Slap, *Doom of Reconstruction*, 1–24.

made similar pleas during his 1869 run for the Senate.[11] Drake had lagged behind other Missouri Republicans on both issues. The animosity between the state's two senators intensified in 1870, when Schurz announced that Benjamin Gratz Brown was his preferred candidate for governor.[12] Brown, who had come out for "universal suffrage and universal amnesty" in 1866 and was also estranged from Drake, seemed to be a paragon of ideological constancy.[13]

Pointing to Brown's record, Schurz could contend that immigrants sought to repeal the loyalty oath – thereby reconciling with former secessionists – for the same reason that they had worked for African-American voting: the abiding German appreciation for equal male citizenship and national unity. The *Westliche Post* told German-speaking St. Louisans that Brown had taken up the "German idea of emancipation" before the war and the "essentially German" cause of black suffrage in 1865. (Schurz's paper conveniently ignored the fact that most German Missourians had not voted for suffrage in the 1868 referendum.) Now, the *Post* editorialized, it was naturally "Brown and only Brown who declared himself clearly and explicitly in favor of the lifting of the test oath and the voting restrictions."[14] The newspaper later wrote, "The Germans of Missouri stand again in the first row among those who are eliminating the dividing line of disfranchisement [and] restoring equal rights to everyone, and are thereby prepared to extend the hand of reconciliation to former enemies."[15] Liberal Republican rhetoric capitalized on ethnic loyalties and depended on the congruity of equal rights and reconciliation in the context of postwar Missouri.

Liberal Republicans' observations of Germany also buttressed their case that a conciliatory attitude toward Confederates was a reformulation of old ideas. Noting the parallels between American and European history, German Americans reckoned that the Liberal Republican movement followed the Civil War as inevitably as the German Empire had followed the Revolutions of 1848. At a speech in August 1870, Arnold Krekel, who had chaired the Missouri constitutional convention five years earlier, commemorated the immigrants who had given their lives to secure "equal justice before the law in the preserved Union." To Krekel, the Northern victory had vindicated "self-determination," a liberal nationalist ideal that

---

11 McKerley, "Citizens and Strangers," 97.
12 Schurz, *Reminiscences of Carl Schurz*, 3: 285; *Woechentlich Westliche Post*, Jan. 13, 20, 1869; Benjamin F. Loan to Schurz, Jan. 7, 1869; Schurz to Benjamin F. Loan, Jan. 7, 1869, reel 3, fr. 566, Schurz Papers, LOC.
13 *Westliche Post*, June 26, 1870, Aug. 24, 1870. The English-language *St. Louis Missouri Democrat* also supported Brown. Parrish, *Missouri under Radical Rule*, 288–89.
14 *Westliche Post*, Aug. 24, 1870.   15 Ibid., Oct. 25, 1870.

encompassed citizen rights and national unity. Although he had countenanced the ironclad oath in the interest of "safeguarding... the achievements of the war" back in 1865, Krekel now believed that only revoking it would "achieve the full recovery of the commonwealth." He found the news from Europe instructive because the German *Volk* had also united behind "self-determination" when it waged war on the French royal family. Krekel was the first to suggest that both Germans in Europe and Germans in Missouri were taking bold new strides in the service of the liberal nationalism to which they had always adhered. For him, both the unification of Germany and the elimination of voting exclusions in Missouri were realizations of the promise of 1848 and the Civil War.[16]

Only time would reveal that German-American Republicans in Missouri would have to compromise their liberal nationalism as German politicians in Europe had theirs. The Republican infighting came to a head at the state convention in September 1870. Although Drake's regulars, a group not unlike the majority in the 1865 constitutional convention, could see that the ironclad oath would not last, they were not ready to renounce it, and they certainly did not plan to nominate Brown.[17] Suspecting that Liberals would try to command the proceedings, the regulars had increased the power of newly enfranchised African Americans. The party's central committee had allocated one delegate for every 150 black men – or fraction thereof – in each county. Since many counties had only very small black populations, the African-American presence at the convention was disproportionately large. The *Westliche Post* calculated that there was one delegate for every 94 African-American men in the state, but only one representative for every 136 white Republican voters.[18] When the meeting convened in Jefferson City, 180 black men held the balance of power in the 781-man-strong body. Accusing regulars of manipulating party rules to block Brown's selection, about 250 Liberal delegates, including the whole German contingent from St. Louis, eventually stormed out.[19] The defectors went on to nominate Brown and draft a platform that included hard money, free trade, civil service reform, and the deregulation of alcohol sales.[20] Most significantly, the new Liberal Republican Party affirmed that "the time has

---

16 *St. Charles Demokrat*, Aug. 18, 1870. See also *Westliche Post*, Aug. 12, 1870.
17 Barclay, *Liberal Republican Movement in Missouri*, 173–75, 184, 188–91.
18 *Westliche Post*, Aug. 3, 1870; Barclay, *Liberal Republican Movement in Missouri*, 235; Parrish, *Missouri under Radical Rule*, 289–90.
19 On the convention, see Barclay, *Liberal Republican Movement in Missouri*, 233–49; Parrish, *Missouri under Radical Rule*, 291–99. It is difficult to trace all of the individuals involved in the walkout, but for a list of the German-American delegates, see *Westliche Post*, Sept. 3, 1870.
20 *St. Charles Demokrat*, Sept. 8, 1870.

come, that the demands of public security, on which the disfranchisement of a great number of citizens could be grounded, have clearly ceased to exist."[21]

After Jefferson City, the issue became whether the former Republicans who now organized around voting rights for Confederate sympathizers would uphold those rights for African Americans. The editor of the *St. Charles Demokrat* knew that race still posed a dilemma. "Far be it from us to want to promote racial prejudice," the editors wrote, "but it was really a bit much [*etwas starker Tabak*] to expect that 90 Negro votes would count for as much as 140 votes from whites."[22] Similar resentment festered at the *Westliche Post*.[23] Could Liberal Republicans declaim black overrepresentation and run against African Americans without promoting prejudice or doubting the right of black men to full citizenship?

Immigrant reactions to the Franco-Prussian War influenced the answer. The Liberal Republican Party formed at the same time as the Third French Republic – the Jefferson City bolt occurred on the very day that German armies captured Napoleon III at Sedan – and the fall election fell at the time of the most cutting descriptions of the French in the German-language press. Editors were busy depicting the French as thoroughly unfit for the responsibilities of citizenship. Doubt that any man, whatever his *Volk*, could become a good citizen pervaded the German-American public sphere as the German-language discussion of African-American citizenship resumed.

Prefiguring the movement's national incarnation, German-American Liberals made the political climate in Missouri more hostile to black citizenship. Still, each individual participant took a different approach. The most explicit turn against African Americans appeared in the pages of the *St. Charles Demokrat* after John H. Bode, a twenty-six-year-old from Hanover, became editor in June 1869.[24] Just before the election in 1870, Bode characterized the speeches of African-American politicians as "the invective of colored stumping billboards."[25] When James Milton Turner spoke in St. Charles, the *Demokrat* reported that "he has a right slimy gift of the gab and so may well have general success with an ignorant and uneducated class of people, such as the colored still is at this time." Local whites met Turner's speech with a barrage of ominous cheers for Brown. If the

---

21 Ibid., Sept. 8, 1870.   22 Ibid., Sept. 17, 1870.
23 *Westliche Post*, Oct. 13, 1870.
24 On the new editor, John H. Bode, see *St. Charles Demokrat*, June 10, 1869; Arndt and Olsen, *German-American Newspapers*, 246; U.S. Bureau of the Census, Population Schedule of the Ninth Census of the United States 1870, St. Charles, Missouri, 352.
25 *St. Charles Demokrat*, Nov. 3, 1870.

regular Republicans wanted the Liberal Republican candidate to win in a landslide, Bode wrote, "they should send over a few more colored house boys."[26] The *Demokrat* had always portrayed most African Americans as crude and ignorant, but the spiteful tone and gleeful anticipation of black failure were new. A newspaper that had imagined a bright future in which education would make admirable citizens of former slaves now interlaced offensive generalizations about black Americans with pessimistic predictions for the "degraded" French masses. If every Liberal organ had been so malicious, the party's commitment to equal manhood suffrage could be judged uncertain indeed.

Most former Republicans, however, could edge away from African-American rights more incrementally, thanks to the Democratic leaders who had acquiesced to the Fifteenth Amendment. Before the Jefferson City convention, Democratic politicians had made it known that they would not run anyone for governor if Brown were nominated. This "possum policy" was aimed at reassuring Liberal Republicans that Democrats eschewed violence and had nothing against universal suffrage if universal amnesty accompanied it.[27] James S. Rollins, a former Whig who was now a Democratic operative, corresponded regularly with Schurz and even sat in on the Liberal Republican convention.[28] Rollins's son wrote to him at the time to agree with his father that the Liberals' platform was "sound and fit."[29] Carl Dänzer at the *Anzeiger* also thought that this platform would "find little contradiction from the ranks of the Democratic Party."[30] For a while, Liberal Republicans could believe that Democrats had come around to Republican arguments and that bipartisan cooperation was a new strategy, not an ideological transformation.

Of course, former Republicans could not take Democratic protestations at face value without a certain degree of credulity. Missouri Democrats were open about their goal of regaining power for themselves. Dänzer wrote that the Liberals were in reality "the liberal wing of the Democratic Party."[31] In the *Anzeiger*, he objected to the removal of racial qualifications for office holding, but told readers that the Liberal plan would not come to much anyway because the Liberal Republicans were merely a

26 Ibid., Oct. 27, 1870. On Turner, see Kremer, *James Milton Turner*. On African-American partisan activity in Missouri, see Parrish, *Missouri under Radical Rule*, 301–04; McKerley, "Citizens and Strangers," 149–69; Astor, *Rebels on the Border*, 208–42.

27 *Westliche Post*, Aug. 16, 1870; Parrish, *Missouri under Radical Rule*, 305. On other newspapers, see Barclay, *Liberal Republican Movement in Missouri*, 251; Curry, "Introduction," in *Radicalism, Racism, and Party Realignment*, ed. Curry, xix.

28 Parrish, *Missouri under Radical Rule*, 297.

29 James H. Rollins to James S. Rollins, Sept. 5, 1870, folder 106, Rollins Papers, WHMC – Columbia.

30 *Anzeiger des Westens*, Sept. 8, 1870.   31 Ibid., Sept. 8, 1870.

"transitional party."[32] Schurz saw only what he wanted in the Democrats' messages. His *Westliche Post* refuted President Grant's argument that Liberal Republicans in Missouri resembled the anti-Republican movements that were returning Virginia and Tennessee to Democratic rule. Schurz himself circulated a statement to the effect that Liberal Republicans sought the votes only of those Democrats who were for "the total realization of the whole Republican program" and "the guarantee of equal rights for all."[33] The German-American senator believed that he could guide the coalition. The results of the cooperation between liberal politicians and Bismarck in Europe gave compromise a certain luster, especially in September and October 1870. Up until the November election, there was some reason to believe that Democrats too dreamed of a peaceful United States in which black and white men elected well educated, fiscally responsible, incorruptible leaders.

While the *St. Charles Demokrat* was reorienting itself against African Americans and Democrats were disarming Schurz, some German-American Missourians candidly grappled with what Liberal Republicanism might mean for the freed people. Black Missourians did not see the state's Democrats in the same light as Schurz did.[34] Frank Blair, Missouri's most effective opposition politician, had used enough racial invective in the 1868 vice-presidential race to position the Democratic Party as one of unrepentant white supremacy.[35] Murderous political violence in parts of the Southern and border states, including Missouri, had corrupted that election, and African Americans still feared for their physical safety.[36] Arnold Krekel probably learned of these concerns in his role on the board of the Lincoln Institute. When he backed Brown and the repeal of the ironclad oath, he admitted, "I have no doubt that a part of our population would strip Negroes' rights if it lay within their power." The immigrant, who now wore a judge's gown on the federal bench, called for an amendment to the state constitution to make African Americans eligible to hold elective office.[37] Krekel supported the Liberals in part because Drake's regulars had not delivered much to African Americans between 1865 and 1870.

Without clarifying whether their party would be antagonistic toward African Americans, follow the lead of the Democrats, or mount a diligent defense of the principle of equal male citizenship, Liberal Republicans set

---

32 Ibid., Nov. 4, 1870.   33 *Westliche Post*, Sept. 22, Nov. 11, 1870.

34 There were a few exceptions, and Frederick Douglass recommended from outside the state that African Americans back the Liberal Republicans. Astor, *Rebels on the Border*, 215–16.

35 Parrish, *Frank Blair*, 256.

36 Foner, *Reconstruction*, 342–45; McKerley, "Citizens and Strangers," 120; Drake, "Betrayal of the Republican Party in Missouri," *Congressional Globe*, 41st Cong., 3rd sess., App. 1–8 (Dec. 16, 1870).

37 *St. Charles Demokrat*, Aug. 18, 1870.

up a German–American base in Missouri. Schurz spoke across the state, asking immigrants to form local organizations. Germans in Lafayette County, east of Kansas City, informed the *Westliche Post* that they were "natural" Liberals. They had been the first "who hurried to the flag at the outbreak of the rebellion," and now they were the first "who extend the hand of reconciliation." Despite the violent reputation of Lafayette Conservatives, local Liberals expected them to be suitably grateful.[38] Farther east along the Missouri River in Chariton County, German Americans also provided Liberal leadership. Louis Benecke, who had naturalized only after he was mustered out of Union service in 1865, ran for election to the state senate. Proud of having walked out of the Jefferson City convention with Schurz, the twenty-seven-year-old thought it "unnecessary to recount" the Liberal platform in his campaign flyer.[39] Corresponding with several Liberal Republicans around the state, Benecke learned that one of his German-speaking friends had formed the "Brown Party" in another Chariton County township. Although the friend considered his own township a Liberal "stronghold," he knew some farmers worried about splitting the Republican Party. Someone would have to "prod them a little."[40]

In the end, the legions of German Republican voters in Missouri supported Brown "in a solid phalanx."[41] Statewide, the Liberal Republican beat his rival by nearly 40,000 votes, despite the influence of about 20,000 African Americans who were voting for governor for the first time.[42] Brown won every precinct in St. Charles and St. Louis, and he dominated the German counties along the Missouri River.[43] St. Louis also returned Gustavus Finkelnburg to the U.S. House of Representatives,

---

38 *Westliche Post*, Nov. 2, 1870. For Schurz's campaign itinerary, see *Mississippi Blätter*, Oct. 23, 1870. On local violence, see Hughs, "Lafayette County in the Aftermath of Slavery"; Astor, *Rebels on the Border*, 230, 237–39.

39 Louis Benecke, "To the Voters," Oct. 19, 1870, folder 1484, Louis Benecke Papers, WHMC – Columbia. For a biography of Benecke, see the online collection inventory. University of Missouri and State Historical Society of Missouri, "Benecke Family Papers Inventory," WHMC – Columbia, http://whmc.umsystem.edu/invent/3825.html (accessed Dec. 4, 2012).

40 Theodore Boehme to Louis Benecke, Sept. 28, 1870, folder 722, Benecke Papers, WHMC – Columbia. On other correspondence, see Schurz to L. Benecke Feb. 29, 1869, folder 713, Benecke Papers, WHMC – Columbia. See also further correspondence in folders 1483, 1484, 1485, 1491, and 1492.

41 James B. Colegan to C. J. Cornoin, Aug. 28, 1871, box 1, folder 9, Records of Governor Benjamin Gratz Brown, Office of Governor, MSA.

42 The referendum against the oath passed even more convincingly. Barclay, *Liberal Republican Movement in Missouri*, 269, 261–62; Parrish, *Missouri under Radical Rule*, 307–08.

43 Appendix, Table 3; *Westliche Post*, Nov. 12, 1870; Office of the Secretary of State, Elections Division, Election Returns, box 12, folders 22, 29, and 36, MSA. On the central counties, see also Barclay, *Liberal Republican Movement in Missouri*, 269.

and Louis Benecke's neighbors sent him to the state senate.[44] German Missourians had established many of the peculiarities of the Liberal Republican movement, including its use of German ethnicity and its esteem for the German state. Former Republicans had vowed that the movement would carry forward the banner of universal manhood suffrage, but they were also beginning to hedge their earlier optimism about African Americans. The act of balancing black rights and white reconciliation would become even more precarious when Schurz tried to transpose the Missouri experience onto the whole country.

THE RISKS OF RECONCILIATION, 1870–1871

Between the Missouri election of 1870 and the presidential election of 1872, the decision to accommodate Democrats would steadily undermine the Liberal Republicans' relationship with African Americans. When Schurz spoke of reconciliation on a national scale, he did not just mean lifting voting restrictions on former Confederates. National reunification, as Liberals saw it, required ending the federal interventions that allowed black men in the South to exercise their political rights. That action would have more profound ramifications than amending Missouri's voting qualifications. Most Liberal Republicans still evinced less malice toward African Americans than Democrats did. They would say that treating the defeated white South magnanimously was one way to ensure order and justice. The reassessment of means and reshuffling of priorities, however, would be as consequential as German liberals' acceptance of Bismarckian militarism. Men who had argued that bolstering the rights of African Americans would save the nation now maintained that it would be preferable to placate the sometimes violent enemies of the freed people. Because bridging sectional and partisan divides was so important to Liberal Republican ideology, it is impossible to understand the significance of the new party for African-American citizenship without investigating the interactions that implicated former Republicans in the racial calculus of the Democrats.

Democrats seized on Schurz's misreading of events in Missouri to manipulate him. As Carl Dänzer noted, polling in the state had given the Democrats an unequivocal "victory."[45] Brown owed his election to Democratic

44 *Westliche Post*, Nov. 11, 1870; G. W. Wood to Louis Benecke, Nov. 16, 1870, folder 1484; Robert Benecke to Louis Benecke, Nov. 15, 1870, folder 724, Benecke Papers, WHMC – Columbia.
45 *Anzeiger des Westens*, Nov. 9, 1870. In the long-term, the *Anzeiger's* assessment proved accurate. Curry, "Introduction," in *Radicalism, Racism, and Party Realignment*, ed. Curry, xix; Kleppner, *Third Electoral System*, 119–20.

voters, who had secured 77 of the 138 seats in Missouri's lower house. (Liberal Republican candidates won just 21.)[46] Knowing that he needed the Democrats, Brown quickly made Frank Blair his personal choice to replace Drake in the Senate.[47] At first, Schurz worried about these omens, but he proved remarkably susceptible to Democratic flattery.[48] Extensive correspondence among Missouri politicians provides a record of how Democrats assuaged the senator's qualms. In a letter to Rollins, Blair laid out his plan to win over German Americans. "If we treat them with consideration," he wrote, "they will unite with me cordially, as they agree with me on the currency[,] taxation & tariff questions." He believed that "backed by the Germans of Missouri we [the Democrats] can carry the other German vote in the next presidential election." Since Blair thought Schurz "as much the leader of the Germans in America, as Bismarck is in Europe," he cultivated a friendship with the man who was now his colleague in the Senate.[49] Blair also enlisted the assistance of Rollins in assuring Schurz that Missouri was "irretrievably lost to the Republicans but that he will be supported & maintained by the Democracy."[50] Brown, increasingly a Democratic partisan, joined in too.[51] Taken in by effusive compliments, Schurz kept repeating, "When the Missouri Democrats voted for the same principles and men that they had previously most ardently fought against, then they certainly went to the Republicans and not these to them."[52] By December 1870, Schurz was shutting out plentiful evidence that the Liberal Republicans were beholden to Democrats.

As Schurz set about designing a national movement, he appeased Democrats and began to speak of Reconstruction as an unreasonable federal imposition on Southern whites. On December 15, 1870, he presented the Senate with a careful blueprint to end the Republican Reconstruction measures that President Grant had made his own.[53] Schurz said that a "conciliatory policy" had been necessary in Missouri so that the "Southern

---

46 Parrish, *Missouri under Radical Rule*, 310.
47 Slap, *Doom of Reconstruction*, 20; Parrish, *Missouri under Radical Rule*, 314.
48 Schurz to Emil Preetorius, Nov. 16, 1870, reel 89, fr. 96–97, Schurz Papers, LOC.
49 Frank Blair, Jr. to James S. Rollins, Dec. 18, 1870, folder 106, Rollins Papers, WHMC – Columbia. See also Blair to James S. Rollins, Dec. 28, 1870, folder 106, Rollins Papers, WHMC – Columbia.
50 Blair to James S. Rollins, Feb. 16, 1871, folder 107, Rollins Papers, WHMC – Columbia; James S. Rollins to Schurz, Dec. 25, 1870, reel 5, fr. 114–15, Schurz Papers, LOC.
51 Benjamin Gratz Brown to Schurz, Nov. 26, 1870, reel 4, fr. 581–85, Schurz Papers, LOC. For further evidence that Brown understood that he had to cultivate German support, see correspondence in box 1, folders 9, 13, 21, 27, and 28, Records of Benjamin Gratz Brown, Office of Governor, MSA.
52 *Westliche Post*, Dec. 2, 1870. See also Sept. 27, Nov. 11 and 26, 1870. For evidence that the praise convinced Schurz, see Schurz to Louis Benecke, Feb. 2, 1871, folder 1492, Benecke Papers, WHMC – Columbia.
53 Schurz to Emil Preetorius, Dec. 12, 1870, reel 89, fr. 105–06, Schurz Papers, LOC.

people" would "identify their interests, aspirations, and hopes with the new order of things." He patently did not count African Americans among "the Southern people." The senator singled them out as symbols of Drake's "arbitrary party despotism." After explaining the role of black delegates at the state convention, Schurz accused the regulars of using "colored agitators" to seduce black voters with "all the artifices of demagogism [sic]." To supplement his rhetorical solidarity with Southern whites, Schurz introduced a bill to lift "disqualifications and disabilities imposed on all persons lately in rebellion."[54] The proposal gave the misleading impression that former Confederates throughout the South faced the same restrictions as secessionists in Missouri. In reality, no national law excluded former Confederates from voting, and only a few hundred Southern leaders were still prohibited from holding office under the Fourteenth Amendment.[55] With his speech and the symbolic amnesty bill, Schurz moved closer to the Democrats who stroked his ego and fed his ambitions.

Schurz's overtures to Democrats became incompatible with a rigorous defense of black suffrage, most obviously because they meant decreasing the power of the federal officials who offset some of the political violence in the South. In his 1865 *Report on the Condition of the South*, Schurz had documented chilling attacks on freed people. At that time, he had seen the vote as a weapon of self-defense. By 1868, however, it was apparent that violence could jeopardize voting rights too. Organizations such as the Ku Klux Klan not only targeted black militia, schools, and churches, they also intimidated Republican voters.[56] Terrorism was at its worst in areas where African Americans were numerous enough to decide elections, but former Confederates also threatened German immigrants in Missouri. A German-born preacher wrote to Schurz in December 1870 to relate what had transpired on election day in Warrenton. An altercation began when a group of "rebels" rode up to the polling place crying out "Hurrah" for Jefferson Davis, the president of the Confederacy. When German Union veterans retorted, " . . . and a rope to hang him," the secessionists took out revolvers and forced the immigrants to take their comment back. The preacher, who said that he valued "human rights," considered it "still far too early to give such people [unrepentant secessionists] the vote." As a Christian, he believed in forgiveness, but "a change of heart must also take place."[57] This

---

54 *Congressional Globe*, 41st Cong., 3rd sess., 118, 121, 120 (Dec. 15, 1870).
55 James A. Rawley, "The General Amnesty Act of 1872: A Note," *Mississippi Valley Historical Review* 47 (1960): 481–82; Foner, *Reconstruction*, 504.
56 Rable, *But There Was No Peace*; Keith, *Colfax Massacre*.
57 Wilhelm Schreck to Schurz, Dec. 12, 1870, reel 5, fr. 33–35, Schurz Papers, LOC. For another warning that the Liberal Republicans' faith in former Confederates was misplaced, see William

incident, which was innocuous compared to depredations against African Americans in other areas, did not move Schurz. By shrugging off reports of violence, the senator showed that he was willing to disregard the spirit of the Fifteenth Amendment.

Schurz's indifference to incursions against voting rights was the lynchpin of the Liberal Republican deal with Democrats. In April 1871, the senator was one of the few Republicans to vote against the third piece of legislation implementing the Fifteenth Amendment. The Ku Klux Klan Act, an ambitious extension of federal power, made it a federal crime for an individual to interfere with citizenship rights. Specifically, the act authorized the president to declare martial law and suspend the writ of habeas corpus to stop terrorism against African-American voters.[58] In explaining his opposition, Schurz said that the likely abuse of federal power outweighed the potential damage of Klan attacks: "I consider the rights and liberties of the whole American people of still higher importance than the interests of those in the South whose dangers and sufferings appeal so strongly to our sympathy." An accord like the one that he had brokered in Missouri would "dissolve that bond of common grievance which binds the law and order loving Democrats of the South to the lawless element." It would "strengthen the influence and power of the honest element in the Republican party of the South."[59] Although Schurz still longed for calm in the states of the former Confederacy, he now saw tending to African-American rights as an obstacle to it.

Liberal Republicans deliberately downplayed the significance of terrorism. In September 1871, as federal prosecutors were moving against the Klan in South Carolina, Schurz reached out to Southern whites in a major speech.[60] Although he condemned "acts of violence and persecution inflicted by a certain class of the Southern population upon Republicans and colored people," he did not think that they were a systematic challenge to the Fifteenth Amendment. Speaking in Nashville, Tennessee, the Liberal leader described the aversion of the white South to African-American politics as a natural one given "all the traditions of her people." He also said

Gilman to Schurz, Feb. 28, 1871, reel 5, fr. 279–80, Schurz Papers, LOC. For Schurz's explicit denial that any such violence occurred in Missouri, see *Congressional Globe*, 41st Cong., 3rd sess., 119 (Dec. 15, 1870).

58 Foner, *Reconstruction*, 454–59; Trefousse, *Carl Schurz*, 196; Wang, *Trial of Democracy*, 83–86.

59 *Congressional Globe*, 42nd Cong., 1st sess., 687, 688 (April 14, 1871). The *St. Charles Demokrat* emphasized that the main problem with the Ku Klux Klan Act was the power it gave to the "tyrannical Grant." *St. Charles Demokrat*, April 20, 1871.

60 On the South Carolina trials, see Lou Falkner Williams, *The Great South Carolina Ku Klux Klan Trials, 1871–1872* (Athens: University of Georgia Press, 1996).

that African Americans were "inexperienced" voters duped by "unscrupulous and rapacious demagogues." Underscoring the importance of "local government," Schurz told his audience that even the atrocities committed by white terrorists did not warrant the Grant administration's actions in South Carolina.[61] He commiserated with Southern whites, whom he believed were subjected to vengeful and corrupt rule by African Americans and their Republican supporters.

Because Schurz was the most visible Liberal Republican during 1871, the senator's withdrawal from the movement for black rights was nationally important. Schurz had never been personally close to African Americans, but he had once been a dogged opponent of prejudice. He had argued that any man could become a valuable citizen. Schurz's new views were on display when he butted heads with Grant over plans to annex the Caribbean country of Santo Domingo early in 1871. The rising Liberal had asked his fellow senators, "Is the incorporation of that part of the globe and the people inhabiting it quite compatible with the integrity, safety, perpetuity, and progressive development of our institutions which we value so highly?" His answer was informed by his assessments of the French and black Southerners. "I trust we have lived too long and seen too much," he said, "to believe that the mere absence of a king is sufficient to make a true republic, and that you have only to place the ballot in the hands of the multitude to make them citizens fit to sustain the fabric of self-government."[62] It turned out that Schurz found consolation in the North American climate, which he believed favored good citizenship in a way that the tropical conditions of the Caribbean did not. But climate could serve as a proxy for race.[63] Schurz insisted that this was not the case, but there was no hiding the fact that he had lost his enthusiasm for extending citizenship. His confidence in uplift disappeared between 1870 and 1872, taking with it his advocacy for a minimum level of federal support for the freed people.

Two other German-born politicians were more conflicted about the racial implications of the Liberal Republican movement. W. W. Coleman and August Thieme both initially shared Arnold Krekel's doubts about former Confederates. Coleman, who succeeded Bernhard Domschke at the *Milwaukee Herold*, wrote in April 1871 that "the South still suffers from

61 Schurz, "The Need for Reform and a New Party," Sept. 20, 1871, in *Speeches, Correspondence and Political Papers of Carl Schurz*, 2: 261, 277, 264, 267, 283–84, 277–78. Also minimizing the violence, see *St. Charles Demokrat*, Jan. 4, 1872.
62 *Congressional Globe*, 41st Cong., 3rd sess., App. 26, 27, 29 (Jan. 11, 1871). For background, see Trefousse, *Carl Schurz*, 186–88, 191–95.
63 Nicholas Guyatt, "America's Conservatory: Race, Reconstruction, and the Santo Domingo Debate," *Journal of American History* 97 (2011): 984.

the old political intolerance" and "is not ready by in large to tolerate and respect freedom of thought and of speech or citizen equality at the ballot box." He enjoined Congress to conduct a thorough investigation before it scaled back the federal role in the South.[64] The following week, however, the *Herold* came out against the Ku Klux Klan bill because, Coleman said, it gave the president too much power to overrule local authorities and might hinder reconciliation.[65] Thieme was even more cautious about Liberal Republicanism, declaring the Ku Klux Klan Act constitutional.[66] During 1871, his *Wächter am Erie* reported positively on the educational and economic progress of black Southerners, and in September it published Jacob Müller's argument that "the existence and strength of the Ku Klux bands in the South" was evidence that "amnesty" and "reconciliation" in truth meant "only expedience and disfranchisement."[67] Thieme endorsed Müller for Ohio's lieutenant governorship that year, but before the 1872 election he critiqued the Republican speeches that warned that Southern whites would not recognize the rights of Southern blacks. They were little more than partisan scaremongering, he implied.[68]

The Liberal Republican movement may have signified slightly different things to different participants, but Schurz's accommodations would define it as a whole. Reunification was at the heart of Liberal Republican ideology, and Democrats made racial concessions the price of that reunification. The German-American senator did not need to disavow the Fifteenth Amendment completely to effect political change. Schurz simply voiced his growing fear that some men would never make good citizens. Against the backdrop of the European war and Southern violence, however, his new politics was freighted with significance. Most Americans – Democrats and Republicans alike – saw that even the most careful retreat from Reconstruction would lower African Americans' chance at defensible political rights. German immigrants, caught up in German unification across the Atlantic, were among the few who failed to notice.

INSTITUTIONAL REFORM, RACE, AND CITIZENSHIP

During 1871 and early 1872, German-American Liberal Republicans attracted a national following. The new party had already benefited from the excitement of the Franco-Prussian War and some of the ideas rippling

---

64 *Herold Wöchentliche Ausgabe*, April 13, 1871.
65 Ibid., April 20, 1871. See also April 27, 1871.   66 *Wächter am Erie*, May 1, 1871.
67 Ibid., Sept. 22, 1872. The report on black Southerners appeared on April 22, 1871.
68 Ibid., March 15, July 11, 1872.

out from it: the more essentialist definition of the German *Volk* and the necessity of reconciling former political foes. (Schurz had entreated Northerners to make their peace with Southerners just as Forty-Eighters had forgiven the Prussian monarchy.[69]) In the debate over reconstructing the former Confederate states, Liberal Republicans trotted out another point of German pride, Prussia's administrative institutions. German-born Liberals were not authoritarians themselves, but the quest for administrative probity led many immigrants to reexamine the liberalism that underpinned biracial Republican governments in Southern states.

Even at the national level, however, the Franco-Prussian War also had some less ideological repercussions. Liberal Republicans used its tug on the emotions of immigrants quite shamelessly. They were aided by bungling in the Grant administration. In 1870, at the climax of the Missouri campaign – and as war raged in Europe – the U.S. Ordinance Bureau sold 100,000 Springfield rifles to an arms dealer who passed them on to the French government.[70] The transaction seemed trivial to English-speaking newspapermen, but with German troops still dying in France, immigrants thought that it merited "serious consideration."[71] Editors who already disliked Grant alleged that he was prolonging the European war. Small groups of Cincinnatians, St. Louisans, and Milwaukeeans staged public demonstrations, and State Representative Peter Deuster even asked the Wisconsin legislature to censure the president.[72] Eventually, Secretary of State Hamilton Fish and Secretary of War William W. Belknap, having received petitions from Schurz, reported that the shipments had stopped. The fuss died down in the spring of 1871.[73]

In 1872, Schurz reignited the "arms scandal" in a stunt devised to convert German-American umbrage into Liberal Republican momentum. He charged Grant's War Department with contravening American neutrality

---

69 *Congressional Globe*, 42nd Cong., 2nd sess., 701 (Dec. 15, 1870).

70 For brief narratives of the affair, see Summers, *The Era of Good Stealings* (New York: Oxford University Press, 1993), 208; Trefousse, *Carl Schurz*, 178–81; Koerner, *Memoirs*, 2: 523–24.

71 *Cincinnati Volksfreund*, Oct. 5, 1870; *Westliche Post*, Oct. 5 and 6, Dec. 22, 1870; *Illinois Staatszeitung*, Jan. 9, 1871; *Wochenblatt der New-Yorker Staats-Zeitung*, Oct. 15 and 29, Nov. 12, 1870; *Banner und Volksfreund*, Oct. 18, Nov. 2, 1870, July 29, 1871; *Seebote*, Nov. 14, 1870, Jan. 9 and 16, March 27, 1871, March 18, 1872. For the response of the English-language press, see *New York World*, Oct. 4 and 5, Nov. 3 and 4, 1870; *New York Tribune*, Oct. 4, 5, and 13, 1870; *New York Times*, Oct. 4 and 5, 1870; *The Nation*, Oct. 4 and 5, 1870; *Cincinnati Enquirer*, Oct. 5, 1870; *Cincinnati Commercial*, Oct. 6, 1870.

72 Listing the protests, see *Cincinnati Commercial*, Jan. 27, 1871; *Cincinnati Volksfreund*, Jan. 10 and 26, 1871; *Illinois Staatszeitung*, Jan. 9, 1871; Hense-Jensen, *Wisconsin's Deutsch-Amerikaner*, 1: 234. On Deuster's resolution, see *Seebote*, Jan. 30, Feb. 6, 1871.

73 Hamilton Fish to Schurz, Jan. 23, 1871; William Belknap to Schurz, Jan. 24, 1871, reel 5, fr. 202–03, 206, Schurz Papers, LOC. Francis Lieber also petitioned Fish. Lieber to Hamilton Fish, Oct. 8, Nov. 17, 1870, Feb. 14, 1871, vols. 73, 74, and 76, Fish Papers, LOC.

and violating the laws that governed the sale of ordinance.[74] Congressional investigations dismissed these accusations, but not before Schurz had inveighed in the Senate, "This great American Republic of ours understands and interprets her . . . neutral duties strictly on the cash principle!"[75] He could both brand Grant as corrupt and paint German immigrants as independent-minded disciples of "honest government." German Americans were owned by no politician, Schurz asserted, "Least of all do they belong to those politicians who will sacrifice truth and right, and justice, and honor, and public interest to the mere advantage of a party." At that, the packed Senate galleries broke into applause.[76] James A. Garfield, the future president, said that the performance was "the most brilliant senatorial speech of [Schurz's] life."[77] The ploy returned the subject of arms sales to the columns of German-language newspapers, solidifying German Americans' opposition to Grant.[78]

Letters from around the country brought Schurz news of his success among German Americans. About a quarter of the correspondence that reached his office during 1871 and 1872 was penned in the careful German script of immigrants writing to "their" German senator.[79] Schurz received about two dozen letters regarding the arms scandal alone. One Ohio man wrote, "After I read your great speech on the 'arms hagglers' in the Cin. Volksblatt through very carefully, I feel compelled & spontaneously drawn to congratulate you from the bottom of my true German heart. That must have struck like a bomb & so hurrah for my countryman & the Herr Senator Carl Schurz!"[80] The proprietor of the *Detroit Abend-Post* requested a translation of a recent speech "in the interests of the whole *Deutschtum*

---

74 *Congressional Globe*, 42nd Cong, 2nd sess., App. 67–74 (Feb. 20, 1872). For Grant's neutrality proclamation, see Grant, *Papers of Ulysses S. Grant*, ed. Simon, 20: 235–50.

75 *United States Congressional Serial Set*, Senate Report 183, 42nd Cong., 2nd sess., vol. 1497, sess. vol. 3 (May 11, 1872); House Report 46, "Sales of Ordnance Stores," 42nd Cong., 2nd sess., vol. 1528, sess. vol. 1 (April 15, 1872); *Congressional Globe*, 42nd Cong., 2nd sess., App. 70, 72 (Feb. 20, 1872).

76 *Congressional Globe*, 42nd Cong, 2nd sess., App. 74 (Feb. 20, 1872).

77 James A. Garfield, *The Diary of James A. Garfield*, ed. Harry James Brown and Frederick D. Williams, 4 vols. (East Lansing: Michigan State University Press, 1967–1981), 2: 21. A St. Louis judge deemed Schurz's speech a cheap but incredibly effective ploy. Napton, Feb. 27, 1872, "Diary Transcription," 719–23, folder 8, Napton Papers, MHS.

78 For a mere sample of the editorial coverage, see *Wächter am Erie*, March 9, 1872; *Cincinnati Volksfreund*, Feb. 14, 17, 27, and 28, 1872; *Columbus Westbote*, March 13 and 16, 1872; *Westliche Post*, Feb. 21, 1872; *St. Charles Demokrat*, March 14 and 21, 1872; *Cincinnati Volksblatt*, Nov. 5, 1872. German-language regular Republican papers that sought to minimize the impact of the scandal include *Illinois Staatszeitung*, March 26 and 27, 1872; *Cleveland Anzeiger*, Aug. 8, 1872; *Toledo Express*, Feb. 29, 1872.

79 German-speakers remained Schurz's main constituency. He engaged Anglo-Americans, but he represented immigrants. Of the 485 letters collected in Schurz's "General Correspondence" between June 8, 1871 and May 6, 1872, 128 (26.4 percent) were written in German. Reels 6 and 7, Schurz Papers, LOC.

80 Louis Phillip Salterbach to Schurz, Feb. 22, 1872, reel 7, fr. 116, Schurz Papers, LOC.

of the state of Michigan."[81] One immigrant in Iowa, who chose to write in English, described Schurz's confrontation with Drake and the Grant administration as a "noble undertaking, and every [R]epublican, who is not blinded by party prejudices must at once see that yours is the right and true position." He added, "Being a German, I feel proud and grateful that you have done so, and think that with but few exceptions, the German element of the [R]epublican [P]arty take the same view." Actually, some Republicans did fear that Schurz was only doing the work of Democrats, but far more thought as the Iowan did.[82]

The national phenomenon of German-American Liberal Republicanism was concentrated in certain localities. It was strong in southwestern Ohio, partly because a revival of *Temperenzlerei* during 1871 made German immigrants uneasy about the Republican Party.[83] That spring, Cincinnati malcontent Friedrich Hassaurek helped found the Central Republican Association of Hamilton County.[84] Like Missouri's Liberal Republican Party, the organization devoted itself to abolishing protective duties, reforming the civil service, and removing the political disabilities "imposed for participation in the rebellion."[85] Liberal Republicanism caught on in other Ohio cities too. In Columbus and Dayton, about 35 percent of party leaders were German-born.[86] By March 1872, Thieme could sweepingly state that German Republicans were "unanimously" arrayed against party regulars.[87] "There is tumult everywhere among the German Republicans," the Democratic *Columbus Westbote* noted approvingly, "and the pleasant time when they all followed the party banner through thick and thin is, thank God, over."[88] Ohio Democrats supposed that men such as Schurz remained "with one foot in the party from which all the trouble now emanates," but Democrats welcomed reconciliation and reform, and they agreed unreservedly with Schurz's economic and ethnocultural policies.[89]

---

81 August Marxhausen to Schurz, April 3, 1871, reel 5, fr. 430, Schurz Papers, LOC.
82 Leavitt J. Lusch to Schurz, April 10, 1871, reel 5, fr. 488, Schurz Papers, LOC.
83 *Cincinnati Volksfreund*, Sept. 9, 16, 27, 29, and 30, Oct. 2, 4, and 10, 1871.
84 Insert in *Cincinnati Volksblatt*, Sept. 19, 1872; Hassaurek to Schurz, March 26, 1871; H. W. Thompson to Schurz, March 27, May 15, 1871; Jacob D. Cox to Schurz, Dec. 27, 1870; Schurz to Jacob D. Cox, April 4, 1871, reel 5, fr. 322–24, 695, 125–27, 433–34, Schurz Papers, LOC. On the Cincinnati organization, see also Horace White to Schurz, Dec. 25, 1870, reel 5, fr. 118–20, Schurz Papers, LOC; Slap, *Doom of Reconstruction*, 22–23; *Westliche Post*, Nov. 1, 1870.
85 See enclosure in Friedrich Hassaurek to Schurz, March 26, 1871, reel 5, fr. 322–23, Schurz Papers, LOC.
86 McGerr, "Meaning of Liberal Republicanism," 308–11.
87 *Wächter am Erie*, March 15, 1872; Sept. 28, 1871.
88 *Columbus Westbote*, Feb. 14, 1872.
89 *Cincinnati Volksfreund*, Nov. 21, 1871. See also Nov. 24 and 30, Dec. 4 and 11, 1871, Feb. 2 and 8, March 19 and 27, April 2 and 8, 1872; *Columbus Westbote*, April 10, 1872; *Anzeiger des Westens*,

Emil Rothe, exasperated with "Democrats who cling to the old and belong to a bygone era," heavily promoted an alliance between German-American Democrats and German-American Liberal Republicans.[90] Such cooperation, in Rothe's mind, had been the point of the Democratic New Departure.

In Wisconsin, German Americans were also part of the nationwide spread of Liberal Republicanism during 1871, and there, New Departure Democrats were more important than disaffected Republicans. Wisconsin's German Democratic editors looked on gleefully as Schurz slowly cut his ties to Grant and fell under the spell of politicians such as Frank Blair. Editorials in the *Watertown Weltbürger*, the *Seebote*, and the *Banner und Volksfreund* all zealously defended Schurz from his Republican detractors.[91] After Schurz's Nashville speech, the *Banner und Volksfreund* commented that the program he had outlined "could be sure of the support of the whole German element of the nation."[92] The *Seebote* was similarly keen to see German Americans unite like their "brothers in the old Fatherland."[93] Meanwhile, the state's largest Republican newspaper, Coleman's *Herold*, endorsed the straight Republican candidate, Cadwallader Washburn, for governor in 1871. It was not until March 1872, after Washburn had signed new legislation affecting alcohol sales, that Coleman turned to Schurz.[94] The *Herold* advertised Milwaukee's Liberal Reform Union Club, a minor organization that formed only at the last minute to choose delegates for the national Liberal Republican convention.[95]

As the movement took root in Ohio and Wisconsin, calls for institutional reform threatened to subvert racial justice. Like many other Americans, German immigrants were genuinely troubled by the abuse of political patronage, but black voting accentuated their discomfort. Many Liberal Republicans argued that African-American voters fueled a cycle of political

---

March 3, 26, and 28, April 11 and 27, 1872. For a survey of newspaper positions, see *St. Charles Demokrat*, May 4, 1871; Wittke, *German-Language Press*, 155–58.

90 *Cincinnati Volksfreund*, Nov. 21, 1871. See also Nov. 10 and 11, 1870.

91 *Banner und Volksfreund*, Nov. 6, 1, 15, and 16, 1870; *Watertown Weltbürger*, Nov. 12, 1870; *Seebote*, Oct. 31, Nov. 14 and 21, 1870. All three newspapers provided extensive coverage of Schurz's performances around the county during 1871. *Banner und Volksfreund*, Aug. 15, Oct. 21, 1871; *Watertown Weltbürger*, Aug. 12, 1871; *Seebote*, May 8, Aug. 21 and 28, Sept. 25, Oct. 2, 1871.

92 *Banner und Volksfreund*, Sept. 22, 1871.

93 *Seebote*, Feb. 2, 1871. Detailing the resistance, see *Banner und Volksfreund*, July 13 and 16, Oct. 28, Nov. 17, 1871; *Watertown Weltbürger*, Nov. 7, 1871; *Seebote*, May 22, June, 12, 1871.

94 Herman J. Deutsch, "Yankee-Teuton Rivalry in Wisconsin Politics of the Seventies," *Wisconsin Magazine of History* 14 (1931): 262–82; Deutsch, "Disintegrating Forces in Wisconsin Politics of the Early Seventies," *Wisconsin Magazine of History* 15 (1931): 168–81; *Herold Wöchentliche Ausgabe*, Sept. 28, 1871, Feb. 15, March 28, 1872.

95 Ibid., March 28, 1872, April 4, 11, and 25, 1872; *Banner und Volksfreund*, April 20 and 21, 1872; Hense-Jensen, *Wisconsin's Deutsch-Amerikaner*, 1: 237.

dysfunction in which politicians rewarded their allies with plum political appointments and the appointees reciprocated with contributions come the next election.[96] Dishonest white Republicans, the *Westliche Post* claimed, had succeeded in "making the colored people, as a race, weak-minded accessories to that outrageous system of robbery."[97] Liberals often conflated the misuse of patronage with excessive public spending. In a racist screed, John Bode at the *St. Charles Demokrat* remarked that "brute-like Negroes and thieving carpet-baggers won the upper hand and drove the Southern states in quick step toward social and financial ruin."[98] Although most formerly Republican German-language newspapers were not so vile, the Liberal Republican movement tended to stigmatize interracial politics as inherently corrupt.

The effort to reform American institutions was not, then, simply a distraction from African–American rights; it was repudiation of the liberal nationalist assumption that robust citizenship rights – specifically male suffrage – fortified a nation. In the new analysis, unfit voters – often African Americans – weakened the American polity. Their influence could be lessened only by curtailing the power of the popular will in the functions of government. Although not always nefarious, this reform definitely was not liberal.

German immigrants widened the gap between institutional reform and liberalism by posing as members of a *Volk* that was *essentially* averse to corruption. The bulletins reporting that Germans were "march[ing] at the head of true civilization" in Europe had reinvigorated but changed the older idea that Germans were uniquely principled.[99] When immigrants located their superiority in German armies, schools, and bureaucracies, they claimed unsullied and efficient institutions – not individual rights or representation – as the hallmark of advanced peoples and great states. To adjust to this new position, former Republicans shook off the earlier connotations of the "freedom-loving German" and ended the practice of comparing themselves to the freed people. One issue of the *St. Charles Demokrat* juxtaposed

---

96 Foner, *Reconstruction*, 497–98; Sproat, *"Best Men,"* 28–36; Summers, *Era of Good Stealings*, 153–79; Masur, *Example for All the Land*, 194–207, 214–24, 248–56. For a historian who interpreted reform instead as a distraction from African-American rights, see Ari Hoogenboom, *Outlawing the Spoils: A History of the Civil Service Reform Movement, 1865–1883* (Urbana: University of Illinois Press, 1961), 39–40. On reform as a means to curb the power of undesirable voters in the North, see Keyssar, *Right to Vote*, 117–71; Sven Beckert, "Democracy in the Age of Capital: Contesting Suffrage Rights in Gilded Age New York," in *The Democratic Experiment: New Directions in American Political History*, ed. Meg Jacobs (Princeton, NJ: Princeton University Press, 2003), 146–74.

97 *Westliche Post*, Aug. 8, 1872. Democratic papers commonly connected race and corruption. For other references by former Republicans, see *Wächter am Erie*, Oct. 26, 1871, Sept. 30, 1872; *St. Charles Demokrat*, April 14, 1870, April 5, July 4, Aug. 8, 1872.

98 Ibid., Dec. 14, 1871.   99 *Westliche Post*, Sept. 5, 1870.

accounts of German immigrants and African Americans. The first article explained that the world had much for which to thank the Germans, listing Martin Luther, Bismarck, Prussian General Helmuth von Moltke, and Schurz. Their special "task" in the United States, according to the *Demokrat*, was not pursuing equal rights but "freeing America from corruption, social hypocrisy, and crazy temperance activism." In an adjacent column, a second piece reported on an African-American convention in New Orleans. The delegates, the *Demokrat* ran, were too foolish to see through "Massa Grant." Their resolutions proved that "the colored population and its ignorance has been used to win votes for corruption through pitiful flattery."[100] A people's supposed disposition toward corruption now seemed more important than a country's defense of equal citizenship. Gone was the notion that a man of any race could become a capable citizen and the idea that citizen rights and representation distinguished a superlative country.

Further accelerating the flight from 1860s liberalism, Liberal Republicans advised Americans to learn from German institutions. Although some German-American leaders did criticize Prussia's *Beamtenstaat* (administrative state), most of them respected it.[101] The Prussian example stalked the Liberal Republican plan for a professional civil service insulated from the whims of public opinion and the scheming of political parties. After 1870, German-language newspapers ran many stories in which the United States stacked up poorly against Germany. John Bode found it remarkable that attempts to tackle official deceit in the United States were met with the response that such defects "are inseparable from our republican form of government." American corruption, he went on, meant "this *Volk* is losing respect in the eyes of all other civilized nations."[102] Rothe at the Democratic *Cincinnati Volksfreund* agreed. He reprinted a New York editorial that said, "In other countries dishonest officials are more summarily prosecuted than here." Every corrupt official in Prussia, the article claimed, was in jail.[103] With Germany on the rise and the United States still recovering from its civil war, transatlantic comparisons seemed especially poignant.

Schurz was the most eminent German immigrant to ask Americans to look abroad as they tried to cleanse public life at home. In January 1871,

---

100 *St. Charles Demokrat*, May 2, 1872.
101 Critics included Friedrich Hecker and Gustav Körner in Illinois. *Westliche Post*, Feb. 7, 1872; *Wächter am Erie*, May 23, 1871; Freitag, *Friedrich Hecker*, 80, 207, 315–17; *Cincinnati Volksblatt*, Aug. 31, 1870.
102 *St. Charles Demokrat*, Sept. 21, 1871.
103 *Cincinnati Volksfreund*, Nov. 9, 1871. For a later interpretation with similar emphasis, see "The Civil Service: Speech of Charles Reemelin: At Defiance, August 22, 1876," undated newspaper clipping from the *Cincinnati Commercial*, Charles Reemelin Papers, CHS.

he told senators to imagine their system from an outsider's perspective. He described the post-election scramble for patronage as an international embarrassment. The speech was part of Schurz's second attempt to form a civil service commission. The latest bill contained an examination system that would, like Prussia's, have made merit, not party loyalty, the criterion for appointment and promotion.[104] Native-born Americans were used to the senator's calls for reforms of all kinds, but now he was recommending that the United States replicate one aspect of European governance.

The German Americans who brought European institutions into the debate over Reconstruction foreshadowed the politics of the Gilded Age. Instead of seeing civil service reform as a matter of classical republican virtue, these immigrants respected professional expertise and elaborate organizations.[105] Their arguments widened the interest of Americans in foreign thinkers and foreign initiatives, especially German ones. During the 1870s, Germany was just becoming a center for the social science research that would encourage governments to act more creatively both to improve residents' welfare (as historian Daniel Rodgers has argued) and to appropriate their labor (as Andrew Zimmerman has emphasized).[106] German-American Liberal Republicans did not want to grant governments greater power in 1872, but they were the first large group of Americans to see Prussia as a leader in public policy.[107] Their transatlantic bent connected Liberal Republicanism to the international eclipse of liberal nationalism in the 1870s.

104 *Congressional Globe*, 41st Cong., 3rd sess., App. 69 (Jan. 27, 1871); Trefousse, *Carl Schurz*, 184–93. On his 1869 attempt, see *Congressional Globe*, 41st Cong., 2nd sess., 61 (Dec. 20, 1869); Hoogenboom, *Outlawing the Spoils*, 71–72; Trefousse, *Carl Schurz*, 184–85; *Woechentlich Westliche Post*, Dec. 29, 1869.

105 Andrew Slap's concentration on select ideologues stresses the importance of classical republicanism. Although this philosophy continued to influence the Anglo-American language of corruption, I consider it secondary to other trends. Slap, *Doom of Reconstruction*, xxii–xxv, 120–25. See also Hoogenboom, *Outlawing the Spoils*, 7; Summers, *Era of Good Stealings*, 9; Summers, *Plundering Generation*, 167–69; Michael Thomas Smith, *The Enemy Within: Fears of Corruption in the Civil War North* (Charlottesville: University of Virginia Press, 2011).

106 Daniel Rodgers, *Atlantic Crossings: Social Politics in a Progressive Age* (Cambridge, MA: Belknap Press of Harvard University Press, 1998); Andrew Zimmerman, *Alabama in Africa: Booker T. Washington, the German Empire, and the Globalization of the New South* (Princeton, NJ: Princeton University Press, 2010). See also Axel R. Schäfer, *American Progressives and German Social Reform, 1875–1920* (Stuttgart: Franz Steiner Verlag, 2000); Daniel Levine, *Poverty and Society: The Growth of the American Welfare States in International Comparison* (New Brunswick, NJ: Rutgers University Press, 1988); Bender, *Nation among Nations*, 263–71. On transatlantic reform more generally, see Leslie Butler, *Critical Americans: Victorian Intellectuals and Transatlantic Liberal Reform* (Chapel Hill: University of North Carolina Press, 2007).

107 The "liberal reform public intellectuals" of the Gilded Age favored government intervention to support corporate capitalism. Cohen, *Reconstruction of American Liberalism*, 17. Older works argue that most reformers espoused laissez-faire. See Sproat, *"Best Men,"* 143–68.

THE ELECTION OF 1872

By 1872, German Americans who had been energetic Republicans had helped style a party of reunion and reform that gambled with African-American rights. The German-language public sphere as a whole was as important as individual German-born leaders to the Liberal Republican Party. At the beginning of May, the immigrants dreamed that their mass movement could anoint a president. But everything hung on a national convention scheduled to meet in Cincinnati.

Germans from around the Midwest gathered in the Queen City fully intending to remake American politics just as decisively as Germans were rewriting European history.[108] From Missouri came Friedrich Münch, Carl Schurz, Louis Benecke, Carl Dänzer, and an ambitious young reporter named Joseph Pulitzer.[109] Illinois sent Gustav Körner, Caspar Butz, and Friedrich Hecker, while W. W. Coleman made the trip from Wisconsin with a slate of delegates that included several German Americans who were new to politics.[110] August Thieme, Friedrich Hassaurek, Charles Reemelin, and J. B. Stallo represented the host state.[111] Some German-American Democrats also came to Cincinnati to attend a competing meeting that was held concurrently. Countless other immigrants awaited telegraph reports from the "extraordinary" convention at home.[112] That spring, only a handful of major German-American leaders remained steadfast Republicans. Jacob Müller would not leave the party until after his term as Ohio lieutenant governor expired in 1873, and nationally, Franz Sigel, Francis Lieber, and Chicago editor Hermann Raster avoided Liberal Republicanism.[113] A German-born delegate from Indiana observed that "nearly all prominent leaders of *Deutschtum*" graced the convention.[114] He was not far wrong.

108 On the convention's organization, see James S. Rollins to Schurz, Feb. 4, 1872, reel 6, fr. 540–44, Schurz Papers, LOC; *St. Charles Demokrat*, March 28, 1872; *Cincinnati Volksfreund*, Jan. 26, 1872; Slap, *Doom of Reconstruction*, 132.

109 For lists of delegates and attendees, see Koerner, *Memoirs*, 2: 557; *Cincinnati Volksfreund*, April 29, May 2, 1872; *St. Charles Demokrat*, Nov. 30, 1871; *Westliche Post*, April 17, 1872; Nagler, "Deutschamerikaner und das *Liberal Republican Movement*, 1872."

110 *Herold Wöchentliche Ausgabe*, April 25, May 9, 1872; Hense-Jensen, *Wisconsin's Deutsch-Amerikaner*, 1: 237.

111 Reemelin, *Life of Charles Reemelin*, 202; Wittke, "Friedrich Hassaurek," 12; Rutherford B. Hayes to S. Birchard, Sept. 15, 1872, reel 172, fr. 1020, Hayes Papers, HPC. On the Democrat-controlled Reform and Reunion Party convention, see *Cincinnati Volksfreund*, May 3, 1872.

112 *St. Charles Demokrat*, May 9, 1872; *Wächter am Erie*, May 1, 1872.

113 *Toledo Express*, Jan. 10, 1872; *Columbus Westbote*, Feb. 21, March 30, April 27, 1872; *Cincinnati Volksblatt*, Aug. 31, 1872; *Cincinnati Volksfreund*, Jan. 12, 1872; *Cleveland Anzeiger*, Aug. 10 and 16, 1872; "Jacob Mueller" in *The Dictionary of Cleveland Biography*, ed. David D. Van Tassel and John J. Grabowski (Bloomington: Indiana University Press, 1996), 324; Wittke, *Refugees of Revolution*, 254.

114 W. A. Fritsch, *Aus Amerika: Alte und Neue Heimat* (Stardgard i. Pom: Verlag von Wilhelm Prange, [c. 1905–1908]), 50.

Despite their numbers, German Americans would lose whatever grip they had had on the third party. Schurz presided over the convention, but he could not stop the nominations of Horace Greeley, the eccentric editor of the *New York Tribune*, for the presidency, and Benjamin Gratz Brown, now ensconced with the Missouri Democrats, for the vice-presidency. No German American was partial to Greeley, a tariffs and temperance man who had not even sided with Prussia during the European war.[115] Remembering the nomination years later, one German American wrote, "A trickster, raised in the slimy politics of *then* Missouri – Gratz Brown – was able, by combining with a few tricksters in other states, to nominate Horace Greely [sic], and turn the whole body into a mockery of itself, I shall never forget that adjournment."[116] The convention was "a total fiasco," the Cincinnati *Wahrheitsfreund* printed, "and with it the entire Liberal Republican movement met a sad end"; it had "committed suicide."[117] Schurz took it all personally, feeling, in Blair's words, "cut to the quick."[118] He was disturbed that Greeley's nomination smacked of back-room dealing, which would suggest to outsiders that the Liberal Republicans were as untrustworthy as any other politicians. In a frank personal letter, Schurz told Greeley that German immigrants, who "cared . . . about the moral tendency of the movement," would not vote for him. The senator wrote that while "the most prominent German leaders of the West" were against the ticket, he would canvass for Greeley.[119]

With the nomination, Liberal Republicans were left with little to campaign on except their antipathy towards Republican Reconstruction. Schurz could not promise that Greeley would fight tariffs or temperance, and the party's reform credentials were damaged. Reconciliation was all that remained, and Democrats largely dictated its meaning, especially after their national convention voted to nominate Greeley too. Reluctantly, German-speaking Democrats at the *Cincinnati Volksfreund*, the *Fremont Courier*, the *Columbus Westbote*, the *Wisconsin Banner und Volksfreund*, the *Milwaukee Seebote*, and the *Watertown Weltbürger* signed on to Greeley's cause.[120] Liberal Republican events increasingly indulged Democratic prejudices. At a

---

115 *New York Tribune*, Aug. 22, Sept. 5, 7, 12, and 27, 1870; Matthew T. Downey, "Horace Greeley and the Politicians: The Liberal Republican Convention in 1872," *Journal of American History* 53 (1967): 727–50.

116 Reemelin, *Life of Charles Reemelin*, 202. See also *Columbus Westbote*, May 15, 1872.

117 *Wahrheitsfreund*, May 8, 1872. See also Rutherford B. Hayes to His Son, May 9, 1872, reel 172, fr. 903–04, Hayes Papers, HPC; *Wächter am Erie*, May 11, 1872; *Cincinnati Volksfreund*, May 6, 1872.

118 Frank Blair, Jr., to James S. Rollins, May 9, 25, 1872, folder 122, Rollins Papers, WHMC – Columbia. See also Koerner, *Memoirs*, 2: 557.

119 Schurz to Horace Greeley, May 6, 1872, reel 7, fr. 607–11, Schurz Papers, LOC.

120 *Cincinnati Volksfreund*, July 3, 1872; *Fremont Courier*, June 20, 1872; *Columbus Westbote*, May 15, 1872; *Banner und Volksfreund*, July 9, 1872; *Watertown Weltbürger*, July 27, 1872; *Seebote*, June 22,

Milwaukee meeting, for example, one man exclaimed, "If someone treated us in Wisconsin like the Southerners, we would without exception be Ku Kluxers!" The *Seebote* reported that this comment was greeted with "wild applause."[121] It was not something that most German Missourians would have said when the movement began in 1870, but it was a predictable extension of the desire to reconcile whites in the North and the South.

A rally in Watertown, Wisconsin, dramatized how German Americans, as bearers of the Liberal Republican message of reconciliation, became complicit in a broader backlash against African-American rights. In September 1872, Schurz, the old Radical Republican based in St. Louis, and Rothe, the New Departure Democrat working in Cincinnati, returned to the Democratic town where they had both begun their American political careers. As many as 8,000 people attended what a local newspaper billed as "the biggest political demonstration that has ever occurred in Wisconsin." The personal reunion of the two immigrants symbolized the political reconciliation that they had come back to Watertown to discuss. At first, Schurz tried to justify the actions of Radicals during the 1860s. "We were obliged," he informed the audience in English, "to protect the new, recently freed citizens – by force if necessary, when such was used against them." The applause line, however, followed: "But no sort of force can be applied by a free government for long." Schurz added, "Force ultimately destroys the freedom of the people." He vilified the army's role in Reconstruction and pushed blacks back from the community of citizens who deserved "freedom." When Rothe rose, he said that "the Negroes in the South are protected and coddled while the white citizens of the South are oppressed." Both men also mentioned civil service reform and the economy, but the glorification of white reunion set the emotional tenor of the gathering.[122]

Federal support for African Americans in the South had become the main issue of the election of 1872. Editors at the formerly Republican *Wächter am Erie, Cincinnati Volksblatt, Westliche Post, St. Charles Demokrat*, and *Milwaukee Herold* stood by black suffrage in principle, but wanted to reestablish "harmony and fraternal feeling" among whites, even if it meant throwing in their lot with apologists for the Ku Klux Klan.[123] German-born politicians who stayed in the Republican Party did not let Liberals forget that reunion would come at a cost for African Americans. Judge Stallo told a

1872. For surveys of the press, see *Cincinnati Volksfreund*, June 13, July 1, 1872. One German-language Democratic newspaper in Missouri apparently did not endorse Greeley. *Anzeiger des Westens*, June 14, 1872. Two German Catholic newspapers opposed him: *Wahrheitsfreund*, May 8, 1872; *Amerika*, Oct. 27, 1872.

121 *Seebote*, Sept. 23, 1872.   122 *Watertown Weltbürger*, Sept. 21, 1872.
123 *Cincinnati Volksblatt*, Sept. 19, 1872.

St. Louis crowd that the only reconciliation that interested him was one that came "with an acknowledgement of the rights of those who were freed by the war" and "a coming together of the races in the South." He asked, "Will the emancipated slaves stand together with their former masters when they [the masters] join . . . with a party whose doctrines only mean oppression and slavery to them?" The *Toledo Express* and two other minor German-language newspapers in Ohio and one in Wisconsin agreed with Stallo's sentiment.[124] Grant loyalists said they wanted "national unity, freedom, and equality," while Greeley stood for terrorism, tariffs, and temperance.[125]

The election of 1872 never quite became a referendum on equal citizenship because Greeley was such an unappealing candidate. He could not have been the vehicle that German-American Liberal Republicans sought without discarding his economic and ethnocultural programs. The polls confirmed what politicians already expected. Grant held on to the presidency with the support of a convincing 55 percent of the nation's voters. Wisconsin almost perfectly reflected the national aggregate. In Milwaukee, where immigrants were already disinclined to support Republicans, four of the five most heavily German wards registered lower returns for the incumbent Grant in 1872 than they had for the candidate in 1868, but little had changed in the state.[126] The sitting president also won Ohio again without much alteration in German-American voting patterns. The *Volksfreund* was probably right, however, that Cincinnati had tipped. Less than half of the city's German Americans now went Republican.[127] All four of the wards that were German Republican strongholds in 1868 gave Grant a smaller proportion of their votes. In one, the Seventh Ward, returns for the president fell from 73 to 48 percent, but Grant still took home majorities in the three others, and he picked up a German ward that had gone for the Democrat in 1868.[128]

---

124 *Toledo Express*, Sept. 21, 1872. On Stallo, see also *Westliche Post*, Sept. 18, 1872; *Cincinnati Volksfreund*, Oct. 3, 1872. Anglo-American Republicans hastily organized the *Cleveland Anzeiger* in August 1872 to represent the party line in German. *Cleveland Anzeiger*, Aug. 5, 1872. On the *Cincinnati Courier*, see *Cincinnati Volksfreund*, July 15, 1872; Arndt and Olsen, *German-American Newspapers*, 438; Burgheim, *Cincinnati in Wort und Bild*, 138. Wisconsin Republicans founded a new paper in Madison and distributed copies of the *Illinois Staatszeitung*. Deutsch, "Disintegrating Forces in Wisconsin Politics," 179; L. F. Frisby to Elisha W. Keyes, Sept. 20, 1872, box 26, folder 1, Elisha W. Keyes Papers, WHS. Keyes's papers indicate Republican concern about the German vote.

125 *Cleveland Anzeiger*, Aug. 5, 2, 6, 9, 10, and 15, Sept. 2, 1872; *Toledo Express*, March 2, Sept. 24 and 26, Oct. 25 and 28, Nov. 1, 1872. On regular Republican papers in other states, see *Cincinnati Volksfreund*, April 24, 1872.

126 Appendix, Table 4.

127 *Cincinnati Volksfreund*, Oct. 14, Nov. 6, 1872. The analysis was partly based on state elections in October.

128 Appendix, Table 2.

Unlike Wisconsin and Ohio, Missouri was one of only six states – four in the border region and two in the South – in Greeley's column. The Liberal Republican won 56 percent of the state's vote, but far fewer German-American voters went for him than had supported Brown for governor two years earlier. Greeley received slim majorities in four of St. Louis's five most German wards, all of which had supported a Democratic governor a month earlier. German immigrants helped end Missouri's Liberal Republican interlude and return the state to Democratic hands. In St. Louis, they would always vote more Republican than the city or state as a whole, but after 1872, German Missourians were no longer a Republican bloc.[129]

The real impact of German Americans on Liberal Republicanism had not been electoral but ideological. A community that had thrown its weight behind African-American citizenship now sanctioned the Democratic position that the whole project of Reconstruction had been corrupt, vindictive, and foolhardy. Immigrants had reframed the controversy over black rights in the United States as they watched Germany's unification. Previously, liberalism had been an end in itself as well as the surest means to secure national unity. Republicans had argued that black rights would strengthen the nation. Now, however, Liberal Republicans maintained that they complicated reconciliation and reform in the United States. This new nationalism would become only more popular as the century progressed. African Americans would continue to fight for citizenship, but the Northern whites who had facilitated Reconstruction would soon leave them to struggle alone. Economic and ethnocultural questions would displace black citizenship in the editorials of German-American newspapers, and the German language of American citizenship would fracture along economic and religious lines.

129 Appendix, Table 3; Burnham, *Presidential Ballots*, 165–229. Six strongly German counties identified by historian Paul Kleppner supported Brown with 75.2 percent of returns in 1870, but gave Greeley only 44.2 percent in 1872. Kleppner, *Third Electoral System*, 111.

7

Class, Culture, and the Decline of Reconstruction, 1870–1876

Milwaukee would become famous for its socialism, but the city's first viable radical working-class newspaper did not begin publication until 1875. In the inaugural issue of the German-language *Milwaukee Socialist*, editor Joseph Brucker promised to "fight all class prejudice, all religious and church influence, every political arbitrariness and abridgment of rights, all weakness of character and deceit, [and] to work for the realization of a genuine people's state."[1] Brucker, a recent immigrant from Austria whom unimpressed locals tagged "a born agitator and hothead," affiliated his modest daily with the International Workingmen's Association (IWA).[2] Some of the Marxists who dominated the organization by that time complained that he was "petit bourgeois" in outlook. They said that he had lost sight of the need for revolution. But Brucker criticized liberalism too, agreeing with his orthodox Marxist critics that wage labor did not make for true freedom.[3] His *Socialist* called on governments to institute minimum wages and an eight-hour workday, establish public works, prohibit child labor, and nationalize public transportation. German-speaking socialists became the Midwest's most relentless campaigners for "economic rights," state guarantees of citizens' economic welfare.[4]

1 *Milwaukee Socialist*, Nov. 15, 1875.
2 Hense-Jensen, *Wisconsin's Deutsch-Amerikaner*, 2: 82; Wisconsin Writers' Program Writings and Research Notes, Works Progress Administration (WPA), box 13, WHS; *Milwaukee Socialist*, Dec. 1, 1875.
3 Hermann Schlüter, *Die Internationale in Amerika: Ein Beitrag zur Geschichte der Arbeiter-Bewegung in den Vereinigten Staaten* (Chicago: Deutsche Sprachgruppe der Sozialist. Partei der Ver. Staaten, 1918), 339.
4 On German Americans' preeminence, see Nadel, "German Immigrant Left," 54–57. My "economic rights" resemble the "social rights" of British theorist T. H. Marshall. Marshall, *Citizenship and Social Class, and Other Essays* (Cambridge: Cambridge University Press, 1950). Marshall's terminology is problematic because Americans applied "social rights" inconsistently to various practices such as the right to avail oneself of public accommodations or to marry whom one chose. Historians have shown that the designation of "social rights" was used after the Civil War to stymie racial equality.

German Americans also found themselves at the center of the fight over cultural rights, another of the great controversies of the 1870s. Although the immigrants' pluralism had always involved a celebration of cultural difference, the language of cultural *rights* included ambitious demands for taxpayer subsidization of separate institutions that both nurtured minority traditions and preserved communal autonomy.[5] Immigrants had long objected that Anglo-American Republicans wanted to instill their version of Protestant values in public schoolchildren, but a select group of Roman Catholics began to challenge the status quo more vociferously around 1870.[6] They lobbied states for funds to support religious schools. The new push had the backing of some non-German Catholics, and plenty of German-born Catholics remained skeptical, but German-American members of the Church were known for holding tight to their cultural distinctiveness.[7] By entering the feud over public education, they helped revive the cultural animosities that had been in abeyance during the 1860s.

Of course, neither Catholicism nor socialism was new to the 1870s. Catholics could point to a centuries-old tradition, and socialists had built up their own canon. Socialist thinkers had never expected that their struggle would end once all men could freely contract their labor and exercise the franchise. They had allied with liberals in 1848 and during the decade of the Civil War because they saw emancipation and suffrage as insufficient yet necessary. With those battles won, socialists could move on to new ones.

Masur, *Example for All the Land*, 9–10, 136–38; Richard A. Primus, *The American Language of Rights* (New York: Cambridge University Press, 1999), 153–60.

5 In the German-American public sphere, Catholics primarily articulated cultural rights in individual, not collective, terms. The scholarly literature, however, theorizes multicultural societies where groups mediate the liberal relationship between the individual and the state. See especially John Rawls, *A Theory of Justice* (London: Oxford University Press, 1971); Michael Walzer, *Spheres of Justice: A Defense of Pluralism and Equality* (New York: Basic Books, 1983); Will Kymlicka, *Liberalism, Community, and Culture* (Oxford: Clarendon Press, 1989); Kymlicka, *Multicultural Citizenship: A Liberal Theory of Minority Rights* (Oxford: Clarendon Press, 1995); Charles Taylor, "The Politics of Recognition," in *Multiculturalism*, ed. Amy Gutmann (Princeton, NJ: Princeton University Press, 1994), 25–73. The cultural sections of the 1948 Universal Declaration of Human Rights have generated a debate similar to the one of the 1870s in the United States. Janusz Symonides, "Cultural Rights: A Neglected Category of Human Rights," *International Social Science Journal* 50, no. 158 (1998): 559–72; Yvonne Donders, "Do Cultural Diversity and Human Rights Make a Good Match?" *International Social Science Journal* 61 no. 199 (2010): 15–35. Historian Rebecca Bennette argues that Catholics in Bismarck's Reich saw respecting regional diversity as essential to national integration. Bennette, *Fighting for the Soul of Germany*.

6 On the education debate and the wider trend of Protestants pursuing social objectives through the state, see Ward M. McAfee, *Religion, Race, and Reconstruction: The Public School in the Politics of the 1870s* (Albany: State University of New York Press, 1998); Gaines M. Foster, *Moral Reconstruction: Christian Lobbyists and the Federal Legislation of Morality, 1865–1920* (Chapel Hill: University of North Carolina Press, 2002).

7 On the worldview of German Catholics, see Conzen, "Immigrant Religion and the Republic," 43–56.

German-American Marxists continued to plan for revolution, but along with other socialists they tried to adapt to postwar America. Economic rights might be "petit bourgeois" insofar as they only reformed the existing state, but they represented workers' immediate concerns and became the basis on which German-American socialists engaged with that state. During the 1870s, socialists concentrated their agitation more squarely on economic rights than they had before.

As different as socialists and Catholics were, both groups contributed to the disputes that strained Northern politics leading into the election of 1876. In the process of making their respective rights claims, they would disrupt the liberal nationalism that was behind the belief that the freedmen could follow male immigrants into voting citizenship. Historians know that labor politics in the North divided the Republican Party during the 1870s,[8] but narrowing in on German socialists in the Midwest and pairing them with Catholics reinforces the main contention of this book. As new Americans and transnational actors, immigrants helped demarcate a period of liberal nationalist supremacy in the mid-nineteenth-century United States.

Socialist and Catholic politics would share three features. First, both sets of actors found liberal nationalism confining. They felt that liberalism's individualism was too rigid to satisfy their needs and the nation-state was too small a scale on which to envision change. Socialists belonged to an international brotherhood of workers, and Catholics to an international church. Second, economic and cultural controversies sparked more self-conscious talk of gender among German Americans. Immigrant women's interest in household solvency and childhood education was more obvious to contemporaries than their investment in black emancipation and suffrage. Finally, although neither socialists nor Catholics specifically targeted African Americans, black Southerners would find it difficult to harness the controversial new movements for economic and cultural rights, and they would suffer in the resulting backlash.

SOCIALISTS AND ECONOMIC RIGHTS

The depression that enveloped the United States from 1873 to 1878 prompted German Americans to articulate their changing ideas of the relationship between economic justice and citizenship. At the same time, they reassessed liberal nationalism and reexamined the status of women and African Americans. In September 1873, the company of Civil War

8 See footnote 11 in the Introduction.

financier Jay Cooke collapsed, triggering a panic. A wave of bank failures escalated into a full-scale crisis that devastated American communities. Within months, railroads, mines, and iron works were laying off workers. After two years, only about one-fifth of those American wage workers who remained employed had steady work, and some saw their wages cut by up to 45 percent.[9] In Cincinnati, hundreds of the least fortunate begged officials for food each day, and tens of thousands of the city's homeless slept in police station basements each night.[10] It was enough to convince some immigrants to contemplate returning to Germany.[11]

Farmers also struggled during the 1870s, as plummeting land prices compounded low agricultural profits. In Wisconsin, the two major railroad conglomerates had exacerbated the situation by raising rates just three days before the panic began.[12] The *St. Charles Demokrat* reported that conditions were tough in rural Missouri too. Farmers in the county just north of St. Louis were falling further into debt despite their obvious productivity.[13] Farther south, some large landowners who could not afford to pay wages to their workers offered them sharecropping contracts instead. Many of the modest number of African Americans who had bought their own farms or paid their rent in cash also accepted this arrangement for the first time during the slump.[14] One federal official estimated that the blacks of low-country Georgia owned less property at the end of the 1870s than they had as slaves.[15] "Times are hard," Carl Schurz recognized in 1875, "business is languishing; our industries are depressed; thousands of laborers are without work; the poor are growing poorer; the country is full of distress; something must be done to afford relief.... The question is what that something should be."[16]

Democrats had a simple answer: vote Republicans out of office and return to strict laissez-faire. Most German Americans still believed that Congress must abandon tariffs, railroad subsidies, and currency manipulation. These

9 Philip S. Foner, *The Great Labor Uprising of 1877* (New York: Monad Press, 1977), 20; Foner, *Reconstruction*, 512–24; Samuel Bernstein, "Labor and the Long Depression, 1873–1878," *Science and Society* 20 (1956): 60–72.

10 Ross, *Workers on the Edge*, 240–44.

11 Several observers mentioned return migration. *Fond du Lac Nordwestlicher Courier*, June 4, 1874; *Amerika*, June 2, 1875; *St. Charles Demokrat*, June 10, 1875; North American Federal Council, "Zweiter Vierteljahresbericht," Oct. 7, 1874, reel 2, fr. 891, IWA Papers, WHS.

12 Thompson, ed., *History of Wisconsin*, vol. 2, *Civil War Era*, by Current, 590–91; Dale E. Treleven, "Railroads, Elevators, and Grain Dealers: The Genesis of Antimonopolism in Milwaukee," *Wisconsin Magazine of History* 52 (1969): 205–22. For a grim portrait of the situation in rural Wisconsin, see *Wöchentliche Appleton Volksfreund*, Sept. 9, 1874.

13 *St. Charles Demokrat*, Nov. 27, 1873.   14 Foner, *Reconstruction*, 537.

15 *Congressional Globe*, 46th Cong., 2nd sess., Senate Report 693, pt. 2, 261. Cited in Foner, *Reconstruction*, 537.

16 Schurz, "Honest Money," Sept. 27, 1875, in *Speeches, Correspondence and Political Papers of Carl Schurz*, 3: 161, 184.

policies skewed markets, increasing the wealth of a few well-connected speculators at the expense of the great majority of Americans, they reasoned. Without them, the thinking went, there would be no need for the sort of economic rights that some socialists were now discussing. The *Cincinnati Volksfreund* reminded its readers that Jay Cooke had profited from the Republican land grants that had underwritten the railroad boom of the 1860s.[17] Editors at Milwaukee's *Seebote*, and Ohio's *Columbus Westbote*, *Fremont Courier*, and *New Philadelphia Deutsche Beobachter* agreed that the panic was the "fruit of Republican domination." They were sure it would persuade Americans of the perils of Republican rule.[18] The *Westbote* coolly pronounced the financial disaster a "beneficent storm, which would bring wholesome lessons and wholesome consequences with it."[19]

Disaffected Republicans were just as quick to blame the depression on President Grant and propose laissez-faire, not economic citizenship, as the antidote. The *Cincinnati Volksblatt*, independent since 1872, asserted that Republicans' "whole system" had caused all the problems: "It is based on inequitable preference and the extortion of the working, farming, and middle classes in the interests of a few finance and stock kings."[20] Other independent but Republican-leaning newspapers such as the *Milwaukee Herold* and the *Wächter am Erie* also excoriated Republicans for their close relationships to financial magnates, while condemning tariffs, railroad subsidies, and inflationary monetary policy.[21] Even Schurz, who was trying to reestablish himself within the Republican Party after the Liberal rout, remained critical of these measures.[22] Leading German independents and Republicans agreed with Democrats that the government should encourage "pecuniary independence" instead of protecting the workers and farmers who bore the risks of industrialization and agricultural consolidation.[23]

Yet a new generation of German-speaking socialists rejected the main parties. The socialist Forty-Eighters who had worked with liberals in the Republican Party had passed from the scene by 1870. Joseph Weydemeyer

---

17 *Cincinnati Volksfreund*, Sept. 24, 1873.
18 *Milwaukee Seebote*, Nov. 10, 1873; *Columbus Westbote*, Nov. 5, 1873; *Fremont Courier*, Oct. 9, 1873; *New Philadelphia Deutsche Beobachter*, Oct. 23, 1873.
19 *Columbus Westbote*, Oct. 1, 1873.
20 *Cincinnati Volksblatt*, Sept. 25, 1873. On the *Volksblatt*'s political independence, see July 5, 1876.
21 *Herold Wöchentliche Ausgabe*, Sept. 24, Oct. 16, 1873; *Wächter am Erie*, Sept. 23, 1873. For German Republicans' continued commitment to hard money policies, see *Cincinnati Volksblatt*, May 31, 1873, Nov. 2, 1876; *Cleveland Anzeiger*, July 24, 1876; *Wächter am Erie*, Oct. 1, 1875; *Westliche Post*, Oct. 6, 1876; *St. Charles Demokrat*, Oct. 7, 1875; *Milwaukee Germania*, Nov. 12, 1877; *Green Bay Wisconsin Staats-Zeitung*, Nov. 12, 1874; *Madison Wisconsin Botschafter*, Sept. 30, 1875; *Stockbridge Union*, June 18, 1873.
22 Schurz, "Honest Money," 3:161–212. For another critical Republican, see Freitag, *Friedrich Hecker*, 348–55, 452–86.
23 *Cincinnati Volksblatt*, Sept. 25, 1873.

had died several years earlier, and August Willich retired to a small town in western Ohio after he returned from Germany in 1871.[24] The break was not complete. Weydemeyer's son Otto was a "worthy heir" to his father's Marxism, acting as corresponding secretary for St. Louis's Section 1 of the International Workingmen's Association during the early 1870s.[25] Friedrich A. Sorge and Adolf Douai remained active in New York, where the IWA's North American Federal Council was located, and Mathilde Anneke held to many socialist precepts. There must have been a cohort of German Americans who followed such leaders through the war years and into the 1870s, but, as one historian put it, the Civil War had "absorbed the idealism of the early German immigrants, and the socialist movement had to begin again in the Sixties."[26] Neither Milwaukee's Joseph Brucker nor Albert Currlin, who would become the leading German-American socialist in St. Louis, had been born at the time of the Revolutions of 1848. Both men had missed the American Civil War too, immigrating to the United States in their twenties, shortly after German unification.[27]

Although the socialists of the 1870s assessed capitalism much like their predecessors, they operated in a new context. Emancipation and male suffrage had made anachronisms of old tactics. The time had passed for postponing working-class revolution and cooperating with liberals under Republican auspices.[28] Any suggestion of compromising with established political parties was abhorrent to the North American Federation of the IWA, which by 1870 boasted nine affiliates.[29] Its first congress in 1872 resolved, among other things, "to rescue the working classes from the influence and power of all political parties and to show that the existence of all these parties is a crime and threat against the working classes."[30] Few tenets were so widely accepted and often repeated within the organization. There

---

24 Easton, *Hegel's First American Followers*, 200.
25 Obermann, *Joseph Weydemeyer: Ein Lebensbild*, 397; reel 2, fr. 656 passim, IWA Papers, WHS.
26 Thomas W. Gavett, *Development of the Labor Movement in Milwaukee* (Madison: University of Wisconsin Press, 1965), 27; Schneirov, *Labor and Urban Politics*, 54; Jentz, "48ers and the Politics of the German Labor Movement," 49, 58–60; Montgomery, *Beyond Equality*, 167; Levine, *Spirit of 1848*, 264; Philip S. Foner, *The Workingmen's Party of the United States: A History of the First Marxist Party in the Americas* (Minneapolis: MEP Publications, 1984), 10; David T. Burbank, "The First International in St. Louis," *Missouri Historical Society Bulletin* 18 (1962): 166; Nadel, *Little Germany*, 141–54.
27 Wisconsin Writers' Program Writings and Research Notes, WPA, box 13, WHS; *Westliche Post*, July 28, 1877; Burbank, *Reign of the Rabble: The St. Louis General Strike of 1877* (New York: Augustus M. Kelley, 1966), 18; Elliot J. Kanter, "Class, Ethnicity, and Socialist Politics: St. Louis, 1876–1881," *UCLA Historical Journal* 3 (1982): 39–40; Schlüter, *Die Internationale in Amerika*, 356.
28 A sophisticated interpretation of the postbellum shift in the city of Chicago, see Jentz and Schneirov, *Chicago in the Age of Capital*.
29 Philip S. Foner, *Workingmen's Party*, 12–14, 19.
30 North American Federal Council to the General Council, Dec. 7, 1872, reel 1 fr. 1053–54, IWA Papers, WHS.

was some contention over whether the IWA should use municipal elections to introduce socialist ideas to urban workers. Lassallians, who were amenable to the political option, were up against Marxists, who favored using trade unions and believed that a "somewhat perfected organization must precede any political movement of the working classes."[31] To reconcile these positions, the Workingmen's Party, which replaced the IWA in the United States in 1876, advised members "to abstain from all political movements in general for the present and to turn their back on the ballot box," but its rules allowed individual sections to take part in local races.[32] Socialists all now opposed the type of accommodation that Weydemeyer and Willich had reached with the Republicans during the 1860s.

Marxist misgivings about conventional politics related to their fear that state recognition of limited economic rights would delay the revolution. Piecemeal concessions might dull workers' appreciation of the injustice inherent in wage labor, socialists thought. It was a long-standing dilemma reframed in the postwar city. With the economic hardships of life in the North now more troubling to German Americans than either slavery or political disfranchisement in the South, immigrants were seriously debating the regulation of hours, wages, and safety, and government aid to the poor. Marxists resisted incremental change, but all socialists used the language of economic rights when they joined the public discussion. By specifying particular entitlements, socialists answered Americans' present distress with a tangible vision of a society reborn. According to the IWA's North American congress in 1872, the workers' state would be characterized by "the elevation of the oppressed to a position where equal rights and duties are enjoyed by every human being."[33] On some level, even the Marxist mission was a search for economic rights.

References to economic rights were ubiquitous in local socialist politics, the sort of mobilization that Radical Republicans such as Weydemeyer and Willich had discouraged during the 1860s. By 1877, the Workingmen's Party in St. Louis had recruited about 600 German-speaking members, begun publication of the *Volksstimme des Westens*, and nominated candidates in municipal elections.[34] The *Volksstimme* described "political rights" as

---

31 North American Federal Council to the General Council, Oct. 10, 1871, reel 1 fr. 1029, IWA Papers, WHS.

32 Philip S. Foner, ed., *The Formation of the Workingmen's Party of the United States: Proceedings of the Union Congress Held at Philadelphia, July 19–22, 1876* (New York: American Institute for Marxist Studies, 1976), 33–34. Philip S. Foner, *Workingmen's Party*, provides details of the party's activities during its brief existence under this name during 1876 and 1877.

33 North American Federal Council to the Workingmen's Assembly of New York, Jan. 29, 1871, reel 1 fr. 1062, IWA Papers, WHS.

34 Burbank, *Reign of the Rabble*, 19; Ross, *Workers on the Edge*, 250.

"only empty words." Party nominees stood on a platform of state owner-ship of railroads, public works relief, a mandated eight-hour workday, and the end of child labor. They pledged to "set out the causes of [the worker's] afflictions and seek moral and material rights."[35] That same year, Milwau-kee's Socialist Democratic Party, another affiliate of the Workingmen's Party, also sought "rights" and "citizenship." Brucker, its leader, was always more partial to the American reform tradition than most of his colleagues. At one recorded speech, he introduced himself as "a citizen of the United States" and presented his ten-point program as a plan to stamp out "injustice" and "hostility to freedom."[36] Socialists in St. Louis and Milwaukee maintained that citizens had rights beyond the political ones that liberals so venerated.

Economic rights were not the only thing that distinguished socialists from liberal nationalists. The IWA announced its internationalism in its name and transatlantic structure. "Workingmen of all countries unite!" took off as a slogan. Sometimes men such as Brucker even felt that workers were indeed "beginning to wake from their dreams" around the world.[37] For social-ists, national institutions served global elites, and national loyalties deluded unsophisticated workers. The Franco-Prussian War had been quite a test. The IWA's largely German leadership in the United States began to criticize "German chauvinism" after France declared itself a republic in September 1870. The North American Federal Council resolved that responsibility for any further bloodshed lay with the Prussians.[38] Such statements had lit-tle influence on Midwestern workers, but a socialist counterdemonstration protested the triumphal nationalism on show at the New York festivities marking the end of the war in May 1871.[39] A more practical example of international fraternity came in donations to the Parisian Commu-nards fleeing France.[40] Where earlier socialists had sometimes disdained but

---

35 *St. Louis Volksstimme des Westens*, Sept. 1, 1877. For enumeration of the Marxists' goals, see Philip S. Foner, *Workingmen's Party*, 34–35; Roediger, "'Not Only the Ruling Classes to Overcome but also the So-Called Mob': Class, Skill and Community in the St. Louis General Strike of 1877," *Journal of Social History* 19 (1985): 213; Ross, *Workers on the Edge*, 250; Schneirov, *Labor and Urban Politics*, 54–55; Burbank, *Reign of the Rabble*, 19.

36 Joseph Brucker, *Die Social-Demokratie und ihr Wisconsiner Wahl-Programm: Ein Vortrag* (Milwaukee: Socialist Printing Company, 1877), 1, 4, 22.

37 North American Federal Council, "To All Trades Unions and Labor Societies," May 21, 1871; North American Federal Council to the Workingmen's Assembly of New York, Jan. 29, 1871, reel 1, fr. 996, 1064, IWA Papers, WHS; *Milwaukee Socialist*, Oct. 17, 1876.

38 North American Federal Council, "Resolutions Submitted to the Anti-War-Meeting," [Sept. 1870], reel 1, fr. 1102, IWA Paper, WHS.

39 North American Federal Council to the General Council, May 21, 1871, reel 1, fr. 999, IWA Papers, WHS.

40 North American Federal Council to the General Council, Nov. 5, 1871, reel 1, fr. 1030, IWA Papers, WHS.

usually manipulated nationalism, the new leaders despised it nearly as much as mainstream political parties.

As they left behind the liberalism and nationalism of the 1860s, socialists took up theories that might have resulted in a more expansive form of citizenship. German-American liberals in the Republican Party had excluded women without much reflection. They had not planned how to proceed if the franchise did not secure economic equality for black Southerners. Socialists' comprehensive critique of American society, on the other hand, could have exposed the norms that subjugated women and perpetuated racial inequality. The politics of Reconstruction America, however, militated against translating theory into practice. Male socialists would be slow to respond to their female colleagues, and their impatience with political rights and the Republican Party set them at odds with black Southerners.

German-American feminists found socialist organizations more conducive to their activism than the Republican Party. As Anglo-American suffragists regrouped in the wake of the Fifteenth Amendment, immigrant women began to work within the institutions of the radical left to build a parallel movement.[41] Mathilde Anneke, never one to miss an opportunity, helped form Milwaukee's all-female Section 3 of the IWA in 1876.[42] The new group often functioned as an auxiliary to the male sections in the city, arranging social and educational activities to "disseminate socialistic ideas."[43] Yet members of Section 3 valued its independent status, using separate membership cards, conducting regular meetings, and corresponding directly with the IWA's international headquarters, which had by then transferred to New York. A couple of surviving letters prove that Anneke and others kept women's suffrage firmly on the local agenda and broached it with the General Council.[44] Anneke also worked with other groups whose membership overlapped with the socialists. The feminist frequently addressed the Freie Gemeinde, a "congregation" of humanist "freethinkers" who were dedicated to "free self-determination in every area of life in accordance with

41 Monica Cook Morris, "The History of Woman Suffrage in Missouri, 1867–1901," *Missouri Historical Review* 25 (1930): 67–82; Carol Lasser, "Party, Propriety, Politics, and Woman Suffrage in the 1870s: National Developments and Ohio Perspectives," in *New Viewpoints in Women's History: Working Papers from the Schlesinger Library 50th Anniversary Conference, March 4–5, 1994*, ed. Susan Ware (Cambridge, MA: Arthur and Elizabeth Schlesinger Library, Radcliffe College, 1994), 134–57. For German-American women's rights activism in New York City during the early 1870s, see Bank, *Women of Two Countries*, 54–61.

42 Ortlepp, "*Auf denn, Ihr Schwestern*," 153–54; Anneke, *Mathilde Franziska Anneke*, ed. Wagner, 357–58; Nadel, "German Immigrant Left," 53–55.

43 *Milwaukee Daily Sentinel*, Feb. 2, 1876; *Milwaukee Socialist*, June 19, 1876.

44 General Council to Milwaukee Section 3, March 28, 1876, reel 1, fr. 834; Emilie Lyser to the General Council, reel 2, fr. 720, IWA Papers, WHS.

progressive common sense and science."[45] Women's suffrage seemed highly rational to the freethinkers. Women writing in their Milwaukee newspaper ascribed gender inequality not to natural difference, but to "human society" and dissected the religious traditions that subordinated their sex.[46]

German-American socialist men, however, were ambivalent about the feminism that proliferated in radical circles during the 1870s. The *Socialist* reflected their general attitudes. One editorial approved of the Republican Party's relative "progressiveness" on gender, but Brucker made female employment an emblem of capitalism's cruelty.[47] He repeatedly idealized the male-headed household, empathizing with workingmen who faced the ignominy of "sending" their wives out to earn wages.[48] At the institutional level, the German-American leaders of the IWA sometimes classified women's suffrage among the frivolous reforms that could distract socialists from revolution. When the German Americans engineered the notorious expulsion of several of New York's English-speaking sections in 1871, gender radicalism was one of the counts against the Yankees.[49] The General Council later told Milwaukee's Section 3, "We have nothing at all against women's suffrage," adding in parentheses that "the equality of women, in every respect, is self-evident in a state based on the rights of workers." The letter then pointed out that the vote had not solved the problems of working-class men, asking Section 3 to focus on the "abolition of the economic exploitation [of the working class], which is the basis for all forms of bondage."[50] A cynical reader might conclude that talk of women's rights was tolerated within the IWA, but fighting for them was not. Female delegates registered a protest when the convention that formed the Workingmen's Party in 1876 endorsed equal wages, but not suffrage, for women.[51] Socialism's promise of gender equality fared poorly in the hands of real socialists.

45 Bundes der Deutschen Fr. Gemeinden von Nord-Amerika, "Beschlüsse der vierten Tagsatzung," Philadelphia, June 26 and 27, 1867, p. 6, box 1, folder 6, Freie Gemeinde Papers, MCHS; Wisconsin Writers' Program Writings and Research Notes, WPA, box 13, WHS.
46 *Milwaukee Freidenker*, Oct. 15, April 1, Sept. 1, Oct. 1, 1872. On the *Freidenker*, see Rampelmann, *Im Licht der Vernunft*, 79–83.
47 *Milwaukee Socialist*, June 17, 1876.
48 Ibid., Nov. 17 and 26, 1875; Brucker, *Die Social-Demokratie*, 8–9.
49 Timothy Messer-Kruse, *The Yankee International: Marxism and the American Reform Tradition, 1848–1876* (Chapel Hill: University of North Carolina Press, 1998); Mari Jo Buhle, *Women and American Socialism* (Urbana: University of Illinois Press, 1981), 1–48; Ortlepp, "Die Entstehung einer deutschamerikanischen Frauenbewegung," in *Die deutsche Präsenz*, ed. Raab and Wirrer, 189–210; Ortlepp, *Auf denn, ihr Schwestern*, 185–86; Schlüter, *Die Internationale in Amerika*, 335; Nadel, "German Immigrant Left," 51–56.
50 General Council to Milwaukee Section 3, March 28, 1876, reel 1, fr. 834, IWA Papers, WHS.
51 Philip S. Foner, ed., *Formation of the Workingmen's Party*, 6.

German-born socialists engaged with race differently than gender. On the face of it, white socialists and black Southerners appeared to be natural allies. Although they had little personal contact, socialist leaders identified African Americans as "the true working people" of the "Southern states."[52] Had Brucker been paying attention, he would have seen that the freed people, like him, imagined a polity in which states served the economic interests of their citizens. Following the war, one of the first priorities of Southern blacks had been "laws protecting our property and labor," as a group of "Colored Citizens" put it in Vicksburg, Mississippi.[53] Once the Reconstruction Act of 1867 had enfranchised black men in the former Confederacy, they had tried to pass their economic ideas into law. African Americans in South Carolina were the most successful. They created a commission that resold land on long-term credit and provided homesteads to about 14,000 black families, as well as some white ones. Other South Carolinian achievements were more typical of the rest of the South. Republicans constructed a public school system, reformed taxation so that landowners paid their share, saw to it that laborers would be remunerated for their work, and overturned the practice of hiring out convicts. (Their attempts to establish minimum wages and maximum hours foundered.[54]) Marxists might have seen these attainments as paltry, but the policies of Southern Republicans bore remarkable similarity to the ones that Brucker proposed for Wisconsin in 1877: compulsory public schooling, progressive taxation, a ban on convict labor, and guarantees of workers' wages.[55]

Despite their common ideological ground, however, the German-American socialists of the 1870s did not ally with black Southerners as the liberals of the 1860s had. Socialists could not stomach the Republican Party, and their understanding of the evolution of citizenship associated any interest in African-American rights with a bygone era. It seemed a vestige of the liberal approach of the previous decade. At one point, Brucker's coeditor at the *Socialist*, Gustav Lyser, told a meeting that the Republicans had "eliminated black slavery through a bloody war," but "that of

---

52 Quarterly Report of the North American Federation, Feb. 3, 1875, clipping, reel 2, fr. 895, IWA Papers, WHS.

53 Hahn et al., eds., *Freedom: A Documentary History of Emancipation, 1861–1867, series 3, vol. 1, Land and Labor* (Chapel Hill: University of North Carolina Press, 2008), 817.

54 Foner, *Reconstruction*, 372–79; Julie Saville, "Grassroots Reconstruction: Agricultural Laborers and Collective Action in South Carolina, 1860–1868," *Slavery and Abolition* 12, no. 3 (1991): 173–82; Saville, *Work of Reconstruction*; Stanley, *From Bondage to Contract*; Barbara Fields, *Slavery and Freedom on the Middle Ground: Maryland during the Nineteenth Century* (New Haven, CT: Yale University Press, 1985); Ira Berlin et al., "The Wartime Genesis of Free Labor," in *Slaves No More: Three Essays on Emancipation and the Civil War*, ed. Ira Berlin et al. (Cambridge: Cambridge University Press, 1992), 152–54, 182–86.

55 Brucker, *Die Social-Demokratie*, 22.

whites, wage-slavery," endured.[56] Immigrant workers had always burdened the term "wage-slavery" with their complicated ideas of race, but this particular comment brought up the issue of change over time. Socialists suggested that although discrimination against African Americans had once justified political action, that time was over. For Lyser and other socialists, economic injustice had become a predominantly white problem.

Socialists' sense that it was time to focus on white workers dovetailed neatly with the idea that civil and political rights were no longer under serious threat and that the next phase in the evolution of citizenship would be economic. Every time that they depreciated voting rights, German-American socialists reinscribed a linear narrative of citizenship: it would progress onward in a series of steps. This view, embedded in the experiences of European men and integrated into the thinking of Marx and other socialists, was later popularized among scholars by social theorist T. H. Marshall. Lecturing on British history in 1949, Marshall outlined a schematic narrative of the unfolding of citizenship rights that began with civil and political rights in the eighteenth and nineteenth centuries and was topped off during the twentieth century with a bundle of "social rights," including "a modicum of economic welfare and security."[57] Although Marshall's work has informed historians of the United States, many of them have noted that it falls short of explaining the status of racial minorities and women, which sometimes regressed even as white men's citizenship forged ahead.[58]

Seeing the development of citizenship as a linear phenomenon was not very useful to the African Americans negotiating Southern politics. That much was clear in the *Milwaukee Socialist's* brief report on a speech that Frederick Douglass gave at the Republican national convention in 1876. Douglass related the Old Testament story of Moses, who had instructed the Israelites to "borrow" crops and jewels from their oppressors when they fled slavery in Egypt. Even Russian serfs, Douglass told delegates, had acquired small plots of land upon emancipation. The freed people of the United States had received nothing. Republicans, he said, had "delivered us to the storm, the whirlwind, and the vengeance of our embittered masters."[59] Douglass's main point, however, was not that Republicans should change

---

56 *Milwaukee Socialist*, Oct. 16, 1876. For another reference to "white wage-slavery," see Dec. 8, 1875.
57 Marshall, *Citizenship and Social Class*, 11, 21.
58 For accounts that emphasize Marshall's limits when it comes to race and gender, see Margaret R. Sommers, "Citizenship and the Place of the Public Sphere: Law, Community, and Political Culture in the Transition to Democracy," *American Sociological Review* 58 (1993): 587–620; Evelyn Nakano Glenn, *Unequal Freedom: How Race and Gender Shaped American Citizenship* (Cambridge, MA: Harvard University Press, 2002), 18–55; Alice Kessler-Harris, *In Pursuit of Equity: Women, Men, and the Quest for Economic Citizenship in 20th-Century America* (Oxford: Oxford University Press, 2001), 10, 12.
59 *Milwaukee Socialist*, June 6, 1876.

their economic policies. He was arguing that it would be premature to abandon Republican Reconstruction, especially since African Americans could sustain the Republican Party in the South if the amended Constitution were enforced. In the absence of land redistribution, Douglass had become more committed than ever to the franchise. He was a loyal Republican representing African Americans.

When the account of Douglass's presentation appeared in the *Socialist*, which routinely harangued the Republicans, it took on a different meaning. In Brucker's hands, Douglass seemed to testify that his party's obsession with suffrage had rendered it irrelevant. Whatever the merits of this interpretation, it was not Douglass's. He had made the pragmatic choice to work within the partisan system to increase African-American power. Brucker was single-mindedly set on economic equality and took political rights for granted. African Americans, although quite conscious of their own economic exploitation, could not be so cavalier about the right to vote. During the 1870s, violence and lax enforcement were jeopardizing the gains of African-American men. Because socialists were uninterested in this fact, their politics was hazardous to race-neutral citizenship.

Brucker never collaborated with African Americans, but the apparent ties between Northern socialists and Southern freed people were of the utmost salience to many white Northerners. The theories of the socialists provided new reasons to question African Americans' fitness for citizenship. Some Northerners were afraid that poor Americans – both black and white – wanted to control governments themselves. To many Northern whites, Reconstruction came to stand for the preferential treatment of the undeserving poor. Although African Americans could not count on white socialists, they bore the brunt of the retaliation against the idea of economic rights.

The counterattacks on socialism ranged in tone from calm and principled to alarmist and irrational. At the reasonable end of the spectrum, a correspondent to the Democratic *Cincinnati Volksfreund* wrote that he did not consider "rights" to be at stake in the economic debate: "Property owners have [no] *legal* [*rechtliche*] obligation to provide for the wellbeing of their less well-off fellow citizens; they are certainly morally obliged to, but no one has the right [*Recht*] to compel them to." In the next paragraph, the writer continued, "However, the property-less working classes have the full right [*Recht*] to demand such laws from the state which secure the fruits of their labor and give them the opportunity to become property owners themselves."[60] This statement was consistent with Democratic and

---

60 *Cincinnati Volksfreund*, June 13, 1872.

Republican editors' disapproval of special considerations for manufacturers, railroad investors, and bankers, but many other German Americans reacted more viscerally to the prospect of a mobilizing working class.[61] During 1871, the *Milwaukee Herold* had run an article warning that some of the more disturbing activities of the IWA had "not yet found their way into the press." New York's Section 10 was holding biweekly meetings "in a small room in an obscure bar decorated with fascinating painted symbols, among which revolvers and daggers play a leading role." Debates "revolved around the overthrow of all established conditions of whatever sort – social or political." The correspondent took particular note of the presence of Victoria Woodhull, a native-born feminist conspicuous for her objections to conventional marriage, and the fact that "even the Negro is represented there."[62]

It did not take long for the socialists' adversaries to combine their dislike for the redistribution of resources with their apprehension of social chaos and turn on the biracial governments of the South. In 1874, a native-born reporter, James S. Pike, wrote a series of articles for the *New York Daily Tribune* alleging that South Carolina's "Black Parliament" was "plundering the property-holders of the state" to aid corrupt politicians and the profligate poor.[63] When Pike's reports came out in a single volume, *The Prostrate State*, the formerly Republican *Milwaukee Herold* distilled the book's contents for its readers. A table highlighted the recent climb in South Carolina's state outlay. The accompanying article stated that the government had "stolen" public revenue and the few white lawmakers who did not "abet the black crooks, had no more influence on the legislature than a seat has on he who sits in it."[64] It is important to emphasize that Pike blended laissez-faire with insulting caricatures and racist arguments that flouted liberalism. Coleman at the *Herold* was slightly more restrained, but he too read supposed economic failings as racial ones. The review in his newspaper not only lambasted

---

61 Sometimes laissez-faire logic led German-speaking Democrats and Republicans to tolerate industrial action and local workers' parties. *Wächter am Erie*, March 31, 1873; *Columbus Westbote*, April 23, Nov. 5, 1873; *Cincinnati Volksfreund*, Aug. 3, 1870, Oct. 28, 1871, Jan. 17, April 13 and 26, June 13, 20, 21, and 25, 1872; *Herold Wöchentliche Ausgabe*, March 27, Oct. 16, 1873; *Wochenblatt der New-Yorker Staatszeitung*, Nov. 22, 1873.

62 *Herold Wöchentliche Ausgabe*, Oct. 5, 1871. See also Dec. 14, 1871; *Westliche Post*, Sept. 18, 1872. A few months earlier the *Herold* had printed that the American sections of the International Working-men's Association would not be as radical as their Parisian counterparts because American workers understood the value of their political rights. *Herold Wöchentliche Ausgabe*, June 20, 1871.

63 James S. Pike, *The Prostrate State: South Carolina under Negro Government* (New York: Loring & Mussey, 1935; reprint, New York: D. Appleton, 1974), 15, 179. For explorations of Pike's work, see Richardson, *Death of Reconstruction*, 104–7; Sproat, *"Best Men,"* 35–36; Foner, *Reconstruction*, 525–26.

64 *Herold Wöchentliche Ausgabe*, Jan. 29, 1874.

African Americans, it made racial equality the central problem facing South Carolina.

In impugning the economic decisions of Republican governments, Pike attacked the legitimacy of African-American politics. He unintentionally showed the wisdom of Douglass's insight that political and economic rights were interdependent, not sequential. For Southern blacks, economic security was impossible without political power. Yet some Americans now wanted to make political power contingent on conformity to certain economic orthodoxies. German-American socialists' belief that citizenship progressed in linear form from the political to the economic did not help African Americans. No one ever suggested that Brucker's views of political economy disqualified him from political citizenship. His socialism did not imperil his access to the ballot box. Black men, however, still could not be sure that they would be seen as rightful political actors. Despite the failure of white socialists to unite with black Southerners, many other Americans argued that both groups were making dangerous claims on the state. These ideological interactions were choreographed to the rhythms of the 1870s. Free labor ideology no longer kept so many German Americans in step with black rights. Neither Brucker nor Coleman approved of liberal solutions. One rejected laissez-faire and the other questioned race-neutral citizenship.

CATHOLICS, CULTURAL RIGHTS, AND EDUCATING THE CITIZEN

While Americans were debating the economic meaning of citizenship, a cultural storm was also brewing. Between the collapse of the Know Nothing Party in the mid-1850s and the ratification of the Fifteenth Amendment in 1870, the sectional crisis had taken over American politics. As 1870 approached, however, pious Catholics and Protestants returned to the ethnocultural scrimmaging of the 1850s. Conservative Catholics wanted state support of denominational schooling, while Protestants thought that state institutions should promulgate what they saw as non-sectarian Christian morality. Religiously inspired public education became so essential to native-born Protestant Republicans that historian Ward McAfee has called it "the soul of the Republican program in the 1870s."[65] Arraying in opposition to both groups, the vast majority of German Americans – non-Catholics and moderate Catholics – were partisans of secular public schooling. African Americans also held a unique position, seeing education as the route to community empowerment. They would try to ignore the

---

65 McAfee, *Religion, Race, and Reconstruction*, 6.

Republicans' new cultural politics, but since it offended immigrant voters and taxed liberal nationalism, they could not insulate themselves from the repercussions.

Unsurprisingly, most German Americans argued that public education should honor ethnic difference. The immigrants overwhelmingly believed that teachers should facilitate a mutually rewarding cultural exchange. Their clamorous defense of German-language instruction presented this pluralism.[66] A correspondent to the Republican *Toledo Express* called German classes in state schools a "right," and the editor of the Democratic *Anzeiger des Westens* stated that they were "in the interests of American citizenship." Yet neither paper was recommending that German-speaking children should be segregated. The *Anzeiger* editorialized that bilingual education would make sure that immigrants "were woven into the whole population." The children of "the older Anglo-Saxon or already American population," the paper ran, "will also be enlightened by the communication between them and the Germans, and through their knowledge of German literature, the Americans will acquire access to the intellectual activity of the German *Volk*, which will allow them to honor and respect newly immigrated people." According to the *Anzeiger*, teachers had no right to inflict Anglo-Protestantism on children, for the state had "nothing to do with the beliefs of its citizens."[67] Pluralism was obviously so fundamental a principle that it did not count as a belief.

Some Roman Catholic German Americans pursued pluralism into the realm of cultural *rights*. Nearly all immigrants, regardless of confession, frowned on Protestant teachers who proselytized in public classrooms. But whereas most immigrants wanted to secularize their neighborhood schools, some Catholics thought that it was impossible to inculcate the "morality and piety" vital to good citizenship without religion.[68] All bishops, most priests, and some lay leaders in the Midwest said that Catholic parents must send their children to Catholic schools. Cincinnati's episcopally sponsored *Wahrheitsfreund* insisted that "no **good** Catholic" could enroll his or her children in a "system of education without a religious purpose."[69] Given this

66 *Herold Wöchentliche Ausgabe*, April 29, 1873. Carolyn R. Toth, *German-English Bilingual Schools in America: The Cincinnati Tradition in Historical Context* (New York: P. Lang, 1990). No German-American editor in Ohio, Missouri, or Wisconsin doubted the benefits of bilingual education.

67 *Toledo Express*, Feb. 21, 1872; *Anzeiger des Westens*, Sept. 11, 1873. See also *Toledo Express*, March 27, 1872; *Cincinnati Volksfreund*, Sept. 28, Oct. 3, 1871; *Milwaukee Germania*, Nov. 12, 1873; *Stockbridge Union*, April 24, May 22, 1873.

68 *Wahrheitsfreund*, July 12, 1865. For a discussion of the Catholic approach to knowledge (*Wissenschaft*) in the context of Germany's educational debates, see Bennette, *Fighting for the Soul of Germany*, 122–56.

69 *Wahrheitsfreund*, July 28, 1869.

injunction, it seemed unfair to tax Catholics for public education: "Is it just to compel someone to pay for something for which he can have no use?"[70] In Missouri, the lay Catholic leader and Democratic politician Henry J. Spaunhorst told fellow state senators, "I do not want the state to dictate the type of education that should be imparted to our children if it is contrary to our conscience and convictions."[71] Representatives of German Catholicism in Ohio and Missouri argued that in order to protect "freedom of religion," the state should "collect the public school funds and distribute them equally among everyone."[72] These Catholics, usually speaking of individual rather than group prerogatives, sought state funding for institutions that conserved their distinctive traditions and provided sanctuaries for their group. They demanded that governments recognize a new set of rights – cultural rights.

When some Midwestern Catholics championed cultural rights, they provoked a furor that radiated out from pulpits and school board meetings to legislatures and presidential campaigns. While the beliefs of this Catholic faction were anything but novel, their latest push unsettled the political patterns of the 1860s. At the end of 1869, members of Cincinnati's Board of Education, including some Catholics, voted to prohibit teachers from using religious texts and songs in class. Thousands of Catholic families in Cincinnati availed themselves of public schools, and they longed for them to be truly secular. After some early indications that the Catholic hierarchy might back the plan, Archbishop Purcell declared it unacceptable.[73] Missouri experienced a similar intra-Catholic schism. In 1872, Henry Spaunhorst founded the *Amerika*, a Catholic weekly that favored state-supported parochial schools. One of his Irish Catholic colleagues in the Missouri legislature had introduced a bill that would have appropriated tax revenue for private schools that offered their services free of charge.[74] Meanwhile, Catholic children attended St. Louis's city schools in about the same numbers as ones run by the Church. At one point, Archbishop Peter R. Kenrick had to restrain priests who were denying absolution to parents

---

70 Ibid., July 14, 1869, Feb. 1, April 19, 1871.
71 Ibid., Feb. 15, 1870. On Spaunhorst, see Isidor Loeb and Floyd C. Shoemaker, eds., *Journal of the Missouri Constitutional Convention of 1875*, 2 vols. (Columbia: State Historical Society of Missouri, 1920) 1: 107–08.
72 *Wahrheitsfreund*, July 12, 1865, July 14, 1869.
73 Harold M. Helfman, "The Cincinnati 'Bible War,' 1869–1870," *Ohio State Archaeological and Historical Quarterly* 60 (1951): 370–71; Bernard Mandel, "Religion in the Public Schools of Ohio," *Ohio Archaeological and Historical Quarterly* 58 (1949): 185–206; White, "Religion and Community," 293.
74 Michael Hoey, "Missouri Education at the Crossroads: The Phelan Miscalculation and the Education Amendment of 1870," *Missouri Historical Review* 95 (2001): 383–84; Lloyd P. Jorgenson, *The State and the Non-Public School, 1825–1925* (Columbia: University of Missouri Press, 1987), 112–14.

who chose public schooling.[75] Wisconsin Catholics, it is worth mentioning, were less combative. Peter Deuster at the *Seebote* printed letters supporting state funding for Catholic schools, but he allocated more space to his own concerns about the anti–Catholic bias in public schools.[76]

The majority of German Americans in Ohio, Missouri, and Wisconsin saw themselves as cultural liberals wedged between Catholic separatists and Anglo-Protestant bigots. Secular German-American leaders, be they Democrats, Republicans, or socialists, restated their long-standing fear of Catholic "Jesuitism" on the one hand and puritanical "Muckerism" on the other.[77] The commotion dredged up into public view feelings that slavery and black suffrage had partially submerged. In Cincinnati, Emil Rothe, the observant Catholic editor of the Democratic *Volksfreund*, proclaimed that secularizing public schools would be a victory over the "fanatical encroachments" of native-born Protestants and "a step toward the implementation of the principles of the Declaration of Independence."[78] Friedrich Hassaurek, the freethinker editing the independent *Volksblatt*, praised the school board's plan because it would weaken the demand for denominational schools that "alienate the citizens of this great republic, who consist of so many diverse elements, from each other."[79] At local elections in 1870, Cincinnatians voted to return the "anti-Bible" representatives to the Board of Education, and in 1872, the Ohio Supreme Court upheld the Bible ban.[80] Down in Missouri, Liberal Republican Joseph Pulitzer, still a protégé of Schurz at the *Westliche Post* and just elected to the state legislature, led the political opposition to Catholic schools.[81] Another German-born Liberal Republican drafted an amendment to the state constitution to outlaw the public funding of any sectarian organization.[82] In 1870, more than 92 percent of

75 *Amerika*, Oct. 17, 1870; *Wahrheitsfreund*, Feb. 15, 1870; Peter R. Kenrick to H. Van der Sanden, Dec. 21, 1866, April 6 and 26, 1869, box 1, folder 4, Archbishop Peter R. Kenrick Papers, ASLA; Hoey, "Missouri Education at the Crossroads," 380.

76 *Seebote*, Aug. 11, 1873, Aug. 14 and 21, 1876. Two small Catholic newspapers that began publication after hopes for public funding had been quashed also avoided the hopeless cause. *Green Bay Concordia*, Aug. 12, 1875; *Milwaukee Columbia*, Jan. 22, 1874.

77 *Milwaukee Socialist*, June 27, 1876; *Milwaukee Freidenker*, April 1, 1872.

78 *Cincinnati Volksfreund*, Aug. 28, 1869.

79 *Cincinnati Volksblatt* quoted in the *Wahrheitsfreund*, July 14, 1869. See also *Anzeiger des Westens*, Sept. 11, 1873; *Westliche Post Wochen-Blatt*, Nov. 10, 1869; *Wächter am Erie*, March 23, 1869; *St. Charles Demokrat*, Sept. 30, 1869. The *Wahrheitsfreund* distanced itself from the school board question. *Wahrheitsfreund*, Feb. 23, 1870.

80 Helfman, "Cincinnati Bible War," 386.

81 *St. Charles Demokrat*, March 3, 1870; Hoey, "Missouri Education at the Crossroads," 385; Saalberg, "*Westliche Post* of St. Louis," 185–228.

82 Loeb and Shoemaker, eds., *Journal of the Missouri Constitutional Convention of 1875*, 1: 85–86; Hoey, "Missouri Education at the Crossroads," 385–86.

Missouri voters approved it in a referendum.[83] German Americans preferred a liberal cultural pluralism to state-funded separatism.

Staunch Catholics such as Spaunhorst had seen to it that cultural rights "stir[red] all of America like a whirlwind," but their attempt to redefine citizenship was overshadowed by the reaction against them.[84] Like the decade's battles over economic rights, Ohio's "Bible wars" and Missouri's school funding fracas presented two contrasting alternatives to the liberal nationalism of pluralism, individual rights, and limited government. Both intransigent Catholics and obdurate Protestants brought the state into matters of religion and culture. Even after the specific controversies were legally settled, Catholics and Protestants kept the underlying issues alive. In this polarized setting, German-American Republicans would reconsider whether cultural diversity and racial inclusion automatically went hand in hand as they had always claimed.

Transnational alliances figured in the cultural and racial calculations of the 1870s in a way that they had not in the 1860s. Catholics felt a new kinship to their coreligionists around the world, and their Protestant antagonists correspondingly saw the Church as an international menace. Germany's *Kulturkampf* fueled both tendencies. Because Bismarck thought that the loyalty of Catholics to Rome endangered the "unity won on the battlefield," he designed a cultural correlate to his military campaign.[85] His chief goal was to subdue the mainly Catholic regions of Alsace and Lorraine in the west and Pomerania in the east. Skillfully coupling his own Lutheran piety with the secular leanings of the Reichstag, the chancellor began an unparalleled offensive on the Catholic Church. After 1871, any priest who communicated a "political" message from the pulpit risked arrest. The next year, members of religious orders were stripped of their traditional role as unpaid teachers in the public schools reserved for Catholics, and the Society of Jesus was expelled from German territory altogether. In 1873, the imperial government started to oversee the training and appointment of Catholic clergy. Amplified by further discriminatory legislation, the *Kulturkampf* sent more than half of Prussia's priests to jail or into exile before 1878.[86] By that

---

83 *Westliche Post*, Sept. 3, 1870; Hoey, "Missouri Education at the Crossroads," 390–91.
84 *Wahrheitsfreund*, Sept. 1, 1869; Joseph Salzmann to Ludwigs-Missionverein, Oct. 29, 1869, box 1, folder 59, Ludwigs-Missionverein Correspondence, Archdiocese of Milwaukee Archives (hereafter AMA), St. Francis, WI.
85 Quoted in Ronald J. Ross, *The Failure of Bismarck's Kulturkampf: Catholicism and State Power in Imperial Germany* (Washington, DC: The Catholic University of America Press, 1998), 7, 11.
86 Erich Schmidt-Volkmar, *Der Kulturkampf in Deutschland, 1871–1890* (Göttingen: Musterschmidt-Verlag, 1962), 73–74; Michael B. Gross, *The War against Catholicism: Liberalism and the Anti-Catholic Imagination in Nineteenth-Century Germany* (Ann Arbor: University of Michigan Press, 2004), 240–43;

point, it was clear that Bismarck's suppression of the Catholic Church went beyond the liberals' ambition to separate church and state.

Reviewing the events of the early 1870s, the editors of the Catholic *Amerika* in St. Louis described the transnational coalitions that were forming for and against Catholicism. A worldwide war seemed to rage between Catholics and their enemies. On one side stood the Vatican, the German bishops, and the faithful, wrote the *Amerika*. On the other massed thinkers as diverse as Charles Darwin, Otto von Bismarck, and German socialist Karl Liebknecht.[87] In the new matrix, cultural rights had displaced political rights as the central object of disagreement and new battle lines cut across the old liberal–conservative divide. Catholicism's reputed foes did not share one view of citizenship. By making partners of Bismarck and Liebknecht, the *Amerika* rearranged the groupings sketched in the *Socialist*. Brucker, of course, divided the world between supporters and opponents of economic rights. The politics of the 1870s was reconfigured along multiple competing axes that superseded the old polarities of 1848 and the 1860s. German Americans had to operate in a world in which new debates, not just new ideas, beset liberal nationalism.

News of the *Kulturkampf* enhanced the fellowship between American Catholics and Catholics abroad. In the years following 1871, Catholic newspapers such as the *Wahrheitsfreund* and the *Amerika* published numerous accounts of the Prussian-led assault on the Church. A new German-language Catholic weekly in Milwaukee, the *Columbia*, compared it to Attila the Hun's war on the "Christian world order" in the fifth century, reminding readers of the age and size of the Catholic Church.[88] Catholics in the United States could also attend lectures detailing Bismarck's latest offences. At one of these in Cincinnati, 750 people listened to an exiled Jesuit describe his persecution.[89] Priests were an important source of information. One American clergyman who was traveling in northern Germany wrote to Archbishop Purcell that "there cannot be another country on the globe, where under the cloak of liberal concessions and national demands the church received harder blows, than in this empire of blood and iron," and a young Cincinnatian at an Austrian seminary reported that Bismarck had set his sights on "the total extinction of Catholic life."[90]

Helmut Walser Smith, *German Nationalism and Religious Conflict: Culture, Ideology, Politics, 1870–1914* (Princeton, NJ: Princeton University Press, 1995), 42–49.

87 *Amerika*, Dec. 31, 1872. See also *Wahrheitsfreund*, Jan. 25, 1871.

88 *Milwaukee Columbia*, Jan. 15, 1874.

89 *Wahrheitsfreund*, Jan. 8, 1873; *Amerika*, Nov. 4, 1872; *Westliche Post*, Aug. 7, 1872; *Cincinnati Volksblatt*, Aug. 5, 1872.

90 Bernhard H. Engbers to John B. Purcell, Jan. 4, 1872; Charles S. Kemper, to John B. Purcell, Nov. 22, 1872, box 27, Purcell Papers, AAC.

The lay immigrants entering American churches must have had their own stories too.

If Catholics identified with the victims of the *Kulturkampf,* some non-Catholic immigrants were tempted to side with Bismarck, another departure in German-American politics since 1870. Forty-Eighters had considered the Church an undemocratic locus of power, sometimes sliding towards intolerance, but in 1848, they had believed in liberal institutions that included and uplifted all Germans. The systematic repression of specific populations ran counter to the means revolutionaries had chosen to cement national unity. The experience of minority status in the United States made cultural pluralism indispensable to their liberal nationalism during the 1850s and 1860s. In the passion of 1870 and 1871, however, Forty-Eighters had demurred to Bismarck in the handling of Alsace, Lorraine, and the Poles. Well into 1872, the *Volksfreund* and the *Volksblatt* in Cincinnati periodically excused Bismarck's conduct of the *Kulturkampf* because the Church obstructed German rule. One *Volksfreund* editorial announced that the Polish subjects of the German Empire were standing in the way of "the one true principle of the advancement of national, political, and religious equality."[91] The newspaper was justifying cultural restrictions that served state cohesion. In this case, it concluded that when liberal ideals came in conflict with national imperatives, the nation must take precedence.

German-American politicians and editors, however, were reluctant to jettison cultural inclusivity. Even the *Volksfreund* later asked, "What, by heaven, do the maintenance of the lessons of their church and the instruction of the youth by the living religious have to do with the future, power, and glory of the German Empire?"[92] Perhaps religious diversity was not in conflict with national unity. According to the *Westliche Post,* "the core of the great controversy" was whether the German administration was responsibly balancing individual religious freedom against the legitimate interests of the empire:

The state has no right to limit citizens' freedom of opinion and conscience. . . . In order to prevent this . . . the constitutions of all free states have outlined the principle that the state have nothing to do with the church as such. But does that give any church the right to misuse its power over the minds of its believers to subvert the necessary authority of the state over its citizens?[93]

The *Post* was not eager to take sides. Among the mainstream German-language newspapers in Ohio, Missouri, and Wisconsin, only Milwaukee's *Germania,* new in 1873 and unusual in its Protestant tone, was unambivalent

---

91 *Cincinnati Volksfreund,* March 7, 1872. See also Aug. 22, 1872; *Cincinnati Volksblatt,* Nov. 1, 1872.
92 *Cincinnati Volksfreund,* June 22, 1872.   93 *Westliche Post,* July 9, 1872.

in its support of the religious crackdown. Although other newspapers reported when the Reichstag approved laws constraining religion, they rarely offered editorial comment.[94]

If the tempest over cultural rights produced new models of transnationalism, it also reawakened the gender tensions that had always accompanied religious politics. Anglo-American women who used their domestic authority to spread Protestantism irked German Americans. Ohio's 1875 gubernatorial race, in which Republican Rutherford B. Hayes made much of the benefits of Protestant public schooling and the detriments of alcohol consumption, was the sort of election that reignited old suspicions. One small German weekly denounced women who supposedly neglected their husbands and children to go from tavern to tavern harassing patrons.[95] The wife of the Republican candidate, Lucy Hayes, not only supported her husband, she was also a well-known *Temperenzlerin* in her own right.[96] A college-educated Methodist from a prominent family, the future first lady never taught school herself, but young women of similar convictions did. German immigrants already disliked the feminization of American education, and the Protestant zeal of many teachers certainly did not help matters.[97] Cultural rights, like economic rights, aggravated immigrants' gender sensibilities anew.

The cultural politics of the 1870s tessellated the illiberal, transnational, and gendered dimensions of the economic politics of the decade, and it also affected black citizenship. Although African Americans generally accepted Protestantism and refrained from talking of cultural rights, they used the segregated schools of the Reconstruction South as incubators of black pride. In some ways, the freed people resembled hard-line Catholics, or at least the German Americans who believed that common citizenship and cultural difference were entirely consonant. Generations of scholars have shown that black teachers led the struggle for equal rights and that African Americans went to great lengths to train more such role models.[98]

---

94 *Milwaukee Germania*, Nov. 8, 1873; *Westliche Post*, July 22, 1872; *Columbus Westbote*, May 3 and 22, 1873; *Cincinnati Volksblatt*, May 12, 1873; *Cincinnati Volksfreund*, Jan. 16 and 17, 1874.
95 Ibid., Oct. 7, 1875.
96 Emily Apt Geer, *First Lady: The Life of Lucy Webb Hayes* (Kent, OH: Kent State University Press, 1984), 3–8.
97 *Westliche Post*, Jan. 1, Feb. 10, 1865; Wittke, *Refugees of Revolution*, 300–09; Bettina Goldberg, "The Forty-Eighters and the School System in America: The Theory and Practice of Reform," in *German Forty-Eighters*, ed. Brancaforte, 206–07; Juliane Jacobi, "Schoolmarm, *Volkserzieher, Kantor,* and *Schulschester*: German Teachers among Immigrants during the Second Half of the Nineteenth Century," in *German Influences on Education in the United States*, ed. Geitz, Heideking, and Herbst, 115–28.
98 Litwack, *Been in the Storm So Long*, 494–95, 497–98; Foner, *Reconstruction*, 96–102; Masur, *Example for All the Land*, 77–85, 188–94. There is a broad literature on black education and Reconstruction.

W. E. B. Du Bois wrote in 1935 that it was because of public education that Negroes "kept their souls in spite of public and private insult of every description; they built an inner culture which the world recognizes in spite of the fact it is still half-strangled and inarticulate."[99] African Americans valued public schools so highly because they vindicated past citizenship claims, undergirded future ones, and created small domains of black sovereignty. For exactly the same reasons, hostile whites sometimes murdered teachers and torched schoolhouses.[100]

Schooling was a partisan issue in former slave states, mainly because Democrats and Republicans all knew that dismantling public education would undercut black citizenship. In 1875, a new constitutional convention in Missouri demonstrated how this could be done. Chosen by an electorate that now included black men and former secessionists, all but seven of the sixty-eight delegates were Democrats, and more than half of them had actively supported the Confederacy.[101] One former Confederate colonel captured the spirit of the body when he said, "The thunder of the Republican party is departing forever, & . . . the glorious negro question on which they have subsisted for ten years in this country is about to die in Missouri."[102] Democrats were not fans of government-funded institutions at the best of times, and they felt especially strongly about those that served African Americans. The 1875 constitution decreed racial segregation in all public schools and set about divesting education.[103] Democrats shortened the period of time that children would be eligible for free schooling, gave local bodies more control over spending, and no longer required that the legislature distribute school funds so as to "equalize the amount appropriated for common schools throughout the state."[104] Within three years,

See Du Bois, *Black Reconstruction in America*, 637–69; Du Bois, *The Common School and the Negro American* (Atlanta: Atlanta University Press, 1911); Ronald E. Burchart, *Schooling the Freed People: Teaching, Learning, and the Struggle for Black Freedom, 1861–1876* (Chapel Hill: University of North Carolina Press, 2010); Heather Andrea Williams, *Self-Taught: African American Education in Slavery and Freedom* (Chapel Hill: University of North Carolina Press, 2005).

99 Du Bois, *Black Reconstruction*, 667.

100 Ibid., 645–47; Burchart, *Schooling the Freed People*, 157–62; Litwack, *Been in the Storm So Long*, 487–98.

101 Shoemaker, "Personnel of the Convention," in *Journal of the Missouri Constitutional Convention of 1875*, ed. Loeb and Shoemaker, 1: 67, 64–65.

102 Ibid., 4: 301. A handful of German Democrats, including Pulitzer, championed comprehensive public education.

103 Loeb, "Constitutions and Constitutional Conventions in Missouri," in *Journal of the Missouri Constitutional Convention of 1875*, ed. Loeb and Shoemaker, 1: 41.

104 Ibid., 1: 40–41; Shoemaker and Loeb, eds. *Debates of the Missouri Constitutional Convention of 1875*, 12 vols. (Columbia: The State Historical Society of Missouri, 1930–1944), 9: 139; Shoemaker, *Missouri and Missourians: Land of Contrasts and People of Achievements*, 2 vols. (Chicago: Lewis Publishing Company, 1943), 2: 664–65. See also Parrish, *Missouri under Radical Rule*, 131–32; *St. Charles Demokrat*, Jan. 28, 1875.

Missouri's superintendent of education reported that many school districts had used their power to reduce their provisions for African Americans. Local officials, especially in rural areas, failed to count black children for the purpose of establishing schools. When challenged, they delayed any inquiry until it was too late in the school year to hire new staff or arrange suitable facilities.[105] Despite such travesties, Missouri was a best-case scenario. It provided more comprehensive education than any other former slave state, leading them all by the end of the century in the proportion of African-American youngsters who attended school.[106]

Democrats in the states of the former Confederacy, which had larger black populations and more federal oversight than Missouri, could move in the same direction because Northern Republicans were losing interest in Reconstruction. The cultural contraction of the Republican Party did not help. Strident Protestantism upset the cultural compromise that had brought Republicans to power during the 1860s. It also interfered with the arguments that intertwined the tolerance of immigrants and the inclusion of African Americans. Ohio's 1875 election season showcased the new politics, with Hayes campaigning on hard money, honest government, and anti-Catholicism, not the rebuilding of the South. To German-American Democrats, it looked as though Republicans were plotting an "American *Kulturkampf*."[107] As one editor declared, the "school question" had overshadowed the "Nigger question."[108] The strategy won Hayes the governorship without mass German-American defections, but August Thieme at the *Wächter am Erie* permanently turned his back on the party of "temperance and crusades."[109] Hayes's disregard for immigrant culture made the Republican Party, which was still the partisan home of African Americans, unappealing to German-American leaders. When the Ohioan ran for the presidency the following year, his campaign would further whittle down the electoral mandate for Reconstruction and hollow out the liberal ideology behind it.

---

105 Henry S. Williams, "The Development of the Negro Public Schools System in Missouri," *Journal of Negro History* 5 (1920): 157–58; W. Sherman Savage, "Legal Provisions for Negro Schools in Missouri, 1865 to 1890," *Journal of Negro History* 16 (1931): 313–15.

106 James D. Anderson, *The Education of Blacks in the South, 1860–1935* (Chapel Hill: University of North Carolina Press, 1988), 151.

107 *Milwaukee Columbia*, Oct. 21, 1875; *New Philadelphia Deutsche Beobachter*, Sept. 16, 1875.

108 *Columbus Westbote*, Oct. 13, 1875. See also *St. Charles Demokrat*, Sept. 9, 1875; Forrest W. Clonts, "The Political Campaign of 1875 in Ohio" (MA thesis, The Ohio State University, 1921); McAfee, *Religion, Race, and Reconstruction*, 178–80.

109 *Wächter am Erie*, Sept. 11, Oct. 1, 1875. Supporting local candidate Hayes and reporting election results, see *Cincinnati Volksblatt*, Oct. 11, 13, and 14, 1875. Predictably opposing Hayes on cultural issues, see *Neuer Philadelphia Deutsche Beobachter*, Sept. 16, Oct. 7 and 21, 1875; *Cincinnati Volksfreund*, Oct. 13 and 14, 1875.

THE PRESIDENTIAL ELECTION OF 1876

Milwaukee socialists made their first foray into presidential politics in 1876. On October 9, Joseph Brucker and hundreds of his comrades interrupted a huge meeting of impassioned Democrats. Cheered on by the others, Brucker stormed the stage and bombarded the Democrats with questions: How would they end the continuing depression? What would they do for suffering workers? Was there really any difference between Democrats and Republicans?[110] In fact, the socialists had already decided that little separated Samuel Tilden from Rutherford B. Hayes.[111] The Democrats sometimes spoke of class struggle, but they proposed to curb special interests rather than recognize economic rights. Republicans, who intended to use high tariffs and tight control of the currency to stimulate industrial growth, were no more receptive to economic citizenship. Socialists acknowledged the cultural distinctions between the two parties. Although Tilden did not want tax revenue to sponsor Catholic schools, he respected the Church, while Hayes played to anti-Catholic Protestants. Neither option satisfied Brucker. In the *Socialist*, he advised voters to reject the choice between "Jesuitism" and the "money bag" and opt instead for the "No-President-at-all-Ticket."[112] In simplified form, Brucker delineated the economic and cultural axes that had realigned Northern politics by 1876.

As political economy and religion eclipsed Reconstruction in the politics of the North, Republicans and Democrats were converging on matters of race. The Democratic platform proclaimed the party's "devotion to the Constitution of the United States with its amendments" and paid lip service to "the equality of all citizens before just laws of their own enactment."[113] It did not, however, reprove the violent disfranchisement of African Americans by some Democrats in the South.[114] Republicans pointed out as much, running on "the full realization of the principle of political freedom and equality for all without respect of descent and race."[115] Yet Republicans' actions did not live up to their rhetoric. Although Northern Republicans were still saddened by outrages such as the murder of 100 black Louisianans at Colfax in 1873, they were less likely than before to do anything about them.[116] Grant had not sent troops to Mississippi to shield the black and white Republicans subject to violence during the 1875 elections. Democrats

---

110 *Milwaukee Socialist*, Oct. 10, 1876.
111 Ibid., Oct 16 and 21, 1876; Hense-Jensen, *Wisconsin's Deutsch-Amerikaner*, 2: 68–69.
112 *Milwaukee Socialist*, Nov. 6, Oct. 18, 1876.
113 Donald B. Johnson, ed., *National Party Platforms* (Urbana: University of Illinois Press, 1973), 49.
114 Gillette, *Retreat from Reconstruction*, 59.   115 *Cleveland Anzeiger*, July 24, 1876.
116 Keith, *Colfax Massacre*.

"redeemed" the state and began to eviscerate the postwar amendments.[117] All the while, the Supreme Court was making it more difficult to enforce Republicans' Reconstruction policies.[118] The differences between the parties on that score were diminishing.

Schurz, one of the few notable German Americans to support Hayes, hoped that the Republicans would retreat still further. The veteran campaigner urged his candidate to substitute the "old war issues" with "the living questions" of the future. Schurz counseled Republicans not to discuss African-American citizenship. "There is at present," he wrote Hayes, "far more strength . . . in the advocacy of a policy of justice and conciliation, than in an attempt to rake up old animosities and in a mere repetition of old cries."[119] Hayes replied that he was uncomfortable with Schurz's allusions to "local self-government." The phrase seemed to Hayes "to smack of the bowie knife and the revolver." He wrote privately, "'Local self-government has nullified the 15th amendment in several States, and is in a fair way to nullify the 14th and 13th." The candidate then floated a compromise: "But I do favor a policy based on the observance of all parts of the Constitution – the new as well as the old, and therefore I suppose you and I are substantially agreed on the topic."[120] Such temporizing – Hayes was gesturing toward the limits of federal authority – allowed Republicans to speak up for African-American rights without having any plan to safeguard them. Republicans had never been of one mind on black citizenship, but African-American political rights had risen in popularity until about 1870. Now they were losing ground.

Schurz wanted Hayes to make more of the economic issues of the 1870s. One of the reasons he had first struck up a relationship with the Ohioan was Hayes's fondness for tight monetary policies. Schurz had argued in 1875 that government-fed inflation would profit only unscrupulous borrowers, "speculators, who, instead of following the path of frugal and steady industry, tried quickly to get rich on their wits." When inflation devalued the dollar, loans could be repaid at a discount. According to Schurz, "worthy laborers" could best be assisted through "the strictest maintenance of the limitations of governmental power."[121] Although most immigrants subscribed to this hard money and free market orthodoxy, they balked when Schurz went on to scorn the very idea that there was a "social question" in the United

117 Foner, *Reconstruction*, 557–63.
118 Benedict, "Preserving Federalism: Reconstruction and the Waite Court," *Supreme Court Review* (1978): 39–79.
119 Schurz to Hayes, June 21, 1876, in *Speeches, Correspondence and Political Papers of Carl Schurz*, 3: 249. See also Schurz to Hayes, Sept. 25, 1876, reel 47, Hayes Papers, HPC.
120 Hayes to Schurz, June 27, 1876, in *Speeches, Correspondence and Political Papers of Carl Schurz*, 3: 254.
121 Schurz, "Honest Money," 3: 190–91, 201, 167, 193.

States.[122] Socialists were aghast. It was hard to remember that men such as Schurz and Weydemeyer had once been Republican colleagues.

Unfortunately for Schurz, German Americans were remembering their partiality for the economic and cultural platforms of the Democratic Party. Republicans were the corrupt lackeys of monied interests and the bigoted opponents of German customs, said German-speaking Democrats. Tilden, the Democrats thought, was a hard-money reformer and friend to the immigrant. Schurz relayed to Hayes that "a large majority of the German voters, and among them very many who always went with the Republicans, are now inclined toward Tilden."[123] Since 1872, more German-born politicians in the Midwest had returned to the Party of Jackson. Thieme was one, along with Gustav Körner in Illinois and Joseph Pulitzer, who had cashed out his investment in the *Westliche Post.*[124] When the shareholders of the *Cincinnati Volksblatt* voted to support hometown favorite Hayes, Hassaurek promptly resigned as editor.[125] Even Sigel and Stallo, who had stumped for Grant in 1872, went over to Tilden.[126] Of course new Republican politicians and editors emerged, and the *Milwaukee Herold, Westliche Post,* and *St. Charles Demokrat* backed Hayes, but by 1876 nearly a whole generation of German-American leaders had written off the Republican Party.[127]

Nevertheless, the swing toward the Democrats hardly suggested that "99 out of 100 Germans vote Democratic," Schurz's newspaper protested.[128] Hayes did just as well among German Cincinnatians as Grant had in 1868, and he polled higher than Grant had among German Milwaukeeans, although immigrants there and throughout Wisconsin voted by and large for Tilden.[129] The Republicans' numbers were down in the German wards of Cleveland and St. Louis, but even so, they received majorities among German-Americans in the latter city.[130] Voters were slower to change than their leaders.

---

122 *Volksstimme des Westens,* Sept. 3, 1877; *Cincinnati Volksblatt,* July 24, 1877; Brucker, *Die Social-Demokratie,* 10.

123 Schurz to Hayes, Aug. 7, 1876, in *Speeches, Correspondence and Political Papers of Carl Schurz,* ed. Bancroft, 3: 280.

124 Koerner, *Memoirs of Gustav Koerner,* 2: 565, 597–98; Saalberg, "*Westliche Post* of St. Louis," 225–26. *Columbus Westbote,* April 16, 1873; *Fremont Courier,* Sept. 14, 1876; *Westliche Post,* Oct. 12, 1876.

125 *Cincinnati Volksblatt,* July 11, 1876. See also July 7, 1876; *Fremont Courier,* July 22 and 29, 1876.

126 *Wochenblatt des Wisconsin Banner und Volksfreund,* Aug. 17 and 24, 1876.

127 For an example of a short-lived German Republican newspaper, see *Cleveland Anzeiger,* July 24, 1876.

128 *Westliche Post,* Oct. 12, 1876.

129 Appendix, Tables 2 and 4. Some commentators believed that there were German-born voters who found Hayes a more convincing defender of hard money and reform than Tilden. *Wochenblatt des Wisconsin Banner und Volksfreund,* Oct. 19, Nov. 2, 1876; Hense-Jensen, *Wisconsin's Deutsch-Amerikaner,* 2: 60–70.

130 Appendix, Tables 1 and 3.

Americans would not learn who would be the next president until 1877, but the election had already proven that economic and cultural questions had supplanted those of race and political rights in the German-language public sphere. In the new environment, which dated back to the ratification of the Fifteenth Amendment and the Franco-Prussian War in 1870, Americans saw the first flickers of the Gilded Age with its intensified transnationalism and mounting discussion of women's roles. African-American men would continue to battle to retain their political rights, but German Americans as dissimilar as Joseph Brucker, Henry Spaunhorst, and Carl Schurz believed that the "living questions of the future" lay elsewhere.[131]

131 Schurz to Hayes, June 21, 1876, in *Speeches, Correspondence and Political Papers of Carl Schurz*, ed. Bancroft, 3: 249.

Epilogue: The Great Strike of 1877

At midnight on July 24, 1877, Sergeant John Finn telegraphed the War Department from St. Louis to warn that revolution was in the air.[1] The great railroad strike had crossed the Mississippi. Nearly two weeks earlier, workers on the Baltimore & Ohio had left their posts in West Virginia to protest the latest in a series of deep wage cuts. Since then, drivers, engineers, and freightmen had brought rail traffic to a halt on lines across North America. The jeers of demonstrators had replaced the clatter of trains in dozens of centers. In St. Louis, as Sergeant Finn explained in his telegram, perhaps ten thousand people had flocked to Lucas Market to show that they stood with the strikers. Loathe to waste this expression of working-class energy, leaders of the local Workingmen's Party inserted themselves at the head of a mass movement that they hoped would secure economic rights and perhaps even build into a more transformative force. Projecting their voices across the crowd, the socialists roared that it was "the duty of the government to enact such laws as will ensure equal justice to all the people of the nation." They demanded – in English and German – that Congress recognize the economic rights of poor Americans immediately, emphasizing, "Every man willing to perform a use to society is entitled to a living."[2] The racially mixed audience thundered its approval at each proposal, and before Finn went to report to his superiors, the call had gone out for a citywide general strike.

1 John Finn to Chief Signal Officer, telegram, July 24, 1877, reel 70, fr. 74, Hayes Papers, HPC; Roediger, "Not Only the Ruling Classes to Overcome," 213–39; Burbank, *Reign of the Rabble*, 53–58; Philip S. Foner, *Great Labor Uprising of 1877*, 171–75. On the Great Strike generally, see Robert V. Bruce, *1877: Year of Violence* (Indianapolis, IN: Bobbs-Merrill, 1959); David O. Stowell, *Streets, Railroads, and the Great Strike of 1877* (Chicago: University of Chicago Press, 1999); Stowell, ed., *The Great Strikes of 1877* (Urbana: University of Illinois Press, 2008).
2 *Westliche Post*, July 26, 1877.

Although the Great Strike of 1877 convulsed the whole nation, what transpired in St. Louis was, in the words of one historian, "unique in the history of the American labor movement."[3] Other cities experienced more violence. In Pittsburgh, for example, state militiamen killed at least twenty unarmed protestors.[4] With outrage at this tragedy snaking through the Midwest, workers in Columbus and Cincinnati picketed and interrupted rail service.[5] Even in the relatively unaffected cities of Milwaukee and Cleveland, rumors of imminent unrest were enough to frighten the authorities.[6] But only in St. Louis did the strike take on the character of a "labor revolution."[7] There, the Workingmen's Party established undisputed – albeit tenuous – control of an estimated twenty thousand strikers and their allies for nearly a week, bringing German-American socialists into direct confrontation with the German-American establishment.[8] The location was especially meaningful to the immigrants. In 1861, Franz Sigel and other veterans of the Revolutions of 1848 had helped capture St. Louis's Camp Jackson, giving martial expression to the myth of the freedom-loving German. Some of the same men had conceived the Liberal Republican movement in the city in 1870. The general strike of 1877 concluded German-American participation in Reconstruction, revealing how the immigrants' fight over economic rights would influence African-American citizenship. Both sides would blame black St. Louisans for the week's excesses.

During 1877, Democrats and Republicans also settled the inconclusive presidential election of the previous year. The outcome rested on contested results in South Carolina, Louisiana, and Florida, where Republican officials had invalidated returns from counties in which black voters had seen the most egregious intimidation. Democrats disputed this decision, setting in motion a flurry of political negotiation. Not until March 1877 did Democratic congressmen finally clear the way for the Electoral College to elect Hayes. The exact terms of the compromise cannot be known, but the new president signaled that Republicans would no longer charge the army with shoring up the citizenship rights of Southern blacks. Hayes ordered troops to stand down in South Carolina and Louisiana, conceding those states to politicians whose return to power depended on suppressing the

---

3 Philip S. Foner, *Great Labor Uprising of 1877*, 157.
4 Ibid., 63–65.
5 *Columbus Westbote*, July 25, 1877; *Cincinnati Volksblatt*, July 23 and 28, 1877; Philip S. Foner, *Great Labor Uprising of 1877*, 130–32, 223–34; James Matthew Morris, "The Road to Trade Unionism: Organized Labor in Cincinnati to 1893" (PhD diss., University of Cincinnati, 1969), 162–70.
6 *Wächter am Erie*, July 31, 1877; *Banner und Volksfreund Demokratisches Wochenblatt*, Aug. 2, 1877.
7 *Westliche Post*, July 26, 1877.　　　　　　　8 Burbank, *Reign of the Rabble*, 167.

African-American vote.[9] In another sign that he was resigned to white rule in the South, Hayes appointed the conciliatory Carl Schurz to his cabinet as secretary of the interior. Finn's telegram reached a Republican administration that included the St. Louis politician who had denied that there was a "social question" in the United States and personified the German community's declining interest in black citizenship.

German-American leaders could be found on both sides of the economic conflict in St. Louis. Albert Currlin was a natural choice for the committee that the Workingmen formed to coordinate the strike. He led the German section of the party, which, with a membership of about 600, was larger than the city's English, French, and Bohemian sections combined. During the weeklong disruption, Currlin attempted to prevent lawlessness, protect property, and negotiate an end to the work stoppage, even as he catalyzed popular support for the Workingmen's Party and its agenda.[10] In daily speeches, the young socialist did not hide his antipathy for Schurz, lashing out at the "capitalists and lawyers" who surrounded Hayes.[11] It is difficult to assess how many immigrants followed Currlin, but German Americans appear to have been overrepresented among the men and women who absconded from their workplaces to attend rallies during July 1877. According to the English-language *St. Louis Times*, more than 60 percent of the people arrested on the last day of the strike were "German."[12] Even Schurz's *Westliche Post* and Carl Dänzer's *Anzeiger des Westens* eventually had to grant that "Germans played a prominent role in the late strike disturbances."[13]

Fearing that all German Americans would suffer by association, St. Louis's German-born Republican and Democratic politicians became the strike's most strenuous opponents.[14] These men aggravated the class tensions that had run high since the panic of 1873. Because it was impossible to pretend

9 C. Vann Woodward, *Reunion and Reaction: The Compromise of 1877 and the End of Reconstruction* (Boston: Little, Brown, 1951); Benedict, "Southern Democrats in the Crisis of 1876–1877: A Reconsideration of *Reunion and Reaction*," *Journal of Southern History* 46 (1980): 489–524; Vincent P. DeSantis, "Rutherford B. Hayes and the Removal of the Troops and the End of Reconstruction," in *Region, Race and Reconstruction*, ed. Morgan Kousser and James McPherson (New York: Oxford University Press, 1982), 417–50.

10 Burbank, *Reign of the Rabble*, 71–73, 82–83, 101–02, 114, 122, 136. German-American socialists also organized mass meetings in Cincinnati and Milwaukee. *Banner und Volksfreund Demokratisches Wochenblatt*, Aug. 2, 1877; *Milwaukee Seebote*, July 26, 1877; *Cincinnati Volksblatt*, July 23, 1877; Philip S. Foner, *Great Labor Uprising of 1877*, 130–32, 223–34.

11 *Anzeiger des Westens*, July 24, 1877; *Amerika*, July 24, 1877.

12 The paper referred to the seventy-three arrests around the strike headquarters on Friday, July 28. Roediger, "Not Only the Ruling Classes to Overcome," 216, 228, 230.

13 *Anzeiger des Westens*, Aug. 2, 1877.

14 For a comparison with the English-language newspapers, see Burbank, *Reign of the Rabble*, 131.

that there were no German-born socialists, members of the German-American elite denigrated them. The *Westliche Post* accused Currlin of "incitement," alleging that he and other socialists "constantly provoke[d] the honest workers into insurrection in the most criminal and damnable ways."[15] In response to such rancor, picketers surrounded the *Post*'s offices. On Thursday, July 26, a railroad executive telegraphed Schurz in Washington to tell him the "mob" was now "threatening" his own newspaper.[16] The following day, "the enmity of the communists" became a point of pride at the paper. It was, the editors wrote, "more agreeable . . . than their friendship."[17] Not to be outdone, the Democratic *Anzeiger des Westens* characterized all of the people involved in the industrial action as "enemies of civil society and public welfare, enemies whom the state must overpower and force to obey."[18] The strike proved what the election of 1876 had already suggested. Neither one of the two major parties was sympathetic to working-class ideas of economic citizenship. Alliances based on economic philosophy were trumping ethnic and partisan bonds.

The Great Strike highlighted preexisting differences between the socialists and other immigrants, but it also pushed the *Westliche Post* and the *Anzeiger* to take a remarkable new position. Both papers abandoned laissez-faire, advocating government intervention to break the strike. The American state was not to remain a neutral observer; it must get the trains running and send the laborers back to work. Dänzer was the first St. Louis editor to request state and federal aid for the city. On the Tuesday that the Workingmen's Party formally called for workers to walk off the job, he wrote that the "disorder" must be stopped. "When it cannot happen in a friendly manner," he went on, "it must happen with the application of all force that the law puts at the disposal of the authorities."[19] "What are we waiting for?" the *Anzeiger*'s lead editorial asked the next day. The newspaper mentioned the law, but it sought action *before* any criminal acts were committed: "There are already signs that the reigning anarchy may turn into robbery, plundering, and bloodshed."[20] Not only did the *Westliche Post* agree that federal troops should move against the striking workers, Schurz himself apparently encouraged Hayes to send six companies of U.S. regulars from

15 *Westliche Post*, July 28 and 26, 1877.

16 James H. Wilson to Schurz, telegram, July 26, 1877, reel 18, fr. 420, Schurz Papers, LOC.

17 *Westliche Post*, July 27, 1877. See also July 31, Aug. 1, 1877.

18 *Anzeiger des Westens*, July 24, 1877. In contrast, the Catholic *Amerika* provided quite balanced coverage, acknowledging the legitimacy of strikers' demands and the seriousness of socialist efforts to maintain order. *Amerika*, July 24, 25, and 26, 1877.

19 *Anzeiger des Westens*, July 24, 1877.   20 Ibid., July 25, 1877.

Fort Leavenworth, Kansas, to St. Louis.[21] In the end, the city fathers did not need this assistance. At three o'clock on Friday, July 27, policemen on horseback led the mayor and volunteer militiamen in a raid on strike head-quarters. At the time, the Workingmen's steering committee was drafting plans to pacify the increasingly restive crowd outside. For all the conster-nation, the strike ended with the police inflicting the only bloodshed. No one was seriously hurt, and even the looting was minimal.[22]

The potential for lawlessness, not the fact of it, had warranted crushing the strike, according to the *Westliche Post* and *Anzeiger des Westens*. Dänzer and Schurz, former revolutionaries themselves, now tasted the foreboding that had seized European authorities when Germans had risen up in 1848 and laid hold of Missouri secessionists when immigrants had taken Camp Jackson in 1861. The editors were terrified to see tens of thousands of working-class St. Louisans organizing under the leadership of the social-ists. Genuine anxiety was surely one motive in their drive to reestablish order. A consistent economic ideology also seemed to motivate Schurz and Dänzer – at least at first. Finding economic *rights* preposterous, they faulted the socialists for pressuring the government to capitulate to two minority groups, self-interested strikers and unemployed workers. Still, the solution that the German-American leaders offered – using government force to stifle dissent, preempt possible violence, and assist businessmen – also meant extending the purview of the state. Although well-off German Americans rejected the socialists' idea that the government ought to guarantee eco-nomic rights, they rationalized state interference on behalf of employers and property owners. The perceived threat of an awakened working class loosened German Americans' ideological commitment to the government restraint of laissez-faire.

The strike had tested whether German immigrants would emphasize the primacy of men's political rights and limited government. As it turned out, neither side did. Rather than choosing between government action and government inaction, St. Louisans had to decide whose interests and whose rights the government should uphold. German-American Democrats and Republicans portrayed themselves as representatives of the great middle of the population, those Americans who worked hard and did not expect any special treatment, but their rhetoric often concealed policies that privileged business. Liberal nationalism as German Americans had known it could

21 James H. Wilson to Schurz, telegram, July 22, 1877, reel 18, fr. 356, Schurz Papers, LOC; Philip S. Foner, *Great Labor Uprising of 1877*, 165; Burbank, *Reign of the Rabble*, 21–22.
22 Ibid., 139–43, 150.

not survive into the Gilded Age. As Thomas Bender argues, "Industrialism effectively brought an end to the practical utility of the republican tradition and laissez-faire political economy."[23]

Democrats who assented to a strike-breaking role for the U.S. Army did so despite having spent the last decade characterizing its work enforcing Republican Reconstruction as an illegitimate exercise of federal power. Dänzer had maintained that it was unconstitutional for federal soldiers, officials, or courts to resist the racist onslaught against African Americans in the South, but he wanted them to *prevent* the possibility of property damage and violence in St. Louis. The urban poor on Dänzer's doorstep seemed more dangerous than the Ku Klux Klan, and the property rights of large employers seemed more valuable than the voting rights of African Americans. The *Westliche Post* remarked on this discrepancy following the strikes. "All the Democratic newspapers," it printed, "shouted themselves hoarse calling for federal protection during the past week; they only felt safe again once federal troops were marching in the streets, and two Democratic governors were the first who urgently telegraphed for the national army."[24] In fact, not all Democrats agreed with Dänzer. In Wisconsin, the *Watertown Weltbürger* published a Chicago piece regretting that the "July Revolution" had created "skepticism in the ability of the republican form of government to endure." By sending troops to quiet the so-called "dangerous classes," the German American wrote, Anglo-Americans had adopted European tactics. "Remember 1849," he cautioned.[25] The Democrats would continue to try to balance social order against popular politics.

German-American Republicans, especially the secretary of the interior, also employed a double standard. Schurz was ready to send agents of the federal government out against striking workers but not against white terrorists. Having retreated from the policy of defending the freed people during the early 1870s, Schurz now supported business owners. Moreover, his seat in the cabinet gave Schurz greater power than Dänzer. German-Missourian Republicans, who had already given up on Reconstruction, now wanted to quash working-class protest. Their accord with Democrats concluded the Civil War era in St. Louis.

The Great Strike makes a fitting epilogue to a study of German-American politics during Reconstruction because of its racial import. In the pages of the *Westliche Post* and the *Anzeiger*, black protestors symbolized the anarchy

---

23 Bender, *Nation among Nations*, 257.   24 *Westliche Post*, Aug. 1, 1877.
25 *Watertown Weltbürger*, Aug. 4, 1877. See also *Cincinnati Volksfreund*, July 25, 1877; *Sheboygan National Democrat*, July 26, 1877; *Amerika*, July 30, 1877.

that socialists had unleashed on the city. On Thursday, July 26, the *Westliche Post* provocatively noted that a column of picketers had attracted "a rear guard of hundreds of colored deck hands and vagabonds of the worst sort." It asserted that "it is an absolute fact that many dark figures who came up out of their dens on the levee joined the demonstrations yesterday so that if there were a disturbance of the peace, they could make off with anything that wasn't riveted or nailed down. The so-called 'roust-abouts' are playing a leading part in the demonstrations and everyone who reads the daily police reports knows what is expected of them if it comes to a disturbance of the peace."[26] In fact, the record of arrests provided no such corroboration.[27] The misleading stereotypes of lawless blacks reinforced the connection in whites' imagination between African Americans and unreasonable claims on government. When the *Post* and the *Anzeiger* said that African Americans took "an opinion-forming role" in the strikes, they linked African Americans and socialists just as James Pike had done in his 1874 commentary on South Carolina.[28]

Many white socialists had accepted the racial logic of the mainstream press before the close of that charged week in St. Louis. As David Roediger has observed, the deteriorating relationship between white organizers and black workers was a key element of the strike in the city. In Cincinnati, African-American socialist Peter H. Clark had helped lead demonstrations.[29] Even in St. Louis, there had been signs of cooperation across racial lines at the beginning of the week. On Monday, African Americans had taken the platform beside Albert Currlin to speak before integrated audiences.[30] At the Tuesday evening rally that so frightened Sergeant Finn, a black steamboat worker asked whether working-class St. Louisans would be true to the strikers regardless of their color. Shouts from the crowd assured him that they would.[31] As the Workingmen's Party struggled to wrangle real concessions from government and businesses, however, racial animosity helped undo the strikes. Currlin offered the most vivid evidence of this turn when, arrested, he faced felony charges of riot. Nasty racial epithets riddled his interview with a *St. Louis Times* reporter. The organizers, Currlin claimed, had just decided to call off the protests when "a gang of niggers" had hijacked them

26 *Westliche Post*, July 26, 1877.
27 Roediger, "Not Only the Ruling Classes to Overcome," 225–26, 232.
28 *Anzeiger des Westens*, July 26, 1877.
29 *Cincinnati Volksblatt*, July 23, 1877; Philip S. Foner, *Great Labor Uprising of 1877*, 130–32, 223–34.
30 Burbank, *Reign of the Rabble*, 33, 73, 118; Roediger, "Not Only the Ruling Classes to Overcome," 225.
31 Burbank, *Reign of the Rabble*, 54; Roediger, "Not Only the Ruling Classes to Overcome," 225.

and the peaceful strike had devolved into a disorderly melee.[32] "We did all we could," he said, "to get the crowd to disperse and to dissuade any white men from going with the niggers."[33] The Catholic *Amerika*, a friend to the white workers, interpreted the whole strike as a spontaneous uprising against competition from "African" and "Chinese" workers.[34] Clearly, the white proponents of economic citizenship in St. Louis did not all identify with African Americans.

Although Currlin's venom was not typical, other German-American socialists also distinguished sharply between working-class whites and blacks. In his analysis of the Great Strike in the *Milwaukee Socialist*, Joseph Brucker did so without slinging hateful slurs. He wrote, "The mouths of the 'pious' politicians – the honest reformers à la Hayes, Schurz, and associates – overflow for the black slaves. For them, they know how to draw the sword and fight!" Brucker contrasted such attitudes with Hayes's treatment of the strikers: "For white slaves, they don't once have a sympathetic word."[35] Demonstrating an outdated reading of Republican policy, Brucker counterposed the rights of poor blacks and poor whites. He paid no attention to the black demonstrators, dismissing African Americans because of their history in the "bourgeois" Republican Party. His stance was so common in the white labor movement that it would scarcely merit comment if some German Americans had not shown in the 1860s that they could participate in a biracial struggle.

As a coup de grace, the fallout from the strike obscured the arcing history of Reconstruction from future generations.[36] Some editors, uncomfortable with the profile of German-American socialists, revised their narrative of the Civil War era. The *Anzeiger* reprinted an unsigned editorial that began this process in unusually abrasive style. The writer began by making a charge at socialism, which he believed had an unfortunate transnational dimension. He stated that "immigrants infected with the sickness of socialism" had obviously had a hand in the recent commotion. Yet most German Americans, the editorial ran, "condemned the socialist delusion." It was safe to say that the "European plant" would "never thrive in this country." The writer guessed that once socialists understood American citizenship, they too would drop their economic appeals to the state. His message was uncomplicated: the simple opportunities of laissez-faire and the ballot box

---

32 Philip S. Foner, *Great Labor Uprising of 1877*, 207–08; Roediger, "Not Only the Ruling Classes to Overcome," 225. This insight inspired Roediger's tremendously influential 1991 book, *Wages of Whiteness*. See especially Roediger, *Wages of Whiteness*, 167–70.
33 Burbank, *Reign of the Rabble*, 72–73.   34 *Amerika*, Aug. 1, 1877.
35 *Milwaukee Socialist*, Aug. 1, 1877.
36 Bruce Levine mentions this revisionism in passing. Levine, *Spirit of 1848*, 263–71.

satisfied German immigrants. All they wanted was to become voting citizens of an ethnically plural American nation.[37]

Part of the editorial's strategy was to juxtapose the disreputable strikers of 1877 with the revered revolutionaries of 1848. The Forty-Eighters were now uncontroversial ethnic icons who had emigrated "to enjoy the blessings of free, constitutional self-government."[38] The anonymous author was not only writing socialism out of the history of the European revolutions and the American Civil War, but also distorting the liberal nationalism of the 1860s. Writing just a couple of days after the strike, he seemed to confuse the liberal Forty-Eighters' earlier confidence in economic individualism with their later promotion of government relief for business. His revolutionaries were not emissaries of national change but bulwarks of national stability. In reality, of course, Forty-Eighters had hitched nationalism to antislavery and pro-suffrage politics, which had ruptured the status quo antebellum, nowhere more than in St. Louis. The course of the Civil War had helped their cause. From 1865 to 1870, German-American Republicans had argued that respecting individual rights would secure the integrity of the American nation and that the naturalization of European immigrant men could be a template for the freedmen's acquisition of citizenship. These immigrants had ultimately preserved the distinctions between race and ethnicity and between principle and practice, but they could take some credit for the Fifteenth Amendment.

The version of this history that appeared in the *Anzeiger* piece reflected, but did not acknowledge, the fact that nationalism had peeled off from liberalism since 1870. During the Franco-Prussian War, the Forty-Eighters had fumbled toward a more essentialist understanding of the German *Volk* and a more generous view of the Prussian state. Although they did not suddenly renounce African Americans or representative institutions, these formerly Republican immigrants subordinated citizenship to sectional reconciliation and bureaucratic reform. As Liberal Republicans, they spoke of the relationship between individual rights and the nation quite differently. Enforcing the constitutional rights of African Americans, they said, would only get in the way of national unity. During the 1870s, economic and cultural politics had further unsettled liberalism. The *Anzeiger*'s paean to the Forty-Eighters ignored the signs that business interests and redeemers were now honoring laissez-faire and equal male suffrage in the breach.

In the decades following the Great Strike, white Northerners would become habituated to stories of privation and violence in the South, but

---

37 *Anzeiger des Westens*, Aug. 2, 1877.   38 Ibid., Aug. 2, 1877.

the specter of urban poverty and radicalized workers in the North disturbed them more than ever. By the 1890s, the agrarian yet hardly backward People's Party, with its program of economic justice through public ownership of monopolies such as railroads, would inspire interracial cooperation in some areas, but it was never designed to dislodge racial injustice.[39] The most acclaimed reformers of the late nineteenth century confronted the hardships of Northern cities, where few African Americans lived. Black Southerners would still argue that racial prejudice and economic exploitation were coconspirators, but as Gilded Age reform grew in strength, segregation would only tighten its legal grip.[40]

The image of the white immigrant man as the archetypal new citizen lived on. In St. Louis's 1906 commemoration of Franz Sigel, for example, the general's naturalization took on a totemic quality. Sigel, of his own volition, had joined the nation that had granted him unprecedented political and economic opportunities. His choice seemingly confirmed that the United States was exceptional. Yet elevating the experience of European men did not always mean extending the advantages that they enjoyed to other groups. Race could carve out states of exception, and the achievements of white immigrants could become a cudgel of reproach against the freed people who had no chance to match them. Events after 1870 illustrated that ethnic politics could accommodate racial exclusion. German constructions of ethnicity in the United States were no longer useful to African Americans. Although many German Americans who had voted for Lincoln would never leave the Republican Party, the Democratic Party reassumed its status as the party of immigrants. Nearly a century would elapse before Democrats such as John F. Kennedy and Lyndon B. Johnson convincingly reconnected the immigrant story and African-American rights.

---

39 Charles Postel, *The Populist Vision* (New York: Oxford University Press, 2007).
40 David W. Southern, *The Progressive Era and Race: Reaction and Reform, 1900–1917* (Wheeling, IL: Harlan Davidson, 2005); McPherson, *Abolitionist Legacy*, 299–394; Elizabeth Lasch-Quinn, *Black Neighbors: Race and the Limits of Reform in the American Settlement House Movement, 1890–1945* (Chapel Hill: University of North Carolina Press, 1993); Ralph E. Luker, *The Social Gospel in Black and White: American Racial Reform, 1885–1912* (Chapel Hill: University of North Carolina Press, 1991); Eileen L. McDonagh, "The 'Welfare Rights State' and the 'Civil Rights State': Policy Paradox and State Building in the Progressive Era," *Studies in American Political Development* 7 (1993): 225–71.

Appendix: Voting Tables

Table 1. *Voting in Cleveland's "German" wards, 1860, 1867, 1868, 1872, and 1876 (%)*

Ward	German-Born among White Males over 21	Lincoln (R) for President, 1860	Black Suffrage Referendum, 1867	Grant (R) for President, 1868	Grant (R) for President, 1872	Hayes (R) for President, 1876
4	32.0	67	68.1	66.3	64.3	58.2
5	37.1	45	31.5	42.1	44.1	36.0
6	54.3	67	59.1	68.5	71.9	63.6
7	47.8	64	45.4	58.1	54.6	49.2
11	60.9	44	37.4	49.3	51.6	44.8
City-wide total	32.3	58	49.7	61.2	64.3	52.6
State-wide total	7.2★	52.3	46	54.0	53.2	50.2

★ Ohio-wide German-born population based on total German-born as percentage of total population according to the 1860 census. U.S. Bureau of the Census, *Abstract of the Eighth Census*, 621–23.

Cleveland "German" wards defined as wards where at least 30 percent of white males over 21 were German-born. Thomas W. Kremm, "The Rise of the Republican Party in Cleveland, 1848–1860" (PhD diss., Kent State University, 1974), 21.

Cleveland results from Kremm, "Rise of the Republican Party in Cleveland," 291; Ohio Secretary of State, *Annual Report, 1873* (Columbus: State Printers, 1874), 103; *Cleveland Leader*, Oct. 9, 1867, Nov. 8, 1876.

Ohio-wide results from Sawrey, *Dubious Victory*, 115; Ohio Secretary of State, *Annual Report, 1868* (Columbus: Columbus Printing, 1869), 47, 103–6, 109–10; Burnham, *Presidential Ballots*, 676–77.

Table 2. *Voting in Cincinnati's "German" wards, 1860, 1867, 1868, 1872, and 1876 (%)*

Ward	Lincoln (R) for President, 1860	Black Suffrage Referendum, 1867	Grant (R) for President, 1868	Grant (R) for President, 1872	Hayes (R) for President, 1876
7	71.8	58.5	72.6	47.7	55.8
9	36.0	19.7	37.5	50.1	56.5
10	69.2	62.9	72.3	56.5	65.4
11	75.9	59.5	78.6	58.2	65.2
12	57.1	48.4	58.1	55.4	67.0
City-wide total	52.3	45.4	56.3	44.7	50.7

Cincinnati "German" wards defined by *Cincinnati Commercial*, Nov. 5, 1868.
Election results from *Cincinnati Enquirer*, Nov. 8, 1860; *Cincinnati Volksfreund*, Oct. 11, 1867, Nov. 6, 1872, Nov. 12, 1876; Ohio Secretary of State, *Annual Report, 1868*, 54.

Table 3. *Voting in St. Louis's "German" wards, 1860, 1868, 1870, 1872, and 1876 (%)*

Ward	German-Born Among Total Population, 1858	Lincoln (R) for President, 1860	Black Suffrage Referendum, 1868	Grant (R) for President, 1868	Brown (LR) for Governor, 1870	Henderson (R) for Governor, 1872	Grant (R) for President, 1872	Hayes (R) for President, 1876
1	58.9	65.5	35.4	71.9	88.1	46.8	46.3	57.4
2	55.4	65.0	22.1	66.2	94.5	45.1	48.5	55.8
3	33.9	44.8	38.7	69.4	92.5	49.8	51.4	50.3
8	31.0	46.3	30.4	50.1	64.4	49.7	49.1	51.6
10	36.8	46.5	32.0	42.7	74.6	37.3	37.0	38.0
City-wide total	33.1	41.6	32.7	54.6	78.7	46.7	45.8	45.9
State-wide total	7.4	10.3	42.7	57.0	62.2	43.7	44.0	41.4

St. Louis "German" wards defined as wards where more than 30 percent of the total population was German-born, based on an 1858 city census. Kellner, "German Element on the Urban Frontier," 320.

Missouri-wide German population according to the 1860 census. U.S. Bureau of the Census, *Abstract of the Eighth Census*, 599, 621–23.

St. Louis results from *Westliche Post*, Nov. 5, 1868, Nov. 12, 1870, Nov. 8, 1872, Nov. 9, 1876.

Missouri results from *Missouri Republican*, Nov. 8, 1860; Parrish, *A History of Missouri*, 3: 3; Parrish, *Missouri under Radical Rule*, 258; Burnham, *Presidential Ballots*, 570–71; Barclay, *Liberal Republican Movement in Missouri*, 269; Shoemaker, *Missouri and Missourians*, 2: 21.

Table 4. *Voting in Milwaukee's "German" wards, 1860, 1865, 1868, 1872, and 1876 (%)*

Ward	German-Born among White Males over 21, 1860	Lincoln (R) for President, 1860	Fairchild (R) for Governor, 1865	Black Suffrage Referen-dum, 1865	Grant (R) for President, 1868	Grant (R) for President, 1872	Hayes (R) for President, 1876
2	74	37.0	17.8	16.6	34.2	22.3	41
6	75	45.1	27.3	23.4	38.2	29.4	48
8	73	56.3	29.7	25.3	52.5	53.1	55
9	79	38.1	17.2	15.6	31.9	29.2	44
City-wide total	49.9	44.3	33.3	30.9	41.8	40.2	46
State-wide total	13.8★	56.6	54.3	45.6	57.1	54.6	50.1

★ Wisconsin-wide German-born population based on total German-born as percentage of total population according to the 1860 census. U.S. Bureau of the Census, *Abstract of the Eighth Census*, 621–23.

Milwaukee "German" wards defined as wards where more than 50 percent of adult males were German-born according to the 1860 census. Richard James Anderson, "The German Vote of Milwaukee in the 1860 Election" (MA thesis, University of Chicago, 1968), 9, 30.

Presidential and gubernatorial election results from *The Legislative Manual of the State of Wisconsin*, editions: 3 (1860), 53; 5 (1866), 187, 198; 6 (1867), 151; 8 (1869), 239, 253; 12 (1873), 334, 354; 16 (1877), 383, 407.

Black suffrage referendum results from *Milwaukee Daily News*, Nov. 9, 1865.

Bibliography

Archival Collections

Archdiocese of Milwaukee Archives, St. Francis, Wisconsin (AMA)
  Ludwigs-Missionverein Correspondence
Archdiocese of St. Louis Archives (ASLA)
  Archbishop Peter Richard Kenrick Papers
Archives of the Archdiocese of Cincinnati (AAC)
  Archbishop John Baptist Purcell Papers
Cincinnati Historical Society (CHS)
  Murat Halstead Papers
  Charles Reemelin Papers
German-Americana Collection, University of Cincinnati
  Fick Pamphlet Collection
Rutherford B. Hayes Presidential Center, Fremont, Ohio (HPC)
  Rutherford B. Hayes Papers (microfilm)
  Schurz-Hayes Papers
Library of Congress, Washington, DC (LOC)
  Hamilton Fish Papers
  Carl Schurz Papers (microfilm)
Abraham Lincoln Presidential Library and Museum, Springfield, Illinois
  Engelmann-Kircher Family Papers
Milwaukee County Historical Society (MCHS)
  Peter Engelmann Papers
  Freie Gemeinde Papers
  Franz Huebschmann Papers
Missouri Historical Society, St. Louis (MHS)
  John Fletcher Darby Papers
  William Napton Papers
Missouri State Archives, Jefferson City (MSA)
  Records of Governor Benjamin Gratz Brown
  Records of Governor Thomas Clement Fletcher
  Office of the Secretary of State, Election Returns

241

Ohio Historical Society (OHS)
  William Henry Smith Papers
  Friedrich Hassaurek Papers
Western Historical Manuscript Collection – Columbia, Missouri (WHMC –
    Columbia)
  Charles D. Drake Papers
  Louis Benecke Papers
  James S. Rollins Papers
Wisconsin Historical Society, Madison (WHS)
  Mathilde and Fritz Anneke Papers (microfilm)
  Gladys Dieruf Papers
  Duecker Family Papers
  Lucius Fairchild Papers
  Germans in the United States Collection
  Timothy O. Howe Papers
  International Workingmen's Association (IWA) Papers (microfilm)
  Elisha W. Keyes Papers
  John Knell Papers
  Carl Schurz Papers
  C. C. Washburn Papers
  Wisconsin Writers' Program Writings and Research Notes, Works Progress
    Administration (WPA)
Wisconsin Historical Society, Milwaukee Area Research Center (WHS–MARC)
  Milwaukee Turners Records

Newspapers and Periodicals

Appleton Volksfreund
Buffalo County (Wisc.) Republikaner
Chicago Tribune
Cincinnati Enquirer
Cincinnati Volksblatt
Cleveland Anzeiger
Cleveland Wächter am Erie
Fond du Lac Nordwestliche Courier
Green Bay Banner
Green Bay Wisconsin Staats-Zeitung
Madison Wisconsin Botschafter
Madison Wisconsin-Staats-Zeitung
Milwaukee Banner und Volksfreund
Milwaukee Freidenker
Milwaukee Herold
Milwaukee Sentinel
Milwaukee Star of Bethlehem
New Philadelphia (Ohio) Deutsche Beobachter
New-Yorker Staats-Zeitung

Der deutsche Pionier [Cincinnati]
Chicago Illinois Staatszeitung
Cincinnati Commercial
Cincinnati Volksfreund
Cincinnati Wahrheitsfreund
Cleveland Leader
Columbus Westbote
Fremont (Ohio) Courier
Green Bay Concordia
La Crosse Nord Stern
Manitowoc Wisconsin Demokrat
Milwaukee Atlas
Milwaukee Columbia
Milwaukee Germania
Milwaukee Seebote
Milwaukee Socialist
The Nation [New York]
New York Amerikanische Turnzeitung
New York Times

New York Tribune
Oshkosh (Wisc.) Deutsche Zeitung
Sheboygan (Wisc.) National Demokrat
St. Charles (Missouri) Demokrat
St. Louis Anzeiger des Westens (briefly Neuer
   Anzeiger des Westens)
St. Louis Westliche Post (Sunday edition
   titled Mississippi Blätter)
Stockbridge (Wisc.) Union
Watertown (Wisc.) Weltbürger

New York World
Sauk City Pionier am Wisconsin
Springfield (Mass.) Daily Republican
St. Louis Amerika
St. Louis Missouri Republican

St. Louis Volksstimme des Westens

Toledo Express
Wausau (Wisc.) Wochenblatt

Published Primary Sources

Anneke, Mathilde Franziska. *Mathilde Franziska Anneke in Selbstzeugnissen und Doku-menten*. Ed. Maria Wagner. Frankfurt am Main: Fischer, 1980.

———. *Memoiren einer Frau aus den badisch-pfälzischen Feldzug*. Newark, NJ: [n.p.], 1853.

———. "Die Sclaven-Auction: Ein Bild aus dem amerikanischen Leben." In *Die gebrochenen Ketten: Erzählungen, Reportagen und Reden, 1861–1873*. Ed. Maria Wagner. Stuttgart: Hans-Dieter Heinz Akademischer Verlag, 1983, 27–48.

Bates, Edward. *The Diary of Edward Bates, 1859–1866*. Ed. Howard K. Beale. Washington, DC: U.S. Government Printing Office, 1933. Reprint, New York: Da Capo Press, 1971.

Börnstein, Heinrich. *Die Geheimnisse von St. Louis*. Cassel: H. Hotop, 1851.

Boernstein, Heinrich. *Memoirs of a Nobody: The Missouri Years of an Austrian Radical, 1849–1866*. Trans. and ed. Steven Rowan. St. Louis: Missouri Historical Society Press, 1997.

Bruce, H. C. *The New Man: Twenty-Nine Years a Slave, Twenty-Nine Years a Free Man*. York, PA: P. Anstadt & Sons, 1895. Reprint, New York: Negro Universities Press, 1969.

Bruce, William. "Memoirs of William George Bruce," *Wisconsin Magazine of History* 16 (1933): 42–65.

Brucker, Joseph. *Die Social-Demokratie und ihr Wisconsiner Wahl-Programm: Ein Vortrag*. Milwaukee, WI: Socialist Printing Company, 1877.

Burgheim, Max. *Cincinnati in Wort und Bild*. Cincinnati: M. & R. Burgheim, 1888.

Constitution of the German Empire (proposed, 1849).

Constitution of the German Empire (1871).

de Hauranne, Ernest Duvergier. *A Frenchman in Lincoln's America*. Trans. and ed. by Ralph H. Bowen. Chicago: R. R. Donnelley & Sons Company, 1974.

Dicke, Peter Heinrich. "Autobiography of Peter Heinrich Dicke: Pastor and Pioneer Missionary." Trans. Eleanor Katherine Daib. *Concordia Historical Institute Quarterly* 78 (2005): 135–61.

Douglass, Frederick. *The Frederick Douglass Papers: Series One, Speeches, Debates, and Interviews*. Ed. John W. Blassingame and John R. McKivigan. 5 vols. New Haven, CT: Yale University Press, 1991.

Eighth Annual Report of the Superintendent of Public Schools of the State of Missouri. Jefferson City, MO: Reagan & Carter, State Printers, 1874.

Erinnerung an Milwaukee die Stadt der Zusammenkünfte deutscher Vereine im Jahre 1877. Milwaukee, WI: Philipp Best Brewing Co., 1877.

Foner, Philip S., ed. *The Formation of the Workingmen's Party of the United States: Proceedings of the Union Congress Held at Philadelphia, July 19–22, 1876.* New York: American Institute for Marxist Studies, 1976.

Frankfurt Parliament, "Gesetz betreffend die Wahlen der Abgeordneten zum Volkshause." April 12, 1849. Available at http://www.documentarchiv.de/nzjh/1849/reichswahlgesetz1849.html. Accessed Dec. 4, 2012.

Fritsch, W. A. *Aus Amerika: Alte und Neue Heimat.* Stardgard i. Pom: Verlag von Wilhelm Prange [c. 1905–1908].

Garfield, James A. *The Diary of James A. Garfield.* Ed. Harry James Brown and Frederick D. Williams. 4 vols. East Lansing: Michigan State University Press, 1967–1981.

German-American Biographical Pub. Co., *Cleveland and Its Germans.* Trans. Steven Rowan. Cleveland, OH: Western Reserve Historical Society, 1998.

Grant, Ulysses S. *The Papers of Ulysses S. Grant.* Ed. John Y. Simon. 32 vols. Carbondale: Southern Illinois University Press, 1967–2012.

Grebner, Constantin. *We Were the Ninth: A History of the Ninth Regiment, Ohio Volunteer Infantry.* Trans. and ed. Frederic Trautmann. Kent, OH: Kent State University Press, 1987.

Hahn, Steven, et al., eds. *Freedom: A Documentary History of Emancipation, 1861–1867.* Series 3. Vol. 1. *Land and Labor.* Chapel Hill: University of North Carolina Press, 2008.

Helbich, Wolfgang, and Walter D. Kamphoefner, eds. *Deutsche im amerikanischen Bürgerkrieg: Briefe von Front und Farm, 1861–1865.* Paderborn: Ferdinand Schoningh, 2002.

———. *Germans in the Civil War: The Letters They Wrote Home.* Trans. Susan Carter Vogel. Chapel Hill: University of North Carolina Press, 2006.

Henni, John Martin, and Anthony Urbanek. "Documents: Letter of the Right Reverend John Martin Henni and Anthony Urbanek." Trans. Peter Leo Johnson. *Wisconsin Magazine of History* 10 (1926): 66–94.

Howard, Benjamin C., ed. *Report of the Decision of the Supreme Court of the United States, and the Opinions of the Judges Thereof, in the Case of Dred Scott versus John F. Sandford.* Washington, DC: Cornelius Wendell, 1857.

Huber, Ernst Rudolf, ed. *Dokumente zur deutschen Verfassungsgeschichte.* 5 vols. Stuttgart: W. Kohlhammer Verlag, 1961–1966.

Johnson, Donald B., ed. *National Party Platforms.* Urbana: University of Illinois Press, 1973.

Kapp, Friedrich. *Vom radikalen Frühsozialisten des Vormärz zum liberalen Parteipolitiker des Bismarckreichs: Briefe 1843–1884.* Ed. Hans-Ulrich Wehler. Frankfurt am Main: Insel Verlag, 1969.

Kargau, E. D. *St. Louis in früheren Jahren: Ein Gedenkbuch für das Deutschthum.* St. Louis: Aug. Wiebuch & Sohn, 1893.

Kircher, Henry A. *A German in the Yankee Fatherland: The Civil War Letters of Henry A. Kircher.* Ed. Earl J. Hess. Kent, OH: Kent State University Press, 1983.

Koerner, Gustav. *Memoirs of Gustav Koerner, 1809–1896.* 2 vols. Cedar Rapids, IA: The Torch Press, 1909.

Koss, Rudolph A. *Milwaukee*. Milwaukee, WI: Herold, 1871.

Lincoln, Abraham. *The Collected Works of Abraham Lincoln*. Ed. Roy P. Basler. 9 vols. New Brunswick, NJ: Rutgers University Press, 1953–1955.

Loeb, Isidor, and Floyd C. Shoemaker, eds. *Journal of the Missouri Constitutional Convention of 1875*. 2 vols. Columbia: State Historical Society of Missouri, 1920.

Mallinckrodt, Anita M. *What They Thought*. Vol. 2, *Missouri's German Immigrants Assess Their World*. Augusta, MO: Mallinckrodt Communications and Research, 1995.

Manitowoc Nord-Westen. "Geschichte der Entstehung und Gründung der deutschen Colonie, St. Nazianz." Trans. J. J. Schlicher. *Wisconsin Magazine of History* 31 (1947): 84–91.

Mann, Horace. *Report of an Educational Tour in Germany, and Parts of Great Britain and Ireland*. London: Simkin, Marshall, and Company, 1846.

Marx, Karl, and Frederick Engels. *The Collected Works of Karl Marx and Friedrich Engels*. Trans. Richard Dixon et al. 47 vols. New York: International Publishers, 1975–2004.

———. *Selected Works of Karl Marx and Frederick Engels*. 2 vols. Moscow: Foreign Languages Publishing House, 1955–1958.

Minor, John D., et al. *The Bible in the Public Schools: Arguments before the Superior Court of Cincinnati in the Case of* Minor v. Board of Education of Cincinnati. Cincinnati: Robert Clarke & Co., 1870.

Missouri Constitutional Convention. *Journal of the Missouri State Convention Held at the City of St. Louis, January 6–April 10, 1865*. St. Louis: Missouri Democrat, 1865.

Möhrmann, Renate, ed. *Frauenemanzipation im deutschen Vormärz: Texte und Documente*. Stuttgart: Philipp Reclam, 1978.

Mueller, Jacob. *Memories of a Forty-Eighter: Sketches from the German-American Period of Storm and Stress in the 1850s*. Trans. Steven Rowan. Cleveland, OH: Western Reserve Historical Society, 1996.

Münch, Friedrich. *Gesammelte Schriften von Friedrich Münch*. Ed. Konrad Ries and Carl G. Rothann. St. Louis: Julius Meyer, 1902.

Ohio Secretary of State. *Annual Report, 1868*. Columbus: Columbus Printing, 1869.

———. *Annual Report, 1873*. Columbus: State Printers, 1874.

Parker, Thomas. *Report of the Superintendent of Public Schools in the State of Missouri to the Twenty-Fourth General Assembly*. Jefferson City, MO: Ellwood Kirby, 1869.

Pike, James S. *The Prostrate State: South Carolina under Negro Government*. New York: Loring & Mussey, 1935. Reprint, New York: D. Appleton, 1874.

Reemelin, Charles. *The Life of Charles Reemelin*. Cincinnati: Weier and Daiker, 1892.

Republican National Convention. *Proceedings of the Republican National Convention Held at Chicago, May 16, 17, and 18, 1860*. Albany: Weed Parsons and Company, 1860.

Rowan, Steven, ed. and trans. *Germans for a Free Missouri: Translations from the St. Louis Radical Press, 1857–1862*. Columbia: University of Missouri Press, 1983.

Salomon, Herman. "The Civil War Diary of Herman Salomon." *Wisconsin Magazine of History* 10 (1926): 205–10.

Schurz, Carl, ed. *Speeches of Carl Schurz*. Philadelphia: J. B. Lippincott & Co., 1865.

————. *The Reminiscences of Carl Schurz*. 3 vols. New York: The McClure Company, 1907–1909.

————. *Speeches, Correspondence and Political Papers of Carl Schurz*. Ed. Frederic Bancroft. 6 vols. New York: G. P. Putnam's Sons, 1913.

————. *Intimate Letters of Carl Schurz, 1841–1869*. Ed. and trans. Joseph Schafer. Madison: State Historical Society of Wisconsin, 1928.

————. *Report on the Condition of the South*. Senate Executive Documents, 39th Cong., 1st sess., no. 2, 1865. Reprint, New York: Arno Press, 1969.

Shoemaker, Floyd C., and Isidor Loeb, eds. *Debates of the Missouri Constitutional Convention of 1875*. 12 vols. Columbia: State Historical Society of Missouri, 1930–1944.

Stewart, Frank M., and E. W. Young, eds. *The Legislative Manual of the State of Wisconsin*, 5th ed. Madison, WI: William J. Park, State Printer, 1866.

Urbanek, Anthony. Report to Archbishop of Vienna, Edward Milde, 1853. In "Documents: Letter of the Right Reverend John Martin Henni." *Wisconsin Magazine of History* 10 (1926): 89.

U.S. Bureau of the Census. *Abstract of the Eight Census*. Washington, DC: U.S. Government Printing Office, 1865.

————. Decennial Census Population Schedules. Manuscript returns for 1860 and 1870.

————. *Ninth Census of the United States, 1870*. 4 vols. Washington, DC: U.S. Government Printing Office, 1872.

U.S. Congress. *Congressional Globe*. 1865–1877.

Welcker, Carl Theodor, and Karl von Rotteck, eds. *Das Staats-Lexikon*. 6 vols. Altona: J. F. Hammerich, 1838.

Selected Secondary Literature

Anbinder, Tyler. *Nativism and Slavery: The Northern Know Nothings and the Politics of the 1850's*. New York: Oxford University Press, 1992.

Arenson, Adam. *The Great Heart of the Republic: St. Louis and the Cultural Civil War*. Cambridge, MA: Harvard University Press, 2011.

Armitage, David, et al. "Interchange: Nationalism and Internationalism in the Era of the Civil War." *Journal of American History* 89 (2011): 455–89.

Arndt, Karl J. R., and May E. Olsen. *German-American Newspapers and Periodicals, 1732–1955: History and Bibliography*. Heidelberg: Quelle & Meyer, 1961. Reprint, New York: Johnson Reprint Corp., 1965.

Arnesen, Eric. "Whiteness and the Historians' Imagination." *International Labor and Working Class History* 60 (2001): 3–32.

Astor, Aaron. *Rebels on the Border: Civil War, Emancipation, and the Reconstruction of Kentucky and Missouri*. Baton Rouge: Louisiana State University Press, 2012.

Baker, Jean H. *Affairs of Party: The Political Culture of Northern Democrats in the Mid-Nineteenth Century*. Ithaca, NY: Cornell University Press, 1983.

Baker, Paula. "The Domestication of Politics: Women and American Political Society, 1780–1920." *American Historical Review* 89 (1984): 620–47.

Bank, Michaela. *Women of Two Countries: German-American Women, Women's Rights, and Nativism.* New York: Berghahn Books, 2012.

Baum, Bruce. *The Rise and Fall of the Caucasian Race: A Political History of Racial Identity.* New York: New York University Press, 2006.

Beckert, Sven. *The Monied Metropolis: New York City and the Consolidation of the American Bourgeoisie, 1850–1896.* Cambridge: Cambridge University Press, 2001.

———. "Democracy in the Age of Capital: Contesting Suffrage Rights in Gilded Age New York." In *The Democratic Experiment: New Directions in American Political History*, ed. Meg Jacobs, 146–74. Princeton, NJ: Princeton University Press, 2003.

Bender, Thomas. *A Nation among Nations: America's Place in World History.* New York: Hill and Wang, 2006.

Benedict, Michael Les. *Compromise of Principle: Congressional Republicans and Reconstruction, 1863–1869.* New York: Norton, 1974.

———. "Preserving the Constitution: The Conservative Basis of Radical Reconstruction." *Journal of American History* 61 (1974): 65–90.

Bennette, Rebecca Ayako. *Fighting for the Soul of Germany: The Catholic Struggle for Inclusion after Unification.* Cambridge, MA: Harvard University Press, 2012.

Bergquist, James M. "The German American Press." In *The Ethnic Press in the United States: A Historical Analysis and Handbook*, ed. Sally M. Miller, 131–59. Westport, CT: Greenwood Press, 1987.

———. "The Mid-Nineteenth-Century Slavery Crisis and the German Americans." In *States of Progress: Germans and Blacks in America over 300 Years.* Ed. Randall M. Miller, 55–71. Philadelphia: The German Society of Pennsylvania, 1989.

Blackbourn, David, and Geoff Eley, eds. *The Peculiarities of German History: Bourgeois Society and Politics in Nineteenth-Century Germany.* Oxford: Oxford University Press, 1984.

Blight, David. *Race and Reunion: The Civil War in American Memory.* Cambridge, MA: Belknap Press of Harvard University Press, 2001.

Bonadio, Felice. *North of Reconstruction: Ohio Politics, 1865–1870.* New York: New York University Press, 1970.

Brancaforte, Charlotte L., ed. *The German Forty-Eighters in the United States.* New York: Peter Lang, 1989.

Brooke, John L. "Consent, Civil Society, and the Public Sphere in the Age of Revolution and the Early American Republic." In *Beyond the Founders: New Approaches to the Political History of the Early American Republic*, ed. Jeffrey Pasley, Andrew W. Robertson, and David Waldstreicher, 207–50. Chapel Hill: University of North Carolina Press, 2004.

Brophy, James M. *Popular Culture and the Public Sphere in the Rhineland, 1800–1850.* Cambridge: Cambridge University Press, 2007.

Brown, Thomas J., ed. *Reconstructions: New Perspectives on the Postbellum United States.* Oxford: Oxford University Press, 2006.

Brubaker, Rogers. *Citizenship and Nationhood in France and Germany.* Cambridge, MA: Harvard University Press, 1992.

Bruce, Robert V. *1877: Year of Violence.* Indianapolis, IN: Bobbs-Merrill, 1959.

Buhle, Mari Jo. *Women and American Socialism.* Urbana: University of Illinois Press, 1981.

Burbank, David T. "The First International in St. Louis." *Missouri Historical Society Bulletin* 18 (1962): 163–72.

————. *Reign of the Rabble: The St. Louis General Strike of 1877.* New York: Augustus M. Kelley, 1966.

Burchart, Ronald E. *Schooling the Freed People: Teaching, Learning, and the Struggle for Black Freedom, 1861–1876.* Chapel Hill: University of North Carolina Press, 2010.

Burg, Robert W. "Amnesty, Civil Rights and the Meaning of Liberal Republican-ism." *American Nineteenth Century History* 4, no. 3 (2003): 29–60.

Burnham, Dean. *Presidential Ballots, 1836–1892.* Baltimore: Johns Hopkins University Press, 1995.

Burton, William L. *Melting Pot Soldiers: The Union's Ethnic Regiments.* Ames: Iowa State University Press, 1988.

Canaday, Margot. *The Straight State: Sexuality and Citizenship in Twentieth-Century America.* Princeton, NJ: Princeton University Press, 2009.

Cohen, Nancy. *The Reconstruction of American Liberalism, 1865–1914.* Chapel Hill: University of North Carolina Press, 2002.

Conzen, Kathleen Neils. *Immigrant Milwaukee, 1836–1860.* Cambridge, MA: Harvard University Press, 1976.

————. "German-Americans and the Invention of Ethnicity." In *America and the Germans: An Assessment of a Three-Hundred-Year History*, ed. Frank Trommler and Joseph McVeigh, 1: 131–47. Philadelphia: University of Pennsylvania Press, 1985.

————. "Ethnicity as Festive Culture: Nineteenth-Century German America on Parade." In *The Invention of Ethnicity*, ed. Werner Sollors, 44–76. New York: Oxford University Press, 1989.

————. "German Catholics in America." In *The Encyclopedia of American Catholic History*, ed. Michael Glazier and Thomas J. Shelley, 571–83. Collegeville, MN: The Liturgical Press, 1997.

————. "Immigrant Religion and the Republic: German Catholics in Nineteenth-Century America." *German Historical Institute Bulletin* 35 (2004): 43–56.

Cott, Nancy F. "Marriage and Women's Citizenship in the United States." *American Historical Review* 103 (1998): 1440–54.

Craig, Gordon A. *The Politics of the Prussian Army, 1640–1945.* New York: Oxford University Press, 1955.

Degler, Carl N. "One Among Many: The United States and National Self-Determination." In *Lincoln, the War President: The Gettysburg Lectures*, ed. Gabor S. Boritt, 91–119. New York: Oxford University Press, 1992.

Dobbert, Guido. "German-Americans between New and Old Fatherland, 1870–1914." *American Quarterly* 19 (1967): 663–80.

Donders, Yvonne. "Do Cultural Diversity and Human Rights Make a Good Match?" *International Social Science Journal* 61, no. 199 (2010): 15–35.

Dowe, Dieter, et al., eds. *Europe in 1848: Revolution and Reform.* Trans. David Higgins. New York: Berghahn Books, 2001.

———. *Aktion und Organisation: Arbeiterbewegung, sozialistische und kommunistische Bewegung in der preußische Rheinprovinz, 1820–1852.* Hanover: Verlag für Literatur und Zeitgeschehen, 1970.

DuBois, Ellen Carol. *Feminism and Suffrage: The Emergence of an Independent Women's Movement in America, 1848–1869.* Ithaca, NY: Cornell University Press, 1978.

Du Bois, W. E. B. *The Common School and the Negro American.* Atlanta: Atlanta University Press, 1911.

———. *Black Reconstruction: An Essay toward a History of the Part which Black Folk Played in the Attempt to Reconstruct Democracy in America, 1860–1880.* New York: Russell & Russell, 1935.

Dudden, Faye E. *Fighting Chance: The Struggle over Woman Suffrage and Black Suffrage in Reconstruction America.* New York: Oxford University Press, 2011.

Düding, Dieter. *Organisierter gesellschaftlicher Nationalismus in Deutschland, 1808–1847.* Munich: R. Oldenbourg, 1984.

Easton, Loyd. *Hegel's First American Followers: The Ohio Hegelians: John B. Stallo, Peter Kaufmann, Moncure Conway, and August Willich.* Athens: Ohio University Press, 1966.

Edwards, Rebecca. *Angels in the Machinery: Gender in Party Politics from the Civil War to the Progressive Era.* New York: Oxford University Press, 1997.

Efford, Alison Clark. "Race Should be as Unimportant as Ancestry: German Radicals and African American Citizenship in the Missouri Constitution of 1865." *Missouri Historical Review* 104, no. 3 (2010): 138–58.

Egerton, Douglas R. "Rethinking Atlantic Historiography in a Postcolonial Era: The Civil War in a Global Perspective." *Journal of the Civil War Era* 1 (2011): 79–95.

Engle, Stephen D. *The Yankee Dutchman: The Life of Franz Sigel.* Fayetteville: University of Arkansas Press, 1993.

———. "Yankee Dutchmen: Germans, the Union, and the Construction of a Wartime Identity." In *Civil War Citizens: Race, Ethnicity and Identity in America's Bloodiest Conflict,* ed. Susannah J. Ural, 11–56. New York: New York University Press, 2010.

Eyck, Frank. *The Frankfurt Parliament, 1848–1849.* London: Macmillan, 1968.

Fehrenbacher, Don E. *The Dred Scott Case: Its Significance in American Law and Politics.* New York: Oxford University Press, 1978.

Fellman, Michael. *Inside War: The Guerrilla Conflict in Missouri during the American Civil War.* New York: Oxford University Press, 1989.

Fleche, Andre M. *The Revolution of 1861: The American Civil War in the Age of Nationalist Conflict.* Chapel Hill: University of North Carolina Press, 2012.

Foner, Eric. *Politics and Ideology in the Age of the Civil War.* New York: Oxford University Press, 1980.

———. *Nothing but Freedom: Emancipation and Its Legacy.* Baton Rouge: Louisiana State University Press, 1983.

———. "Rights and the Constitution in Black Life during the Civil War and Reconstruction." *Journal of American History* 74 (1987): 863–83.

————. *Reconstruction: America's Unfinished Revolution, 1863–1877*. New York: Harper & Row, 1988.

————. *Free Soil, Free Labor, Free Men*, rev. ed. Oxford: Oxford University Press, 1995.

Foner, Philip S. *History of the Labor Movement in the United States*. Vol. 1, *From Colonial Times to the Founding of the American Federation of Labor*. New York: International Publishers, 1947.

————. *The Great Labor Uprising of 1877*. New York: Monad Press, 1977.

————. *The Workingmen's Party of the United States: A History of the First Marxist Party in the Americas*. Minneapolis: MEP Publications, 1984.

Foster, Gaines M. *Moral Reconstruction: Christian Lobbyists and the Federal Legislation of Morality, 1865–1920*. Chapel Hill: University of North Carolina Press, 2002.

Fraser, Nancy. "Rethinking the Public Sphere: A Contribution to the Critique of Actually Existing Democracy." In *Habermas and the Public Sphere*, ed. Craig Calhoun, 109–42. Cambridge, MA: MIT Press, 1991.

Fredrickson, George M. *The Inner Civil War: Northern Intellectuals and the Crisis of the Union*. New York: Harper and Row, 1965.

————. *The Black Image in the White Mind: The Debate over Afro-American Character and Destiny*. New York: Harper & Row, 1971.

Freitag, Sabine. *Friedrich Hecker: Biographie eines Republikaners*. Stuttgart: Steiner, 1998.

Frizzell, Robert W. *Independent Immigrants: A Settlement of Hanoverian Germans in Western Missouri*. Columbia: University of Missouri Press, 2007.

Gabaccia, Donna R. "Is Everywhere Nowhere? Nomads, Nations, and the Immigrant Paradigm of United States History." *Journal of American History* 86 (1999): 1115–34.

Gazley, John G. *American Opinion of German Unification, 1848–1871*. New York: Columbia University, 1926. Reprint, New York: AMS Press, 1970.

Geitz, Henry, ed. *The German-American Press*. Madison, WI: Max Kade Institute for German-American Studies, 1992.

Gerber, Richard A. "The Liberals of 1872 in Historiographical Perspective." *Journal of American History* 62 (1975): 40–75.

————. "Carl Schurz's Journey from Radical to Liberal Republicanism: A Problem in Ideological Consistency." *Mid-America* 82 (2000): 71–99.

Gillette, William. *The Right to Vote: Politics and the Passage of the Fifteenth Amendment*. Baltimore: The Johns Hopkins Press, 1969.

————. *Retreat from Reconstruction, 1869–1879*. Baton Rouge: Louisiana State University Press, 1979.

Gjerde, Jon. *The Minds of the West: Ethnocultural Evolution in the Rural Middle West, 1830–1917*. Chapel Hill: University of North Carolina Press, 1997.

Goyens, Tom. *Beer and Revolution: The German Anarchist Movement in New York City, 1880–1914*. Urbana: University of Illinois Press, 2007.

Gross, Michael B. *The War against Catholicism: Liberalism and the Anti-Catholic Imagination in Nineteenth-Century Germany*. Ann Arbor: University of Michigan Press, 2004.

Gunderson, Joan R. "Independence and Citizenship and the American Revolution." *Signs* 13 (1987): 59–77.

Guterl, Matthew Pratt. *American Mediterranean: Southern Slaveholders in the Age of Emancipation.* Cambridge, MA: Harvard University Press, 2008.

Guyatt, Nicholas. "America's Conservatory: Race, Reconstruction, and the Santo Domingo Debate." *Journal of American History* 97 (2011): 974–1000.

Habermas, Jürgen. *The Structural Transformation of the Public Sphere: An Inquiry into a Category of Bourgeois Society.* Trans. Thomas Burger. Cambridge, MA: MIT Press, 1989.

Hahn, Steven. *A Nation under Our Feet: Black Political Struggles in the Rural South.* Cambridge, MA: Belknap Press of Harvard University Press, 2003.

Hannaford, Ivan. *Race: The History of an Idea in the West.* Washington, DC: The Woodrow Wilson Center Press, 1996.

Harzig, Christiane. "The Ethnic Female Public Sphere: German-American Women in Turn-of-the-Century Chicago." In *Midwestern Women: Work, Community, and Leadership at the Crossroads,* ed. Lucy Eldersveld Murphy and Wendy Hamand Venet, 141–57. Bloomington: Indiana University Press, 1997.

Hattam, Victoria. "Ethnicity: An American Genealogy." In *Not Just Black and White: Historical and Contemporary Perspectives on Immigration, Race, and Ethnicity in the United States,* ed. Nancy Foner and George M. Fredrickson, 42–60. New York: Russell Sage Foundation, 2004.

———. *In the Shadow of Race: Jews Latinos, and Immigrant Politics in the United States.* Chicago: University of Chicago Press, 2007.

Hawgood, John H. *The Tragedy of German-America: The Germans in the United States of America during the Nineteenth Century – And After.* New York: G. P. Putnam's Sons, 1940.

Heater, Derek. *A Brief History of Citizenship.* New York: New York University Press, 2004.

Heideking, Jürgen, and James A. Henretta, eds. *Republicanism and Liberalism in America and the German States, 1750–1850.* Cambridge: Cambridge University Press, 2002.

Helbich, Wolfgang, and Walter D. Kamphoefner, eds. *German-American Immigration and Ethnicity in Comparative Perspective.* Madison, WI: Max Kade Institute for German-American Studies, 2004.

Hense-Jensen, Wilhelm. *Wisconsin's Deutsch-Amerikaner bis zum Schluß des neunzehnten Jahrhunderts.* 2 vols. Milwaukee, WI: Verlag der Deutschen Gesellschaft, 1900.

Herzog, Dagmar. *Intimacy and Exclusion: Religious Politics in Pre-Revolutionary Baden, 1803–1849.* Princeton, NJ: Princeton University Press, 1996.

Hochgeschwender, Michael. *Wahrheit, Einheit, Ordnung: Die Sklavenfrage und der amerikanische Katholizismus, 1835–1870.* Paderborn: Ferdinand Schöningh, 2006.

Hoerder, Dirk, and Jörg Nagler, eds. *People in Transit: German Migrations in Comparative Perspective.* Cambridge: Cambridge University Press, 1995.

Hoey, Michael. "Missouri Education at the Crossroads: The Phelan Miscalculation and the Education Amendment of 1870." *Missouri Historical Review* 95 (2001): 372–93.

Honeck, Mischa. *We Are the Revolutionists: German-Speaking Immigrants and American Abolitionists after 1848.* Athens: University of Georgia Press, 2011.

Horsman, Reginald. *Race and Manifest Destiny: The Origins of American Racial Anglo-Saxonism*. Cambridge, MA: Harvard University Press, 1981.

Huber, Ernst Rudolf. *Deutsche Verfassungsgeschichte seit 1789*. 8 vols. Stuttgart: W. Kohlhammer, 1957–1991.

Hyman, Harold M., and William Wiecek. *Equal Justice under Law: Constitutional Development, 1835–1875*. New York: Harper & Row, 1982.

Ignatiev, Noel. *How the Irish Became White*. New York: Routledge, 1995.

Isenberg, Nancy. *Sex and Citizenship in Antebellum America*. Chapel Hill: University of North Carolina Press, 1998.

Jacobson, Matthew Frye. *Whiteness of a Different Color: European Immigrants and the Alchemy of Race*. Cambridge, MA: Harvard University Press, 1999.

Jeffrey, Julie Roy. *The Great Silent Army of Abolitionism: Ordinary Women in the Antislavery Movement*. Chapel Hill, University of North Carolina Press, 1998.

Jentz, John B. "The 48ers and the Politics of the German Labor Movement in Chicago during the Civil War Era." In *The German-American Radical Press: The Shaping of a Left Political Culture, 1850–1940*, ed. Elliott Shore, Ken Fones-Wolf, and James P. Danky, 49–62. Urbana: University of Illinois Press, 1992.

———, and Richard Schneirov. *Chicago in the Age of Capital: Class, Politics, and Democracy during the Civil War and Reconstruction*. Urbana: University of Illinois Press, 2012.

Kamphoefner, Walter D. "St. Louis Germans and the Republican Party, 1848–1860." *Mid-America: An Historical Review* 57, no. 2 (1975): 69–88.

———. *The Westfalians: From Germany to Missouri*. Princeton, NJ: Princeton University Press, 1987.

———. "German-Americans and Civil War Politics: A Reconsideration of the Ethnocultural Thesis." *Civil War History* 37 (1991): 232–45.

———. "'Auch unser Deutschland muss einmal frei werden': The Immigrant Civil War Experience as a Mirror on Political Conditions in Germany." In *Transatlantic Images and Perceptions: Germany and America since 1776*, ed. David E. Barclay and Elisabeth Glaser-Schmidt, 87–107. Cambridge: Cambridge University Press, 1997.

Katz, Philip. *From Appomattox to Montmartre: Americans and the Paris Commune*. Cambridge, MA: Harvard University Press, 1998.

Kaufmann, Eric. "American Exceptionalism Reconsidered: Anglo-Saxon Ethnogenesis in the 'Universal' Nation, 1776–1850." *Journal of American Studies* 33 (1999): 437–57.

Kazal, Russell. "Irish 'Race' and German 'Nationality': Catholic Languages of Ethnic Difference in Turn-of-the-Century Philadelphia." In *Race and the Production of Modern American Nationalism*, ed. Reynolds J. Scott-Childress, 149–68. New York: Garland Publishing, 1999.

———. *Becoming Old Stock: The Paradox of German-American Identity*. Princeton, NJ: Princeton University Press, 2004.

Keil, Harmut. "German Immigrants and African-Americans in Mid-Nineteenth Century America." In *Enemy Images in American History*, ed. Ragnhild Fiebig-von Hase and Ursula Lehmkuhl, 137–57. Providence, RI: Berghahn Books, 1997.

————, ed. *German Workers' Culture in the United States, 1850–1920.* Washington DC: Smithsonian Institution Press, 1998.

Keith, LeeAnna. *The Colfax Massacre: The Untold Story of Black Power, White Terror, and the Death of Reconstruction.* New York: Oxford University Press, 2008.

Keller, Christian B. *Chancellorsville and the Germans: Nativism, Ethnicity, and Civil War Memory.* New York: Fordham University Press, 2007.

Kerber, Linda K. "The Meanings of Citizenship." *Journal of American History* 84 (1997): 833–54.

Kessler-Harris, Alice. *In Pursuit of Equity: Women, Men, and the Quest for Economic Citizenship in 20th-Century America.* Oxford: Oxford University Press, 2001.

Kettner, James H. *The Development of American Citizenship, 1608–1877.* Chapel Hill: University of North Carolina Press, 1978.

Keyssar, Alexander. *The Right to Vote: The Contested History of Democracy in the United States.* New York: Basic Books, 2000.

Kistler, Mark O. "German-American Liberalism and Thomas Paine." *American Quarterly* 14 (1962): 81–91.

Klement, Frank L. "Catholics as Copperheads during the Civil War." *Catholic Historical Review* 80 (1994): 36–57.

Kleppner, Paul. *The Cross of Culture: A Social Analysis of Midwestern Politics, 1850–1900.* New York: The Free Press, 1970.

Kloppenberg, James T. *The Virtues of Liberalism.* New York: Oxford University Press, 1998.

Kocka, Jürgen, ed. *Bürger und Bürgerlichkeit im 19. Jahrhundert.* Göttingen: Vandenhoeck & Ruprecht, 1987.

Kocka, Jürgen, and Allan Mitchell, eds. *Bourgeois Society in Nineteenth-Century Europe.* Oxford: Berg, 1993.

Kolbeck, M. Orestes. *American Opinion on the Kulturkampf, 1871–1882.* Washington, DC: The Catholic University of America Press, 1942.

Koselleck, Reinhart. "Volk, Nation, Nationalismus, Masse." In *Geschichtliche Grundbegriffe: Historisches Lexikon zur politisch-sozialen Sprache in Deutschland,* ed. Otto Brunner, Werner Conze, and Reinhart Koselleck. Vol. 7, 380–89. Stuttgart: Ernst Klett Verlag, 1992.

Kruman, Marc W. *Between Authority and Liberty: State Constitution Making in Revolutionary America.* Chapel Hill: University of North Carolina Press, 1997.

Kymlicka, Will. *Liberalism, Community, and Culture.* Oxford: Clarendon Press, 1989.

————. *Multicultural Citizenship: A Liberal Theory of Minority Rights.* Oxford: Clarendon Press, 1995.

Langewiesche, Dieter. *Liberalism in Germany.* Trans. Christiane Banerji. Princeton, NJ: Princeton University Press, 2000.

Levine, Bruce. *The Spirit of 1848: German Immigrants, Labor Conflict, and the Coming of the Civil War.* Urbana: University of Illinois Press, 1992.

Lipp, Carola, ed. *Schimpfende Weiber und patriotische Jungfrauen: Frauen im Vormärz und in der Revolution 1848/49.* Moos: Elster, 1986.

Litwack, Leon. *Been in the Storm So Long: The Aftermath of Slavery.* New York: Knopf, 1979.

Luebke, Frederick C., ed. *Ethnic Voters and the Election of Lincoln.* Lincoln: University of Nebraska Press, 1973.

Mahar, William J. *Behind the Burnt Cork Mask: Early Blackface Minstrelsy and Ante-bellum American Popular Culture.* Urbana: University of Illinois Press, 1999.

Maltz, Earle M. *Civil Rights, the Constitution, and Congress, 1863–1869.* Lawrence: University of Kansas Press, 1990.

Marshall, T. H. *Citizenship and Social Class, and Other Essays.* Cambridge: Cambridge University, 1950.

Masur, Kate. *An Example for All the Land: Emancipation and the Struggle over Equality in Washington, D.C.* Chapel Hill: University of North Carolina Press, 2010.

McAfee, Ward M. *Religion, Race, and Reconstruction: The Public School in the Politics of the 1870s.* Albany: State University of New York Press, 1998.

McCormick, Richard L. "Ethno-Cultural Interpretations of Nineteenth-Century Voting Behavior." *Political Science Quarterly* 89 (1974): 351–77.

McDaniel, W. Caleb, and Bethany L. Johnson. "New Approaches to Internationalizing the History of the Civil War Era." *Journal of the Civil War Era* 2 (2012): 145–50.

McGreevy, John T. *Catholicism and American Freedom: A History.* New York: W. W. Norton, 2003.

McKerley, John. "Citizens and Strangers: The Politics of Race in Missouri from Slavery to the Era of Jim Crow." PhD diss., University of Iowa, 2008.

McLellan, David. *Karl Marx: A Biography.* New York: Palgrave Macmillan, 2006.

McManus, Michael J. *Political Abolitionism in Wisconsin, 1840–1861.* Kent, OH: Kent State University Press, 1998.

McMillan, Daniel A. "Germany Incarnate: Politics, Gender, and Sociability in the Gymnastics Movement." PhD diss., Columbia University, 1997.

McPherson, James M. "Grant or Greeley: The Abolitionist Dilemma in the Election of 1872." *American Historical Review* 71 (1965): 43–61.

———. *The Abolitionist Legacy: From Reconstruction to the NAACP.* Princeton, NJ: Princeton University Press, 1985.

Mehta, Uday. "Liberal Strategies of Exclusion." *Politics and Society* 18 (1990): 427–54.

Messer-Kruse, Timothy. *The Yankee International: Marxism and the American Reform Tradition, 1848–1876.* Chapel Hill: University of North Carolina Press, 1998.

Mohr, James C., ed. *Radical Republicans in the North: State Politics during Reconstruction.* Baltimore: Johns Hopkins University Press, 1976.

Moltmann, Günter. *Atlantische Blockpolitik im 19. Jahrhundert; die Vereinigten Staaten und der deutsche Liberalismus während der Revolution von 1848/49.* Düsseldorf: Droste Verlag, 1973.

Mommsen, Wolfgang J. *Das Ringen um den nationalen Staat: Die Gründung und der innere Ausbau des Deutschen Reiches unter Otto von Bismarck, 1850 bis 1890.* Berlin: Propyläen Verlag, 1993.

Montgomery, David. *Beyond Equality: Labor and the Radical Republicans, 1862–1872.* New York: Knopf, 1967.

Nadel, Stanley. *Little Germany: Ethnicity, Religion, and Class in New York City 1845–80.* Urbana: University of Illinois Press, 1990.

———. "The German Immigrant Left in the United States." In *The Immigrant Left in the United States.* Ed. Paul Buhle and Dan Georgakas, 45–76. Albany: State University of New York Press, 1996.

Nagel, Daniel. *Von republikanischen Deutschen zu deutsch-amerikanischen Republicanern: Ein Beitrag zum Identitätswandel der deutschen Actundvierziger in den Vereinigten Staaten, 1860–1861.* St. Ingbert: Röhrig Universitätsverlag, 2012.

Nagler, Jörg. *Fremont contra Lincoln: Die deutsch-amerikanische Opposition in der republikanischen Partei während des amerikanischen Bürgerkrieg.* Frankfurt am Main: Peter Lang, 1984.

———. "Deutschamerikaner und das *Liberal Republican Movement,* 1872." *Amerikastudien / American Studie*s 33 (1988): 415–38.

Nathans, Eli. *The Politics of Citizenship in Germany: Ethnicity, Utility and Nationalism.* Oxford: Berg, 2004.

Neeley, Mark E., Jr. *The Boundaries of American Political Culture in the Civil War Era.* Chapel Hill: University of North Carolina Press, 2005.

Ngai, Mae. "The Architecture of Race in American Immigration Law: A Reexamination of the Immigration Act of 1924." *Journal of American History* 86 (1999): 67–92.

———. *Impossible Subjects: Illegal Aliens and the Making of Modern America.* Princeton, NJ: Princeton University Press, 2004.

Nipperdey, Thomas. *Germany from Napoleon to Bismarck, 1800–1866.* Trans. Daniel Nolan. Dublin: Gill & Macmillan, 1996.

Obermann, Karl. *Joseph Weydemeyer: Pioneer of American Socialism.* New York: International Publishers, 1947.

———. *Joseph Weydemeyer: Ein Lebensbild, 1818–1866.* Berlin: Dietz Verlag, 1968.

Öfele, Martin. *German-Speaking Officers in the United States Colored Troops, 1863–1867.* Gainesville: University of Florida Press, 2004.

Ortlepp, Anke. *"Auf denn, Ihr Schwestern!": Deutschamerikanische Frauenvereine in Milwaukee, Wisconsin, 1844–1914.* Stuttgart: Franz Steiner Verlag, 2004.

Paludan, Phillip S. *A Covenant with Death: The Constitution, Law, and Equality in the Civil War Era.* Urbana: University of Illinois Press, 1975.

Parrish, William E. *Missouri under Radical Rule, 1865–1870.* Columbia: University of Missouri Press, 1965.

Perman, Michael. *The Road to Redemption: Southern Politics, 1869–1879.* Chapel Hill: University of North Carolina Press, 1984.

Peterson, Brent O. *Popular Narratives and Ethnic Identities: Literature and Community in Die Abendschule.* Ithaca, NY: Cornell University Press, 1991.

Pflanze, Otto. *Bismarck and the Development of Germany.* Vol. 1. *The Period of Unification, 1815–1871.* Princeton, NJ: Princeton University Press, 1990.

Pickle, Linda Schelbitzi. *Contented among Strangers: Rural German-Speaking Women and their Families in the Nineteenth-Century Midwest.* Urbana: University of Illinois Press, 1996.

Pochmann, Henry A. *German Culture in America: Philosophical and Literary Influences, 1600–1900.* Madison: University of Wisconsin Press, 1957.

Potter, David M. "The Civil War in the History of the Modern World: A Comparative View." In *The South and the Sectional Conflict,* ed. David M. Potter, 287–99. Baton Rouge: Louisiana State University Press, 1968.

Primus, Richard A. *The American Language of Rights.* New York: Cambridge University Press, 1999.

Quigley, David. *The Second Founding: New York City, Reconstruction and the Making of American Democracy.* New York: Hill and Wang, 2004.

Raab, Josef, and Jan Wirrer, eds. *Die deutsche Präsenz in den USA: The German Presence in the U.S.A.* Berlin: LIT Verlag, 2008.

Rawley, James A. "The General Amnesty Act of 1872: A Note." *Mississippi Valley Historical Review* 47 (1960): 480–84.

Rawls, John. *A Theory of Justice.* London: Oxford University Press, 1971.

Reidel, Manfried. "Bürger, Staatsbürger, Bürgertum." In *Geschichtliche Grundbegriffe: Historisches Lexikon zur politisch-sozialen Sprache in Deutschland,* ed. Otto Brunner, Werner Conze, and Reinhart Koselleck, vol. 1, 676–78. Stuttgart: Ernst Klett Verlag, 1972.

Richardson, Heather Cox. *The Death of Reconstruction: Race, Labor, and Politics in the Post-Civil War North, 1865–1901.* Cambridge, MA: Harvard University Press, 2001.

———. *West from Appomattox: The Reconstruction of America after the Civil War.* New Haven, CT: Yale University Press, 2007.

Roberts, Timothy Mason. *Distant Revolutions: 1848 and the Challenge to American Exceptionalism.* Charlottesville: University of Virginia Press, 2009.

Rodgers, Daniel. *Atlantic Crossings: Social Politics in a Progressive Age.* Cambridge, MA: Belknap Press of Harvard University Press, 1998.

Roediger, David R. "Racism, Reconstruction, and the Labor Press: The Rise and Fall of the St. Louis Daily Press, 1864–1866." *Science and Society* 42 (1978): 156–77.

———. "'Not Only the Ruling Classes to Overcome but also the So-Called Mob': Class, Skill and Community in the St. Louis General Strike of 1877." *Journal of Social History* 19 (1985): 213–39.

———. *Wages of Whiteness: Race and the Making of the American Working Class.* London and New York: Verso, 1991.

Rosen, Hannah. *Terror in the Heart of Freedom: Citizenship, Sexual Violence, and the Meaning of Race in the Postemancipation South.* Chapel Hill: University of North Carolina Press, 2009.

Ross, Ronald J. *The Failure of Bismarck's Kulturkampf: Catholicism and State Power in Imperial Germany.* Washington, DC: The Catholic University of America Press, 1998.

Saalberg, Harvey. "The *Westliche Post* of St. Louis: A Daily Newspaper for German-Americans, 1857–1938." PhD diss., University of Missouri, 1967.

Samito, Christian G. *Becoming American Under Fire: Irish Americans, African Americans, and the Politics of Citizenship during the Civil War Era.* Ithaca, NY: Cornell University Press, 2009.

Saville, Julie. *The Work of Reconstruction: From Slave to Wage Laborer in South Carolina, 1860–1870.* Cambridge: Cambridge University Press, 1994.

Sawrey, Robert D. *Dubious Victory: The Reconstruction Debate in Ohio.* Lexington: University Press of Kentucky, 1992.

Saxton, Alexander. "Blackface Minstrelsy and Jacksonian Ideology." *American Quarterly* 27 (1975): 3–28.

———. *The Rise and Fall of the White Republic: Class Politics and Mass Culture in Nineteenth Century America.* London: Verso, 1990.

Schäfer, Axel R. *American Progressives and German Social Reform, 1875–1920.* Stuttgart: Franz Steiner Verlag, 2000.

Schlüter, Hermann. *Die Anfänge der deutschen Arbeiterbewegung in Amerika.* Stuttgart: J. H. W. Dietz Nachfolger, 1907.

———. *Die Internationale in Amerika: Ein Beitrag zur Geschichte der Arbeiter-Bewegung in den Vereinigten Staaten.* Chicago: Deutsche Sprachgruppe der Sozialist. Partei der Ver. Staaten, 1918.

Schneirov, Richard. *Labor and Urban Politics: Class Conflict and the Origins of Modern Liberalism in Chicago, 1864–97.* Urbana: University of Illinois Press, 1998.

Schulte, Wilhelm. *Fritz Anneke: Ein Leben für die Freiheit in Deutschland und in den USA.* Dortmund: Historischer Verein Dortmund, 1961.

Schwalm, Leslie A. *Emancipation's Diaspora: Race and Reconstruction in the Upper Midwest.* Chapel Hill: University of North Carolina Press, 2009.

Sexton, Jay. "Toward a Synthesis of Foreign Relations in the Civil War Era, 1848–1877." *American Nineteenth Century History* 5 (2004): 50–73.

Sheehan, James J. *German Liberalism in the Nineteenth Century.* Chicago: University of Chicago Press, 1978.

———. *German History, 1770–1866.* Oxford: Clarendon, 1989.

Shore, Elliott, Ken Fones-Wolf, and James P. Danky, eds. *The German-American Radical Press: The Shaping of a Left Political Culture, 1850–1940.* Urbana: University of Illinois Press, 1992.

Simpson, Brooks. *The Reconstruction Presidents.* Lawrence: University of Kansas Press, 1998.

Slap, Andrew L. *The Doom of Reconstruction: The Liberal Republicans in the Civil War Era.* New York: Fordham University Press, 2006.

Smith, Helmut Walser. *German Nationalism and Religious Conflict: Culture, Ideology, Politics, 1870–1914.* Princeton, NJ: Princeton University Press, 1995.

Smith, Michael Thomas. *The Enemy Within: Fears of Corruption in the Civil War North.* Charlottesville: University of Virginia Press, 2011.

Smith, Rogers. "The 'American Creed' and American Identity: The Limits of Liberal Citizenship in the United States." *Western Political Quarterly* 41 (1988): 225–51.

———. *Civic Ideals: Conflicting Visions of Citizenship in U.S. History.* New Haven, CT: Yale University Press, 1997.

Snay, Mitchell. *Fenians, Freedmen, and Southern Whites: Race and Nationality in the Era of Reconstruction.* Baton Rouge: Louisiana State University Press, 2007.

Sperber, Jonathan. *Popular Catholicism in Nineteenth-Century Germany.* Princeton, NJ: Princeton University Press, 1984.

———. *Rhineland Radicals: The Democratic Movement and the Revolutions of 1848–1849.* Princeton, NJ: Princeton University Press, 1991.

———. *The European Revolutions, 1848–1851.* Cambridge: Cambridge University Press, 1994.

———. "Churches, the Faithful, and the Politics of Religion in the Revolutions of 1848." In *Europe in 1848: Revolution and Reform,* ed. Dieter Dowe et al., trans. David Higgins, 708–30. New York: Berghahn Books, 2001.

Spickard, Paul. *Almost All Aliens: Immigration, Race, and Colonialism in American History and Identity.* New York: Routledge, 2007.

Sproat, John G. *"The Best Men": Liberal Reformers in the Gilded Age*. New York: Oxford University Press, 1968.

Stauffer, John. *The Black Hearts of Men: Radical Abolitionists and the Transformation of Race*. Cambridge, MA: Harvard University Press, 2002.

Stowell, David O. *Streets, Railroads, and the Great Strike of 1877*. Chicago: University of Chicago Press, 1999.

———, ed. *The Great Strikes of 1877*. Urbana: University of Illinois Press, 2008.

Summers, Mark W. *The Plundering Generation: Corruption and the Crisis of the Union, 1849–1861*. New York: Oxford University Press, 1987.

———. *The Era of Good Stealings*. New York: Oxford University Press, 1993.

Symonides, Janusz. "Cultural Rights: A Neglected Category of Human Rights." *International Social Science Journal* 50, no. 158 (1998): 559–72.

Taylor, Charles. "The Politics of Recognition." In *Multiculturalism*, ed. Amy Gutmann, 25–73. Princeton, NJ: Princeton University Press, 1994.

Timpe, Georg, ed. *Katholisches Deutschthum in den Vereinigten Staaten: Ein Querschnitt*. Freiburg im Breisgau: Herder & Co., 1937.

Toll, Robert C. *Blacking Up: The Minstrel Show in Nineteenth-Century America*. New York: Oxford University Press, 1974.

Trefousse, Hans L. *Carl Schurz: A Biography*, 2d ed. New York: Fordham University Press, 1998.

Trelease, Allen. *White Terror: The Ku Klux Klan Conspiracy and Southern Reconstruction*. New York: Harper & Row, 1971.

Trommler, Frank, and Joseph McVeigh, eds. *America and the Germans: An Assessment of a Three-Hundred-Year History*. 2 vols. Philadelphia: University of Pennsylvania Press, 1985.

Tuchinsky, Adam. *Horace Greeley's New-York Tribune: Civil War Socialism and the Crisis of Free Labor*. Ithaca, NY: Cornell University Press, 2009.

Unger, Irwin. *The Greenback Era: A Social and Political History of American Finance, 1865–1879*. Princeton, NJ: Princeton University Press, 1964.

Ural, Susannah J., ed. *Civil War Citizens: Race, Ethnicity, and Identity in America's Bloodiest Conflict*. New York: New York University Press, 2010.

Valentin, Veit. *Geschichte der deutschen Revolution von 1848–1849*. 2 vols. Berlin: Ullstein, 1930–1931.

Vick, Brian E. *Defining Germany: The 1848 Frankfurt Parliamentarians and National Identity*. Cambridge, MA: Harvard University Press, 2002.

Wagner, Maria. "Mathilde Anneke's Stories of Slavery in the German-American Press." *MELUS* 6 (1979): 9–16.

Walzer, Michael. *Spheres of Justice: A Defense of Pluralism and Equality*. New York: Basic Books, 1983.

Wang, Xi. *The Trial of Democracy: Black Suffrage and Northern Republicans, 1860–1910*. Athens: University of Georgia Press, 1997.

Wawro, Geoffrey. *The Franco-Prussian War: The German Conquest of France in 1870–1871*. Cambridge: Cambridge University Press, 2003.

Wehner-Franco, Silke. *Deutsche Dienstmädchen in America, 1850–1914*. Münster: Waxmann, 1994.

Welke, Barbara Young. *Law and the Borders of Belonging in the Long Nineteenth Century United States*. Cambridge: Cambridge University Press, 2010.

Wellenreuther, Hermann, ed. *German and American Constitutional Thought*. Oxford: Berg, 1990.

Williams, Lou Falkner. *The Great South Carolina Ku Klux Klan Trials, 1871–1872*. Athens: University of Georgia Press, 1996.

Wittke, Carl F. *Tambo and Bones: A History of the American Minstrel Stage*. Durham, NC: Duke University Press, 1930.

————. "The German Forty-Eighters: A Centennial Appraisal," *American Historical Review* 53 (1948): 711–25.

————. *The German-Language Press in America*. [Lexington]: University of Kentucky Press, 1957.

————. "Friedrich Hassaurek: Cincinnati's Leading Forty-Eighter," *Ohio Historical Quarterly* 68 (1959): 1–17.

————. *Refugees of Revolution: The German Forty-Eighters in America*. Philadelphia: University of Pennsylvania Press, 1952. Reprint, Westport, CT: Greenwood Press, 1970.

Woodward, C. Vann. *Reunion and Reaction: The Compromise of 1877 and the End of Reconstruction*. Boston: Little, Brown, 1951.

————. "Seeds of Failure in Radical Race Policy." In *New Frontiers of American Reconstruction*, ed. Harold M. Hyman, 125–47. Urbana: University of Illinois Press, 1966.

Yellin, Jean Fagan. *Women and Sisters: The Antislavery Feminists in American Culture*. New Haven, CT: Yale University Press, 1989.

Zimmerman, Andrew. *Alabama in Africa: Booker T. Washington, the German Empire, and the Globalization of the New South*. Princeton, NJ: Princeton University Press, 2010.

Zucker, A. E., ed. *The Forty-Eighters: Political Refugees of the German Revolution of 1848*. New York: Columbia University Press, 1950.

Index

261